The Immigrant Left in the United States

D1562480

SUNY Series in American Labor History
Robert Asher and Amy Kesselman, Editors

Other books in this series include:

The Immigrant Left in the United States

Edited by
Paul Buhle
and Dan Georgakas

State University of New York Press

Published by
State University of New York Press, Albany

© 1996 State University of New York

For information address State University of New York Press, State
University Plaza, Albany, NY 12246

Production by Laura Starrett
Marketing by Dana Yanulavich

Library of Congress Cataloging in Publication Data

The immigrant left in the United States / edited by Paul Buhle, Dan
  Georgakas.
      p.   cm. — (SUNY series in American labor history)
    Includes bibliographical references and index.
    ISBN 0-7914-2883-4 (cloth) — ISBN 0-7914-2884-2 (pbk)
    1. Radicalism—United States. 2. Immigrants—United States-
  -Political activity.   3. Socialism—United States.   4. Right and
  left (Political science) I. Buhle, Paul, 1944– . II. Georgakas,
  Dan. III. Series.
  HN90.R3I47   1996
  303.48′4—dc20   95-19955
                                                                CIP

10   9   8   7   6   5   4   3   2   1

Contents

Introduction

The full history of the American Left has yet to be unearthed, let alone written. Perhaps the greatest single obstacle to such a project has been the inability of scholars to utilize the wealth of material generated by immigrants whose daily language and intellectual discourse were not in English. Indeed, with a handful of exceptions, histories of leftist currents among these groups remain unwritten. *The Immigrant Left in the United States* provides preliminary studies of groups never analyzed in this context and seeks to revise and elaborate histories of groups with considerable documentation. It also suggests the scope and nature of research yet to be undertaken.[1]

Study of the immigrant Left is far from new. As early as 1911, veteran German-American socialist editor Hermann Schlüter's volume, *Die International in Amerika: Ein Beitrag zur Geschichte der Arbeiter-Bewegung in den Vereinigten Staaten* [The International in America, a Contribution to the History of the Workers' Movement in the U.S.], was published in Chicago. This important monograph, which examined the first wave of immigrant socialism, was followed by a handful of books, nearly all in Yiddish, published by leftist and fraternal groups to commemorate their movements' pioneers.[2] English-language historians of American radicalism, never numerous until the 1960s, generally took little notice of such volumes or of the movements that produced them. Because the emerging scholarship directed attention almost entirely toward English-language radicalism and the famous personalities of the Left, it tended simply to bypass subjects that required both language skills and a particular expertise in specific immigrant cultures.[3]

This neglect persisted until the 1970s. By that time, labor and social historians such as Herbert G. Gutman had revitalized social history by looking directly at the everyday life of the American masses, immigrants emphatically included.[4] Although they had limited language tools themselves and less interest in the Left than in the working class per se, their methods and their sensitivity had an enormous impact upon younger graduate students interested in radical history. These students, including many second- or third-generation immigrant descendents eager to uncover the "hidden history" of their specific cultural tradition, meanwhile drew strength from other developments.[5] Major research repositories, most notably the Immigration History Research Center in Minnesota, aggressively collected, categorized, and made available materials from a wide spectrum of ethnic groups. Diaspora studies, increasingly popular in the home nations of the emigrants who had left for America, added considerably to the resources of the combined archival effort.[6]

The political climate of the 1960s and 1970s also fed the new ethnic and radical scholarship. Interest in various ethnic histories proved a natural corollary to the drive to recover black history (or "roots"). Fortuitously, as various social movements of the period began to lose their momentum, many talented former activists undertook work in public history. They often sought out the aging veterans of earlier radical movements. Such individuals, eager for historical vindication after the trials of McCarthyism and decades of forgetfulness, eagerly spoke about their past and personally donated a large body of hitherto inaccessible material, published and unpublished.

The interaction of radical generations produced a rich flow of public forums, documentary films, oral histories, museum exhibits, memorial meetings, and scholarly volumes. Among the archival projects most significant in the recovery of immigrant history, the Oral History of the American Left (housed at New York University's Tamiment Library) taped, collected, and catalogued hundreds of interviews, stirring still more veterans to write their memoirs or to collect material from their own circles.[7] The documentation resulting from all these activities not only filled in categories for sympathetic scholars but actually reorganized categories, as the insights of research were modified by the voices of those who had experienced events first hand. That more and more new books showed real insight into the lives of ordinary radicals was, perhaps, the greatest of tributes to the footwork of a generation.

By the 1990s, most veterans of the movements that had reached their peak in the New Deal and World War II eras had passed from the scene, and the young scholars of the 1960s had themselves become middle-aged. Social history meanwhile suffered a certain loss of prestige; academic interest in European immigration and the industrial working class declined significantly. The memoirs so recently published now seemed to recall a time long past. Although serious research on earlier immigrants and colonized cultures such as Mexicans, Native Americans, and Puerto Ricans continued, more attention began to be directed toward groups whose immigration patterns were linked to the momentous 1965 revision of immigration laws, a revision that opened the doors to groups previously discouraged or excluded from entry in large numbers into the United States.

Most of the new immigrants came from Latin America, Asia, and, to a lesser degree, the Middle East. If they faced a more complex America than their predecessors had, they also confronted many of the same conditions, from sweatshops to discrimination based on racist assumptions. Sooner or later—sooner in many cases—the new immigrants organized to make demands on their adopted nation and on an ethnic hierarchy, which now sometimes privileged ethnic groups such as eastern or southern Europeans considered inferior only a generation or two earlier.

These newcomers also frequently came from lands gripped by social upheaval related to the collapse of the governing system in Russia and the reverberations as far away as Asia and Latin America. Most obviously in the case of the Haitians but in many other cases as well, immigrants and their American-based organizations were also certain to play an influential role in the immediate fate of the homeland. These developments represented a reprise of sorts for familiar paradigms, the Haitians behaving, for instance, much like turn-of-the-century Cubans who had organized revolutionary and support movements from Florida strongholds. Filipinos, Iranian and South Korean students, Puerto Ricans, and many others had occupied in recent decades or would now certainly occupy a similar status. Various immigrant Lefts also asserted themselves—sometimes loudly and in the name of their own politics but usually more quietly, under a broader rubric—within U.S. labor, liberal, and civil rights coalitions. Once more, like their predecessors, activists found class and ethnic issues inextricably entangled with language, race, gender, and religious concerns.

Seen in this way, a large narrative commencing with the arrival of German radicals during the Civil War era and continuing on to the present exhibits remarkable continuity and equally remarkable paradoxes. Social patterns recurred in very different populations, even as the confidence of the Left in their (and its own) ultimate destiny has flagged. If Marxists—traditionally the most systematic thinkers of the immigrant Left—invariably anticipated that early patterns of social disorder and eclectic dissent would grow into a cohesive socialist vanguard, today's interpreters understandably foreswear any definitive "before" and "after." If rather than becoming more dysfunctional in its own terms, capitalism seems instead to increase its mastery of planetary resources even while despoiling them, then ethnically specific working classes are forever newly produced out of groups of impoverished emigrants fleeing their homes for cities or a new land. Rather than producing a happy ending in a world consumer society, capitalism continually reproduces differentiations and degradations at its commercial and industrial centers, with no end necessarily in sight. Exploitation and great suffering may be safely predicted, while alternatives seem more elusive than they did a half century or century ago.

The essays presented in this collection reflect, in some ways, the exhaustion of traditional Left perspectives. But they also challenge the traditional scholarship of immigrant life, which assumes upward mobility and inevitable assimilation. Neither of these theoretical models—each suited in its own way to the European immigrant experience—fits the actual experience of most groups past or present. Economic success no more demonstrates cultural vitality, for instance, then a lack of upward mobility reveals some defective quality in specific cultures. The rags-to-riches myth suffers further from the general perception of the mid-1990s that ordinary Americans are less and less likely to live as well as (let alone better than) their parents. Assimilation has also become increasingly problematic. Spanish-speaking cultures, some of which preexisted what is now the United States, can hardly be said to have become assimilated or to present the prospect of doing so. Public controversies over "multiculturalism" and "English-first" reflect a deep uneasiness about the day-to-day conditions of life in a society where the traditional sources of cohesion have evidently worn thin.

All this is not to deny that some groups have fared, and will doubtless continue to fare, better than others. Nor is it to deny the more paradoxical prospect that Left mobilizations may very well take shape in the middle rather than the poorest range of immigrant culture (as they have also tended to do in the past). Germans were surely more fortunate than Italians at the opening of the twentieth century and natives of Trinidad or Hong Kong more fortunate than Filipinos or Salvadorans at century's end. Each group has its own unique historical situation and its own cards to play; the Left often makes an important contribution to how the hand dealt is actually used.

The relatively recent appearance of a "transnational" field or approach casts new light upon the experience of immigrants. As early as the 1910s, Randolph Bourne had described "Trans-National America" in place of the melting pot, and the precocious revolutionary intellectual Louis C. Fraina described a "new racial type" destined to arise from the mixing of Old and New Worlds.[8] But only with the steady advance of business globalization and fresh currents of immigration did leading scholars begin to turn away from the sturdy myths of "American exceptionalism" to a picture always more complex in real life. Ongoing developments such as the ecological crisis are global in nature and seem certain to intensify the turn toward a transnational perspective.[9]

That said, little of the transnationalist discussion thus far has been historical in character, and still less has concerned the subject at hand. Labor history, which long suffered from the generalization that American workers were so "unique" as to defy (European) Marxist models of behavior, has only recently begun to recover from the narrowness of "exceptionalism," the idea of America as a nation entirely different from others.[10] Social scientists exploring similar territory conclude erroneously but similarly that the contemporary experience of post-1965 immigration is likewise utterly distinct from everything preceding it.[11]

The promise of transnationalism, for this book's subject in particular, is thus unfulfilled. Indeed, basic definitions have yet to be laid out. Historical judgments on the impact of immigrant Lefts within their communities and the nation (or world) at large are inevitably constrained and compromised by an uneven historiographical landscape.

Where documentation is substantial, as in the case of Germans and Jews, broad overviews can be devised and intertextual observations made about past scholarship. From the complex history of Mexican-Americans to the intense case of Jewish garment workers, studies here plumb forgotten, distorted, neglected, and once controversial moments of ethnic experience. More commonly, however, no full-length study has been published. Even such relatively large ethnic groups as Italians, Irish, and Poles, let alone such smaller but significant groups as Armenians, Hugarians, Lithuanians, Latvians, non-Jewish (or assimilated Jewish) Russians, Bulgarians, West Indians (French-Creole-, or English-speaking), Portuguese, Filipinos, or French-Canadians have yet to find their ethnic Left major scholars. Work has only begun or remains mostly in unpublished sources on south Slavs (Croats, Slovenes, Serbs), Swedes and Norwegians, Ukrainians, Arabs, Puerto Ricans, Cubans, and a variety of Asian groups.

The essays in this volume are the first known to focus on radicalism along immigrant Poles, Ukrainians, Haitians, Arabs, and Greeks. They likewise make an opening effort to comprehend "transnational" experience, the transatlantic or transpacific political dialogue, which played a key role in immigrant life but which scholars have so rarely grappled with hitherto. They push the limits of existing scholarship by seeking to provide an overview of scattered studies in so large a conceptual area as Asian immigration. And they seek, in some cases, to comprehend the little understood role of first- and second-generation immigrants in American letters and American popular culture. Despite the limitations of existing available data and the incapacity of any one volume to encompass so vast and complex a subject as the immigrant Left, these essays collectively challenge the standard accounts of immigrant life and indicate where future research may fruitfully be directed.

—Paul Buhle and Dan Georgakas

Notes

1. The best available resource for overviews and further suggestions for reading is the *Encyclopedia of the American Left* (New York, 1990), edited by Mari Jo Buhle, Paul Buhle, and Dan Georgakas. A complete bibliography of material on the immigrant Left, written in various nations and in various languages, would be impossible to compile at this date. The second edition of the *Encyclopedia* (projected for 1997) will, however, contain an updated and thorough survey of recent scholarly advances.

2. Hermann Schlüter's history of the First International in the U.S., *Die Internationale in Amerika* (Chicago, 1918), was characteris-

tically published by the *Deutsche Sprachgruppe der Sozialistishe Partei der Vereinigten Staaten* [German Language group of the Socialist Party of the U.S.]. Of later histories, perhaps the most outstanding are A. Sh. Sachs, *Di Geshikhte fun Arbeter Ring* 2 vols. (New York, 1925), published by the Workmen's Circle; Kalmon Marmor, *Moris Vinchefsky, Zeyn Lebn un Verk* (New York, 1928) (volume 1, a close study of the Yiddish socialist editor described at length in Paul Buhle's essay below, was published by the communist *Morgn Freiheit*); *Dovid Edelshtott Gedenk-Bukh* (Los Angeles, 1952), a collection of anarchist memoirs about the late nineteenth-century Yiddish poet and editor; *Geshikhte fun der tsienistisher arbeter vavegung in Tsofen Amerike* (New York, 1955), a two-volume history of labor Zionism; and the survey of the Yiddish-language socialist movement, J. S. Hertz, *Di Yiddishe Sozialistishte Bevegung in Amerike* (New York, 1954).

In addition to these sources, the memoir literature of individual Yiddish-language anarchist, socialist, and communist veterans is sizable, published in small editions and financed by "publication committees" of the authors' friends. A far larger Yiddish scholarship on Left-tinged Yiddish fiction, theatrical, and poetry writers exists. Fictional treatments of the Yiddish-language Left are also plentiful, especially in short fiction.

3. The major exception to this rule is Melech Epstein, *Jewish Labor in the United States* (New York, 1950), written by a former staff member of the Yiddish communist *Morgn Freiheit* newspaper. Theodore Draper's *Roots of American Communism* (New York, 1957) and his *American Communism and Soviet Russia* (New York, 1960) showed a passing familiarity with a number of Left language groups, but little understanding of their unique character and little real interest beyond the leadership decision making in each group.

It is striking, furthermore, how equally distant the once standard communist and anticommunist histories are from the immigrant experience: William Z. Foster, *History of the Communist Party, USA* (New York, 1952) and Lewis Coser and Irving Howe, *The American Communist Party, 1919–1957, a Critical History* (New York, 1958) evidence little interest in the ethnic-cultural element of the Left, let alone its worldview. Studies published decades later, which, however, remain stolidly in the traditional vein, such as Harvey Klehr, *The Heyday of American Communism* (New York, 1984), seem likewise oblivious to virtually all developments in this field even now, with a variety of primary and secondary materials abundantly available. James Weinstein's *Decline of Socialism in America, 1912–1924* (New York, 1967) is remarkable, in this respect, mainly for its listing of ethnic socialist newspapers and their circulation, and for the author's frank suggestion that more research on the immigrant groups was badly needed.

4. Herbert G. Gutman, *Work, Culture and Society in Industrializing America* (New York, 1976) collects his massively influential essays. Gutman himself was called before a Congressional investigating committee to explain his life as a former counselor at a left-wing summer camp with a Yiddish emphasis. A posthumous second collection, *Power & Culture: Essays on the American Working Class* (New York, 1987), edited by Ira Berlin, offers a broader selection with a sensitive introduction by the editor, noting Gutman's effort to address the questions of class hegemony as well as those of history "from the bottom up."

5. A short list of outstanding works on the immigrant Left from this generation would include first of all, several major collections on German-Americans, such as Hartmut Keil, ed., *German Workers' Culture in the United States, 1850–1920* (Washington, D.C., 1988); Bruce C. Nelson, *Beyond the Martyrs: A Social History of Chicago's Anarchists, 1870–1900* (New Brunswick, 1988); and James Dankey et.al., eds., *The German American Radical Press* (Urbana, 1990). It would also include Michael G. Karni and Douglas J. Ollila, Jr., eds., *For the Common Good: Finnish Immigrants and the Radical Response to Industrial America* (Superior, Wisconsin, 1977); the more eclectic collection, Dirk Hoerder, ed., *"Struggle a Hard Battle": Essays on Working-Class Immigrants* (DeKalb, 1986); and volumes with important sections on the immigrant Left, such as Mari Jo Buhle, *Women and American Socialism, 1870–1920* (Urbana, 1982) and Paul Buhle, *Marxism in the United States* (London, 1991 edition).

The following, post-1960s generation of historians has produced many case study labor histories with important Left ethnic sidelights, such as Salvatore Salerno, *Red November, Black November: Culture and Community in the Industrial Workers of the World* (Albany, 1989), and Ardis Cameron, *Radicals of the Worst Sort: Laboring Women in Lawrence, Massachusetts, 1860–1912* (Urbana, 1993). Unfortunately, in most cases the immigrant material was examined secondhand, through English-language sources only.

6. Beyond the Immigration History Research Center (at the University of Minnesota), the reader is directed to the YIVO

Institute Library, New York City, for Jewish materials; the Minnesota Historical Society for Scandinavian and Finnish materials; the State Historical Society of Wisconsin for the Socialist Labor Party papers; and the Cornell University Library for the papers of the International Workers Order and other relevant collections. Scattered libraries have individual collections of great value, but not even those with considerable collections of English-language Left archives are likely to have significant non-English-language materials. The U.S.-related materials in non-U.S. libraries have yet to be assessed, but consist mainly in complete runs of serials produced within the U.S. by groups from the particular nation or culture.

7. A published *Guide* is available from the Tamiment Collection, Bobst Library, New York University, including outtake footage from some of the outstanding documentary films of the 1970s–1980s covering immigrant Left subjects.

8. Randolph Bourne, "Trans-National America," in Bourne, *The History of a Literary Radical and Other Papers* edited by Van Wyck Brooks, (New York, 1956), 283; Louis C. Faina, "Literary Gleanings: The Chasm," *Daily People,* April 9, 1911.

9. See the discussion in the *American Historical Review* 96 (October 1991): Ian Tyrrell, "American Exceptionalism in an Age of International History," 1031–55; McGerr, "The Price of the 'New Transnational History,' " 1056–67; and "Ian Tyrrell Responds," 1068–72. Unfortunately, far too much of this discussion hinges upon redefinitions of "exceptionalism," in large part because "transnationalism" is more concept than practice in scholarship as yet.

10. See Sean Wilentz, "Against Exceptionalism: Class Consciousness and the American Labor Movement, 1790–1920," *International Labor and Working Class History* 26 (Fall 1984); 1–24, along with the accompanying comments by Nick Salvatore and Michael Hanagan, 26–36; and Steven Sapolsky, "Response to Sean Wilentz's 'Against Exceptional: Class and the American Labor Movement, 1790 to 1920,' " *ibid.* 27 (Spring 1985); 35–38.

11. See *Towards a Transnational Perspective on Migration*, edited by N. G. Schiller et.al. (New York, 1992), in which the "Old Migration" becomes a straw man, utterly irrelevant to post-1965 trends except as contrast.

ONE

Fence Cutters, Sedicioso, and First-Class Citizens: Mexican Radicalism in America*

Douglas Monroy

Mexican culture was deeply rooted in the Southwest long before it became part of the United States, long before Mexican people became *extrajenos* (aliens) in their native lands, and long before the grand waves of twentieth-century immigration swelled the Mexican-American population into the millions. The first immigrants were people of mixed Indian and Spanish blood, seventeenth-century settlers of New Mexico and eighteenth-century settlers of Texas, southern Arizona, and California, who fought (with various degrees of success) and also intermixed (in various ways) with the Pueblos, the Navajos, the Apaches, the Comanches, the Pimas, the Papagos, the Shoshone, and the Chumash peoples. The maintenance of local prerogatives largely defined their political concerns. As citizens of a new and troubled Republic of Mexico, those in the departments of the northern frontier also participated in the battles over federalism versus centralism. They rebelled against efforts by the government to consolidate control in the capital, most successfully in 1831 in California, decidedly less successfully in 1837 in New Mexico.[1]

---

*This essay is dedicated to Dorothy Healey.

I.

When considering Mexicans within the context of American immigrant radicals, they must first be understood as a local people who rebelled against other immigrants and against what became the Anglo-American tide. Characteristic of situations where settler invasions follow military triumph, the rebellious activities of Mexicans in the freshly acquired lands of the American Southwest cannot be separated from the unfolding conquest following the Mexican-American War of 1846–1848. Nor can such endeavors be deemed simply "radical." Some combination of desperation, revenge, self-defense, millenarian deliverance, and fate usually motivated the participants. These actions established a tradition of resistance, celebrated in the *platica,* or popular legends, of the Southwest.

Locals revolted against both the American conquerors and the Mexican capitulators. What the *aguardiente*-laced *populacho* began in September of 1846 as a rebellion against the "despotic and arbitrary laws" of the occupying army in Los Angeles, the pastoralist *caballeros* finished with a stirring but short-lived and ceremonial victory over their conquerors in a battle of sabres and lances at nearby San Pascual a month later. In January 1847, an alliance of Taos Indians and New Mexican peasants, with the shadowy participation of such important New Mexican leaders as Padre Antonio Jose Martinez, Tomas Ortiz and Colonel Diego Archuleta, rose in rebellion against Governor Charles Bent, killing him and five of his cohorts. Although brutally repressed, the Taos Revolt became a potent symbol of resistance for the Puebloan and Hispanic New Mexicans.[2]

Racial animosity still simmering from the war, the need to forcibly pacify the local Mexican population, which occasionally evidenced aspirations for revenge, and a situation of frontier lawlessness all spawned a reign of terror by Anglos who "surrounded" Mexicans, especially in California and south Texas. This is one reason *la gente* generated relatively few leaders for nearly a century after the conquest, and why their immediate protests proved more significant as myth or symbol than as practical politics. Race revenge, privateering, religious crusading, clan politics, legal injustice, and the transfer of economic opportunity to the war's victors combined to shape a context in which social banditry became an alternative for Mexican men in the years following the Treaty of Guadalupe-Hidalgo.

"The murderer who murdered the murderers and died for our honor" may aptly characterize not only the most fabled and frightening *bandido* of California, Joaquin Murieta, but others of that state such as desperado Joan Flores and the classic social bandit Tiburcio Vasquez. Each suffered exclusion or outright expulsion from the unfolding American economic organization, from social and amorous opportunities, and from significant political recourse. They were, in Eric J. Hobsbawm's now well-established view, "considered by their peoples as heroes, as champions, avengers, fighters for justice, perhaps even leaders of liberation." Rather than being labeled "primitive rebels" or "prepolitical" (or for that matter primitive or pre-anything), they might better be considered what they were: men imbued with a sense of face-to-face references who responded to what was preoccupying their lives, namely conquest and lost opportunity. They often successfully engaged their conquering adversaries, and attracted allies on the battleground of myth and symbol in the most elemental terms—who was "good" and who was "bad."[3]

The Cortina War of 1859 continued some of these themes without the mercenary aspects of the California *bandidos*. For Mexicans living in the Rio Grande Valley of south Texas, the river marked not a dividing line as much as a basin, which united peoples on both sides. These *nortenos* so fervently attached to place and culture were determined to obstruct people or institutions that threatened their acquisitive and patriarchal ways.

Juan "Chino" Cortina, born into a family with substantial land holdings on both sides of the river, led his people against the Anglo Texans, a populace very quick to back up its white supremacy with violence. In the first skirmish, two months after defending a drunken compatriot from a "gringo" sheriff, Cortina led some sixty patriots into Brownsville, where he raised the Mexican flag and proceeded to release all *mexicano* prisoners from jail, execute several flagrantly unpunished murderers of Mexicans, and plunder the stores of offending merchants. After leaving the city, Cortina issued a declaration justifying his actions. Arguing for "the sacred right of self-preservation," he contrasted the "vile avarice" that led Americans to violate his own race, "which you see filled with gentleness and inward sweetness." Cortina articulated Mexicans' grievances about their loss of land through legal chicanery, the actual and remarkable impunity with which Anglos shot so many of them down, and "ostentatious" Texas racism.

As tensions escalated, over a thousand men were attracted to rebel ranks. When the local Anglo militia and a force lent by the

Mexican government attacked Cortina's riders on October 22, the insurgents defeated them resoundingly. Texas Rangers, the ultimate symbol of Anglo ferocity in the eyes of the Mexicans, now joined the fray but likewise retreated in disarray after their first encounter. His ranks now continuously swelling with the poor and discontented, Chino's army controlled the lower Rio Grande Valley for two months. Finally the U.S. Army arrived and defeated the insurrectionists on December 27, 1859, driving Cortina into exile in Mexico and unleashing a terrorist revenge against the Mexican people of the Rio Grande. (Cortina himself became an ardent supporter of Benito Juarez, fought the French and the Battle of Pueblo—celebrated as *Cinco de Mayo*—and served as military governor of Tamaulipas.) Although Cortina claimed that "the voice of revelation whispers to me," his efforts to liberate the land from the "gringos" or, at least, to force redress of grievances, succeeded mainly in escalating tensions between the well-armed Anglo minority and the Mexican majority.[4]

The prerogatives of Anglo private property provoked other revolts. In 1862 the Mexican people of El Paso discovered a salt bed, which they mined for their own use and for trade to the interior of Mexico, as tradition had hitherto entitled them. Fifteen years later an Anglo who claimed the beds for himself tried to charge them money for removing the salt. The El Paso Salt War of December 1877 was the people's response to the imposition of private property. This nearly spontaneous uprising brought the usual bloodletting at the hands of the Texas Rangers and local Anglos organized into a posse.[5] A decade later, to the north, in San Miguel County, Hispano farmers and rancheros took to their horses, union halls, and even the polls to cast out the interloping Anglos and their commercial ways.

The vast *ejido*, or communal lands, granted to villages of New Mexico did not immediately attract the attention of Anglo America as did the fertile expanses of California and south Texas. But on January 1, 1879, when the Atchison, Topeka, and Santa Fe Railroad arrived in Las Vegas, the situation changed dramatically. What had been pasturage for subsistence farmers could now become grazing lands for commercial beef ranchers as the railroad dramatically enhanced the exchange value of cattle by connecting the *llano*, the plains, to the depots of Kansas. Texas cattlemen and speculators challenged the validity of these traditional community grants with a variety of techniques. The *pobladores*, or villagers, who understood neither Anglo-American land law nor the aggressive spirit of the Anglos, nor for that matter English, soon found themselves alienated from their native lands. *Esta tierra,* this land, which had given them subsistence, also underpinned their entire cultural fabric. Where they once lived lives of communal independence, they were now pressed increasingly into dependence on wages. In spring 1889, armed and masked horsemen began to cut down the gleaming new fences of San Miguel County.[6]

These men who called themselves *las Gorras Blancas* or "the White Caps," were well known to the general population, but few would willingly identify them to authorities. Hispano elites, some of whom had made the transition to market agriculture, opposed lawlessness and a loosening of their own political control over *los pobres.* The Anglos were, of course, aghast at the threat to commercial development. Authorities in Las Vegas, the county seat, largely opposed the fence cutting as well, but kin ties and the hunting skills of the riders discouraged active opposition. Nonetheless, May 1889 saw 21 men indicted for fence cutting and released on bail. Just before their November trial, 63 riders, armed and masked, rode through Las Vegas, menacing the courthouse and district attorney. The grand jury dismissed the charges. That December, 47 more were indicted, but at the spring 1890 trial, the prosecution's witnesses did not materialize, and the charges were once again dropped. Meanwhile, *las Gorras Blancas* had engaged in several rides through Las Vegas and, during one ride, boldly posted copies of their platform:

> Our purpose is to protect the rights and interests of the people in general; especially those of the helpless classes. We want the Las Vegas Grant settled to the benefit of all concerned, and this we hold is the entire community . . .
>
> We want no "land grabbers" or obstructionists of any sort to interfere. We will watch them.
>
> We are not down on lawyers as a class, but the usual knavery and unfair treatment of the people must be stopped.
>
> There is a wide difference between New Mexico's "law" and "justice." Justice is God's law, and that we must have at all hazards.
>
> If the fact that we are law abiding citizens is questioned, come out to our homes and see the hunger and desolation we are suffering; and "this" is the result of the deceitful and corrupt methods of "bossism."[7]

Juan Jose Herrera, district organizer for the Knights of Labor, headed the list of indictees. In the areas where he established his twenty assemblies, there did *las Gorras Blancas* ride. The national Knights leadership disavowed Herrera and *las Gorras Blancas'* alleged violence, and local Anglo Knights did not support their ethnic politics. Nonetheless, the overlapping concerns over wage rates, eventual membership in the People's Party, backing of the local newspaper, *La Voz del Pueblo*, and the geographic location of support for such programs all strongly suggest that *las Gorras Blancas* and *los Caballeros de Labor* were actually one and the same.[8]

The raids suspended politics as usual and Anglo economic development in San Miguel County. In this situation of disarray arose *El Partido del Pueblo Unido*, the People's Party. The local conservative newspaper appropriately called it a "mongrel" party as middle-class Hispanos and Anglos who were disillusioned with the regular parties, Anglo workers angered by old-fashioned *jefes*, politicos, and the masses of increasingly delanded *gente* of San Miguel County all joined it. Members and leaders, often with contrary grievances and goals, were inspired by the national People's Party but remained distinct. *El Partido del Pueblo* swept the elections of 1890 and 1892, though support declined in the latter year. Typical of other populist revolts of the early 1890s, the insurgent political party threw Democrats and Republicans out of office, and then quickly devolved into factional squabbling. After 1892, White Cap activity declined dramatically. Battles over the land grants went into the courts, while class, local, and factional loyalties shattered *La Vox del Pueblo's* vision of a united *mexicano* people. Only sporadic cases of fence cutting, a classic case of "the so-called primitive accumulation" proceeded after the demise of *las Gorras Blancas*.[9]

The people's revolts looked backwards to an increasingly idealized past of economic independence, a time when men's sense of honor and loyalty guaranteed their prerogatives in the family and village. They were defying the imperial marketplace, recoiling at Ango-American racism, and resisting becoming wage workers. One famed rebel was Gregorio Cortez, a good and quiet ranchero of south Texas who shot a sheriff in a misunderstanding over a stolen horse, a story told in one of the most famous *corridos*, or Mexican folk ballads, of the border region.

Cortez became the people's hero when he eluded posses, troops, and Rangers, literally hundreds of men who chased him over five hundred miles over a ten-day period. This well-publicized event, with lots of shooting—particularly of innocent Mexicans upon whom the Rangers took their revenge—further convinced both the Anglos of the Mexicans' vicious character, and Mexicans of their own moral superiority and the Anglos' wickedness. According to a famous telling of the story, one of his people told Gregorio Cortez that "your own people are suffering, and all because of you. . . . You have killed many sheriffs. . . . The Rangers cannot catch you, so they take it out on other people like you." Cortez decided to give himself up, but before he could do so, one of his own people betrayed him for the thousand dollar reward.[10]

Four years of trials ensued. Acquitted on several counts of murder, Cortez was eventually convicted on one count and sentenced in 1905 to life imprisonment (though pardoned in 1913). Cortez was a man who knew, according to the *corridos*, that he would be betrayed and that he would lose his righteous fight. Gregorio Cortez was beloved, not only because he eluded so many Rangers, but because this "good" man sacrificed himself to the physically superior forces of the evil ones whose mastery was becoming more and more inescapable. It proved a costly symbolic victory in what was actually the conclusion of the Mexican-American War, a much larger defeat pervaded by an increasingly acknowledged sense of victimization. As for Gregorio Cortez, "that was the way men were in this country along the rivers," according to one telling of the story. "That was the way they were before these modern times came, and God went away."[11]

II.

The immense numbers of Mexican immigrants who began arriving after the turn of the century transformed parts of the Southwest into "México *afuera*," or "Mexico outside." Whether they were political exiles or people who simply came to work, they believed that someday they would return to *la madre patria*. Thus Mexicans of all persuasions concerned themselves politically with matters in Mexico foremost. Naturally enough, as opposition to the Porfirio Diaz regime swelled and eventually erupted, Mexico's *afuera* experienced many of the same convulsions and explosions. Although partisans of all sides of the Mexican Revolution agitated north of the border, the anarchist ideas associated with Ricardo Flores Magón and the *Partido Liberal Mexicano* dominated Mexican revolutionary politics in the American Southwest.

Mexico's most revered president, the Zapotec Indian Benito Juarez, led his people in the name of liberalism against conservative tyrants such as Santa Ana and against the French invaders. In 1876 Diaz overthrew Juarez and opened Mexico wide to outside capital. Young Mexican intellectuals perceived that the problems of Mexico associated with the *Porfiriato* derived from the regime's and the foreigners' corruption of liberalism. In the 1890s one such student, Ricardo Flores Magón, began to criticize the regime for its favoritism toward English and American companies, and, particularly, for crushing the freedom of the press and electoral democracy. Diaz expelled Flores Magón in 1903 and the rebel joined numerous other exiles in the southwestern U.S., a model of liberalism in these idealistic Mexicans' eyes.

Soon, Librado Rivera, Ricardo and his brother Enrique Flores Magón, Juan Sarabia, Antonio Villareal, and a few others began to organize for revolution in Mexico. From St. Louis in 1905, Flores Magón and others organized the *Partido Liberal Mexicano,* which espoused a vague socialism upholding the sovereignty of the people above all else, while asserting the harmony of all classes. Mexicans on both sides of the border flocked to the liberal clubs the PLM organized, and its newspaper, *Regeneración,* quickly grew in circulation to between fifteen thousand and twenty thousand. The adherents, like the leaders predominantly journalists, craftsmen, and teachers, were mostly petty bourgeois or skilled workers, particularly miners. They were the ones who had most profoundly experienced proletarianization at the hands of American and British capital. The great leader of the Tarascan Indian people, Primo Tapia, from the village of Naranja, Machoacan, which had suffered the destruction of its common lands at the hands of the world market, thus joined the PLM in Los Angeles, allegedly lived in its housing, and actually worked at its newspaper office during 1910–1911.[12]

The American police and Mexican agents constantly harassed the PLM with jailings, confiscations of its press, and physical intimidation. This treatment and the racism they saw reflected so profoundly in the super-exploitation of Mexican workers, ended whatever illusions the *Liberales* retained about U.S. liberalism and reform. Following their arrest in Los Angeles for violation of neutrality laws in 1907, the PLM junta became something of a cause célèbre of Anglo radicals. Although these charges were dropped after a strong legal defense had been mounted, the junta was shipped to Arizona and convicted of violating neutrality laws in May 1909, and sentenced to eighteen months in jail. Meanwhile, during the summer of 1908, the PLM had launched several attacks across the border from Texas, an effort that resulted only in failure and more arrests, leaving the *Liberales* in utter disarray.

In this context, the writings of such anarchists as Michael

Bakunin, Enrico Maltesta, Carlos Malato, and Peter Kropotkin, along with the presence in PLM circles of Emma Goldman and the Spanish anarchist Florencio Bozora, among others, influenced Flores Magón in the direction of anarchy. Likewise from spring 1908 but definitively and publicly in the "*Manifesto de 23 de Septiembre 1911,*" Ricardo Flores Magón, the junta, and *Regeneración* proclaimed themselves and their organization for anarchist revolution in Mexico.[13]

These extraordinary people, their vision as compelling as it was utopian, brought ideology and analysis to their peoples' rebellions against the rule of capital and the market. Like most anarchists, the PLM vociferously condemned bourgeois society, explicitly declaring *guerra al Autoridad, guerra al Capital, guerra al Clero,* and then sought to strike the matches that would ignite revolution in the masses they politicized. The *Liberales* believed that since workers produced wealth, it naturally belonged to them. If wealth came mainly from the land, it too belonged to the people.

This worldview renewed a familiar perspective and resonated with those in Mexico and the Southwest who understandably saw capitalism as an interloper that altered patterns, often from an idealized past of independence and subsistence production. Capital and bourgeois legality enslaved people by keeping them from wealth that was morally theirs. The clergy betrayed the people because it fooled them and kept them from reason and creativity, which was their destiny as human beings. Only through propaganda and direct action, not political maneuvering or strategy, would people overturn the capitalist system. They would then replace this system with self-governing institutions in which local autonomy and cooperation would reign. To these ends, the PLM propagandized vigorously and widely, mostly in the no less than thirty *magonista* newspapers published in the U.S.; formed many clandestine and open "liberal clubs"; and organized workers into unions. They believed this activity would ultimately precipitate *the* general insurrection from which the people would take power.[14]

Such thinking explains the otherwise quixotic invasion of Baja California in 1911. From Los Angeles, the junta planned the uprising to spark the great revolt. Bands composed of *Liberales,* Wobblies, Italian-American anarchists, and assorted adventurers succeeded in taking both Mexicali and Tijuana. But Baja California did not erupt in flames of revolution. The PLM leadership, especially Ricardo Flores Magón who did not take the field, lost credibility. Splits further shook, jumbled, and shattered the organization.[15]

In matters of culture, PLM ideology proved engaging, controversial and sometimes contradictory. Ricardo Flores Magón was a Mexican nationalist who railed at foreign domination of his country, yet also preached international solidarity of the "disinherited of the earth." The people were sovereign and capable of lives of reason, love, and beauty, but presently they were ignorant and apathetic. They had to be educated away from religion and the patriarchal nuclear family, two mainstays of Mexican culture.

The *Liberales* sought to be cönsistent in their own personal ways. Between 1914 and 1916, the Flores Magón brothers and several other *Liberales* rented five acres just north of downtown Los Angeles, where they lived and farmed communally. Ricardo and Enrique lived with their *compañeras* María Talavera and Teresa Arteaga in relationships based on love, not bourgeois marriage. Everyone worked together in the orchard, but the women maintained the household and rolled the newspapers while the men wrote. The subscriptions and fruit they sold downtown could not support *Regeneración,* so several women formed *Luz y Vida* in November 1915. This all-women's PLM adjunct held dances and benefits and sold food to support the paper and the propaganda effort.[16]

Richardo's practice reflected his ideology, elucidated in his famous essay, "*A La Mujer,*" published in September 1910. "Humiliated, degraded, bound by chains of tradition to an irrational inferiority indoctrinated in the affairs of heaven by cleric . . . " woman was "suddenly caught in the whirlwind of industrial production which above all requires cheap labor to sustain the competition created by the voracious 'princes of capital' who exploit her circumstances." Educated and prepared, women would "spit in the face of those who refused to pick up a weapon against oppression." But on the other hand, woman's duty was also to "help man; to stand by his side when he suffers; to lighten his sorrow; to laugh and to sing with him when victory smiles." A second famous essay on women by Praxedis Guerrero, a junta member and field commander killed in battle in 1911, argued more strongly that "feminism" was associated with the "masculine female . . . divorced from her sweet mission." The revolutionary alternative drew strongly on an anarcho-Rousseauean vision of a return to nature that Guerrero associated with nurturing, mysterious, and superior Woman.[17]

What women thought about all this, or how they participated in PLM activities, is more difficult to ascertain. At least one activist of Laredo, the literary figure Sara Estela Ramírez, whose home actually served as the first PLM headquarters upon the Flores Magóns' arrival in Texas, expressed similar Rousseauean notions of womanhood: "woman lives for ever and this is the secret of her happiness, life." "Only action is life," and women should "arise radiant and powerful," she wrote. Apparently Mexican women's pro-female ideologies remained essentialist ones in spite of such inflammatory claims as that of the Los Angeles *Times* that María Talavera, the *compañera* of Ricardo, was a "brilliant and bold woman anarchist who dared more than any of the men" and an "expert assassin." Her own activities got her arrested on several occasions, and she was only one of numerous woman who propagandized for revolution in the American Southwest and the Mexican north. Teresa and Andrea Villareal organized campaigns in support of imprisoned *Liberales* and founded their own newspaper in San Antonio, *La Mujer Moderna*.[18]

In the context of all this agitation, the excitement of the Mexican Revolution (1911–1920), and the penetration of "gringo" capitalism, Mexicans in *México afuera* fought their own revolution. "Supporters of all factions," noted a leery observer in 1914 of La Placita, the old town plaza of Los Angeles, "are to be found among them and adherents of the Industrial Workers of the World and of the Mexican Liberal Party may be heard in the general discussion." Demonstrations, street fighting, consular intrigues, invasions of Mexico, and in south Texas, insurrection against domination by both the *Porfiriato* and Anglo supremacy, all marked political life in *México afuera* during those times of revolution in *la madre patria*.

Rebellion in south Texas coalesced under the banner of *El Plan de San Diego*. The plan's rhetoric and actions bear resemblance to a millenarianist movement, a last ditch effort to regain the ancestral lands and be delivered from evil. Then, too, recent research has shown the close ties that the leadership and adherents had with the PLM through widespread reading of *Regeneración*. Politicking between Woodrow Wilson and Mexican president Venustiano Carranza, with some insinuations about German machinations, also entered the picture as did elements of a race war. Thus this episode of 1915–1916 defies clear-cut analysis. Obviously, different people joined the movement, used it, and interpreted it for different reasons. At any rate, in January 1915, Bacilio Ramos, one of four recently arrived proprietors of a politically inflammatory beer hall in San Diego, Texas, was captured and taken to Brownsville. Among his papers was found a copy of "El Plan de San Diego," a document calling for an armed uprising by Mexicans to take place on February 20 to return all the lands "robbed in a most perfidious manner by North American imperialism," to "put to death every North American over sixteen years of age" (except women and the elderly), to return Indian lands, and to establish sovereign territories for blacks. Only people of "the Latin, Negro, or Japanese race" could enroll.[19]

Instead of an uprising, February 20 marked a substantial revision of the document in which anarchist notions of "universal love," the "proletariat," communal property, and "social revolution" replaced race revenge. Indeed PLM ideology proved appropriate, and present, in the context of polarizing south Texas race relations. In 1904 the arrival of the railroad and irrigation seriously upset the population balance of the south Texan counties. More and more Anglos came to own farms and many, many more Mexicans came to work on them. Only now instead of some marital mixing on the part of the better off, both sides began to maintain exclusive social relations. Less and less did a group of mixed families and a complicated system of *compadrazgo* (godparentage) maintain a tenuous peace. In other words, not only did capitalist ways penetrate all the more deeply, divisions between Mexicans and Texans become more distinct. The approximately sixteen hundred copies of each issue of *Regeneración* circulating in south Texas helped its readers to analyze this situation in political-economic terms. For example, Aniceto Pizaña, founded a PLM group in Brownsville in 1904, followed Ricardo Flores Magón in his evolution to anarchism, and read the paper aloud to illiterates at his ranch. Similarly, Pizaña's best friend, Luis de la Rosa, a butcher and former county sheriff, founded several PLM *grupos* in the area. In 1915, however, the PLM *grupos* divided into two camps, the moderates, associated with Pizaña, and *los sediciosos*, associated with de la Rosa. Typically, petit proprietors in south Texas subscribed to *Regeneración*, again the backbone of the anarchist activists. Constituting something of an intellectual elite, they criticized the new commercial ways but did not simply harken back to the good old days. It is not clear what they thought about the idea that "God went away."[20]

On July 4, 1915, crossing back and forth across the border, armed riders sacked Anglo ranches and businesses, raided livestock, and clashed with Ranger forces. They rode under the banner of *"El Plan de San Diego"* and the leaders were generally considered to be Aniceto Pizaña and Luis de la Rosa. South Texas had become a war zone with both sides committing atrocities. Most of the Anglos fled the southern counties and about forty percent of the Mexicans sought refuge on the other side of the border. Vigilantes and Rangers executed at least 150 Mexicans in retaliation. After de la Rosa led an attack on a train in October, which killed several Anglos amid much antigringo rhetoric, the furor rose to such a pitch that Woodrow Wilson increased troops sufficiently to drive the armed adherents of the plan underground or across the border. The violence was renewed in spring 1916, but by then Carranza had secured enough control in Mexico for a full-fledged assault on all anarchists, including those on his northern periphery. The combined military forces of Mexico and the United States, which stationed fifty thousand troops in south Texas, finally quieted the border. Ironically, Ricardo Flores Magón dismissed the actions in Texas as mere self-defense and denied the existence of the plan, while American radicals attributed *El Plan de San Diego* to a plot to justify American intervention in Mexico.[21]

Consistent with its discourses on "the disinherited of the earth," and for the tactical reason of rallying the masses to the cause and politicizing them, the *Partido Liberal Mexicano* sought to organize Mexican workers into unions, often in cooperation with the Industrial Workers of the World. In its Fresno Local 66 during 1909 and 1910, the IWW, for example, while unable to create an ongoing union, organized many Mexican migratory agricultural and railroad workers. The legendary Frank Little headed the Fresno organizational efforts and the Mexican IWW organizer, Jesus González Monroy, was also a PLM activist. In Los Angeles in 1910–1911, the IWW exerted influence in strikes of Mexican street railway and gas workers. One PLM activist estimated that at its height before the war "the Los Angeles local alone had nearly 400 active members in its Latino wing, mostly Mexicans." Primo Tapia organized Rocky Mountain unskilled miners and migratory wheat laborers for the IWW. He fled back to Mexico in early 1920 after he and some village *compañetos* led a remarkable but unsuccessful effort to organize Mexican beet workers in Nebraska.[22]

After the generals pushed out the anarchists from postrevolutionary Mexico, and Flores Magón died in Leavenworth prison in 1921, Los Angeles involuntarily hosted the remnants of these *Liberales*. These colorful and certainly provocative speakers in La Placita made "many fiery and sometimes vile accusations against religion and capitalism." In the 1920s, reformers concerned with "stopping these 'Reds!' typically cited a "cross-eyed agitator . . . haranguing some two hundred idle, ignorant Mexicans." That these orators spoke against "that old Roman Church opposite us [which] is a nest of deceivers," and against "clergy, law, [and] capital," quickly established their identity.[23]

These inflammatory words did not fall on deaf ears. The people understood that the Catholic Church, the greatest monopolizer of land, opposed the Mexican Revolution. Many Mexicans, while certainly Catholic, were intensely anticlerical, a sentiment the *libre-pensadores* (free-thinkers) exploited in their tirades at La Placita. Of course, the church was not without its equally vehement backers. Luis Tenorio, a street paver of the late 1920s, described how "on Sundays I go to the little square to hear some of the fellow workers. That is where I have gotten socialistic ideas and I read the papers which these friends sell. . . . " From the same period, construction worker Guillermo Salorio said:

> I am studying books and I now lack very little of being well convinced that God doesn't exist. I first became acquainted with these ideas because I went to the square on Sundays and there heard some of the comrades make some speeches. They said nothing but the truth, that the capital is what steals everything and that money isn't good for anything, that it is necessary for everyone to work. I believe the same in everything and that is why I liked their ideas and I began to read papers and books and go to the IWW hall.

Many Mexican workers in the United States, so long admired for their alleged passivity, often revealed themselves as dangerous revolutionaries.[24]

Victims of savage repression as well as ideologies that failed to promote an ongoing organization, the anarcho-syndicalist tradition in the Southwest had faded by the early 1920s. Nevertheless, in Mexico Primo Tapia became the leader of the League of Agrarian Communities in Michoacan, an organization that sought the return of the peoples' *ejido* lands and saluted the Bolshevik Revolution. Through political and military means, Tapia and his followers succeeded in restoring many of the lands and the communal methods of harvesting them, though the government quashed the movement and assassinated him.[25]

The IWW/PLM tradition of class-conscious, nondiscriminatory, industrial unionism remained alive in the north, and motivated organization and strikes through the 1920s and 1930s. The PLM's continuing influence resurfaced in the *Confederación de Uniones de Obreros Mexicanos* (CUOM) organized in 1928 in Los Angeles. A variety of *colonia* and community leaders, including the Mexican consul, called for a union of all Mexican workers in the area, rural and urban. PLM ideology clearly surfaced in the CUOM, which made for an uneasy alliance with the consul who represented a Mexican government eager to push such class-conscious revolutionary agitation into the dustbin of history. One suspects *mutualista* and *colonia* leaders for whom "unity constitutes strength" simply hoped for the unification of as many sectors of the Mexican community as could be achieved.[26]

Ringing the One Big Union bell of the PLM/IWW, the CUOM stated in March 1928:

> That the exploited class, the greater part of which is made up of manual labor, is right in establishing a class struggle in order to effect an economic and moral betterment of its condition, and at last its complete freedom from capitalist tyranny . . . That the corporations, possessors of the natural and social wealth, being integral parts of the international association of industry, commerce and banking, the disinherited class must also integrate by means of its federations and confederation into a single union all the labor of the world.

While the CUOM modified its program of resistance in order to be "in accord with the rights which the laws of this country concede to native and foreign workers," the PLM/IWW tradition resonates soundly through these principles.[27]

The CUOM did not meet with success until, prompted by the important El Monte berry pickers' strike of June 1933, it was reorganized as the *Confederación de Uniones de Campesinos y Obreros Mexicanos* (CUCOM). This organization also continued to carry traces of Magónista anarcho-syndicalist ideology in its organization of Mexican workers in Los Angeles. This philosophy and tradition traveled not merely amorphously in the spirit of Mexican labor organization and struggles, but physically in the baggage of the CUCOM leadership. Representative was its vice president, William Valarde, an IWW member whose father had organized for the IWW and who had "personal and political ties" with the PLM.[28]

Raza y los Rojos

After 1919 the anarchists had new competition in their efforts to win the hearts and minds of Mexican workers. That eventful year saw not only the establishment of Soviet power in Russia, and briefly in Bavaria and Hungary, but also a strike in February of Mexican citrus workers in the San Gabriel Valley just east of Los Angeles. A relatively minor affair in retrospect—the pickers struck because of miserable housing conditions and because the market forced wages below what they could live on—the names of those arrested and their political affiliations provide a window into a remarkable revolutionary moment in Mexican-American history. The press associated those with Spanish last names, such as Manuel Sastre or "Francisco Zamora . . . one of the leading I.W.W.," with that organization. Those with Jewish last names were the *agitadores Rusos*, one of whom allegedly stated that their group was "like a Russian Soviet or committee." The usual array of police power, arrests, stacked juries, and vigilantes forcibly removing organizers from the fields, defeated the strike. But internationally affiliated leaders of the class struggle, anarchists, and communists (apparently without rivalry in this case), had attempted to lead, politicize, and focus the spontaneous, "econo-mist" strike actions of Mexican workers.[29]

Mexicans certainly knew plenty about the notion of the strike, in large part because of all the tumult of the revolution and the harangues of the various politicos. It's impossible to know exactly what produces a specific strike. During the nominal and formal depressions of the 1920s and 1930s, Mexican agricultural workers often refused the wages that the allegedly hard-pressed growers and the labor market assigned them. Workers struck, in part, to establish the market rate for their labor by temporarily withdraw-ing it from the market to determine its exchange value. They also believed that their families' subsistence required a certain minimum remuneration, and only a strike could achieve this. Their labor was not some commodity, but their means of supporting their families, fundamentally a conservative application of their bodies' work. That something as impersonal as the market could establish how much money would be paid them for their families' subsistence was a notion either hateful, immoral, or incomprehen-sible. Thus they could agree with most of what their CUCOM or Communist-affiliated Cannery and Agricultural Workers Industrial Union leaders told them about capitalism, if not always about the church. They usually joined a union and went on strike not from ideology or vision but from a sense of necessity. This was the same mindset with which they migrated to the north in the first place, and then took on work as onerous as stoop labor in the sweltering fields. One did what family survival required on a week-to-week, even day-to-day, basis. This meant taking dreadful jobs, which paid enough to maintain the family, and then going on strike when the market pushed that pay below what was minimally necessary. From their precarious position in the labor market, summoning up the courage to challenge their bosses and the police in order to provision and conserve their families, we see the radicalism of everyperson's challenge both to the domination of the capitalist labor market and to white society's presumptions about racial hierarchy. In addition, there were extraordinary persons who entered the scene to lead confrontations and to introduce radically new ways of thinking about, and eventually organizing, production and social relations.

Few non-Mexicans (usually radicals of some stripe) supported the efforts of Mexicans to redress their grievances. This pattern continued through the interwar years. With the demise of the IWW and the PLM, and the hostility and chauvinism of the AFL towards organizing farm laborers, especially ones of color, not much happened in the area of militant Mexican union activity until the Communist Party's Trade Union Unity League arrived on the scene. There had been work stoppages, like those in 1928 in the Imperial Valley, but they surfaced out of mutual aid societies and were usually defeated. But, in early 1930 when Mexican workers again struck California's great agricultural valley, the TUUL seized upon the situation to organize an industrial, multi-ethnic agricultural union—the Agricultural Workers Industrial League. The strike collapsed and the Communists were arrested and incarcerated in San Quentin for violation of criminal syndicalism laws. A year later the Communist Party established the Cannery and Agricultural Workers Industrial Union, which sprouted in the summer of 1932 in a series of small strikes. While these efforts were defeated, 1933 saw the blossoming of the C&AWIU as well as an intensification of legal and extralegal arrests, violence, and extensive intimidation seeking to stamp unionism out of the fields of California. During 1933 and 1934 Mexican workers and the growers of California engaged in class struggle fought with brass knuckles, guns, clubs, and tear gas, which the growers and their thugs, in and out of uniform, freely wielded. Crushed in July 1934, the C&AWIU succeeded, briefly and with mixed outcomes, in bringing unionism to Mexican field workers. In 1933 the C&AWIU led 24 of the reported 37 agricultural strikes in California, and of those 24, 21 resulted in partial wage increases.[30]

C&AWIU organizer Dorothy Healey has claimed that the strikes "usually broke out spontaneously and then the workers would come and find us." She describes the Mexican workers as "very anti-clerical, very sophisticated politically, and very anarcho-syndicalist in orientation." They told her " 'don't bother us with meetings all the time. . . . Just tell us when the revolution is ready.' " Another faithful party organizer has stated that the leadership from the above-mentioned CUCOM El Monte strike of 1933 stemmed "from the old anarcho-syndicalist unions in Mexico . . . who never reached out to the public in general . . . [because] it was strictly a Mexican union, trade union affair." In its own analysis of the failure of the El Monte strike, the party noted that "the strikers were more apt to give confidence to the leadership of their own fellow workers in carrying through the decisions of the C. and A.W.I.U." Another organizer noted that in the Imperial Valley, "at the most we had 20 to 25 people who signed a card, and they never actually became our conception of the Communist Party member. They drifted away. . . . "[31] Were these radical Mexicans, who organized themselves based on their anarcho-syndicalist heritage and then procured some help from earnest, sometimes effective, sometimes imprudent, "gringo" Bolsheviks? Were they Mexican pickers who merely sought wages adequate to put food on the table? Or were these Mexicans potential recruits for the communist revolutionary vanguard? Individually and collectively, these Mexican pickers were all three, at different places, at different moments, for different agendas.

During the Popular Front period, when the reds supported and organized antifascist and democratic movements rather than their own "revolutionary offensive" organizations such as the C&AWIU, the party produced an outline analysis and strategy on "The Mexican Question in the Southwest." Emma Tenayuca, state chair of the Texas Communist Party, and her husband, Homer Brooks, state secretary, authored the document in 1939. Tenayuca, known as *La Pasionaria*, was a remarkable activist in the Mexican community of San Antonio and leader of the 1938 strike of pecan shellers there. These two activist-theoreticians understood how "The Mexican population of the Southwest is closely bound together by historical, political and cultural ties" because "from the very beginning they were robbed of their land." They also knew how Mexican workers "uniformly received lower wages than those paid Anglo-American workers" and labored in "only the most menial work." Tenayuca and Brooks concluded that:

> Historically the Mexican people in the Southwest have
> evolved in a series of bordering though separated, commu-

nities, their economic life inextricably connecting them, not only with one another, but with the Anglo American population in each of these separated Mexican communities. Therefore, their economic (and hence, their political) interests are welded to those of the Anglo American people of the Southwest.

Mexicans did not actually or potentially constitute a nation according to "Comrade Stalin's classic definition," but racial oppression clearly had much to do with their condition as super-exploited workers. A movement for Mexican liberation would struggle:

(1) Against economic discrimination—extra-low wages; expropriation of small land holders. (2) For educational and cultural equality . . . [including] the use of Spanish as well as English in the public schools. (3) Against social oppression—for laws making illegal the various forms of Jim Crowism (This struggle must be linked with that of the Negro people), and (4) Against political repression.

In such a movement "the leading role will undoubtedly be played by the proletarian base of the Mexican population, its overwhelming majority."[32]

Such a strategy and program both reflected party practice and guided it. With the formation of the Committee for (later Congress of) Industrial Organizations (CIO) in 1935, Communists and Mexicans who had migrated into industrial jobs found themselves interacting with one another in substantial ways. A little over ten percent of the party's recruits in California during 1936–1937 were "Spanish and Mexican workers," though a few months were as long as most sojourned. Leading Mexican unionists sometimes joined the party and stayed, and many Mexicans were organized into Communist-led or -influenced CIO unions, where they gained exposure to many of the national and international political issues associated with the Popular Front. Further, as Mexicans started to concern themselves more with political life in the United States, the reds of the Popular Front involved themselves in, or instigated, such organizations as the Spanish-Speaking Peoples Congress and the *Asociación Nacional México-Americana*. This political activity pushed aside whatever remained of anarchy as a political persuasion among radical Mexicans.[33]

Many Mexicans in California and the Southwest joined, organized, and led such classic Popular Front unions as the United Furniture Workers; the United Cannery, Agricultural, Packinghouse, and Allied Workers of America (UCAPAWA); and the International Union of Mine, Mill, and Smelter Workers, among others. Such unions passed resolutions supporting republican Spain, raised money for the *People's World,* most adamantly sustained the no strike during World War II, and supported Henry Wallace in 1948.

A profound shift in Mexican aspirations transpired in these multi-ethnic organizations. No longer did they only involve themselves in nationalist, community-based defensive strikes; Mexicans now demanded equality in treatment and wages through their unions. Aware that racially exclusive organizations provided employers with willing strike-breakers and doomed the labor movement to defeat, the CIO largely supported racial equality, and the Communists did so enthusiastically. "The companies around here have always been afraid of Anglo-Mexican unity," stated Juan Chacon, president of the Mine, Mill local, about which the famous film *Salt of the Earth* was made. "For a hundred years our employers have played up the big lie that we Mexicans are 'naturally inferior' and 'different,' in order to justify paying us less and separating us from our brothers."[34]

Out of this association between the Communists and the unions with a large Mexican rank-and-file emerged a number of Mexican Party members. "The only hope for the American worker lay in the workers' party," stated a local president of the Steel Workers Organization Committee who, at that time, saw "no essential difference between the Democratic and Republican parties." Communist leadership against fascism in Europe proved particularly compelling in this case. Others seem to have had a more pragmatic attraction: Party membership "made it possible for me," stated an organizer for the United Furniture Workers, UCAPAWA, and the ILGWU, "to work in the labor movement or in socially oriented problems or issues with much better resources." Many Mexican-American ex-communists who spent any time in the party seem to feel either that the party duped and used them in spite of the politics and skills they developed; or that it became "ineffective . . . and thrashed about" when it was attacked, and therefore was no longer relevant to their main purpose of organizing workers. Others stand in support of the positions they took.[35]

Most of the interesting political activity happened within Popular Front organizations that were formally non-party. There was much overlap between such unions as UCAPAWA and the Workers Alliance, for example, depending on whether one was employed in agriculture or out of work. Luisa Moreno, Guatemalan-born labor activist, organized for UCAPAWA, and is generally considered the organizer of *El Congreso del Pueblo de Habla Española,* or the Spanish-Speaking Peoples' Congress, which was founded in Los Angeles with the help of the Communist Party in April 1939. Fifteen hundred people, including delegates representing 105 mostly Mexican-American and *mexicano* organizations attended the convention. In strong contrast to middle-class organizations, the congress stressed unity between those workers from Mexico and Mexican-Americans. It viewed Mexicans in the United States as an oppressed national minority, but allied itself with "all democratic forces among the Anglo-American and minority groups." Josefina Fierro de Bright assumed the position of executive secretary at age eighteen and was an energetic, pragmatic leftist. (Her mother, a restaurant owner in Los Angeles, was an exiled follower of Ricardo Flores Magón.) She told the *People's World,* "The fight against discrimination and deportation, for economic liberty, for equal representation in government, for the building of a better world for our youth—this is our Congress's answer."[36]

The congress's practical work, essentially confined to Los Angeles, consisted of agitating about police abuse, enabling Mexicans access to low-cost housing, helping with residence and citizenship forms and job applications, affirming equality for women in the organization, guaranteeing equal education for Mexican youth, and supporting access for Spanish-speaking people to defense jobs and unionization. The membership included a genuine cross section of *la gente,* and the leadership stretched from liberal-moderate to radical-Left. The congress's history was brief. In 1942, like most Popular Front organizations, it disbanded to promote unity for the war effort.[37]

The two decades following World War II are associated with the "Mexican-American generation," a time of accommodation and assimilation both culturally and politically. Mexican-Americans sought to integrate themselves into the American system rather than to substantively change it. While this categorization obscures much about Chicano history, it also carries some truth: "Radicalism" but not "militancy" faded to the background until "Chicano nationalism" arose in the late 1960s. But those were exciting times. The notion of a Popular Front organization still breathed in the form of the *Asociación Nacional México-Americana* (ANMA), founded in October 1949. A convention to coordinate chapters of *Amigos de Wallace,* which the Mine, Mill had been organizing, provided most of the impetus and initial delegates in the founding of ANMA. The organization sought the political unification of Mexicans in the United States, basic democratic rights, and ethnic and political awareness, including a renewal of ties with Mexicans south of the border. It analyzed the Mexican population of the U.S. as fundamentally working class, but recognized the potency of racial discrimination in the Southwest. Some two thousand people, mostly CIO unionists, belonged to ANMA. Josefina Fierro ran for Congress in 1951 as a candidate of the Progressive Party, and the newspaper *Progreso* served as the official mouthpiece of the organization.

ANMA was enmeshed in cold war and international politics. It advocated peace, disarmament, and opposition to the Korean War, which, the Denver chapter noted, killed Mexican-American soldiers well out of proportion to their numbers. It opposed the Bracero Program, which imported thousands of Mexican nationals to work in agriculture, on the grounds that it simply provided employers cheap labor, divided the working class, and thus undercut wage levels in the Southwest. At the same time, ANMA opposed discrimination against and deportations of Mexican nationals. Because of ANMA's connections with Mine, Mill (the descendent of the Western Federation of Miners), its leaders and members were well aware of the anti-union and anti-alien nature of so much of the antisubversive legislation associated with Truman-McCarthyism. The organization and its publications publicly opposed such repressive legislation. Similarly, ANMA denounced police brutality, cultural stereotyping of Mexicans, and supression of the Spanish language, all of which crushed Mexican-American aspirations for what they called "first-class citizenship." Such positions opened ANMA to charges of control by the Communist Party. The FBI investigated and infiltrated ANMA, prepared evidence, and, in 1954, the attorney general listed it as a subversive organization under the Internal Security Act (McCarran Act) of 1950. This effectively spelled its doom.[38]

The same sort of fate had already befallen the Mine, Mill; the Food, Tobacco, Agricultural, and Allied Workers Union (what UCAPAWA became); and the United Furniture Workers. "In line with the principles of the Communist Party," stated the orders expelling it from the CIO, "Mine, Mill has opposed the Truman doctrine and fought against the Marshall Plan." Their "false claims of autonomy cannot justify adherence to the foreign policy of the Soviet Union and a betrayal of the American workingman." The FTA's policies "show only one undeviating parallel—the damning parallel between the policies of FTA and the Communist Party."

The CIO expelled the Mine, Mill and the FTA (though it was a shell of a union when it happened), and the UFW was re-admitted only when it ousted its left-wing leaders and rejected its Popular Front ideology.[39] Truman-McCarthyism had trampled what remained of the Mexican-American peoples' left-wing union and community organizations.

Anticommunism obviously repressed the Left in America. It busted unions, intimidated Popular Front organizations, and hounded and jailed leaders. (Josefina Fierro de Bright and Luisa Moreno exiled themselves to Mexico). In the greater scope of Mexican radicalism in the United States, the red scares had a less obvious consequence, but one of no less importance. By aiming not only at leaders, but at the most articulate, well-positioned, astute, and thoughtful representatives of the Mexican-American working class and communities (what Antonio Gramsci called "the organic intellectuals"), a crucial transmission belt for the dissemination of socialist or other radical ideologies was severed. Mexican resistance could not get very far when it merely lashed out at the most visible emblems of its oppression, fences and "gringos" for example, or engaged in quick work stoppages. It took a Ricardo Flores Magón, or the leaders of the Popular Front, to listen to the peoples' miseries, to explain their oppression to them, to help them organize effective unions and community organizations, and to help them transcend their harsh, sometimes brutalizing, world with a vision of more benevolent ways to organize production and human relations. The red scares meant no more PLM *grupos;* no more Left-led unions like the C&AWIU or the Mine, Mill; no more Popular Front organizations like the Spanish-Speaking Peoples' Congress and ANMA, or the Workers' Alliance and the International Labor Defense; and no more newspapers like *Regeneración* or *Progreso.* No doubt there was much foolishness in all that anarchist talk about the perfectability of humankind, and even more in all that about the Soviet Union, but ideas had circulated. They traveled to the shop floors, the agricultural fields, neighborhoods, bars, street corners, and even Tarascan Indian villages. Sometimes people listened, sometimes they agreed, sometimes they were moved to oppose what threatened their familiar ways, yet ideas about new politics were not segregated into the hands of sectarians or the academy.

Mexican radicalism was not without its ongoing effects, though. The unions, which were usually radical ones if they organized Mexicans, provided an important means for the structural integration of Mexicans into the United States. It was they who not only affirmed the "radical" notion of equality, but acted upon it. Most Mexicans immigrated to the United States to work, but they often did not have a sense of themselves as workers. They might be petit proprietors, *peones,* peasants, or, quite typically, people who shifted in and out of different categories. For better or for worse, radicals in the United States, Mexican and Anglo, exposed them to working-class consciousness and organized them into working-class associations. Such provided the ideological complement to the structural proletarianization that capitalism brought.

Rural folk and students generated the next radical upsurge. César Chavez and the United Farmworkers Union (UFW), in particular, triggered a renaissance of oppositional activity. The first Mexican-American of true national stature, Chavez organized the UFW in 1962. For a while the UFW succeeded in bringing some justice to the fields of California. The demand for decent working and living conditions in the fields, like African-American demands during the civil rights movement of the 1960s, threatened to "revolutionize" the usual social relations between growers and pickers, the call's consistency with, say, the Declaration of Independence, notwithstanding. Achieving a living wage, the availability of water and toilets in the fields, and some protection from pesticides meant a new life for many agricultural workers. Initially organizing Mexican workers as families and as a community, the UFW's strenuous efforts moved increasingly in the direction of the famous consumer boycotts of lettuce and grapes. While sometimes criticized for centralizing too much control around his suffering and charismatic persona, Chavez inspired a new era of oppositional politics on the part of Mexican Americans.[40]

In the late 1950s, Reies Lopez Tijerina (b. 1923) resurrected efforts to restore the ancestral lands of New Mexico, which had been granted before 1846. Trying to enlist the support of the Mexican government, the United Nations, and the American courts, Tijerina wanted to enforce the Treaty of Guadalupe-Hidalgo and the legality of the land grants. As legal channels produced only frustration, the spirit of *las Gorras Blancas* was reborn. In 1963 he organized the *Alianza Federal de Mercedes,* which attracted hundreds of barrio dwellers in Albuquerque who had been pressured off the land and onto welfare or wage dependency, and thousands of Hispano farmers from northern New Mexico and southern Colorado who barely subsisted on the remains of their ancestral lands. Through marches on the New Mexico capitol, this organization brought mass pressure, albeit futile, on the state government to recognize their cause.

In October 1966, Tijerina and 350 *Aliancistas* occupied a portion of Kit Carson National Forest, which they understood to be part of the San Joaquin del Rio Chama grant. Arresting two rangers for trespassing, they elected a traditional *alcalde* and *ayuntamiento.* After being turned out of the forest, Tijerina was arrested and released on bail. The state's establishment—Anglo and Mexican—called him a communist and a "creature of darkness." On June 5, 1967, Tijerina and twenty armed *Aliancistas* captured the Tierra Amarilla Courthouse in an effort to place District Attorney Sanchez under citizen's arrest. The ensuing shoot-out seriously wounded two officers. The rebels fled to the hills as a two thousand man army terrorized the countryside searching for them. Tijerina was eventually acquitted of charges arising from this affair, but he was jailed for the previous incident, effectively causing the demise of the *Alianza.*[41]

The Crusade for Justice in Colorado, *El Partido de la Raza Unida* in Texas, the high school student strikes ("blow-outs") in East Los Angeles and later in south Texas and Denver, and *el Movimiento Estudiantil Chicano de Aztlán* (MEChA) on college campuses, represented a new nationalism that challenged both Anglo cultural and political dominance as well as the accommodationist views of the 1950s generation of Mexican-Americans. The youth took the word *Chicano* to distinguish themselves from assimilationists. (The word may derive either from the Nahuatl pronunciation of *Mexicano,* or from the state name Chihuahua, and usually denoted someone of rough, lower-class origins.) They also took the phrase in use in Mexican communities since the nineteenth century to denote the Mexican people—*La Raza.*

Rodolfo "Corky" Gonzalez, boxer and author of the inspirational epic poem "I Am Joaquin," founded the Crusade for Justice in Denver in 1966. Vigilant in its attempts to "nationalize every school in our community" and in its defense of the Chicano community against the police, the crusade founded its own school, newspaper, and social center. The movement sought to reclaim *Aztlán,* the mythical northern origin-place of the Aztecs, as the homeland for Chicanos. Emphasizing the organic ties of family, language, and "hands in the soil," Gonzalez projected a flowering of patriarchal nationalism that would ultimately bring about self-determination for a "mestizo nation . . . , a union of free pueblos."[42]

In 1967 college students in San Antonio founded the Mexican

American Youth Organization, which gained financial assistance from the Ford Foundation. Challenging the Democratic Party in that city, it lost its funding, and one of MAYO's organizers and main spokesperson, José Angel Gutiérrez, then went to Crystal City in south Texas to put MAYO's principles into action in his hometown. In mid-1969 his organization and strategy began unfolding as the majority Chicano population began taking over the school board, city council, and even a few businesses through boycotts, and, with the founding of *La Raza Unida* Party in the spring 1970 elections. By 1974, Crystal City and *Raza Unida* had become the pride of the Chicano movement in Texas. Gutiérrez's efforts changed forever the attitude of Mexican-American politics in Texas. There would no longer be the old deference: "Psychologically," he stated, "if you give in to one of those bastards (the Rangers), you've had it. That's been the life of our parents. That's why they go around with their hats in their hands. This has to be stopped. We've got to be just as arrogant."[43]

In 1972, other nationalists such as Corky Gonzalez grabbed hold of the idea and, against Gutiérrez's wishes, thrust the party into national politics. Its zealous supporters' demands for a Chicano third party factionalized Chicano political leaders and essentially doomed *La Raza Unida*. In California and New Mexico, this third party succeeded only in dividing the Chicano vote and helping elect conservatives to municipal offices previously held by Chicano Democrats. The national *Raza Unida* Conference of September 1972 in El Paso marked the split between Gonzalez and Gutiérrez over leadership and ultimately the end of the national third party effort.[44]

In March 1968, fifteen thousand students walked out of five East Los Angeles high schools protesting the lack of Chicano teachers, the irrelevance of their Anglo-oriented classes, and the general disrespect for their culture. The police and arrests and trials of the leaders eventually restored order, but not before students perfected the tactic, using it for two more years to insure the responsiveness of school authorities.

Fall 1966 to spring 1967 saw the emergence of the first Chicano student groups on California college campuses. Concerned primarily with issues of cultural identity and a sense of obligation to the barrios from which they came, these students later formed the United Mexican-American Students (UMAS) in summer and fall of 1967 at UCLA, from which it quickly spread to other Southwestern campuses. Moving away from a service orientation towards political agitation in UMAS and later MEChA, into which some UMAS chapters had transformed, students redefined the goals of education for Chicanos away from preparation for assimilation to "service to the Chicano community . . . and for the purpose of realizing political, social, and economic change." The First Annual Chicano Youth Conference in Denver, which Corky Gonzalez called forth in 1969, had an attendance of over two thousand and proved the highpoint of this movement, producing the ringing statement of the values of Chicanismo, *El Plan Espiritual de Aztlán*. By the mid-1970s, MEChA chapters had begun to divide between nationalists, often affiliated with *Raza Unida;* marxists, who also joined Marxist-Leninist groups; and those who wanted a cultural and fraternal emphasis.[45]

Toward the mid-1970s, many Chicano activists came to reject notions of Chicanismo because it divided those who lived north of the border from those who lived in Mexico. Bert Corona (b. 1918), the remarkable veteran of the CIO and organizer of MAPA, in 1968 organized *Centro de Acción Autonoma-Hermandad General de Trabajadores* (CASA) in Los Angeles to unite all *Mexicanos* against abuses of undocumented workers. The organization, and its newspaper, *Sin Fronteras,* spread to other cities, but new leadership and reorganization as a vanguard group split CASA in 1975 and sent it down the fruitless road of factionalism. A few Marxist-Leninist groups (particularly the Socialist Workers Party, which controlled some *Raza Unida* chapters, and the Maoist August 29th movement) gathered in a few militants floundering about in the context of all these ideological and personalist splits.[46]

Mexican radicalism in the United States offers us a remarkable history of land issues, social revolution, dual unions, Popular Front and union alliances, and ethnic nationalism. All of these movements live in the *plática* of the barrios and pueblos, and in the people who participated in and led them. While most Mexican-Americans have been working class, oppositional politics cannot expect the simple horizontal reordering of *la gente* into proletarian organizations. Nationalist movements split over personal and class differences. Efforts to remain upon and return some of the ancestral lands have had only minor successes. Mexican immigrant radicalism has been expressed in a wide array of oppositional movements, forms, and demands. History shows that no traditional theory of oppositional movements will easily categorize or explain this experience. Perhaps, too, this analysis of Mexican-American movements shows that history moves neither slowly nor convulsively, neither consciously nor impersonally, towards something we usually call "progress," be that a revolutionary or evolutionary transformation.

Notes

1. For the Spanish and early Mexican history of *el norte* see Ramón A. Gutiérrez, *When Jesus Came the Corn Mothers Went Away: Marriage, Sexuality, and Power in New Mexico, 1500–1846* (Stanford: Stanford University Press, 1991); Douglas Monroy, *Thrown among Strangers: The Making of Mexican Culture in Frontier California* (Berkeley: University of California Press, 1990); David J. Weber, *The Mexican Frontier, 1821–1846: The American Southwest under Mexico* (Albuquerque: University of New Mexico Press, 1982). For the specific revolts see Hubert Howe Bancroft, *History of California.* 1884. (Santa Barbara: Wallace Hebberd, 1963), 3:181–212; and Janet Lecompte, *Rebellion in Rio Arriba, 1837* (Albuquerque: University of New Mexico Press, 1985).

2. Bancroft History of California, 5:305–347; Monroy, *Thrown among Strangers,* 177–80; Nash Candelaria, *Not by the Sword* (Ypsilanti: Bilingual Press, 1982), though fiction, contains the best account of the Taos Revolt. The remains of the old church at Taos Pueblo, leveled by Yankee cannon fire after the insurgents had retreated into it, is still a tourist attraction.

3. Pablo Neruda, *Splendor and Death of Joaquín Murieta,* trans., Ben Belitt (New York, 1973), 143–45; Richard G. Mitchell, "Joaquín Murieta: A Study of Social Conditions in Early California" (master's thesis, University of California, Berkeley, 1927), and Ernest May, "Tiburcio Vasquez," *Historical Society of Southern California Quarterly* 29 (1947), are both excerpted in Pedro Castillo and Albert Camarillo, eds., *Furia y Muerte: Los Bandidos Chicanos* (Los Angeles: Aztlán Publications, 1973), 17–51; Monroy *Thrown among Strangers,* 211–18; Robert J. Rosenbaum, *Mexicano Resistance in the Southwest: "The Sacred Right of Self-Preservation* (Austin: University of Texas Press, 1981), 58–67; J. Gregg Layne, "Annals of Los Angeles," part 2, "From the American Conquest to the Civil War," *California Historical Society Quarterly* 13 (December 1934): 328; Leonard Pitt, *The Decline of the Californios: A Social History of the Spanish-Speaking Californians, 1846–1900* (Berkeley and Los Angeles: University of California Press, 1966), 167–71; Robert Glass Cleland, *The Cattle on a Thousand Hills: Southern California, 1850–1880* (San Marino: The Huntington Library, 1975), 250–63 and 274–79, conveniently re-

prints many of the *Los Angeles Star* articles on the exploits of the Flores gang and the famous interview with Vásquez which appeared in the *Los Angeles Star,* May 16, 1874.

4. Rosenbaum, *Mexicano Resistance,* 42–45: Rodolfo Acuña, *Occupied America: A History of Chicanos,* 3rd ed. (New York: Harper and Row, 1988), 43–47; Charles W. Goldfinch, "Juan N. Cortina, 1824–1892: A Re-appraisal" (master's thesis, University of Chicago, 1949), excerpted in Castillo and Camarillo, eds., *Furia y Muerte,* 91–109; Cortina's declaration, from 36th Congress, one Session, House Executive Document No. 52: "Difficulties on the Southwestern Frontier," 79–82, is reprinted in Wayne Moquin, ed., *A Documentary History of Mexican Americans* (New York: Bantam Books, 1972), 272–76.

5. Acuña, *Occupied America,* 47–49; David Montejano, *Anglos and Mexicans in the Making of Texas, 1836–1986* (Austin, 1987), 33.

6. Rosenbaum, *Mexicano Resistance,* 99–105; Acuña, *Occupied America,* 60–65; Mario Barrera, *Race and Class in the Southwest: A Theory of Racial Inequality,* (Notre Dame: University of Notre Dame Press, 1979), 23–30; William deBuys, *Enchantment and Exploitation: The Life and Times of a New Mexico Mountain Range* (Albuquerque: University of New Mexico Press, 1985), 171–92; Frances Leon Swadesh, *Los Primeros Pobladores: Hispanic Americans of the Ute Frontier* (Notre Dame: University of Notre Dame Press, 1974), 68–72.

7. Rosenbaum, *Mexicano Resistance,* 103-18, and "Nuestra Plataforma" is reprinted on page 166; see Fabiola Cabeza de Vaca, *We Fed Them Cactus* (Albuquerque: University of New Mexico Press, 1979), 89–92, for the view of the "respectable citizens."

8. Rosenbaum, *Mexicano Resistance,* 118–24; Acuña, *Occupied America,* 72–73; Cabeza de Vaca, *We Fed Them Cactus,* 89. *La Voz del Pueblo* denied the charge that there existed any connection between Herrera, the Knights, and *las Gorras Blancas.*

9. Rosenbaum, *Mexicano Resistance,* 125–45.

10. Américo Paredes, *"With His Pistol in His Hand": A Border Ballad and its Hero* (Austin: University of Texas Press, 1973), 48–79.

11. Paredes, *"With His Pistol in His Hand",* 87–100, 114–25, 36.

12. W. Dirk Raat, *Revoltosos: Mexico's Rebels in the United States, 1903–1923* (College Station, Texas: Texas A & M University Press,

1981), 25–31; Juan Gómez-Quiñones, *Sembradores, Ricardo Flores Magón y El Partido Liberal Mexicano: A Eulogy and Critique* (Los Angeles: Aztlán Publications, 1973), 13–31, which also reprints the 1906 founding manifesto of the PLM on 95–98; James A. Sandos, *Rebellion in the Borderlands: Anarchism and the Plan of San Diego, 1904–1923* (Norman and London: University of Oklahoma Press, 1992), 8–12; Paul Friedrich, *Agrarian Revolt in a Mexican Village* (Englewood Cliffs, New Jersey: Prentice-Hall, 1970), 64.

13. Calling himself a "chicken thief and a revolutionist" too, Jack London told a Los Angeles PLM meeting in February, 1910, how "we socialists, anarchists, hoboes, chicken thieves, outlaws, and undesirable citizens of the United States are with you heart and soul in your efforts to overthrow slavery and autocracy in Mexico." Emma Goldman spoke at Burbank Hall "in hearty sympathy" with the Mexican Revolution with proceeds going to the PLM. Ethyl Duffy Turner edited the fourth page of *Regeneración* in English while her husband bought and shipped guns to Mexico in the winter of 1911 to fight the revolution. *Regeneración*, 11 *de febrero*, 1 *de octubre*, 1910, 6 *de mayo*, 22 *de abril*, 1911, 13 *de enero*, 1912; Ethel Duffy Turner, *Writers and Revolutionists, an Interview Conducted by Ruth Teiser* (Berkeley: University of California Press, 1967), 10, 22–23; Gómez-Quiñones, *Sembradores*, 32–45, and the manifesto is reprinted on pages 120–25; Sandos, *Rebellion in the Borderlands*, 12–23.

14. *Regeneración*, 23 *septiembre*, 1911; Gómez-Quiñones, *Sembradores*, 41–45; Raat, *Revoltosos*, 33–35.

15. Lowell W. Blaisdell, *The Desert Revolution: Baja California* (Madison: University of Wisconsin Press, 1962), Jesus González Monroy, *Ricardo Flores Magón y Su Actitud en la Baja California* (Mexico, D.F.: Editorial Academia Literaria, 1962); Ratt, *Revoltosos*, 56–59. Agnes Smedley, *Daughter of Earth* (New York: Feminist Press, 1973), 186, and Elizabeth Gurley Flynn, *The Rebel Girl: An Autobiography, My First Life, 1906–1926* (New York: International Publishers, 1973), 181, both mention men going off to fight in Mexico.

16. For an example of Ricardo's railing at apathetic workers see "Manifesto a Todos los Trabajadores del Mundo," *Regeneración*, 3 *abril*, 1911, which is reprinted in Gómez-Quiñones, *Sembradores*, 116–18; Sandos, *Rebellion in the Borderlands*, 128–29; Emma M. Pérez, " 'A La Mujer'': A Critique of the Partido Liberal Mexicano's Gender Ideology on Women," in *Between Borders: Essays on Mexi-*

cana/Chicana History ed. Adelaida R. del Castillo (Encino, California: Floricanto Press, 1990), 468–69.

17. Ricardo Flores Magón, "A La Mujer," *Regeneración,* 24 *septiembre,* 1910, is reprinted in Gómez-Quiñones, *Sembradores,* 110–12 and in English translation in Magdalena Mora and Adelaida R. Del Castillo, eds., *Mexican Women in the United States: Struggles Past and Present* (Los Angeles: Chicano Studies Research Center Publications, 1980), 160–62; Praxedis Guerrero, "La Mujer," in *Regeneración,* 6 *noviembre,* 1910, is reprinted in Gómez-Quiñones, *Sembradores,* 105–08; Pérez, " 'A La Mujer,' " 464–67.

18. Emilio Zamora, "Sara Estela Ramírez: Una Rosa Roja en el Movimiento," in *Mexican Women in the United States,* 163–67; Ramírez's words are from her essay "!Surge!" from *La Crónica,* April 10, 1910, reprinted in *ibid.,* 168; *Los Angeles Times,* September 19, 1907, quoted in Pérez, " ' 'A La Mujer,' " 468–69; Raat, *Revoltosos,* 32; Pérez, " 'A La Muger,' " 470–71.

19. Sandos, *Rebellion in the Borderlands,* 80–81; *El Plan de San Diego* is reprinted in Juan Gómez-Quiñones, "El Plan de San Diego Reviewed," *Aztlán* 1, no. 1 (Spring 1970): 128–31.

20. Sandos, *Rebellion in the Borderlands,* 58–81; Carlos Larralde, *Mexican-American Movements and Leaders* (Los Alamitos, California: Hwong Publishing Company, 1976), 126–27.

21. Sandos, *Rebellion on the Borderlands,* 86–111, 154–63; Montejano, *Anglos and Mexicans in the Making of Texas,* 117–27.

22. González Monroy, *Ricardo Flores Magón,* 18, 64, plate following 64, 88, 110; Juan Gómez-Quiñones, "The First Steps: Chicano Labor Conflict and Organizing, 1900–1920," *Aztlán* 3, no. 1 (Spring 1972): 28–31; Gómez-Quiñones, *Sembradores,* 41; Melvin Dubofsky, *We Shall Be All: A History of the Industrial Workers of the World* (Chicago: Quadrangle Press, 1969), 184–87; Friedrich, *Agrarian Revolt in a Mexican village,* 67–70.

23. Vernon Monroe McCombs, "Stopping the Reds," *El Mexicano* 7 (January–March, 1919): 1, 7; Douglas Monroy, "Anarquismo y Comunismo: Mexican Radicalism and the Communist Party in Los Angeles during the 1930s," *Labor History* 24 (Winter 1983): 36; William Wilson McEuen, "A Survey of the Mexicans in Los Angeles," (master's thesis, University of Southern California, 1914), 69–70.

24. Samuel M. Ortegon, "The Religious Status of the Mexican

Population of Los Angeles," (master's thesis, University of Southern California, 1932), 22–23; Manuel Gamio, *The Mexican Immigrant, His Life Story* (Chicago: Dover Press, 1931), 127, 129.

25. Friedrich, *Agrarian Revolt in a Mexican Village*, 119–30.

26. Francisco E. Balderrama, *In Defense of La Raza: The Los Angeles Mexican Consulate and the Mexican Community, 1929 to 1936* (Tucson: University of Arizona Press, 1982), 91–92; Ricardo Romo, *East Los Angeles: History of a Barrio* (Austin: University of Texas Press, 1983), 154–55; Governor Young's Fact Finding Committee, *Mexicans in California* (State of California, San Francisco, 1930), 123.

27. The CUOM platform is reprinted in Governor Young's Fact Finding Committee, *Mexicans in California*, 123–24.

28. Ronald W. López, "The El Monte Berry Strike of 1933," *Aztlán* 1, no. 1 (Spring 1970); Devre Anne Weber, "The Organizing of Mexicano Agricultural Workers: Imperial Valley and Los Angeles, 1928–1934, An Oral History Approach," *Aztlán* 3, no. 2 (Fall 1972), 323, 328, 330; Louis Reccow, "The Orange County Citrus Strikes of 1935–1936: The 'Forgotten People' in Revolt" (Ph.D. diss., University of Southern California, 1972), 107–08; interview with LaRue McCormick, former executive director of the International Labor Defense, Los Angeles, conducted by the author in January 1977.

29. *Los Angeles Times*, February 1 and 9, March 2, 1919; *Los Angeles Record*, February 5; *El Heraldo de México*, 6 febrero, 1919; Nelson S. Van Valen, "The Bolshiviki and the Orange Groves," *Pacific Historical Review* 22 (1953): 39–50.

30. Carey McWilliams, *Factories in the Field: The Story of Migratory Farm Labor in California*. 1939. (Santa Barbara: Peregrine Press, 1971), 211–29; Weber, "The Organizing of Mexicano Agricultural Workers, 313–33; Dorothy Healey and Maurice Isserman, *Dorothy Healey Remembers: A Life in the American Communist Party* (New York: Oxford University Press, 1990), 42–58; Irving Bernstein, *Turbulent Years: A History of the American Worker, 1933–1941* Boston: Houghton Miflin Company), 160–170.

31. Healey and Isserman, *Dorothy Healey Remembers*, 42–46; interview with LaRue McCormick; Ross Lawrence, "Lessons from the Southern California Strike," *Western Worker*, August 7, 1933; statement of Stanley Hancock quoted in Healey and Isserman, 46; Monroy, "Anarquismo y Comunismo," 41–42, 46–47. Frankly, my

own friendship with Dorothy Healey makes me doubt that she would have waited for anyone to come and ask her to join their struggle—she would have been there already.

32. Emma Tenayuca and Homer Brooks, "The Mexican Question in the Southwest," *The Communist* 18 (1939): 257–68; Roberto R. Calderón and Emilio Zamora, "Manuela Solis Sager and Emma Tenayuca: A Tribute," in *Between Borders,* 269–78; Victor B. Nelson-Cisneros, "La Clase Trabajadora en Tejas, 1920–1940," *Aztlán* 6 (1975), 253–54. Dorothy Healey notes that "Some years later there would be a big inner-Party battle over whether Mexican-Americans should be considered an oppressed national minority, the same way we had traditionally regarded Blacks." Healey and Isserman, *Dorothy Healey Remembers,* 70; see also the various "Draft Resolutions on the Mexican Question" as well as the party's analysis of their *Cinco de Mayo* celebrations of the 1950s in the Dorothy Healey papers at California State University Long Beach.

33. Monroy, "Anarquismo y Comunismo," 51–59; The California State Membership Committee, "Building the Party in California," *The Party Organizer* 10, no. 3–4 (March–April 1937), 19. The same publication acknowledged that "we still lose the majority of new Party members within a few months," and Mexicans were probably no exception to this. William Schneiderman, "New Advances in California," *The Party Organizer* 10, no. 8 (August 1937), 47.

34. Monroy, "Anarquismo y Comunismo," 51–52; Juan Chacon, "Union Made," *California Quarterly* 11 (Summer 1953), 70. Juan Chacon also starred in the film.

35. These quotes are from interviews with Frank Lopez, June 1976, Jaime González Monroy, May 1976. My conclusions are based on these interviews and a brief scolding I received from Emma Tenayuca in April 1984 at the National Association for Chicano Studies Conference in Austin for critical remarks I had made about the party and "The Mexican Question in the Southwest."

36. García, *Mexican Americans,* 145–57; *Peoples' World,* December 4, 1939.

37. García, *Mexican Americans,* 159–73.

38. García, *Mexican Americans,* 208–27; Larralde, *Mexican-American Movements and Leaders,* 186.

39. Congress of Industrial Organizations, *Official Reports on the Expulsion of Communist Organizations from the CIO* (Washington D.C., 1954), 15, 21, 31; Art Preis, *Labor's Giant Step: Twenty Years of the CIO* (New York: Pathfinder Press, 1972), 410–11.

40. Peter Matthiessen, *Sal Si Puedes: César Chávez and the New American Revolution* (New York: Random House, 1973); Sam Kushner, *Long Road To Delano* (New York: International Publishers, 1975).

41. Peter Nabokov, *Tijerina and the Courthouse Raid* Berkeley: Ramparts Press, 1970); Patricia Bell Blawis, *Tijerina and the Land Grants: Mexican Americans in Struggle for their Heritage* (New York: International Publishers, 1971); "Reies Tijerina's Letter from the Santa Fe Jail," *El Grito del Norte*, September 26, 1969, reprinted in Moquin, ed., *A Documentary History of Mexican Americans*, 484–87.

42. Tony Castro, *Chicano Power: The Emergence of Mexican America* (New York: Staurday Review Press, 1974), 129–47; Rodolfo Gonzalez, *I Am Joaquín/Yo Soy Joaquín* New York: Bantam Books, 1972).

43. Castro, *Chicano Power*, 148–66, and Gutiérrez is quoted, 160; Ignacio M. Garcia, *United We Win: The Rise and Fall of La Raza Unida Party* (Tucson: Mexican American Studies and Research Center, 1989).

44. Juan Gómez-Quiñones, *Chicano Politics: Reality and Promise, 1940–1960* (Albuquerque: University of New Mexico Press, 1990), 131–38; Alberto Juarez, "The Emergence of El Partido de la Raza Unida: California's New Chicano Party," *Aztlán* 3, no. 2 (Fall 1972): 189–99.

45. Juan Gómez-Quiñones, *Mexican Students Por La Raza: The Chicano Student Movement In Southern California, 1967–1977* (Santa Barbara, California, 1978), 11-38; Chicano Coordinating Council on Higher Education, "El Plan de Santa Barbara," (Oakland: La Causa Publications, 1969).

46. Gómez-Quiñones, *Chicano Politics*, 146–53.

TWO

The German Immigrant Left in the United States*

Stan Nadel

German immigrants created one of the largest, most complex, and longest-lived of all the varieties of American radicalism, one whose ideas and institutions of were often adopted by later groups of immigrant leftists.[1] There have been times when German-American radicalism seemed to be the only class-conscious radicalism in the U.S., and no history of the American Left could be complete without the Socialist Labor Party, the left wing of the American Federation of Labor, or the Chicago anarchists—all predominantly German. Still, even these familiar episodes take on a different cast when explored within the framework of the German-American immigrant Left.

The German-American immigrant Left was the product of a distinctive immigrant culture based in the artisanal and skilled labor sectors of the American economy. German artisans seeking better lives in the United States created the core of this culture by adapting their old cultural traditions to their new homes. One of the most important aspects of their original culture was the weak hold of religious institutions in German towns and cities by the

---

*Thanks to Alex Yard for sharing his expertise on St. Louis.

middle of the nineteenth century. German migrants going from rural areas in Germany to rural America might form their new institutions around their churches, but the German immigrant culture that developed in American cities was fundamentally secular, and it opened up other possibilities for developing the new urban immigrant culture.[2]

Not only was the new urban culture secular, it was based on a dense network of social organizations. Americans were known as a nation of joiners, but the German immigrants' mania for organizing associations put the Americans to shame. German immigrants banded together for all kinds of ostensible purposes and vast networks of working-class *Vereine* rapidly formed a cultural context, which first promoted and then long sustained a vital leftist subculture—one that bore some similarities to the subculture formed later around the Socialist Party in Germany.[3]

The history of the German-American Left has largely been the preserve of Marxist historians who have tended to present it as divided into two basic parts, one before and one after Marxism became dominant. The reality was never so simple. From beginning to end the German-American Left contained a mixture of ideological influences and trends imbedded in a radical counterculture. The relative weights of various formal ideologies and different varieties of cultural radicalism changed over time, but there were always many shades of red in the German-American Left. Sharp ideological positions are hard to find.

I. The Formative Years

German-American radicalism had deep roots in Europe even before it was transplanted to American soil. Old craft traditions had broken down and revolutionary France had become a beacon beaming revolutionary ideas across Europe by the early years of the nineteenth century. Paris was also a training ground for German journeymen seeking to perfect their skills in the fashion and skills center of Europe. By the 1830s, Parisian artisans were developing a new and more radical version of republicanism, a social republicanism—called socialism. Hundreds of thousands of German journeymen learned the language and skills of social revolution along with the techniques of their crafts—and brought them back to Germany.[4] Economic and political crises in Germany then brought all sorts of German revolutionaries to the United

States, where they would lay the groundwork for a German-American radical movement.

The movement began with the 1845 arrival of Hermann Kriege, a revolutionary associated with the League of the Just.[5] Kriege sought to promote communism among German immigrants beginning to establish themselves in the U.S. He created a *Sozialreformassoziation* as a public arm of the secret league, one which drew large numbers of members by combining political activism with the sponsorship of a large variety of social activities. The Social Reformers sponsored picnics, men's choral societies, women's auxiliaries, sickness-and-death benefit associations, theatrical productions, masked balls, military companies, and all sorts of other ancillary activities.[6] In doing so, they established a left-wing subculture or counterculture destined to be replicated and extended by other German-American leftist organizations from the *Turnvereine* of the 1850s to the Milwaukee German socialist clubs of the twentieth century.

The *Sozialreformassoziation* soon had branches in a number of cities, including New York, Philadelphia, Newark, St. Louis, Milwaukee, Baltimore, and Cincinnati.[7] Although they soon declared that they were no longer communist and tried to establish themselves as the "left wing of Tammany Hall," they continued to be part of a German-American Left.[8] In New York, at least, the Social Reformers and the *Sozialreform* Hall were conspicuous in the labor movement for another 25 years.[9]

Before moving to the right, the *Sozialreformassoziation* invited Kriege's mentor, Wilhelm Weitling, to come to America. A highly skilled journeyman tailor, Weitling was also the premier ideologue of German socialism before Marx. His communism had been forged in the crucible of the Paris labor movement and combined the Christian socialist tradition of Lamennais, Cabet, and Proudhon with a class-conscious appeal for workers to make their own revolution by any means necessary.[10]

Weitling fled to the U.S. after the 1848 revolutions in Germany, established a newspaper, and threw himself into the effort to revolutionize America. He encouraged a surge of union activity in New York in 1850, and soon found thousands of followers among the city's German immigrant workers, who had him represent their union federation at the citywide Industrial Congress. Weitling and his radical allies among the city's German immigrant workers played a prominent role in the great strike wave of 1850, but the unions proved unable to retain their members after the strikes ended.[11]

Weitling organized his followers into a national *Arbeiterbund* in the fall of 1850. With local branches in most of the major centers of German immigration, the *Arbeiterbund* promoted Weitling's paper and his vision of cooperatives, a trade-exchange bank to buy their products with "a new workers' paper money" based on labor, and a utopian colony in Iowa.[12]

The *Arbeiterbund* prospered for a few years and local affiliates opened workers halls with the usual range of German social activities (theater, singing, dancing, bowling, and beer) along with radical politics, but Weitling's influence began to fade after 1853. First his *Arbeiterbund* faced the competition of a "Marxist" rival, and then it fell apart in a bitter struggle over responsibility for the bankruptcy of the utopian colony. Weitling continued to publish his newspaper until mid-1855, but was finally forced to give up radical political activity.[13]

The *Turnvereine*, or Gymnastics Unions, meanwhile became the largest and possibly the most important expression of German-American radicalism in the 1850s. The *Turner* movement had its roots in a nationalistic physical culture movement, which arose in Napoleonic Germany. By the 1840s, republicanism and Free-thought (a religious movement ranging from something like Unitarian Universalism to militant atheism) were central to *Turner* ideology, the movement was largely working class in composition, and socialist ideas had spread through the movement from artisan *Turner* working in Paris. After providing shock troops for the revolutionary cause in Germany, thousands of *Turners* headed for American exile.[14]

In exile, radical *Turners* created a Socialist Gymnastics League in 1851, one whose socialism spanned the spectrum from a social republicanism, which was mainly atheist and republican, to Marxian communism.[15] If the purity of the *Turners'* doctrines might be challenged, thousands of German immigrants in large cities and small towns across the United States joined and read the *Turn-Zeitung*, its newspaper. They were instructed on the history and meaning of socialist ideas, and the *Turnvereine* and *Turn-Zeitung* proved central to spreading the basic ideas of European radicalism across German-America in the early 1850s.[16]

Many *Turners* and other radicals were soon galvanized by the American struggle against slavery, seeing it as a continuation of their long struggle for freedom in Germany. *Turners* provided defense squads for anti-slavery meetings and took the lead in opposing the pro-slavery propaganda of Democratic Party activists. Many radical social Republicans became Radical Republicans over the course of the next decade, and some activists laid claim to Republican patronage in later years.[17]

If the radical impetus of the Social Reformers and *Turners* lost much of its fervor after their first few years, both associations continued to support labor unions and other radical causes for decades. The *Turners* came to the aid of blacklisted labor activists in 1872 and played an active role in protests against the 1874 police riot in New York's Tompkins Square Park.[18] They mobilized again in defense of the Haymarket martyrs in 1886, a defense that was particularly spirited because one of the martyrs was *Turner* activist August Spies (and Chicago's social revolutionaries used the *Turn-vereine* as a cover for their activities in the repression that followed the Haymarket bombing).[19]

Karl Marx's close associate Joseph Weydemeyer brought a version of Marxism to America at the end of 1851. Anxious to spread the doctrines of "scientific" socialism to the New World, he found an outlet in the *Turn-Zeitung*. There he enlightened German-American workers about "class-consciousness" and the "dictator-ship of the proletariat," while stressing the importance of trade unions and strikes as basic forms of class struggle.[20] Soon he had enough followers to form a tiny organization, which he claimed was influential among *Turners*.[21]

German-American unionists had seen their organizations collapse after the victories of 1850, but inflation was driving down the real value of wages sharply by 1853. While Weitling's *Arbeiterbund* said that only communism could solve the workers' problems and opposed the revival of wage-conscious unions and strikes as useless diversions, Weydemeyer's group prepared to throw themselves into the union struggle.[22]

In Baltimore, New York, Philadelphia, Pittsburgh, Cincinnati, Dayton, Cleveland, Milwaukee, and Chicago, German workers in dozens of trades formed unions and went out on strike in the spring of 1853. Class-conscious positions replaced the utopianism of the earlier unions as the failure of the cooperatives, which had grown out of the 1850 strikes, convinced the revived unions to adopt a more wage-conscious approach.[23]

In March, Weydemeyer called for a mass meeting to establish a new "broad workers' alliance . . . on a modern basis." Attracting many of Weitling's former followers and others, a new *Amerikani-sche Arbeiterbund* was formed in close association with the trade unions (several of which formally affiliated with the new League of the Just), the Social Reformers, and the *Turners*.[24]

Proclaiming the irreconcilability of labor and capital, and com-

mitting itself to resist wage cuts and other attacks on workers'
conditions, the new organization's program focused on "practical"
reforms like ten-hour day and child labor laws, a homestead act, a
mechanic's lien law, and an end to Sabbatarian and temperance
laws that "interfere with the workers' enjoyment of their freedom"—all to be implemented by a new political party of labor.[25]
At its peak, in addition to branches throughout the New York City
area, it had affiliates from New Haven to Cincinnati—by way of
both Philadelphia and Buffalo.[26] Then, weakened by Free-thinker
defections, both the League and the unions were crushed by the
economic crisis and mass unemployment of 1854–1855.

Just before the crash, Weydemeyer and his associates sought
to unite both the *Amerikanische Arbeiterbund* and the German-
speaking unions with their English-speaking equivalents. Such
a merger, however, threatened to reduce the German-speaking
workers to a tongue-tied minority in organizations dominated by
English-speakers, whom the Germans considered culturally and
politically backwards. Finding German-American workers less
class-conscious than he had hoped and with the *Arbeiterbund* in
ruins, Weydemeyer gave up and headed west.[27]

Free-thinkers and *Turners* led the unemployed in mass demonstrations demanding public works that winter, as they did again in
the panic of 1857.[28] But, with the anti-slavery mobilization following the proposed Kansas-Nebraska Act, many Free-thinkers and
Turners were en route to the Republican Party and they didn't tarry
long with the cause of labor.[29]

There was one other current in the German-American Left—
equal rights for women. Mathilde Franziska Anneke had been a
champion of women's rights in Germany before she married
radical activist Fritz Anneke in 1847 and edited the *Neue Kölnische
Zeitung* with him and Karl Marx. After Marx fled and Fritz was
arrested, she ran the paper until it was suppressed. Then, Mathilde published the first radical women's paper in Germany until
she left to join her husband on the battlefield in the Baden revolt.
When the revolutionary forces were defeated, the Annekes fled
to America.[30]

Mathilde Franziska immersed herself in the writings of American women's rights activists and tried to publish translations in
the German-American press. In 1852 she revived the *Frauenzeitung*
and undertook a major lecture tour (sponsored mainly by *Turner-
bund, Arbeiterbund*, and Free-thinker societies) to generate subscribers for her new paper. The tour failed to generate the national
German-American women's rights organization she had hoped

for, but it did win enough subscribers to finance her paper for a few years.

Mathilde Anneke saw the causes of women and proletarians as inseparable.[31] She joined Weitling's *Arbeiterbund* in 1852, moved over to Weydemeyer's *Amerikanische Arbeiterbund* in 1853, and was associated with a revived League of the Just later in the decade.

All of these organizations, along with the *Turners* and Free-thinkers, paid at least some lip service to the cause of women's equality, but a very strong strain of hostility towards women's equality remained among the men. Women were encouraged to embroider banners or organize and supply food for organizational picnics and social events, but they were discouraged from raising questions of gender equality in the movement or in the home. While Mathilde Franziska and her readers got little encouragement, the American women's movement was frequently ridiculed by German-American men of the Left. Subscribers to the *Frauenzeitung* found the climate too hostile to do much more than read the paper and attend occasional lectures. The hostility also provided yet another barrier to mutual understanding and cooperation between German-American and Anglo-American radicals, given the strong women's rights component of many Anglo-American reform campaigns from abolitionism to populism.

The Civil War mobilized much of the German immigrant Left into the anti-slavery cause. Many *Turnvereine* enlisted en masse in the Union army, as did many socialist activists. Friedrich Sorge recalled that wartime losses paralyzed the socialist movement until 1867.[32]

II. The Era of German-American Leadership

After the Civil War, the establishment of vital and sometimes lasting labor organizations at the local and national level thrust German-Americans into a potentially pivotal social role. These socialist immigrants had the industrial skills and, even more important, the organizational know-how to show others the way forward. They confronted, however, not only the expected resistance of various authorities, but serious internal fractures and a rightward tow within the labor movement itself. German socialists took advantage of several major uprisings to attempt to generalize the developing class-consciousness, to give it political substance and direction. They learned, to their dismay, that political successes were evanescent, but they could and did continue to build socialist-leaning institutions for themselves. When they joined wider America, they did so on less socialistic terms, sometimes compromising their own values.

The labor movement began to revive in the later years of the war as wartime profits tempted employers to avoid prolonged conflicts with unionizing workers and wartime inflation encouraged workers of all nationalities to unionize. German-American workers participated in the labor boom and organized rapidly. In Chicago, newly arrived German immigrants turned to Irish and English union leaders, but in older centers of German immigration from New York to St. Louis, they had no need for others to lead them.[33] In New York City alone, at least 26 German unions operated by 1864, and they formed their own citywide German central labor organization.[34] By the time the National Labor Union organized in 1867, German unions were heavily represented and German immigrants dominated two of the six national unions.[35]

In purely structural terms, German-American workers felt compelled to move to the forefront of the American labor and radical movements. Very large numbers of literate and highly skilled German artisans had come to dominate a large number of skilled trades, including many of the trades most often subjected to revolutionary transformations in the second half of the nineteenth century. The expansion of regional and national markets opened the possibility of massive profits for employers who could increase the scale and cut the cost of production. Factories with ever greater divisions of labor diluted skills, allowed employers to rapidly increase the rate of work, and then financed the introduction of new machines, which accelerated the process.

Some skilled workers managed to maintain or even improve their conditions through these transformations, but most workers in the German trades faced a long struggle against the degradation of their skills, working conditions, and pay.[36] Over the years, this struggle would make them more and more receptive to radical ideas and organizations and repeatedly pushed them to the lead in labor and radical organizations.

German-American radicals turned their attention back to the labor question. Veterans of the old *Kommunisten Klub* revived their association and soon joined with a small group of recently arrived followers of Ferdinand Lassalle to create a Socialist Party. *Klub* member Friedrich Sorge was prevailed upon to give up his secretaryship of a Free-thinker's league to lead the new party, and Weitling was invited to join the executive committee.[37]

The new party did poorly, but the labor movement benefited

from an economic boom and grew rapidly. In New York, the cabinetmakers' union called upon all the German unions to join them in sponsoring their own newspaper. An Association of United Workers, composed of five major German-American unions and led by the cigarmakers' president, sponsored the weekly *Arbeiter Union* newspaper. When the paper's first editor proved insufficiently devoted to the union cause, he was replaced by the leader of New York's Free-thinkers' League, Sorge's friend Adolph Douai.

A well-known Forty-Eighter, Douai had gone from abolitionism into the Republican Party. He started his career with the *Arbeiter Union* as an advocate of solving the labor problem through currency reform.[38] He did, however, begin running excerpts in the paper from the newly published *Das Kapital*.[39] Soon afterwards, the *Arbeiter Union* came out for government expropriation of all monopolies and large factories—moving from reformism and utopian socialism towards Marxian socialism.[40] By mid-1869, the German labor movement in New York was strong enough to turn the *Arbeiter Union* into a daily, and the workers of Chicago followed their lead, organizing a citywide German central labor union with its own newspaper.[41]

The socialists responded to the unions' growth by gaining charters as National Labor Union Local 5 and as Section 1 for North America of the International Workingmen's Association. They still had only about fifty members, but they were now closely tied to the *Arbeiter Union*.[42] Many leaders of the German unions (including a large number from the increasingly influential cigarmakers' union) joined Section 1. Samuel Gompers recalled "in those early days of the 'seventies the International dominated the labor movement of New York"—and Sorge reported that Chicago and other cities took their lead from New York.[43]

The socialists experienced a setback during the Franco-Prussian War. Internationalists in the United States condemned the war and enlisted their union allies. Both New York's *Arbeiter Union* and Chicago's *Deutsche Arbeiter* joined in denouncing the war (as did many Free-thinker and reform organizations), but an overwhelming majority of German immigrants were swept up in a nationalist fervor for Germany. Both union papers (and the Freethinkers' *Neue Zeit*) collapsed from the loss of readers outraged by the papers' lack of patriotism. But German-American union leaders stood by the International and the unions retained their strength even though they lost their newspapers.[44]

Around 1870 the German immigrant unions moved to the

forefront of the American labor movement. English-speaking workers had prompted the organizing drives of the postwar years, the creation of the National Labor Union, the growing eight-hour day movement, and the eight-hour strike waves, which swept across the country between 1867 and 1870.[45] By the 1870 strike wave, though, Germans shared fully in the leadership of the growing movement.

In 1872, German-American unions associated with the International initiated and guided the largest strike wave yet seen. In New York City alone, more than a hundred thousand struck for the eight-hour day, and German unionists led similar mass strikes in Chicago and Philadelphia. Only a well-organized and determined employer resistance combined with numerous arrests and unprecedented levels of police violence defeated the strikers.[46]

Even before the great struggle of 1872, however, the American internationalists had begun to crash onto the rocks of the Woman Question. Many Free-thinkers of the 1848 generation had backed Mathilde Anneke in the 1850s, and Adolph Douai took his support for women's rights into the pages of the *Arbeiter Union*.[47] But when Augusta Lilienthal, the wife of a Free-thought congregation speaker in New York, pressed the issue in the pages of the *Neue Zeit* in the 1870s, she got a hostile response from the internationalists.[48] They responded that "the granting of the right to vote to women does not concern the interests of workers."[49] As the German-American Left became increasingly class-conscious and more genuinely proletarian, it seemed less open to cultural radicalism.

While Lilienthal and her supporters had little impact on the German-American Left, some American reformers were drawn to the International by news of the Paris Commune. The Woodhull and Claflin sisters, who published a weekly that advocated women's rights, free love, and spiritualism, in addition to labor reform issues, formed Section 12 of the International and began promoting their own causes as those of the International.[50]

When the Germans brought charges against them, they placed the Woman Question at the head of their list. Cigarpacker Fred Bolte said "All this talk of theirs is folly, and we don't want their foolish notions credited as the views of this society. . . . Female suffrage and free love, may do . . . in the future, but the question which interests us as workingmen is that of labor and wages." The split cost the Germans most of their Anglo-American allies and left them even more hostile to women's rights than they had been before.[51]

When the International itself fell apart in a battle between European socialists and anarchists, socialists transferred the general council to New York to prevent an anarchist takeover. That put Sorge, Bolte, and other leaders of Section 1 in charge of what was left of the entire socialist International. They had some success in rebuilding the organization in the U.S., as seen in the eight-hour strikes of 1872, but the defeat of the eight-hour strikes left the movement temporarily exhausted.[52]

A financial disaster hit the U.S. in late 1873 that ushered in one of the worst depressions in history. Mass unemployment undermined all sorts of workers' associations from trade unions and socialist organizations to workers' fraternal orders, though German-American leftists in Chicago bucked the trend by founding the successful weekly *Vorbote* in 1874.[53]

Sorge and the International decided to return to the tactics of 1857 and organize the unemployed.[54] Meetings began in New York and German-American radicals across the country followed suit.[55] By the end of December, unemployed councils in New York reportedly had over ten thousand members, mostly German, and were planning a mass demonstration for January.[56]

Their Chicago colleagues had such a successful turnout at a Turner Hall meeting that they decided to march the next day. Twenty thousand workers paraded to city hall beneath American and red flags and a frightened municipal government promised to work with the Labor Committee to develop a relief program—a promise later broken.[57] Internationalists engaged in similar actions in Newark, Philadelphia, Cincinnati, Louisville, and other cities with large numbers of German immigrants.[58]

The denouement took place where the movement had begun. The New Yorkers called for a mass protest in Tompkins Square—center of the city's main German neighborhood. The night before the protest the police cancelled the permit, but few heard the news and thousands showed up. Using tactics perfected against the eight-hour strikers two years before, masses of club-wielding policemen charged into the peaceful crowd. The police smashed the demonstration in the name of preventing a second Paris Commune and then abandoned all pretext of legality, invading private indoor meetings to beat and disperse would-be protesters.[59] The organized movement of the unemployed was crushed in its New York stronghold and lost heart in other cities as well.

With labor unions eviscerated by mass unemployment and municipal governments violently resisting demands for relief, only electoral action seemed to offer a solution. This alternative was avidly promoted by socialists who had been identified with the doctrines of Ferdinand Lassalle. When the Chicago government reneged on its relief promises, some Germans took the initiative in forming a Workingmen's Party of Illinois. Hoping to appeal to a wide base of support, including dissatisfied farmers associated with the Grange, the new party's platform showed few signs of radicalism and denounced trade unions that "never led to any lasting betterment . . . "[60] Electoral advocates in the East followed closely behind their Chicago comrades. Founding a Social Democratic Workingmen's Party based mainly in New York and Philadelphia, they launched the *Sozial-Demokrat* and tried to create a national political party.[61] After two years without much electoral success, the two parties moved closer to Sorge and his remaining loyalists. By then, most radicals had concluded that socialism would make little headway unless some form of unity could be reestablished.[62]

By 1876, what little remained of the International was also seeking a broader unity (as had just been achieved by the merger of Marxist and Lassallean organizations in Germany). The unification of the three major socialist organizations—the last remnants of the International, the Workingmen's Party of Illinois, and the Social Democratic Workingmen's Party—quickly followed.[63] Not one of the three had over fifteen hundred members and the overwhelming majority of each's membership was of German origin, though all had non-German elements. The Lassalleans' newspapers became the official organs of the new Workingmen's Party. The *Sozial-Demokrat* was renamed the *Arbeiter-Stimme* and, with the *Vorbote*, gave the party two German-language newspapers to its one in English (a proportion that lasted for years).[64]

The merger was based on compromises. Electoral advocates influenced by Lassalle got the internationalists to accept a call for the government to transfer the ownership of industry to producers' cooperatives. On the other hand, the internationalists forced the electoral factions to agree to put primary emphasis on economic struggles and discourage electoral campaigns—"to abstain from all political movements for the present and to turn their back on the ballot box."[65]

Having disparaged electoral activity, all agreed to oppose women's suffrage. Rejecting an appeal from a women's section of the International for an unequivocal commitment to women's equality, they asserted that the "emancipation of women will be accomplished with the emancipation of *men*, and the so-called woman's rights question will be solved with the labor question."[66]

The experience with Anglo-American women's rights advocates in the International left them determined to squelch any such ideas in their own movement.

While the party platform discouraged electoral activity, some sections ran political campaigns anyway. As the new party rapidly turned to electoral campaigns, many leaders of the old International, "withdrew more and more . . . and so cleared the field for the pure socialistic agitation of the younger immigrants . . . "[67]

As the Workingmen's Party focused on electoral campaigns and internal disputes, the great strike wave of 1877 swept across the country. The strikes centered on the railroads, where German immigrants had rarely found work, but they also sparked mass movements in several cities that were heavily German. The predominantly German St. Louis local sponsored a march to support a strike by railroad workers and organized a mass meeting that declared a general strike. The committeemen elected to lead the strike were mostly German-American socialists and trade unionists.[68] Over the next three days the entire city was shut down, municipal officials fled the city, and the strike committee ran the city from their headquarters at Turner Hall.

The leaders of America's nearest approach to the Paris Commune were unnerved by the mob violence, which had swept through other cities. They were revolutionaries, but they were also disciplined and skilled workers who partook of a German culture that emphasized order, even in revolution.[69] So they were frightened by the spectre of mobs of bloodthirsty Irish or African-American "savages" rising from the lower depths. When militants called for arms, the committee called off mass marches and tried to calm their followers. Even as a "citizen's militia" prepared to attack strike headquarters, the committee was unwilling to arm its supporters.[70] On the fifth day of the general strike, police raiders seized the strike headquarters and arrested many of the key leaders—the St. Louis Commune was over.[71]

That summer's events in Chicago set the German-American Left on track to produce America's most revolutionary movement. When the railroad workers struck, Chicago's property owners got the city to deputize twenty thousand special policemen to "preserve order." Confrontations between strikers and a militarized police force escalated into a major street battle after three days of scattered fighting. Having dispersed the strikers, police and specials invaded Turner Hall and broke up a peaceful gathering of the *Möbelarbeiter* (cabinetmakers') union, killing a union official.[72] These events contributed to a rapid growth of workers' militias in

Chicago—not to make a revolution but to defend the workers' right to assemble peacefully.[73]

In the aftermath of the strikes, Workingmen's Party votes grew rapidly in municipal elections (especially in Chicago, Cincinnati, and Buffalo), so the party changed its program to promote electoral campaigns and changed its name to the Socialist Labor Party.[74]

The end of the depression made a revival of the trade union movement possible, and German radicals played a leading role. Internationalists who had been active in their unions in the early 1870s rapidly rebuilt the cigarmakers', furniture makers', tailors', pianomakers', bakers', and brewers' unions in New York and other major cities.

Determined to strengthen their unions against future depressions, they increased initiation fees and dues to create financial reserves and combined sickness-and-death benefits with union activities to make membership more stable. They also centralized power by giving national officers control over all union strike funds. Some, like cigarmakers' union president Adolph Strasser and his protégé Samuel Gompers, also thought they could avoid the brutal repression that they had witnessed in 1872, 1874 and 1877 if their unions focused exclusively on wages and avoided "political" issues.

In 1881, the national unions formed a Federation of Trade and Labor Unions, later renamed the American Federation of Labor. Although some of the German-American leaders drifted away from socialism, unionism and socialism remained closely linked for many other leaders of German-American unions—a disagreement that led to serious conflict in the federations.[75]

The German-American Left revitalized and greatly expanded its press during the postdepression recovery. When the *Arbeiter-Stimme* spun off a daily New York *Volks-Zeitung* in 1878, it opened a new era for the Left. Leading German-American socialist journalists like Adolph Douai, Alexander Jonas, and Sergius Schewitsh created a major socialist daily newspaper, which was able to compete with the nonsocialist German-language papers.[76] Its success rested on its ties to the network of left-wing unions, fraternal organizations, and social-cultural associations, which were vastly greater in membership than any socialist party.[77] These organizations grew rapidly with their paper and New York City saw the flourishing of a German-American socialist counterculture, comparable to that of Germany.

New York set the pace and the *Volks-Zeitung* was the intellectual leader for the rest, but comparable daily papers served large leftist subcultures in all of the largest German-American centers (with weeklies serving similar constituencies in smaller communities). The Philadelphia *Tageblatt* had been created even before the *Volks-Zeitung*, but it grew rapidly in circulation only after it began to emulate the New York paper.[78] In Chicago, the weekly *Vorbote* began issuing the daily *Arbeiter-Zeitung* in 1879.[79] The *Volks-Zeitung*, *Arbeiter-Zeitung*, *Tageblatt* trio of successful dailies (joined by similar papers in Cincinnati, Indianapolis, and St. Louis) remained at the heart of the German immigrant leftist counterculture for the next generation.

While national unions were the wave of the future, the vitality of the labor movement often remained with citywide organizations. German radicals took the lead in creating powerful and often anticapitalist central labor unions. German unions predominated in the creation of New York's radical Central Labor Union in 1882. With over forty unions affiliated, the CLU led most of the labor movement and generated several independent labor political campaigns even before it sparked the famous Henry George campaign of 1886.[80] In Chicago German unionists walked out of the conservative Anglo-American-dominated Trade and Labor Assembly to form "a Central Labor Union after the pattern of the CLU in New York." Even more German than its New York model, the Chicago CLU (which grew to forty thousand members) was a major force in the development of Chicago radicalism leading up to the Haymarket crisis.[81]

Another form of labor organization existed in the specifically German central labor councils that had sprung up in every period of labor organization since 1850. In 1885 a dozen German unions in New York rallied to the support of the *Volks-Zeitung*, and the German labor press in general, and created a new German organization, the United German Trades. It later grew to about fifty unions and was often regarded as a major factor in the strength of the city's German unions. In this too, New York was widely copied and German labor councils were set up in many cities. There was even some talk of forming a national confederation of the German union councils in 1887.[82]

Many historians maintain that the largest labor organization of the 1880s, the Knights of Labor, had little appeal for German immigrant workers, but that is misleading.[83] While some former socialist activists like Adolph Strasser had turned their energies away from the SLP to build trade unions, others joined the Knights of Labor.

Shortly after New York District Assembly 49 formed in 1882, it reportedly fell under the influence of a socialist group called the Home Club. The Home Club has generally been identified as Lassallean, though what that term means when applied to this group of union leaders is somewhat obscure. In any case, that put the second largest Knights assembly with about sixty thousand members (and later the Knights' executive board as well), under the influence of a faction of the German Left.[84] In Chicago, District Assembly 24 included German tanners', shoemakers', printers' and cigarmakers' assemblies—with the German printers represented by August Spies and Oskar Neebe of Haymarket fame.[85]

This gave German radicals an opportunity to resist the rightward drift of America's young craft unions when a socialist faction of the cigarmakers' union organized a successful opposition to Strasser's and Gompers' increasingly conservative leadership. Gompers and Strasser moved to suppress this challenge to their new antipolitical approach (and to their leadership of the union) by forcing the socialist New York local out of the CMIU, but the insurgents formed a rival Progressive Cigarmakers' Union and radical cigarmakers in other cities followed suit. For a while, the progressives had more members than did Strasser's official union.

In New York, the progressives joined District Assembly 49 and the battling German cigarmakers helped widen and embitter the rift between the Knights and the federation (and between the leaders of the American Federation of Labor and the socialists).[86] So it is clear that the role of German immigrants in the Knights of Labor was significant, though the topic requires further investigation.

In the 1870s, the collapse of the trade unions and the repression of the unemployed councils had led many to conclude that force would have to be met by force or no radical organization would be viable. With state militia units reportedly being armed to back up the police, and relief demonstrators in Chicago subjected to the same sort of billy club rule that had demoralized so many in New York, the Chicago *Vorbote* had suggested that workers would be justified in defending themselves with arms.[87]

Activists throughout the movement responded and began to form armed groups. [88] In 1875 Chicago took the lead when a group of militants formed a *Lehr- und Wehr-Verein* (Study and Defense Union) to defend workers' rights.[89] The organization began to grow rapidly after the violent antilabor repression in 1877 and the *Lehr- und Wehr-Verein* (along with similar workers' militias in other cities) reintroduced a component committed to the display and use of armed force into the German immigrant Left—a form of militancy that had not been seen since the *Turnvereine* fighting squads of the 1850s.[90]

Meanwhile the leaders of the Socialist Labor Party, having driven those who placed union organizing before political action out of the party, began a campaign against the armed defense organizations. When the *Vorbote* and the Chicago sections of the SLP defended them, the national committee ordered all SLP members to withdraw from armed groups—beginning a campaign that soon drove a majority of the strongest SLP local in the country (Chicago) out of the party.[91] The split widened when the Chicagoans refused to follow SLP leaders into the Greenback Labor coalition of 1880. The bolters were further disillusioned with elections when their independent socialist ticket did poorly.[92]

The split, which drew most of the German socialists in Chicago and their newspapers out of the SLP, had parallels in other cities as well. A group of New York dissidents formed a Social Revolutionary Club in 1880, and similar clubs formed in other cities over the next year. After participating in an attempt to revive the anarchist IWPA in Europe, the Social Revolutionary Club called a national meeting of like-minded organizations. They met in Chicago's Turner Hall and created a Revolutionary Socialist Party.[93] A German-American social revolutionary movement, often referred to as anarchist, was taking form.

At that point Johann Most, formerly a leading socialist Deputy in the *Reichstag* and then a leading spokesman for anarchism, arrived in New York and provided an impetus for further organization by the social revolutionaries and anarchists. Still, although the gifted Most was a dramatic and popular speaker whose lecture tours were well attended everywhere, his brand of violent anarchism found its greatest support in the new International Working People's Association in the East, where the organization was weakest. In Chicago, where the bulk of the German immigrant Left was associated with the IWPA, vague socialist-revolutionary doctrines tended to prevail against purer anarchist ones.[94]

What remains striking is how similar the German immigrant Left milieu in Chicago in the 1880s was to that in New York, despite the "anarchist" affiliation of the former and the socialist affiliation of the latter. Both based themselves on foundations of dense networks of social, political, and cultural institutions linked by a hyperactive *Vereinswesen*, the counterculture of the German-American Left.[95]

As the German-American Left flourished in the years before the upheaval of 1886, it witnessed the rise of a socialist women's movement. While *Frauenvereine* had long been active in supporting the men's movement through social activities, only in the mid-1880s did women's organizations emerge that were politically active in their own right. The formation of New York's *Frauenbünd* around 1883 began a national movement to organize women of the German immigrant Left.

The *Frauenbünde* had begun to address women's issues and even to criticize the SLP's lack of attention to such issues when Johanna Greie made her debut with a devastating critique of men, even socialist men, as "the enemy of women's emancipation." Backed by a growing number of *Frauenbunde* in 1888, Greie led a campaign to form a nationwide German-American socialist women's organization. Just as the campaign seemed on the verge of success, the SLP executive committee (reeling from the rapid collapse of the Left in 1888) called off the plans for a national women's association and asked the women of the *Frauenbünde* to dissolve their own organizations and reinforce declining party sections. Greie made the transition to regular party activity and continued to be a prominent figure, but most *Frauenbünde* activists abandoned their activism when their associations were disbanded.[96]

Once again the mainstream of the German-American Left had missed a chance to broaden its base by appealing to women. And once again its leaders had reinforced the cultural divide that separated them from Anglo-American radicals who were laying the groundwork for the Populist insurgency of the 1890s.

Events surrounding the Haymarket bombing are too well known to bear repeating here. What needs to be stressed is that even extreme demoralization did not mean wholesale collapse of the German-American socialist culture. The tenacious local press survived, embodying and unifying political communities of neighborhood clubs, unions, shared holidays, martyrs, and surviving hopes. If aging immigrants were increasingly likely to lament the loss of their past days of glory, especially in Chicago, they were still around in rather impressive numbers to do the lamenting.[97]

III. The Long Decline

Sectarian warfare on the Left—the usual result of larger disappointments—demoralized many, and the decline of German-American socialist organizations was exacerbated by the onset of a new depression in 1893. But the renewed crisis of capitalism also confirmed what many had long predicted, and veteran socialists put their shoulders to the wheel of rebuilding a political and union movement.

In a way, it wasn't so much that the German immigrant Left declined in the 1890s, as that the appearance and rapid growth of newer immigrant Lefts associated with the southern and eastern European immigrants of the 1880s–1890s created a relative decline as the Germans became senior figures in a much broader radical movement. Socialist Jews (aided by assimilated German Jews who edited some of the most important German newspapers), along with Hungarian, Polish, South Slav, Finnish, and Russian radicals, had admired German socialist success in the Old World and learned from it in the New. The new immigrants modeled their Free-thought, fraternal, and insurance societies; their labor-propaganda circles and their newspapers, as well as their explicitly political groups, on institutions German-Americans had created before they had arrived.

German-Americans still played a key role in the American Left. As Daniel De Leon's high-handed policies began to alienate many socialists, one of the first organized defections consisted of Milwaukee German-Americans led out of the SLP by Victor Berger. They joined with Eugene V. Debs and his associates to form a new Social Democratic Party. Then, the editors of the New York *Volks-Zeitung* and their supporters split the SLP again and moved to ally with the social democrats. Thus, members of the German immigrant Left played leading roles on both sides in the formation of the Socialist Party in 1901.[98]

Still, the members of the German immigrant Left grew older. With their base in the skilled working class and with an ingrained respect for ideas and education, they had major problems passing their oppositional culture on to their own children. While some of their American-born children moved into the most attractive of the skilled trades, second-generation German-Americans showed a tendency to move into white-collar occupations, which accelerated towards the end of the nineteenth century.[99] Upward mobility was not necessarily a total bar to socialist activism, but it did have a strong tendency to lead many of the most able second- and third-generation German-Americans in other directions.[100]

In Milwaukee, a left-leaning central labor union continued to grow in size and influence after the end of the 1880s. From 1893 to the 1930s, the Trades Council gave financial aid to the city's socialist press, starting with Victor Berger's *Wisconsin Vorwärts*, and the labor and socialist movements grew together in the most

German city in America. With the strong union support, Berger's Social Democratic Party played a dominant role in German working-class wards, and then took over the city administration and elected Berger the nation's first socialist congressman in 1910.[101]

A variety of factors combined to bring about the victories in Milwaukee, victories which would see another socialist elected mayor in 1916 and kept in office until 1940, while Berger was elected to Congress again in 1918, 1924, and 1926. One was the extent to which German immigrants and their children dominated the city. The political organization, which established hegemony among the Germans, was thus well on its way to local predominance.

Milwaukee was exceptional in having a second generation of German-American socialists expanding rather than contracting the socialist base. All three of the city's socialist mayors, for example, were American-born. The predominance of the German Immigrant leftist culture in the city by the early twentieth century helped assure the socialization of the immigrants' American-born children as socialists, but so did the exceptionally large proportion of the children who followed the skilled trades of their parents' generation.

Aging German radicals played an important role in the Socialist Party's organization and politics right through the 1919 split which let to separate Socialist and Communist Parties. Berger continued to play an important role in the rump Socialist Party until he died in 1929. His successor, second-generation German-American Milwaukee mayor Dan Hoan, played a major part in Norman Thomas' rise to leadership and the displacement of the Socialist Party's old guard in the 1930s.

Nor were Germans only important in Milwaukee. In New York, where immigrants from eastern and southern Europe had transformed the Socialist Party base, Germans continued to be the largest single group in the party as late as 1916.[102] After the 1919 split, while the Milwaukee Germans stuck with the old guard, the German Socialist Federation joined the newly developing Communist Party.[103]

New York editor Ludwig Lore played an important role in the split, and he took the *Volks-Zeitung* and its readers with him into the communist movement—where they remained until they were expelled in 1925. Lore and the *Volks-Zeitung* maintained an independent left-wing perspective until the paper, with "only" 23,000 subscribers left, dropped down to weekly publication in 1932.[104] The weekly *Neue Volkszeitung* continued to be an important anti-

Nazi publication for another decade and drew left-wing refugees from Nazi Germany into its circle.[105]

After the demise of the *Volks-Zeitung,* the German immigrant Left continued in the form of benefit societies, singing societies, unions, and old age homes. In 1938 and 1939, the venerable *Arbeiter Kranken-und Sterbe Kasse* (model for the Jewish Workmen's Circle) put out the *Volkskalander,* which had been an annual feature of the *Volks-Zeitung* since 1882. These last issues continued to report a wide range of German immigrant Left counterculture activities, so many that some of them must have extended well into the 1940s.[106] A century after Hermann Kriege founded the *Sozialreformassoziation,* a remnant of the German immigrant Left was still hanging on in the city of its birth.

Historical evaluations of the German-American Left have not tended to be kind. Judged against its own standard, the creation of a class-conscious revolutionary movement to transform capitalism into socialism, it has necessarily been considered a failure. But in a world where socialism is clearly not on the immediate historical agenda and where the vision of a united proletarian movement solving all of the world's problems has lost most of its plausibility, historians must apply different standards.

In the 1850s, Joseph Weydemeyer was so disgusted by the insularity of the German immigrant Left that he abandoned his attempt to create a revolutionary movement.[107] In the 1880s, Friedrich Engels repeatedly condemned the dogmatism, rigidity, and insularity of the German immigrant socialists, demanding that they abandon their culture ("doff every remnant of their foreign garb") and become "out and out Americans."[108] Politically, the German immigrant Left often tried to do just that. Its labor unions always participated in multi-ethnic citywide and national organizations, and the internationalists had encouraged the formation of "American" sections (at least for a while). The Germans of the SLP tried to Americanize the party when they turned its leadership over to a series of Americans, and they finally allied with the quintessentially American Gene Debs in the Socialist Party.

The problem remained at the core of the movement that was tied to the counterculture of the German immigrant left—Bruce Nelson's "Dancing Socialists, Picknicking Anarchists." But that counterculture, not the appeal to revolution, is what made the movement viable. The promised socialist revolution had a certain appeal to be sure, but the daily solidarity of the workplace and its unions, struggles for union wages and human dignity, ethnic neighborhoods, socialist picnics and anarchist dances—leftist songs, poems, stories and plays to nourish the spirit—these made daily life bearable. A shared dream like the ideal of socialism, could bring large numbers of people into the movement for short periods of time, but only a sense of community and shared culture kept people going and sustained the movement over the long haul. And it was there that the German immigrant Left showed the way for generations of American radicals.

Notes

1. Czechs, Hungarians, and Eastern European Jews were the groups who most explicitly copied or borrowed from the Germans, but it would be hard to identify any immigrant Left drawn from continental European sources, which didn't draw to some extent on the experience of the German-American Left. See Paul Buhle, "German Socialists and the Roots of American Working Class Radicalism," in Hartmut Keil and John Jentz, eds., *German Workers in Industrial Chicago, 1850–1910* (DeKalb, Ill., 1983), 224–35; Thomas Čapek, *The Čechs (Bohemians) in America* (New York, 1920), 125–27, 137–40, 254–61; Thomas Čapek, *The Čech (Bohemian) Community of New York* (New York, 1921), 21, 49–50, 59–75; Ronald Sanders, *The Downtown Jews* (New York, 1969), 46–48, 56–62, 90–91; Moses Rischin, *The Promised City* (New York, 1970), 76–81, 95–111, 150–51, 174–79; Morris U. Schappes, "The Political Origins of the United Hebrew Trades, 1888," *Journal of Ethnic Studies* 5 (1977): 13–41. Even the vital Yiddish theater had German-American leftist roots and the first Yiddish theater production in America took place on the stage of the *Turn-Verein* Hall in New York according to Irving Howe and Kenneth Libo, *World of Our Fathers* (New York, 1976), 461–62. For immigrant Left cultures in late nineteenth-century Chicago and their relationships to the Germans, see Bruce C. Nelson, *Beyond the Martyrs: A Social History of the Chicago Anarchists, 1870–1900* (New Brunswick, N.J., 1988), 127–52, 216–23.

2. For rural German immigrants see Frederick Luebke, *Germans in the New World* (Urbana, Ill. 1990) and Walter Kamphoefner, *The Westfalians: From Germany to Missouri* (Princeton, 1987). For urban culture see Stanley Nadel, *Little Germany: Ethnicity, Religion and Class in New York City, 1845–1880* (Urbana, Ill. 1990); Kathleen N. Conzen, *Immigrant Milwaukee, 1836–1860: Accommodation and Community in a Frontier City* (Cambridge, Mass. 1976); Lesley Kawa-

guchi, "The Making of Philadelphia's German-America: Ethnic Group and Community Development, 1830–1883" (Ph.D. diss., UCLA, 1983); Hartmut Keil, "German Immigrant Workers in Nineteenth-Century America: Working-Class Culture and Everyday Life in an Urban Industrial Setting," in *America and the Germans, v. 1* ed., Frank Trommler and Joseph McVeigh (Philadelphia, 1985), 189–206; and Guido Dobbert, *The Disintegration of an Immigrant Community: The Cincinnati Germans, 1870–1920* (New York, 1980).

3. Nadel, *Little Germany*, 104–21; Conzen, *Immigrant Milwaukee*, 152–91; Richard Oestereicher, *Solidarity and Fragmentation: Working People and Class Consciousness in Detroit, 1875–1900* (Urbana, Ill. 1986), 43–52; Keil, "German Immigrant Workers"; Nelson, *Beyond the Martyrs*, 127–52.

4. For more on this see Stanley Nadel, "From the Barricades of Paris to the Sidewalks of New York: German Artisans and the European Roots of American Labor Radicalism," *Labor History* (Winter 1989): 47–75.

5. Werner Kowalski, *Vorgeschichite und Entstehung des Bundes der Gerechten* (Berlin, 1962), 57–81; Ernst Schraepler, *Handwerkerbünde und Arbeitervereine, 1830–1853* (Berlin, 1972), 41–78, 98–103, 117, 122–23, 129–38, 151–63, 181–202, 299–300, 316, 335–36, 384, 432; Carl Wittke, *The Utopian Communist* (Baton Rouge, 1950), 20–22, 29, 34, 39, 48, 101, 108, 111, 115–16, 122–26, 189; P. Hartwig Bopp, *Die Entwicklung des deutschen Handwerksgesellentums im 19. Jahrhundert* (Paderborn, 1932), 99–132.

6. Nadel, *Little Germany*, 118.

7. Philip S. Foner and Brewster Chamberlin, eds., *Friedrich A. Sorge's Labor Movement in the United States* (New York, 1977) 76–77; Hermann Schlüter, *Die Anfänge der deutschen Arbeiterbewegung in Amerika* (Stuttgart, 1907) 23–40; Wittke, *Utopian Communist*, 116–19.

8. Schlüter, *Anfänge*, 40–41.

9. Nadel, *Little Germany*, 119.

10. Nadel, "European Roots," 59; Christopher Johnson, *Utopian Communism in France: Cabet and the Icarians, 1839–1851* (Uthaca, 1974); Edward Berenson, *Populist Religion and Left-Wing Politics in France, 1830–1852* (Princeton, 1984); K. Stephen Vincent, *Pierre-Joseph Proudhon and the Rise of French Republican Socialism* (Oxford, 1984); Wittke, *Utopian Communist*; Hans-Arthur Marsiske, "Wider

die Umsonstfresser" Der Handwerkerkommunist Wilhelm Weitling, (Hamburg, 1986); Ellen Drünert, "Die religiös-ethische Motivation des Kommunismus bei Wilhelm Weitling. Versuch einer Analyse," (Päd. Diss., Bonn, 1979).

11. Nadel, "European Roots," 60–63; Schlüter, *Anfänge,* 79–80, 131; Foner and Chamberlin, *Sorge's Labor Movement,* 91–93; Bruce Levine, *In the Spirit of 1848: German Immigrants, Labor Conflict, and the Coming of the Civil War* (Urbana, Ill. 1992), 125–36.

12. Foner and Chamberlin, *Sorge's Labor Movement,* 89–91; Schlüter, *Anfänge,* 71–79; Wittke, *Utopian Communist,* 220–25; Marsiske, *Wilhelm Weitling,* 96–100; *Republik der Arbeiter,* January, 1850; Wittke, *Utopian Communist,* 188–275; Levine, *Spirit of 1848,* 137.

13. Wittke, *Utopian Communist,* 188–275; Schlüter, *Anfänge,* 79–127; Foner and Chamberlin, *Sorge's Labor Movement,* 89–94.

14. Nadel, "European Roots," 64; "History of the Turners," *Turn-Zeitung,* I (1851–1952), 274–76; H.C.A. Metzner, *Geschichte des Turner-Bundes* (Indianapolis, 1874), 1–20; Levine, *Spirit of 1848,* 91.

15. Schlüter, *Anfänge,* 199–200; Metzner, *Turner-Bundes,* 21–23; Nadel, "European Roots," 65.

16. *Turn-Zeitung,* I (1851–1952), 18–19, 187–89, 203–04, 294, 297, 325, 329–48.

17. Levine, *Spirit of 1848;* Nadel, "European Roots," 67.

18. Nadel, *Little Germany,* 121, 204.

19. Nelson, *Beyond the Martyrs,* 217; Philip Foner, ed., *The Autobiographies of the Haymarket Martyrs* (New York, 1969), 70–71.

20. Karl Obermann, *Joseph Weydemeyer: ein Lebensbild, 1818–1866* (Berlin, 1968); *Turn-Zeitung,* I, 10, 18–19, 114–15.

21. Franz Mehring, "Neue Beitrag Zur Biographie von Karl Marx und Friedrich Engels," *Die Neue Zeit* 25 (1907): 99; Obermann, *Joseph Weydemeyer,* 270.

22. Schlüter, *Anfänge,* 88–93.

23. *New Yorker Staats-Zeitung,* March 3, April 1, 8, and May 6, 1853; Schlüter, *Anfänge,* 132–34; Obermann, *Joseph Weydemeyer,* 297–303.

24. Schlüter, *Anfänge,* 138.

25. *Turn-Zeitung*, I, 220–21; *Die Reform*, March 26, July 13, and October 12, 1853.

26. Schlüter, *Anfänge*, 149.

27. Schlüter, *Anfänge*, 135–56; Obermann, *Joseph Weydemeyer*, 318–40.

28. Levine, *Spirit of 1848*, 143–44; *New Yorker Staats-Zeitung*, January 9, 1855; Nadel, "European Roots," 71–73.

29. Much of Levine's *Spirit of 1848* consists of an argument that this was a continuation of their leftist activity and should not be treated as a diversion. There is a strong element of truth to that proposition as far as the 1850s are concerned, but most of those who became Republicans basically ceased to be part of the active German-American Left after the Civil War.

30. Dora Edinger, "A Feminist Forty-Eighter," *American-German Review* 8 (June 1942): 18–19; Maria Wagner, ed., *Mathilde Franziske Anneke in Selbstzeugnissen und Bilddokumenten*, (Frankfurt/Main, 1980); Gerhardt Friesen, "A Forgotten German-American Pioneer in Women's Rights," *Journal of German American Studies* 12, no. 2 (1977): 34–46; Annette P. Buss, "Mathilde Anneke and the Suffrage Movement," in *The German Forty-Eighters in America*, ed. Charlotte Brancaforte (New York, 1989), 79–92.

31. Buss, "Mathilde Anneke," 82.

32. Socialist leaders who fought included Joseph Weydemeyer, August Willich, and Fritz Jacobi. Jacobi, "one of the brightest and most promising young men of the Communist Club," was killed at Fredericksburg. Morris Hillquit, *History of Socialism in the United States* (New York, 1971), 154–55.

33. John Jentz, "The 48ers and the Politics of the German Labor Movement in Chicago during the Civil War Era: Community Formation and the Rise of a Labor Press," in *The German-American Radical Press: The shaping of a Left Political Culture, 1850–1940* ed., Elliott Shore, Ken Fones-Wolf, and James Danky (Urbana, Ill. 1992), 55; though orthodox marxist historians follow Sorge (Foner and Chamberlin, *Sorge's Labor Movement*, 152) in claiming that the Chicago movement was developed under the influence of the marxists Joseph Weydemeyer and Hermann Meyer.

34. Lawrence Costello, "The New York Labor Movement, 1861–1873," (Ph.D. diss., Columbia University, 1967), 173 & ap-

pendix II; New York *Daily News,* July 9 and October 8, 1864; Foner and Chamberlin, *Sorge's Labor Movement,* 109.

35. John R. Commons, ed., *A Documentary History of American Industrial Society,* IX, 69–71.

36. Nadel, *Little Germany,* 62–74; Hartmut Keil, "Chicago's German Working Class in 1900," in Keil and Jentz, *German Workers in Industrial Chicago,* 19–36; Clyde Griffin and Sally Griffin, *Natives and Newcomers* (Cambridge, Mass., 1978), 182–84; Steven J. Ross, *Workers on the Edge* (New York, 1985); Olivier Zunz, *The Changing Face of Inequality: Urbanization, Industrial Development, and Immigrants in Detroit, 1880–1920* (Chicago, 1982), 36–38, 220–24.

37. Weitling declined. Friedrich Adolph Sorge, *Briefe und Auszüge aus Briefen an F.A. Sorge und Andere* (Stuttgart, 1906), 4–5; Samuel Bernstein, *The First International in America* (New York, 1965), 37–38; Hermann Schlüter, *Die Internationale in Amerika* (Chicago, 1918), 80–90.

38. Kelloggism was the inflationary scheme adopted by the NLU and the Greenback party. Edward Kellogg, *A New Monetary System* (New York, 1861); *Workingmen's Advocate,* December 17, 1867; and Chester McArthur Destler, *American Radicalism, 1865–1901* (Chicago, 1961), 50–77.

39. *Arbeiter Union,* October 31, 1868 et. seq.

40. *Arbeiter Union,* May 1, 8, 1869.

41. Foner and Chamberlin, *Sorge's Labor Movement,* 153; Jentz, "The 48ers and the German Labor Movement in Chicago," 59.

42. Sorge, *Briefe,* 4–5; Bernstein, *First International,* 37–39; Schlüter, *Internationale,* 80–90.

43. Bernstein, *First International,* 162–63; Schlüter, *Internationale,* 421–23; Samuel Gompers, *Seventy Years of Life and Labor* (New York, 1925), 48–49, 57, 60, 82–84; Foner and Chamberlin, *Sorge's Labor Movement,* 152.

44. *Arbeiter Union,* July 30 and August 12, 1870; N.Y. *World,* November 20, 1870 and January 7, 1871; *Workingmen's Advocate,* December 3, 1870, January 14 and 28, 1871; Foner and Chamberlin, *Sorge's Labor Movement,* 152; Bernstein, *First International,* 43–49; Schlüter, *Internationale,* 115–25; Mari Jo Buhle, *Women and American Socialism, 1870–1920* (Urbana, 1981), 3.

45. David Roediger, "Ira Steward and the Anti-Slavery Origins

of American Eight-Hour Theory," *Labor History* 27 (Summer 1986): 410–26; David Montgomery, *Beyond Equality: Labor and the Radical Republicans, 1862–1872* (New York, 1967), 238.

46. Nadel, *Little Germany*, 143–48; Stanley Nadel, "Those Who Would Be Free: the Eight-hour Day Strikes of 1872," *Labor's Heritage* (April 1990): 70–77; Ken Fones-Wolf and Elliott Shore, "The German Press and Working-Class Politics in Gilded-Age Philadelphia," in *The German-American Radical Press*, 66–69.

47. See, for example, *Arbeiter Union*, January 9, 1869.

48. M. J. Buhle, *Women and American Socialism*, 2–3.

49. Foner and Chamberlin, *Sorge's Labor Movement*, 157.

50. Bernstein, *First International*, 112–17.

51. Bernstein, *First International*, 117–18.

52. Bernstein, *First International*, 186.

53. Bernstein, *First International*, 197–204, 215–18; Philip Foner, *History of the Labor Movement in the United States, Volume I* (New York, 1947), 439–41: Nadel, *Little Germany*, 153, 210; Bruce C. Nelson, "Arbeiterpresse und Arbeiterbewegung: Chicago's Socialist and Anarchist Press, 1870–1900," in *The German-American Radical Press*, 82.

54. Sorge had helped the *Kommunisten Klub* organize the demonstrations of the unemployed in New York in 1857 and Bernstein (*First International*, 221) notes the similarity between the plans of 1873 and 1857.

55. *Arbeiter-Zeitung*, November 29, 1873; *New York Times*, December 1, 1873.

56. Bernstein, *First International*, 220–27; Foner, *Labor Movement, I*, 445–47; Herbert G. Gutman, "The Tompkins Square 'Riot' in New York City on January 13, 1874: A Re-Examination of Its Causes and Its Aftermath," *Labor History* 6 (1965), 44–62.

57. Bernstein, *First International*, 227–29; Foner, *Labor Movement, I*, 448–49.

58. Bernstein, *First International*, 223–24.

59. Gutman, "The Tompkins Square 'Riot', 44–62; Bernstein, *First International*, 229–40, Samuel Gompers, *Seventy Years of Life and Labor* (New York, 1925), I, 96–97.

60. *Arbeiter-Zeitung,* February 7, 1874: *Vorbote,* February 14 and June 7, 20, 27, 1874; Nelson, *Beyond the Martyrs,* 53–55; Bernstein, *First International,* 248–51; Foner, *Labor Movement, I,* 448–49; Hillquit, *History of Socialism,* 184.

61. Like the German-Americans of the International, the social democrats were hostile to women's rights. Augusta Lilienthal fought unsuccessfully to keep the new party from calling for a ban on employment for mothers of children under fourteen and for placing severe restrictions on the employment of other women—though she did get the Party to agree to support equal wages for equal work. M. J. Buhle, *Women and American Socialism,* 12–13.

62. Bernstein, *First International,* 245–48.

63. Bernstein, *First International,* 274–87; Philip Foner, *The Workingmen's Party of the United States: A History of the First Marxist Party in the Americas* (Minneapolis, 1984); and Philip Foner, ed., *The Formation of the Workingmen's Party of the United States: Proceedings of Union Congress Held at Philadelphia, July 19–22, 1876* (New York, 1976).

64. Of the 24 papers associated with the WPUS over the next two years, fourteen were in German and only eight were in English. Of the 55 sections of the party in October 1876, 33 used German, sixteen English, four Czech, one Scandinavian (Dano-Norwegian), and one French (Bernstein, *First International,* 286–90). Sorge claimed that ninety percent of the WPUS "was made up of German workers" (Foner and Chamberlin, *Sorge's Labor Movement,* 199).

65. Bernstein, *First International,* 285.

66. Schlüter, *Die Internationale in Amerika,* 306; Foner and Chamberlin, *Sorge's Labor Movement,* 163; Bernstein, *First International,* 286–87; Foner, ed., *Formation of the Workingmen's Party,* 34.

67. Foner and Chamberlin, *Sorge's Labor Movement,* 200.

68. The Germans, with about six hundred members, had by far the largest section of the WPUS in St. Louis in 1877. David Burbank, *Reign of the Rabble: The St. Louis General Strike of 1877* (New York, 1966), 19; and the *St. Louis Daily Times,* June 18, 1877; Foner and Chamberlin, *Sorge's Labor Movement,* 201.

69. A culture embodied in the German joke: Why can't there

be a successful revolution in Germany? Because, outside the Reichstag there is a sign that says "Do Not Step on the Grass."

70. This interpretation is based on David Roediger's "Not Only the Ruling Classes: Class, Skill and Community in the St. Louis General Strike," *Journal of Social History* 19 (Winter 1985): 213–39.

71. On those arrested see the *St. Louis Globe Democrat* and the *St. Louis Daily Times*, July 28, 1877. For more see Burbank, *Reign of the Rabble;* Roediger, "Not only the Ruling Classes"; Philip Foner, *The Great Labor Uprising of 1877* (New York, 1977), 160–88, 208; Elliot Kanter, "Class, Ethnicity, and Socialist Politics: St. Louis, 1876–1881," *UCLA Historical Journal* 3 (1983): 43–45.

72. The union turned to the courts for redress and the policemen were convicted, but they were then fined only six cents each. Foner and Chamberlin, *Sorge's Labor Movement,* 198, 201; Christine Heiss, "German Radicals in Industrial America: The Lehr- und Wehr-Verein in Gilded Age Chicago," *German Workers in Industrial Chicago,* 214–15; Foner, *Labor Movement,* I, 470–71.

73. And not just in Chicago, David reports similar organizations in Cincinnati and San Francisco *(The History of the Haymarket Affair,* 61), and Kanter ("St. Louis Socialists," 46) reports that two hundred members of a Socialist Workingmen's Protective Association were drilling regularly in 1878.

74. This drift was regularly condemned by Marxists and historians in that tradition as a diversion from the key struggle to create unions, but it must be remembered that municipal victories would give workers control over the police who had just been used brutally against them in those cities. Therefore, it was often the same men who advocated both electoral action and organized workers' militias—as with Currlin (general strike leader and editor of the *Volkstimme des Westens*) in St. Louis and the *Vorbote* in Chicago. Kanter, "St. Louis Socialists," 46–57; and Heiss, "Lehr- und Wehr-Verein," 214–15.

75. Sorge reported that "the Germans were the driving, progressive element in the large and small unions . . . " Even Strasser and his protégé Samuel Gompers may have been far slower to abandon socialism than is generally supposed. Gompers (who was a product of the German immigrant community in New York even if he wasn't actually German) was still talking about the need to abolish the wage system and private ownership of the means of

production well into the 1890s. Foner and Chamberlin, *Sorge's Labor Movement*, 199; Foster Rhea Dulles and Melvyn Dubofsky, *Labor in America: A History* (Arlington Heights, Ill., 1984), 142–49; Foner, *Labor Movement, I*, 512–18.

76. Carol Poore, "The *Pionier* Calendar of New York City, Chronicler of German-American Socialism," in *The German-American Radical Press*, 111.

77. Paul Buhle, "Ludwig Lore and the *New Yorker Volkszeitung*: The Twilight of the German-American Socialist Press," in *The German-American Radical Press*, 169–70; Hillquit, *History of Socialism*, 206–07.

78. Ken Fones-Wolf and Elliott Shore, "The German Press and Working-Class Politics," 70; Foner and Chamberlin, *Sorge's Labor Movement*, 201; Hillquit, *History of Socialism*, 204–06.

79. Nelson, "*Arbeiterpresse und Arbeiterbewegung*," 82–83.

80. Hillquit, *History of Socialism*, 260–61; Foner, *Labor Movement, II*, 33–34; Foner and Chamberlin, *Sorge's Labor Movement*, 201; Hillquit, *History of Socialism*, 174–75.

81. Nelson, *Beyond the Martyrs*, 40–44, 228.

82. Hillquit, *History of Socialism*, 262–63.

83. Following F. A. Sorge, see Foner and Chamberlin, *Sorge's Labor Movement*, 199. But Richard Oestereicher's, *Solidarity and Fragmentation: Working People and Class Consciousness in Detroit, 1875–1900* (Urbana, Ill., 1986), gives a very different picture.

84. Foner, *Labor Movement, II*, 78–79; though Hillquit (*History of Socialism*, 268) says that the SLP take-over wasn't until a decade later.

85. Nelson, *Beyond the Martyrs*, 44–48.

86. Foner, *Labor Movement, I*, 517–18 and *II*, 132–44; Sorge (Foner and Chamberlin, *Sorge's Labor Movement*, 203) attributed the formation of "progressive" unions of cigarmakers and others to recent refugees from Germany's antisocialist campaign who were not yet adjusted to American conditions, but Nelson's account of the cigarmakers' split in Chicago (*Beyond the Martyrs*, 38–39) gives no indication of that being a factor, at least not there.

87. Christine Heiss, "Lehr- und Wehr-Verein," 210–11.

88. Schlüter, *Die Internationale in Amerika*, 308.

89. Henry David, *The History of the Haymarket Affair: A Study in the American Social-Revolutionary and Labor Movements* (New York, 1963), 60; Heiss, "Lehr- und Wehr-Verein," 211–12.

90. It is probably not a coincidence that one of the better-known members of the *Lehr- und Wehr Verein* was *Turner-Bund* activist August Spies. Heiss, "Lehr- und Wehr-Verein," 220.

91. Heiss, "Lehr- und Wehr-Verein," 215–16; Hillquit, *History of Socialism*, 213.

92. Foner and Chamberlin, *Sorge's Labor Movement*, 202; Foner, *Labor Movement, I*, 495; David, *History of the Haymarket Affair*, 63; Nelson, *Beyond the Martyrs*, 66–70.

93. Nelson, *Beyond the Martyrs*, 71, 155; David, *Haymarket*, 70–77.

94. Nelson, *Beyond the Martyrs*, 73, 154–73; David, *Haymarket*, 88–138; Paul Avrich, *The Haymarket Tragedy* (Princeton, 1984). On the other hand, it must be noted that Most's pamphlet *Revolutionaire Kriegswissenschaft* was the bible of the cult of revolutionary violence which "centered around *Die Anarchist*, Engel, Fischer, Lingg and Gruppe Nordwestseite." Nelson, *Beyond the Martyrs*, 161–63.

95. That is brought home by Nelson's *Beyond the Martyrs*. Compare that with Nadel's *Little Germany*.

96. M. J. Buhle, *Women and American Socialism*, 33–40.

97. Nelson, *Beyond the Martyrs*, 201–42; Klaus Ensslen and Heinz Ickstadt, "German Working-Class Culture in Chicago: Continuity and Change in the Decade from 1900 to 1910," in *German Workers in Industrial Chicago*, 236–52.

98. Hillquit, *History of Socialism*, 294–309; Ira Kipnis, *The American Socialist Movement, 1897–1912* (New York, 1952).

99. This pattern appeared early in Eastern cities like New York and Philadelphia, but it was true of Detroit and Chicago as well by the later years of the century—with Keil noting a particularly rapid development of this pattern between 1880 and 1900. See Nadel, *Little Germany*, 66; Stephanie Greenberg, "Industrialization in Philadelphia: The Relationship Between Industrial Location and Residential Patterns, 1880–1930" (Ph.D. diss., Temple University, 1977); Zunz, *Changing Face of Inequality*, 36–38, 220–24; and Keil, "Chicago's German Working Class in 1900."

100. The socialist career of Joseph Weydemeyer's son Otto is a conspicuous exception here.

101. Sally M. Miller, "Milwaukee: Of Ethnicity and Labor," in *Socialism and the Cities*, ed. Bruce Stave (Port Washington, N.Y., 1975), 41–71.

102. Paul Buhle attributes this conclusion to an unpublished manuscript by Charles Leinenweber on "Urban Socialism" ("Ludwig Lore and the *New Yorker Volkszeitung*," 171).

103. P. Buhle, "Ludwig Lore and the *New Yorker Volkszeitung*," 171–78.

104. More than twice as many subscribers as it had had in 1880.

105. P. Buhle, "Lugwig Lore and the *New Yorker Volkszeitung*," 171–78; Poore, "The *Pionier* Calendar," 111; Moses Rischin, "Envoi," in *The German-American Radical Press*, 209.

106. Poore, "The *Pionier* Calendar," 111, 119.

107. Obermann, *Joseph Weydemeyer*, 318–40.

108. Marx and Engels, *Letters to Americans 1848–1895* (New York, 1953), 166, 285–91.

THREE

Themes in American Jewish Radicalism

Paul Buhle

In an often brilliant study of personality and aesthetics in American *Yiddishkayt* (Yiddishness, a particular quality of Jewish life in the diaspora), noted Yiddish scholar Ruth Wisse stumbles across the conjuncture of poetics and politics. Jewish social democracy in the United States appears a sort of Old World hangover, politically primitive and economically mistaken but understandable as a transitional worldview for the immigrant generations en route to liberal pluralism. Jewish revolutionary socialism or communism seem, by contrast, a combination of the conspiratorially subversive and the simply monstrous. The idea that dedicated revolutionaries could ever have played important and respected roles in American Jewish culture, among Yiddishists and mainstreamed artists, poets, or moviemakers alike, becomes well-nigh inconceivable, either a bad dream or a blood libel.[1]

This view has long been offered from many different corners. Irving Howe, a mild if persistent socialist, devoted chapters of his best-selling *World of Our Fathers* to describing the world of the Jewish Left in a broadly similar fashion. Jewish socialism was a transitional phenomenon; it had drifted ineluctably into Jewish liberalism during the same era if not in precisely the same way that life in New York's Lower East Side turned into life in the Upper West (or even Upper East) Side and the suburbs. Momentary flashbacks—Howe evidently meant aggressive leftism of all kinds—showed "a streak of madness, the purity of messianic yearning [shadowed] by an apocalyptic frenzy." He added shrewdly and with distinct understatement that fanaticism and the bursts of creativity could always not be separated from each other.[2]

But Howe regarded only one major strand of Jewish socialism as legitimate, treating others from the 1890s to the 1970s as either transitory exotics or destructive invaders. Howe thus decisively narrowed Jewish radicalism's richness and variety (or perhaps he merely confirmed a historical neglect). This was a distinct loss for several reasons. So numerous were the Jewish Left publications, groups, tendencies, and factions that hardly a characteristic of other immigrant radical groups is not somehow represented here, in Jewish form, as a barometer of trends and possibilities. More important, Howe failed to indicate the degree to which a demographically Jewish Left influenced both the entire post–1890 U.S. radicalism and important progressive trends within American popular culture.

Jewish radicals uniquely, among immigrant groups, operated in predominantly gentile as well as Jewish circles. They supplied over the generations a disproportionate number of leaders and often rank-and-file to labor, cultural, and other ostensibly non-Jewish progressive and radical organizations, not only among "Americans" but also among German, Russian, Hungarian, and Polish immigrants. Moreover, if a few highly insular groups can claim more intense support of their own community for the Left, their impact was almost exclusively within the immigrant generation.[3] Jewish political staying power, as well as education and organizational skill, put their activists at the center of the Left's political picture between 1920 and 1960. Rather than disappearing with the eclipse of the Jewish working class and the appearance of Israel, Jewish radicalism has continually revived, albeit in continually changing forms. If the Jewish Left has grown weaker in time, so has the organized Left at large, and the ratio of Jews within the progressive movements or subscribing to progressive publications remains disproportionate by any standard.

A singular source of strength can be found in a peculiar cosmopolitanism. The Jewish Left of the United States has been a conscious part of a physically (and not just emotionally) international movement, in several senses different from other immigrant radicalisms. Its intimate international relationships included not only the European emigrant homelands and Soviet Russia (as did many of the other groups' origins and contacts) but every land where Yiddish speakers gathered, including the young colony in Palestine, which could never have survived without a certain socialistic idealism. Coupled with their own sense as a persecuted people and sympathies for others similarly pressed, Jews could see the possibilities and indeed the outline of a future cooperative world system, to be built in part through their connected efforts in Moscow, Vilna, Budapest, Paris, Sofia, London, Buenos Aires, Cairo, Jerusalem and, New York, all the way across wide America to the chicken farms of Petaluma, California.

Several streams, intimate and intermixed but conceptually distinct, have flowed into the wide currents. One of the main streams, from the movement's earliest beginnings, has been a repugnance for capitalist values and for the wealthy Jews who embrace them. Amid continued upward mobility and centrist institutional leadership from the first immigrant generation onward, an antiphilistine and antibourgeois shadow lurks unbidden, like the bohemian cousin at a family reunion of assorted arrivistes (in the Yiddish patois, *alrightniks*).

Thus if the most powerful figure in the Yiddish-speaking world, Abraham Cahan, gradually relinquished socialist hope and accepted Jewish success among the American gentiles as a more than acceptable fate, he had also eloquently anticipated the moral consequences. In his bildungsroman, *The Rise of David Levinsky*, the wealthy protagonist's worldly success brings spiritual emptiness.[4] The nearly constant theme of the American Jewish novel, play, and cinema, as critic J. Hoberman identified its trace in one of the final Yiddish-language films, can be seen in the melancholic aftereffects of abandoning redemptive expectations. Jewish emotions, in that all too real life experience, have been reduced to the "struggle between middle class hypocrisy and cultural despair."[5]

The countervision of redemption somehow redeemed against all odds has survived among large numbers of Jews as an *ethical* imperative, and for good reasons. It has marked both Jewish resistance and accommodation to the modern world. Left-wing Jews fought for he economic survival of their people (and all the poor and working classes) within the heart of modern capitalism. But they simultaneously recognized very early that their European brethren could not survive *without* a drastic change in the international social order. History and the structures of power weighed against socialist promise, however it might at times coincide with popular Jewish aspiration. But radical groups and individuals nevertheless found ways to inject themselves, their cooperative ideals, into the continuous remaking of Jewish life.

At times openly political, at other times this attitude or ethical commitment expressed itself as a subtextual politics of daily life. American Jews with a left-wing element active among them did much to create a dynamic, multicultural and even multiracial popular commercial culture and have continued to play an extraordinarily influential role. The emerging jazz, films, sports, and pulp press certainly drew attention away from Yiddish culture and Jewish communal institutions as such, as it did from all discrete immigrant cultures, the more so with each passing generation. But the inherent linguistic adaptability of *Yiddishkayt* and its immanent content, what a distinguished scholar of American Yiddish literature calls the "painful dual process of separation and hunger for roots," evoked a will and capacity to seek and borrow, adapt and resynthesize from every available source. A feeling for various cultural styles, along with the contacts and skills to train and market talent, made them indispensable impresarios as well as fans.[6]

Finally, in a political parallel with marked internal contradictions, Jews were virtually the only European-style "social democratic" constituency of lasting importance in twentieth-century United States. Their concentration in greater New York, tens of thousands alone in the sweated clothing industry, made possible an industrial dynamic not accidentally linked to corners of popular culture, i.e., popular attire. Here, in the needles trades, socialists quickly formed the leadership of large sections of the workforce, and remained for generations eminently respectable, indeed widely considered necessary for the stability of both labor and capital. Nowhere else within the American socialist world did or could a consolidation of unionism and journalism take the form of a fixed bureaucracy with socialistic sentiments, wedded far more to the matter of business unionism than to any vision of a future cooperative society. Early on a major base of socialist support from within labor and then for industrial unionism, this tendency nevertheless played an equally key role in the defense of conservative labor leadership *against* perceived radical intrusions.

The drift of older socialistic notions into cold war liberalism reversed rather than eradicated the historical tradition. As Michael Harrington's biographer Robert A. Gorman has quipped, the "most rightwing socialist party in the world" and the most Jewish one outside Israel found its widest influence and maximum financial patronage within the Reagan administration, the very prototype of those regimes once denounced by Jewish intellectuals as the kingdom of the privileged.[7] Similarly, as generations of Jews found their bête noire, in capitalism and their hope in the vision of socialism, later Jewish institutional leaders bridge the intellectual gap between social democracy and the security state, viewing resistance movements against an American empire as de facto anti-Semitism and resurgent U.S. capitalism as Judaism's lasting salvation. From the 1940s on, few right-leaning liberal gentiles and still fewer conservatives had such needs for claims on the history of socialism, or the inspiration of a manqué Marxism in support of such imperial aims as control over markets and raw materials. Nor did any have the need to mobilize large treasuries and public relations teams to discredit the cousins who remained active in the antiwar, antiracist, and environmental movements.

In the end, irony piled upon irony. The political descendents of those who proposed to defend trade unionism against left-wing socialism sacrificed the unions to their own international objectives, abandoning the growing sectors of the workforce (women and minorities) to the vagaries of the market. Meanwhile, former communists or near-communists continued, in their last phase, to articulate the deepest assumptions of Jewish ethics as universal humanist principles and Jewish aesthetics as a guide to modern culture. If we look carefully, we will find the various underlying assumptions steadily remade along the way. But we should resist oversimplified explanations and especially the temptation to read the outcome as inevitable in the logic of Jewish life at large.

I.

Jewish radicalism's origins, if not all the sources of its peculiar American trajectory, lie squarely in Europe. Many scholars have identified the obvious facts of *shtetl* life in the East European Pale or permitted Jewish areas of the nineteenth century. At the depth of the Pale, industrialization and urbanization seemed to break in upon an almost timeless society, judged by the biblical references in daily life and personal expectations for messianic salvation. Jewish culture, always divided by class and by geopolitics—its urban, educated, and semiassimilated central European petty bourgeoisie starkly different from the *shtetl* dwellers in the East— faced extraordinary stresses, both threats and opportunities, in the last half of the century.[8]

A growing sense of class oppression, the legacy of (male) education and the spectre of anti-Semitism combined in strange and unexpected ways, as socialist ideals swept across large sections of the continent with industrial development. The efforts of Jewish liberalism or enlightenment (the *haskalah*) to banish religion and Yiddish alike for rationalism and German (or Russian) were resisted most ferociously by the insular Hasidic communities, the most thoroughly "out of time." Yiddish itself was viewed as "jargon," a mongrel language unsuited to civilized development. Yiddish "literature" existed only in the *T'sena Urena*, or women's bible, practically the only published Yiddish volume for centuries. But the *haskalah* never had a serious chance among the growing diaspora moving into urban, industrial districts across Europe and elsewhere. Middle-class values did not suit the experience or the needs of such masses. Jewish socialists came to learn that if they inherited the Enlightenment tradition, even more (and despite their own fervent atheism) they had inherited the messianic sensibility of emotion, the communal instinct, and the suspicion of the *Yehudim* (or German-assimilated) Jewish elite, which set out the rules for progress on both sides of the ocean.

The birth of Yiddish socialism (and of the Jewish cultural intelligentsia as well) could be concentrated into the experiences of one extraordinary individual, Morris Winchevsky. He personally unified the threads of messianic tradition, the contemporary currents of socialist-anarchist praxis, and the requirements of a Yiddish political culture coming onto history's stage. By no accident, he became the prophet of Jewish socialism in America.

Born in 1856, Winchevsky was the grandson of a great rabbi martyred by German invaders of Poland. Radicalized in a Vilna Jewish school, he fell under the cosmopolitan literary influences of the German Romantics and of Russian critics and poets. And yet he held onto the dream of becoming a Jewish-language writer. In London, physically separated from the *shtetl* but intimately tied to Eastern European Jewry and its diaspora, he found his destiny among the gathering East End ghetto of Jewish tailors, factory operatives, and beggars. He had only to remake himself as a journalist in their spoken language, neither Hebrew nor English but Yiddish, and to interpret for them the socialist ideals and practice of the day.

Winchevsky established in 1881 the *Poylishe Yidl* (the Little Polish Jew), the first radical Yiddish paper anywhere, and after its failure, created the historic *Arbeter Fraint* (the Workers' Friend) in 1884. Overnight, the *Fraint* became what budding Yiddish writers and working-class Yiddish readers had wanted, an organ for their own expression. As would historic Left Yiddish papers in the U.S., the *Fraint* built the radical movement around itself. It devoted itself above all to the spiritual uplift of its readers from their current misery to hopes for a golden tomorrow. Unlike the German-, English-, French-language, and most other socialist papers of the time, it had no skilled worker constituency but only the seated and despised masses of Jews, fresh from the *shtetls*. They saw in the modest Winchevsky a poet, a savior, a demigod.[9]

Apart from his willingness to endure poverty along with the faithful, Winchevsky imbibed a special quality that charmed his readership. As Aaron Lansky has pointed out, the first popular Yiddish writers of the 1880s–1890s characteristically employed a version of wry humor and satire to encompass the tragedy of the Jewish situation, the credulous naivete of the masses and the philistinism of the Jewish wealthy classes.[10] Winchevsky, the *"meshugina filosofer"* (crazy philosopher) asked in the first of many similar monologues:

> What? The world has gone crazy? . . . Is 1848 a dream, no more than a dream? . . . Is it possible that the century which roared like a lion, gave forth a mouse? Have the forces that brought forth socialism also given birth to that monster, anti-semitism? What? The great republic on the other side of the Atlantic makes Jews slaves of gold? What? Does the . . . telephone, wonder-gift of modern times, come into the world only to transmit the cries of Jews, new songs of agony, from one part of Israel to another? And the trains, the new ships? Are they made only so that every land shall contain a section of suffering Jews? What? Victor Hugo dead and Bismark alive? Has the world gone to the devil?[11]

Winchevsky overlaid socialist expectations upon this *Weltschmerz*, but tragic irony remained the key emotion. The "crazy philosopher" is truly mad—or the world must be healed and suffering redeemed.

The rise of industrial capitalism's consumer outlet, the ready-to-wear garment market directed at the new middle classes but also at the working class, made the mass Jewish migration to the United States economically feasible. The nature of the trade also facilitated, by the later 1890s, the organization of a political culture allowing a series of unprecedented institutional breakthroughs. The vicious character of the subcontracting system (where a petty entrepreneur turned over the product of a larger contractor) lent itself to the perpetuation of *shtetl* ties. *Landsmanshaften* sickness-

and-death benefit associations of immigrants from the same districts eased the way for the *Arbeter Ring*, or Workmen's Circle to be founded in 1890, ultimately becoming the most successful of all the Left-led immigrant benefit societies, and an independent center of socialistic worker self-education.

The arrival of tens and then hundreds of thousands of impoverished Jewish immigrants to 1890s New York also coincided with a shattering economic crisis. Driving down already low prices for finished goods and prompting near total unemployment during the "slack season," the depression seemed to identify a diasporic Jewish misery with the ruthlessness of capitalism. The spread of tuberculosis—the *proletarishe krank* (workers' disease) well known to be rooted in the bad circulation and starvation diets of ghetto dwellers—only deepened the desperation and rage.

Neighborhood sentiment against the horrors of tenements meanwhile reinforced a class sensibility. The bosses and slumlords often enough were also Jewish, clawing their way to the top over the bodies of their fellow immigrants, craving at once assimilation into American capitalism and (especially later) a Jewish identity such as nationalism suitable to their own notions of power and authority. In this climate, poor Jews easily sympathized with non-Jewish workers who did not stigmatize them, and simultaneously utilized communitarian traditions against the Jewish capitalists who seemed hell bent on exploiting their own people.

An "internationalism" of cross-ethnic connections quickly emerged alongside Jewish fraternal ties and the launching of specifically Jewish organizations such as the United Hebrew Trades of 1888. The presence of socialist-influenced German and Bohemian immigrants in some better part of the needle trades emphasized a connection that German socialist intellectuals (a sprinkling of them actually Jewish, albeit thoroughly identified with their Germanness) made from above. German-Americans had much to teach in the formation and development of unions, the relationship of the press, fraternal sector, and party to the labor movement.[12]

The presence of European-trained radical intellectuals, themselves thoroughly proletarianized by their conditions, meanwhile gave definite and unique voice to the sense of urgency and hopes for release. Poets, anarchist and socialist alike, met the Jewish masses with voices of millennial inspiration in foredoomed but heroic strikes. But they also made clear that they meant to speak in a cultural voice and with a Jewish accent. The earliest Yiddish socialist newspaper in the U.S. claimed that it would contain "more reading matter than any other Jewish newspaper, EVER published," placed itself in succession of the prophets and protectors of the Jews from Moses onward, bemoaned the vaunted freedom of American as a swindle, and swore the vindication of true Art in the happy days to come.[13] A few years later, Morris Rosenfeld, the "teardrop millionaire" Yiddish poet whose lyrics apotheosized suffering, would blend these same themes, becoming simultaneously and without contradiction a Jewish nationalist and ardent socialist.

The same circle of intellectuals produced the first regular socialist journal (the monthly *Tsukunft*, or future, from 1890) full of ruminations as well as popularization, and even the first aesthetics journal of the U.S. Left (*Der Naier Geist*, the new spirit, 1897–1899).[14] Critics in the pages of the latter, keen to the conceptual problems already posed for Jewish radicalism, debated ardently whether Rosenfeld was a proletarian poet or a people's poet of suffering Jewry.[15] It was a good theoretical question but missed a deeper synthetic truth that anarchist critic B. Rivkin later emphasized. Rosenfeld helped make Yiddish itself a sort of imaginary homeland of a people who could not imagine a secure home without the victory of world socialism.[16]

The complex relations of class and ethnicity worked themselves out differently in the realms of mass culture, with important secondary influences upon the course of socialist politics. German Jews central to the creation of Tin Pan Alley helped devise a synthetic Americanism of borrowed and adapted jazz (they introduced black music and black composers into the sheet music repertoire, albeit by featuring demeaning novelty songs). On the lively, chaotic streets of the Lower East Side, Jewish gangsters rounded up bets on horses, street musicians played "A Bicycle Built for Two," and some of the earliest available experiments in popular film were shown in makeshift moviehouses. Yiddish theater, inevitably founded by socialists, soon softened and blended its radical message into a vibrant commercial drama touched with both Jewish and social concern. The Yiddish radical press, torn almost at once between socialist and anarchist factions and then different factions within the socialist movement, sorted itself out with the victory of the most popular and commercially viable of the competitors.[17] Morris Winchevsky was central to the last initiative.

Arriving in 1894, "the *zeyde*" (or "grandfather," as he was widely known by age forty to the young immigrants) surveyed the doctrinaire ranks of the SLP and set out to publish an artistic-minded socialist Yiddish newspaper. His first effort, *der Emes*, truth, showed signs of revolt but failed in Boston. He relocated to New York, where frustration at the lack of socialist political progress was increasingly directed at Socialist Labor Party leader Daniel De Leon. The former Columbia professor and Sephardi of Dutch West Indian background had a reputation as the first serious Marxist among English-language socialist leaders, and (for a short time) as a great secular rabbi of the radicalized Jewish masses. Like the atmosphere of many a ghetto institution, his SLP regime was famous for its political and intellectual intolerance.[18]

Winchevsky placed himself in the midst of a complex rebellion. He demanded artistic freedom in the Yiddish press, in effect an unhindered opening into American ethnic, popular life. Jewish unionists within the SLP wanted an equal degree of freedom, but with the somewhat different purpose of protecting their organizational investments in the American Federation of Labor. A section of Jewish anarchists during the middle 1890s had already defected to Samuel Gompers' side against De Leon, in return for the AFL leader's patronage. This development marked one major tendency within Jewish radical life, the preservation of philosophical ideals alongside bureaucratic and even cynical institutional arrangements.

The role of Jewish women in this moiling political mixture is of especial interest. Far more rarely permitted education than Jewish men and confined by tradition to a secondary social role at best, ever rebellious-minded Jewish women faced formidable odds. Significant numbers nevertheless educated themselves and yet remained within or close to the working class. A handful of progressive doctors and pioneering birth control advocates emerged naturally from these ranks. Meanwhile, ordinary women workers had been critically placed for labor struggles by their overwhelming presence in large sections of the needles trades. For almost a generation, AFL "Jewish" unions expressed only pessimism and disinterest in their mobilization. Not surprisingly, when the Socialist Labor Party issued a call in 1895 for a Socialist Trades and Labor Alliance to replace the depression-staggered AFL and embrace all workers, such women leaders as young socialist Theresa Serber responded heroically from the shop floor. Crushed by economic hopelessness and by the savage hostility of AFL leaders (and unaided by most male socialists), they were forced to retreat. The failure of the women's unions, during the 1890s, meant the failure of the SLP.[19]

Traditional scholars, from official union chroniclers to Irving Howe, have erred as they framed the consequent political imbroglio of the socialist movement one-sidedly. Seeing the "extreme" socialism of the SLP to blame for the socialist factional crack-up of the 1890s, they have made De Leon into a mere fanatic or a protocommunist. An altogether typical ghetto political combatant in his demand for personal loyalties and his rule-or-ruin behavior, De Leon unquestionably drove the sympathizers of Winchevsky and many other ardent socialists into the arms of the compromised unionists. But De Leon, early and accurately, also identified the undertow of business unionism. By insisting on political loyalty rather than challenging the exclusionary economic basis of the AFL toward unskilled workers, racial minorities, and women, he failed to elaborate the kind of alternative that the Industrial Workers of the World later offered.[20]

At any rate, anti-De Leon rebels closed ranks to form in 1897 the new tabloid, *The Jewish Daily Forward*. The *Forward's* editors aligned themselves with other anti-De Leonists who joined Eugene Debs' alliance of variegated radicals in 1901 to form the Socialist Party of America. Meanwhile, the *Forward* proceeded to carry its own weight as the flagship of Jewish life in the new land. Unlike the German-American press, which inevitable strived to replicate the powerful homeland example right down to the print styles, the American Yiddish experiment demanded fresh approaches, and stirred them in blends of close reportage and even sensationalism with a reform-minded perspective—a moderately Left forerunner of the 1930s *New York Post* or 1940s *PM* with greater actual circulation and more intimate assumptions about the audience. The one-column short story provided the ideal medium for social realism, and authors like Leon Kobrin ("the Jewish Zola") showed the pathos of slum life with poverty, sickness, family, and sexual longing as part of the American bargain. Here, at least for the moment, the question of didactic socialist messages versus Jewish self-centeredness versus popular culture entertainment seemed to have answered itself in practice.[21]

But the *Forward* also buried political socialism in its back columns except at election times and during occasional mass strikes. It admired Eugene Debs as it would admire Norman Thomas in a lower key, decades later, because its readers idolized the socialist leaders. But is subtextual politics often pointed in other directions. Unlike the SLP's flagging Yiddish press, which denounced the contemporary lure of American expansionism, the *Forward* tried to put itself at the head of neighborhood enthusiasm for the Spanish-American War. It urged revenge against the Spanish for wrongs done to Jews four centuries earlier, but it also noticeably revelled in the military victories of American expeditionary forces.[22]

The *Forward*'s editors remained indifferent to the real fate of Cubans or Filipinos placed under the American thumb and, in the Filipino case, slaughtered in vast numbers for seeking independence. The *Forward* quietly dropped its enthusiastic editorials without retracting its position that primitive peoples were best served by American domination.[23] A seed for a later generation's manqué or imperial Marxism had nevertheless been firmly planted. Returning to the paper in 1902 and less interested than before in socialism's prospects, Cahan laid down his own aesthetic rules for Yiddish theater and literature, foreshadowing in still another way the post socialist era of the Jewish-American intelligentsia.

Winchevsky, for his part, was shocked and increasingly repelled at the journalistic and aesthetic consequences of the *Forward*'s militaristic zest and Cahan's high-handedness. By that time, however, the *"zeyde"* represented a great historic figure whose time had passed. Cahan was the present, if not necessarily the future. And Jewish socialism, suffering an era of internal weakness following the splits in the SLP in the late 1890s to 1907 or so, dwindled to hardly more than a literary movement. Although Left publications scraped by, few socialists remained active in the early years of the Socialist Party. Nowhere except among the older generation of Germans, perhaps, were there so many ex-socialists or "retired" socialists who had given up on politics or buried their socialist pasts within the day-to-day life of trade union affairs.

Viewed sympathetically, veteran Jewish unionists heading smallish bodies of mostly craft workers yielded unconsciously, in a lethargic political moment, to the internal logic of the AFL. Until the middle 1930s, many needle trades unions endorsed socialist political candidates as a matter of course, and a handful of these unions exerted themselves when socialists seemed capable of winning a race here or there.

Viewed less sympathetically, however, no sector of nominal or erstwhile socialists waged more ruthless war against the Industrial Workers of the World than did the garment workers' leaders. They joined local police and manufacturers in appealing to Wobbly strikers to return to work (at some times even providing strikebreakers) very much as they would wage war on the communists, albeit without the later rationale of fighting totalitarianism's American representatives. Scarcely anywhere among officials of the Jewish ghetto could the generous and farsighted call for "One Big Union" of all races and groups be heard. If Hungarian, Croatian,

Russian, Greek, and other immigrant socialists adapted ideology and tactics at least partway to accommodate the IWW, the Jewish labor establishment closed ranks against competitors, quashed resistance, and dampened community idealism.

Seen still differently, the Jewish leaders had made their peace with the existing division of authority in American business life, allotting to themselves a unique degree of influence over trade, but ruling out further and more fundamental challenges as bad for stability. Were their socialist commitments still sincere? Difficult to pose properly, the question would be impossible to answer, for craft union movements across Europe operated with the same principles while conducting more vigorous socialist education of their members. While the predominant socialism of the Second International accepted colonialism's racial implications, American Jewish labor leaders (socialist or not) shared the common AFL view that most unskilled immigrants from eastern and southern Europe were unsuited to create a proper unionism or vehicles for self-emancipation. Jewish spokesmen felt compelled only to draw the line at the immigration restriction that Samuel Gompers and most AFL unions eagerly sought. After all, that would bar the door to Jews as well.

II.

Revival of the Jewish Left as of the labor movement at large nevertheless came precisely through new immigration. The upswing of the economy after the depression of the 1890s invited all-time high levels of entrants from southern and eastern Europe, Jews included. Unlike their predecessors, European Jewish radicals had often been involved in the intensely organized politics of the Jewish Bund, a socialist movement with a deep sense of ethnic identity (but no faith in Zionism, the small new entity on the horizon). Many of them had also imbibed the literary-cultural *Yiddishkayt*, ratified in the Chernowitz conference of 1903 by the prince of Yiddish, I.L. Peretz. The *"gantzer yid"* (a phrase perhaps best translated as the "complete Jew"), scarcely a socialist, nevertheless viewed the rise of a solid and lasting Yiddish culture cotangent with a humanist movement against the evils of the world:

The whole world must be redeemed. If justice means redemption from suffering and pain, then therefore, justice must come to reign over the entire world. . . . If, therefore, the Hebraic people are scattered and dispersed, if they suffer in exile, the Divine Presence accompanies them and suffers everywhere with them. Canaan is too small for God's children. The Hebraic land is to spread through all lands! If God is the God of the universe and his people a world people, dispersed to all ends, then the Redeemer must come not to one land but to all lands, the Messiah must come for the entire earth.[24]

A new class of intellectuals, touched as much by the spirit of this Yiddish ethicism as by the pogroms of 1903 and the Russian Revolution of 1905, found their way with ordinary working people to American shores. Self-taught or well-educated, they revived and sustained the Jewish Left for a generation, meeting considerable resistance along the way.

This time, the mass strikes of unskilled workers, which swept from Slavs in the Pressed Car Company of McKees Rocks, Pennsylvania in 1909 to the famed Lawrence and Paterson textile strikes of 1912–1913, also drew the Jewish worker into action. The Shirtwaist Strike of 1909, its participants young women considered too inexperienced for unionization, stunned the Jewish quarter with its solidity and effectiveness. Women workers had figured in the Jewish socialist press since the 1890s as pathetic victims, helpless to alter their fate. It was often hinted, none too subtly, that with adequate pay for Jewish men, they could be retired to the domestic circle once and for all. Welcomed ambivalently as unionists, they were regarded by the dominant socialist faction with mistrust, a potentially destabilizing element. A few years later the new Amalgamated Clothing Workers broke the lock that the conservative United Garment Workers (with Cahan its faithful supporter) had held over organizing in menswear. A new era had truly begun.

Jewish socialism now also revived, but with many uncertainties. Young radicals, at once more self-consciously Jewish and more anticapitalist than their elders, struggled to create new institutions or to take over old ones. Besides the ACW—which drew into its ranks many Jewish as well as Italian former Wobblies and anarchist-minded revolutionaries—the new generation, or *yunge*, founded a Jewish Socialist Federation of a few thousand members, and in another quarter published fresh genres of experimental literary magazines. Within the *Arbeter Ring* they urged Yiddish day classes, something that the immigrant of 1890s vintage had considered hopelessly retrograde. Resisting the assimilation-mindedness of Cahan and the Jewish establishment but resisting also the pure nationalism of the Zionists, these youngsters sought a secular culture of *Yiddishkayt*, a diaspora consciousness big enough for world Jewry and subtle enough to be part of an improved, multicultural socialist America.[25]

World war brought what one might call the second day of revolutionary ghetto socialism, extending from the middle 1910s to the middle 1920s. For the first time we see what Howe described as a rejection of Jewish establishment corruption, resulting not in a simple return to some kind of Jewish soul or purity but a swing toward avid participation in a popular culture that featured jazz dancing, movies, and necking. The Yiddish aesthetic documents themselves, more aesthete than political, express a desire to live free of didacticism and political commands, to fashion a new kind of existence in an environment so mixed with religious and folklore background and dance hall reality that it immediately suggests themes of postmodernism.[26]

It was in any case a scene too complex for any existing vision of socialism. The fact that news appeared each day of the terrible suffering of European Jewry—the worst until the Holocaust—underlined a feeling of hopelessness and of escape into Yiddish literature, American popular life, or both, alongside the call to action. As ghetto pessimist Moshe Nadir wrote for the emerging audience of the middle-class Yiddish reader, one watched with fascination at the movie theater scenes of human slaughter in Europe, meanwhile enjoying the cool atmosphere, drinking a seltzer, and eating a chocolate bar. He ended his ironic mediation, "And tomorrow, if we live, let's go to the beach!"[27] Nadir, known as the "Great Cynic," would in a few years become a prophet of political redemption, still later the brightest light of Yiddish literary communism.

The news of revolution in Russia, in March and then again in November of 1917, brought ecstasy to the Jewish quarter. The very home of czarist oppression had been turned into a world center for change with Jews central to its operation.[28] Doubters like the Mensheviks, including the Jewish Bund, looked like poor guides to events. The minority of radical leaders like the anarchist editors of the *Freie Arbeter Shtimme* who supported the world war now felt the rage of erstwhile followers.[29] Noncommunists from Labor Zionist David Ben-Gurion to Cahan himself at first supported the Bolshevik regime, both because of mass American Jewish enthusiasm and because it was almost certainly better than the anti-Semitic alternatives.

Of the various sixty thousand or so ethnic socialists who in 1919 voted a communist slate in the Socialist Party, it is safe to say that Jews (classified variously as Jews, Hungarians, Russians, or "Americans") constituted more than a quarter and perhaps half. But an instructive division became obvious among the future Jewish-American Bolsheviks. As ghetto youngsters plunged ahead, wrecking the socialist infrastructure with little notion of creating their own counterpart, the future leaders of the Jewish communist sector mostly held back. Older, steeped in community institutions and sentiments, these experienced writers, organizers and artists shared the intense feeling that the world might possibly be redeemed shortly, but if not, a European Jewry might still be protected from the worst by a Russian-sponsored world movement. They negotiated the merger of the Jewish Socialist Federation and the party in the early 1920s, and took charge of burgeoning Yiddish institutions. Only the Finnish immigrants, with their cooperatives, community theatre, and summer camps, brought nearly so much with them into the new movement.[30]

Of course, American Communism looked unacceptably narrow to Jewish skeptics of all kinds. Middle-aged socialists who spent the dreams of their youth, radical-minded men and women upwardly bound and successfully integrated into American life often shared a revulsion at the moral compromises of the Jewish institutions. Abe Cahan had often been featured in caricatures of the popular weekly comic paper *Groysser Kundes* as personified by the *Forward* building, elevating his cash flow over all other concerns. But world revolution was clearly not around the corner, especially not in prosperous and politically conservative America. Culture, as for many disaffected gentiles in the country, largely substituted. These were notoriously the years of speak-easies, jazz, and record sports crowds, but also of the "Yiddish Renaissance," with actors on Second Avenue more radical, talented, and also better paid than on *goyishe* Broadway.[31]

The emerging radical intelligentsia saw things from a higher line of vision. Not many Jews had actually taken major roles in pre–1920 Greenwich Village, where mostly gentile figures like Max Eastman, Floyd Dell, and Margaret Sanger had been outstanding. But a handful of Jewish artists and critics just coming of age— Maurice Becker, Waldo Frank, and Lewis Mumford among others—keenly understood the need of their generation to cross over from culture to politics and back. They conceived of their own task as a matter of assimilating what modernism had to offer and redrawing the large picture of civilization amidst the grab bag of ideologies and methods available to them. As the twenties wore on and even exile radicalism fell out of fashion, the WASP bohemians faded as a group. Jews, along with African-Americans, occasional Italian-Americans, and assorted others seemed to have more to say about dissent and newer cultural possibilities. Jewish intellectuals had the sympathies and universality to put the pieces together. *Modern Quarterly* editor V.F. Calverton, a German-American who made himself the impresario of a younger radical intelligentsia, was mistakenly but understandably placed in a biographical dictionary of notable Jewish-Americans.

To these intellectuals as to many ordinary Jews, the aching poverty of the surviving ghetto locked into the "sick industry" of garmentmaking—seen by Jewish communists as a cauldron of class struggle—seemed more than a place to escape by one means or another. Al Jolson's *The Jazz Singer*, which apotheosized the Jewish portrayal of African-American emotion and stylized it into a fixed form of generic entertainment, symptomized in one way the continuing experimentation with popular styles. The thin but brilliant genre of Yiddish film took the same problem from another angle, showing Jewish jazz babies fighting their backward and grasping fathers to escape the oppressiveness of communal ties into pop-modernist freedom.[32]

Out of this cultural maelstrom, a generation of radical mass cultural innovators began to take shape. E.Y. "Yip" Harburg offers powerful testimony to their rise. Childhood and City College pal of Ira Gershwin, Harburg successfully pulled himself out of youthful poverty with a commercial career, only to decide, as he said later, that "I had my fill of this dreamy abstract thing called business, and I decided to face reality by writing lyrics."[33] He and a collaborator launched their first musical hit in 1929. With three years of life experience in depression America, he wrote "Brother, Can You Spare a Dime?" an eloquent hymn to disillusionment about the American Dream. Conservative calls to ban the tune from the radio fell short when Bing Crosby and Al Jolson made enormously popular recordings of it. As Harburg's biographers say, the lyricist had "personalized the social" with immense political effect, and set the stage for such later career triumphs as *The Wizard of Oz* and *Finian's Rainbow*. Within a few years, a heavily Jewish Composer Collective gave rise to the talent of Marc Blitzstein, Earl Robinson, Aaron Copland, Charles Seeger, and more indirectly the Folk Song movement.[34]

Communists could be forgiven for imagining a future New York Soviet because antibourgeois sentiment, with Russian communism an ambivalent secondary element, remained so vivid. Jewish communalism operated here as the ethnic face of class consciousness and art as a weapon at best. Primitivist in their sheer faith in the power of phrases and deeds to overcome the vast world power of American capital, Communists proposed (at least for themselves) an answer not only to poverty and exploitation but also to the banality of upward-bound American-Jewish life. Solidarity with the Latin Americans under the U.S. heel, solidarity with coal miners in West Virginia or with black tenement dwellers in Harlem gathered furious energies of one kind, as the organization of Jewish choruses, the creation of summer camps, and a new fraternal order gathered equally furious energies of another. Communist commitment assumed its characteristic nonstop quality, along with its frenetic projection of revolutionary reconstruction to distant parts of the world. In the process, the Communists also made themselves the most determinedly antiracist formation in American (including Jewish-American) life.[35]

Not surprisingly, this Jewish Left had most meaning for the rank-and-file garment workers trapped for one reason or another behind the surge of assimilation and upward mobility, and for those young people and intellectuals willfully choosing a revolutionary destiny. Yiddish-language cultural activists and recent immigrants ground down by deteriorating work conditions found each other under red banners. The daily *Morgn Freiheit*, publishing many of the finest Yiddish writers of the day, might have less than ten thousand daily readers, but they lived mostly around New York and could create a social and labor presence. For a few years, they posed major challenges to most of the needles trades union leaderships. Meanwhile, their comrades mounted a unique experimental art theater *(Artef)* for a mostly autodidact proletarian audience, formed a series of folk choruses, created schools and filled them with children and pedagogues. More than any other major labor force in the semiskilled industry of America, the Communist-led needle trades Left won the forty-hour week in the midst of conservative 1920s. More than any other cultural force, the Yiddish Left seemed to epitomize the energetic youth and idealism of a Jewish survivalism.[36]

Downfall came quickly. A combination of economic pressures and a relentless internecine warfare nearly destroyed garment trades unionism. Meanwhile, the Yiddish Left slipped several notches downward. Terribly damaged by Communist manhandling of the ethnic institutions and publically reviled for the Communist refusal to condemn the Palestinian uprising (or Pogrom) of 1929, it lost few of its cadre but most of its nonparty following. Of the eighteen thousand Communist Party members and perhaps thirty thousand fraternalists enrolled after a decade of internal squabbling and increasing bureaucratization, Jews still must have been more than half. But American Communists generally, like the Socialist Party faithful (now largely restricted to older New York Jews, including many union officials, and some other ethnic bases "out west"), had receded into near irrelevance.

III.

The depression raised more doubts in the viability of capitalism than Americans had felt since at least the 1910s. By undercutting the drive to upward mobility, denying a large part of a generation the hope of college education and a profession (still problematic for Jews, excluded or restricted by quotas in many quarters), it also raised the possibility of reconciling modernist and Left impulses, the striving of the artist or middle-class intellectual, and the Jewish lower classes. As the early depression years emphasized the familiar communal struggles—rent strikes, for instance, in many neighborhoods led by bold Jewish women Communists—so the later years highlighted the rise of the middle-class Left milieu with its search for meaning in world events and the possibilities for cultural change.[37]

The familiar Left narrative here features the clash of ideologies (Communist, Trotskyist) and personalities (Earl Browder or Norman Thomas) with distinct and hostile Jewish followings, mass mobilization of industrial unions, the rise and fall of the proletarian novel, and the remarkable experiment in radical theater. Against this undoubted reality, Warren Susman and more recent historians have noted the generally conservative cultural subthemes of the era, the search for security in familiar gender roles, for instance, and the increasing celebration of vintage Americana in the WPA murals for public places. After a brief stage of apocalyptic expectations, Communists and sympathetic intellectuals or artists sought to reconcile the mass desire for stability with the sense—more and more filtered through the New Deal—that some great drift away from the profit system had already begun to take place.[38]

Several wings of Jewish intellectuals, most allied ambiguously or for only a limited period with the Popular Front, tried hard to work creatively on this problem. Playwright Clifford Odets, for instance, illustrated in play after play of the middle 1930s the grinding tension of Jewish lower-middle-class life, relieved at times by the hope for hope, for determination and courage against adversity. Communism on the Russian model had already receded into symbolic irrelevance as ghetto characters envisioned an unnameable something better—a mirror to Odets' own Popular Front views. Similarly, vaunted urban critic Lewis Mumford saw visionary new cities of technological sophistication and democratic rule and a revived but now democratic regionalism replacing the framework of capitalist values. Left-wing painters Ben Shahn or the Soyer brothers, Max Weber, William Gropper, and many others in the visual arts reformulated traditional Jewish themes of urban life, mixing modernist forms with semitraditionalist, semipolticized content.[39]

Others threw themselves into Popular Front institutions and causes, from the American Labor Party to the Teachers Union to the publication *New Masses* to fundraising for the Spanish Civil War's Lincoln Battalion. By 1938, when the Communist Party reached its peacetime peak of around eighty thousand, internal statistics revealed that nearly half of the membership lived in New York State, and that nearly half of those were white-collar and a majority of them were Jewish. The International Workers Order, successful by this time in creating a multicultural fraternal association of some sixteen groups and more than one hundred thousand members, was still more Jewish and New York-centered. (Indeed, the Jewish People's Fraternal Order, nearly half the IWO, overshadowed the Workmen's Circle in size and membership benefits for a few years.) The Communist Left had thus become, within that limited scope, a mass party of sorts, although definitely not of the sort that any Leninist had previously had in mind.

It would be equally difficult to exaggerate the degree to which the Left-wing intellectual as a modern, large-scale social type came into existence in just this period. Previously, radical thinkers mainly served as parttime political and labor functionaries, or made their career as journalists. Few had college appointments, and only the rarest landed government jobs where they could present in one form or another some creation of their efforts. By the 1930s, even in the midst of the depression, white-collar ranks had swollen and radicals among them grown apace; book company offices were a favorite hangout at first, but more prestigious locations soon included New Deal "alphabet" agencies and enough colleges to bring back the World War I era pubic fear of the subversive professor. If Jews suffered from informal quotas, they were also the largest single group seeking entry, which came by the ones and twos to Marxists as to nonradicals.

These intellectuals provided a significant part of the audience for the more dynamic and innovative cultural developments. Jewish artists, but also folklorists, fraternal organizers, and summer camp directors, among others, fostered and developed the idea of a transitional democratization with recognition of pluralistic folk values alongside an inclusive popular culture (and usually, with themselves as the impresarios). A revivification of Old World language, music, and dance matched the "discovery" of African-American spirituals by a Left heretofore hostile to church music; Popular Front and New Deal symbolic events celebrated this diversity as an antidote to fascism. It would be impossible to imagine, for instance, Woody Guthrie, or the field work of the musical folklorists in the South who recorded a vital musical heritage, brought Leadbelly (among many others) north to concert fame, and staged the concert "From Spirituals to Swing," without the enthusiasm of Jewish Popular Front support at every level.[40]

It is possible to argue also that the modern American conception of itself as a national community was formulated here, with the Left as a formidable influence upon the process. Themes branded "multiculturalism" a half century later had their first day, if briefly and sans the political reductionism of a future identity politics. Without in any way romanticizing the stylization of images, it was a remarkable accomplishment.[41] All this was tied fatally, however, to the Communist Party's orientation on international events.

Searing attacks from the noncommunist Left and liberals (both weighted heavily with Jewish intellectuals) increasingly exposed the tyranny of Stalin and the robot-like response of American Communists to changing lines. But these criticisms almost never effectively captured any real working sense of the Popular Front, let alone proposed a serious substitute for its mode and content. The famous flight of the New York intellectuals to high (i.e., European) culture evaded the problems of culture and mass society for personal solutions. Besides, and more importantly, what later cold war critics described as an insidious construction of a rhetoric—the transformation of politics into a hated mass culture—missed several crucial details. Popular Front composers, magazine, radio, and film writers or technicians, and similar innovators lent their talents to forms that liberals in assorted media had already prepared for them, much as cold war socialists and liberals would a decade or so later. And these were, if not inherently "Jewish" messages, ones especially dear to Jewish populations, from whom the messages gained their ablest articulators.[42]

From another angle, the popular culture intervention of the Left brought together a postponed reassessment of political reality. Not long after 1936, the prospect of American revolution had decisively receded, both because the voting propletariat had overwhelmingly endorsed Roosevelt and because the class issues seemed displaced by international ones. Not even the sit-down strikes could restore the sense that capitalism was, for the moment, past its crisis and that labor struggles involved a demand for recognizing existing forces rather than for prefiguring some prerevolutionary conclusion. Substituting in a broad sense from dramatic change in the U.S.—safely postponed until the end of the Roosevelt regime—world events would provide the revolutionary breakthroughs, or at least stave off fascism. Spain, Russia, and China (and for Labor Zionists, Palestine) thus became the grand arenas of action. America, in all these instances, was the homefront where funds were raised, ethnic and popular opinion contested, symbols turned into supportive action.[43]

The Party and its (mostly gentile) top leaders accepted the overwhelmingly Jewish element in this entire drama very uncomfortably, as uncomfortably as did the Jewish community at large. Communist internal statistics continued to exaggerate the "industrial" base of the party, and at the least sign of reversion to older class struggle models, the vintage rhetoric returned like some ghost of the Marxist past or of an old relative still oddly on hand. Jewish institutional leaders wavered between total hostility and a willingness to see the Left carry out the footwork for Roosevelt's reelection, antifascist mobilization, and ever-growing service to exiles. The Jewish People's Fraternal Order was even admitted to the inner circles of Jewish organizations shortly before the Hitler-Stalin Pact. In the shrinking world of Yiddish, meanwhile, the formation of the *Yiddishe Kultur Farband* in 1937 (even amidst the Moscow Trials) was the last new sign of organized *Yiddishkayt*, welcomed by many noncommunists and even anticommunists.

At the announcement of the pact, large numbers of Communist followers and some of the most famous divided from Popular Front ranks. Moshe Nadir, whose published work as a Communist continued to thrill literary-minded Yiddish readers in newspaper columns and almost a dozen volumes, dropped from sight and died alone. In a Midwest college town like Madison, Wisconsin, where the CP consisted of a handful of skilled Jewish journalists at one of the nation's most ardent liberal dailies, the local party branch folded *sine die*. Still, a surprisingly small proportion of leaders or functionaries followed the embittered radicals out. In truth, they had nowhere to go, and like so many liberal Democrats in so many periods of moderate and conservative party domination, they played a waiting game instead.

A world nevertheless may be said to have ended in 1939, one including, but also far larger then, the communist or any political realm. The challenge posed by the last large "new" immigrant generation during the 1910s had lasted a quarter century, and extended from industrial unions to *Yiddishkayt* to the Jewish version of Popular Front culture. Abroad, the same years saw the rise and destruction of Yiddish cinema, centered in Warsaw; the success and then degeneration of the Soviet regime and its early encouragement of Jewish culture; and the trials of the Jewish Labor Bund, a final noncommunist alternative outside the United States to Zionism's claims as the solution to Jewish homelessness. Within the U.S., and notwithstanding the immense emotional involvement of Jews in their relatives' fate and the continuing trickle of refugees, the fate of assimilation was now well-nigh sealed. The war experience raised admiration for the Russians up to previously inconceivably heights, especially after Stalingrad. But it also suffused among its American participants a cultural homogeneity, even as the older generation of immigrants mobilized themselves on the Left one last time. Not to rush the story, the participants would remain Jewish—but in a strikingly different sense.

Something more subtle than the horrors of the Moscow Trials and the disappearance after 1940 of serious hopes for a farmer-labor party had also happened to the socialist dream. Jewish Communists and Socialists who looked to the Roosevelt administration for a vehicle of transition to a higher social order inadvertently reinforced a particular, evolving belief in the necessity for massive mobilization under a capitalist government, which had never abandoned its political links with a system of race privilege or its impulses toward the militarization of society. In the name of antifascism, socialism as a voluntary, up-from-below or regional democratic possibility utterly faded away. The behemoth state would henceforth play the main hand, and if the state fell to powers less benevolent than Roosevelt, the Jewish Left would play the new master's game, or be crushed.

No wonder that the emerging noncommunist or anticommunist Jewish intellectual coming of age sought different things for himself (in rare instances, herself)—neither political redemption in revolutionary anticapitalism nor the perpetuation of a uniquely

Jewish, Yiddishist world. We are more than halfway to the perspectives of a Ruth Wisse in which such dynamic nineteenth- and twentieth-century impulses become less real than events in a Middle East saga thousands of years earlier.

The main path, however, was hardly Zionism, which had great support among American Jewish leaders but little popularity. Rather, it was mainly an intellectual's response in a new key: a political detachment and skepticism, sometimes coupled with an emerging high modernism. As Alan Wald has shown with great depth and precision, the "New York intellectuals" of overwhelmingly Jewish backgrounds and interests passed through phases of sympathy with Trotskyism. The striving for a more avowedly revolutionary and pure Marxist doctrine—replicating, in a microcosm, the repeated striving for purity—yielded swiftly to other political consequences.

By the early to middle 1940s, the small but dynamic and well-connected group centered at the *Partisan Review* had begun to reveal their own longstanding doubts. Lionel Trilling, destined to be the most prestigious critical scholar among them, evinced in a series of forgotten short stories the revelation that the lower (gentile) classes lacked the interest and the capacity to take over the levers of society. The Jewish attachment to socialism had been, if one read out the implications, a historic joke at best. Young socialist Irving Howe, in a prophetic stroke for his own trajectory, rushed in to defend Trilling, on aesthetic grounds, against the inevitable political criticisms of Trilling from Trotskyist true believers.[44]

Bellow's *The Dangling Man* (1944) was still closer to the mark in its protagonist's (and author's) sense of relief at having given up the weight of historical (and no doubt, Jewish) destiny. Popular Front culture—by that time quickly fading from reality but still vivid in the minds of its critics—had become the object of particular outrage. It not only fastened democratic labels upon totalitarian movements, but worse, perhaps, smelled of kitsch. Critics such as Clement Greenberg, embracing an abstract expressionism, which burst past all boundaries of subject matter and treatment, arguably directed their blows unconsciously against the very merger of Jewish culture and popular culture, which marked the New Deal and the Popular Front as something to be effaced and forgotten. Disposing of Popular Front culture, as Andrew Ross comments shrewdly, was also a way of pushing out of sight a Jewish lower middle class whose tastes and manners embarrassed its children, the critics themselves.[45]

Not quite paradoxically, the embrace of liberal humanism by a generation of Jewish liberal critics reflected the emergence of the Jewish intelligentsia into the colleges and universities where the most notable or powerful of them almost at once perceived their role as defenders of the canon against challenges on all sides. Leading members viewed with pride their role in an intelligentsia that seemed no longer alienated from society. Others, who made the analysis of alienation and similar social phenomena into a major academic expertise of the 1950s, nevertheless agreed with the description of the Left's obsolescence. Jewish socialism had by now receded into a warm recollection of immigrant times long past, or—when attached to Jewish Communism—an embarrassing reminder of disloyalty to the American promise and to Jewish destiny. The trial and execution of the Rosenbergs, indeed, stirred more furious essays on Jewish deradicalization than any American subject before or since.[46]

By the same token, as the "Jewish unions" steadily ceased to be Jewish except in their leadership, and non-whites filled the thinning ranks of garment workers, union leaders had for the most part completed a cycle of radicalism. Aging giants who remained in control of their ranks, above all David Dubinsky of the ILGWU, established themselves as partners with intelligence agencies in foreign operations, fleeing (one could say) the historic ghosts of socialism. Apart from their hatred of communism prepared through decades of conflict and amply justified (in their minds) by the shape of postwar Europe, they had set their star upon the *Pax* Americana as surely as the *Forward,* a half century earlier, had enthused over the capture of Cuba and the Philippines.[47] "Socialism" had become obsolete, save as a receding memory of egalitarian visions, no longer ridden with troubling suggestions of expropriating the expropriators. Indeed, the slender threads of dissent still alive in the Liberal Party, child of the anticommunist garment unions, featured a vision of racial equality hinged upon the implicitly upward-bound middle-class citizen. Any other possibility had become unwanted.[48]

IV.

After the invasion of Russia, and with the U.S. declaration of war on Germany and Japan, one of the most curious episodes of American Left history and one of the last in Jewish Communism swiftly unfolded. Communists experienced newfound respectability, great enough to obscure a recent legacy of bitterness, in the community at large if not among specific individuals. Once again, as in the early 1920s and the 1930s, the cadre rebounded. The conversion of the CP into the Communist Political Association in 1943 accelerated tendencies already alive in the Popular Front, the more so now with the men gone and women actually in the CPA majority of 85,000. These were, of course, disproportionately Jewish women, some of them older returnees to the factories but often the younger generation involved in traditional "women's" sectors (such as rent stabilization campaigns) never accorded the respect an egalitarian movement would have given them. With the heavy emphasis on war support and domestic matters, American Communism almost became a Jewish women's movement.

But this would be putting too strongly, of course, how the already mythical muscular proletariat had been replaced once and for all by the antifascist warrior and how the gendered interpretation of women's new importance would be put aside doubly at the moment that the head of the household returned to the proletarian home. Slav Left novelist Tom Bell, choosing a Jewish site for *All Brides Are Beautiful* (1940), had ironically created the background for one of Hollywood's finest realist films, *From This Day Forward* (1946), about the return of a Jewish veteran to the Bronx and his family's life as they prepared successfully or unsuccessfully for upward mobility. The very neighborhood base of the Left itself shortly dissolved into memory with the GI Bill and the destruction wrought by the new highways. Revivals of *Yiddishkayt* and of leftism in the South Bronx, such as the formation of newer Left *shules* and the election of Progressive Party candidate Leo Isaacson to Congress in 1948, were final bursts of cultural-political energy. Quite apart from the cold war with its omnipresent FBI intimidation and other calamitous effects, dusk had come to the idea of the Jewish proletarian revolution.

And yet, even as the catastrophe yawned in front of a Communist movement self-tortured by abrupt international shifts, expulsions, and defense of indefensible Stalinist actions abroad, odd moments of optimism and creativity continued to unfold. Most clearly, for Jewish radicals especially, they opened in Hollywood. There, a decade or more of self-sacrifice and of shrewd deployment of talent brought a wave of unionization, with Communists or near-communists in the leadership, save in the gangster-run craft unions. A counterplan spearheaded by conservative and even anti-Semitic gentiles went into action at once to break or neutralize the unions, with Ronald Reagan its FBI informant within the unions and Walt Disney its chief industry booster. But Communists had won the loyalty of people of great talent and integrity. As screen-writers and directors in particular, they also began to get the idea that they could create a truly different cinema. For a few years they succeeded modestly; as Marxists working in the center of popular culture creation, they also thought aloud about the possi-bilities.

Albert Maltz, Samuel Ornitz, Budd Schulberg, Paul Jarrico, Bobby Lees, Edward Dmytryk, Joseph Losey, Abraham Polonsky (a former radio writer for Gertrude Berg), and Lester Cole, to recall only some of the most famous, were not all Jewish. But they lived in an intensely Jewish creative world of mass entertainment. Like the cultural impresarios of the 1930s, they conceived of a democra-tized American culture in which a variety of themes could be seriously and popularly portrayed in implicitly radical terms. One might say that in them the future possibilities of mass cultural intervention first came alive. In the first few years of the *Hollywood Quarterly*, begun in 1946, Marxism mixed with technical expertise to suggest society's foremost popular culture dialogue in an cryp-tically Jewish ambience.

Indeed, a few dozen films, (from drawing room comedy to war action to film noir to slapstick) made between 1938 and 1950 suggest how influential the Left was and how searing critiques of capitalist values could be when a writer-director like Abraham Polonsky's got his chance in *Body and Soul, Force of Evil*, and *I Can Get It For You Wholesale*. (Later he would turn this critique into a plea for civil liberties in greylisted episodes of *You Are There*.) Communist Party aesthetic guidance had nothing to do with these efforts; indeed, the very discussion of Marxism always tended to veer off from the project at hand. At most, party leaders' efforts to give political commands finished off a demoralized and black-listed crew.[49]

The studio blacklist in 1947, persecutory government hearings, and the scurrilous campaigns of gossip columnists and profes-sional witnesses (coordinated, as always, by the FBI) combined to drive the Hollywood radicals underground. As it turned out, *The House I Live In* (1946), a much heralded Hollywood short featuring then leftish Frank Sinatra singing a song of racial brotherhood penned by Abel Meeropol was, like the various prestigious "pro-gressive" political bodies supporting vice president Henry Wallace, the last uncontested shot before Harry Truman's successful com-mand of the cold war demonized the Left. The launching in 1947 of *Commentary* magazine, mildly liberal but ferociously anticommu-

nist and quite supportive of the blacklist, marked the new day
coming in the Jewish world. The shellacking defeat of Henry
Wallace in 1948 verified the irreversibility of the direction of things,
quite as much as the disillusionments suffered by Jewish Communists and the much heightened appeal of Jewish nationalism.
(Ironically, Communists briefly emerged as among the strongest
supporters of the Jewish state, and a large handful of them fought
in Israel's war of independence.)[50]

So long as the Left held any positions of strength, a *kulturkampf*
accelerated, nearly realizing its aim of silencing the Jewish radicals
and driving them from organized Jewish life. If Jewish radicals
from the small-town Yiddish chorus of Petaluma, California to the
best-known Jewish artists, idolized black singer-actor Paul Robe-
son as a great hope for American democracy, *Commentary* writers
rationalized that gentile crowds attacking his audience violently in
Peekskill, New York, had been provoked beyond their capacity to
remain tolerant. If the Anti-Defamation League had worked quietly with the FBI since the 1930s, by 1950 it opened a new front in
Hollywood to pinpoint individual (Jewish) Communists of the film
world. Arthur Schlesinger, Jr., part-Jewish cold warrior often seen
as Jewish spokesman for liberal causes, branded the Hollywood
blacklistees "hacks" who deserved their fate. Hardly anyone chose
to remember, by that time, how effectively the same Communists
had worked for Jewish war relief only a few years earlier, and how
florid the public praise had been for the role of "progressives" in
Roosevelt's final reelection. By the early 1950s, communism had
ceased to be the issue, save in rhetorical terms; the loyalty of Jews
to American nationalism and its assorted programs had been put
on the docket.[51]

Driven almost entirely out of labor in 1949 with the internal
purges and the exclusion of surviving Left-led unions, their major
fraternal society, the Jewish People's Fraternal Order, dissolved
under government order in 1952, Jewish radicals were still not
quite finished. Other Left ethnic groups with few exceptions grew
steadily older and virtually went underground. Jews became, if
anything, more prominent among the small Left of the invisible
political generations.

From a half dozen campuses where free speech remained
more or less free (if intensely monitored), little branches of the
Labor Youth League sprouted with some of the brightest Jewish
young people of the day. They knew (and so did the FBI) that the
civil rights movement gradually sweeping the South was led at
local levels by trainees of historic Left institutions like the High-

lander School in Tennessee, with steady northern Jewish support. If they still tied their star to the Soviet Union until 1956 and imagined the revival of a corrupt and moribund labor movement, they remained, in certain ways, placed to react to the coming events.

And so it proved, from campus hottenannies (featuring Pete Seeger or a host of other Popular Front refugees) to civil rights fund-raising to ban-the-bomb and similar rallies of the early to middle 1960s. The Jewish undergraduate, seizing the gauntlet dropped by an aunt or uncle in some previous college episode or even a grandparent on the picketline of a garment strike, showed the gentiles how to organize. From Bob Dylan (aka Zimmerman) to Abbie Hoffman, they also proposed cultural terms both more obviously American and more politically oriented than anything offered by the Beatles. If a latter-day successor to the forgotten beloved lyricist Morris Winchevsky could be found in this era, it would more likely be Dylan or Hoffman than the culture critics of the Jewish written word. Like the poets of old, the folksingers walked the picketlines and went to jail with their listeners. On the peripheries, surviving leftish Jewish-led institutions, like the Hospital Employees Local 1199, rallied minority workers, and thousands of former Communists still loyal to the Left provided logistical back-up for the civil rights movement and the emerging campus New Left.

Mainstream Jewish leaders who might be properly regarded by now as the logical successors to the garment union dynasty did not at first place their institutions entirely outside these influences, from civil rights and folk music to youth culture and antiwar sentiments. Hopeful for broadening the alliance with historically black organizations like the NAACP (long funded disproportionately by Jewish individuals) and often in awe of Martin Luther King, Jr., middle-aged Jewish liberals with New Dealish and socialist or communist memories looked to idealistic young people to take up banners of social justice. At campus Hillel Foundations, they sponsored coalitions, primed advanced thought, and urged the awakening to conscience of a new Jewish generation.

The older generation of institutional leaders was very largely committed, however, to the Johnson administration's vision of the Great Society as reform from the commanding heights of the post-New Deal coalition. Like the aging Jewish Communists (who numbered by now only a few thousand), they could not imagine the future arriving in any other way. Those more and less progressive discovered that the decline of labor and of the old-time

Democratic political machine put professional fund-raising more and more in charge of campaigns, allowing individual Jewish activists and empowered groups greater influence in the Democrats' inner circles than ever before. For a moment, the antiwar sentiment in the Jewish community allowed a new brand of liberal a place between the combatants of the Old Left and a career opportunity in Congress. Inclusion of African-Americans into the southern Democratic state parties, a Jewish hope for thirty years to break the back of Dixiecrat racism and transform the Democratic Party nationally, was almost brokered by Allard Lowenstein, cold war socialist and protege of Irving Howe.[52]

But the impulse failed and with it the penultimate gasp of the Jewish Old Left-cum-liberalism could be palpably heard. Feeling close to a liberal victory that fate had somehow stolen from them, key players could not bring themselves to desert familiar cold war positions on the Vietnam War, especially after the Six Day War in the Middle East. Indeed, Jewish leaders in the Americans for Democratic Action (ADA) and the AFL-CIO increasingly tested each other on the Vietnam issue. Weakness signalled disloyalty, with leaders increasingly convinced they were fighting Truman's good fight once again, destined for victory simultaneously abroad and at home. Some of the hardest of the hard-liners on Vietnam were formerly leading socialist youth and later labor functionary, Gus Tyler of the ADA, and his generational successors like Albert Shanker of the United Federation of Teachers.[53]

Here and there, exceptional personalities and issues could yet be found to bridge liberalism and the new dissent. The birth of feminism (and later, lesbian feminism) stirred deep sentiment among fair-minded liberals, quite as deep in its way as the inveterate hostility of grizzled cold war AFL–CIO leaders toward the feminism and homophilia of George McGovern's 1972 campaign. Bella Abzug and Gloria Steinem, respectively the last grand mainstream political figure of Old Left and the former Left union journalist become first feminist best-selling author, spoke for generations of women who had scarcely been heard in any sector of the Jewish Left during previous generations. Both feminism and gay rights had a continued trajectory in Jewish life, evoking a suppressed past and creating leftish public figures.

Perhaps, however, these final impulses leftward had been only an illusion? Secure physically if not emotionally in suburbia, more proportionally affluent than any other identifiable group in American society, Jews seemed (according, certainly, to Jewish Republicans) to have no more necessary links to the poor and oppressed.

Yet they did emotionally, for reasons rooted in personal and collective pasts, for undying resentments against WASP racism and evangelicalism, and for a certain need to place themselves *against*, if only against a disappointing century. The campus New Left was, in its most cerebral but also often its most countercultural element, very substantially their children and grandchildren. The next generation of peaceniks, and to a lesser extent environmentalists, carried on a familiar family or clan saga.

The campus confrontations and ghetto uprisings of 1967–1971, the New York Teachers' Strike, and above all the Mideast war had meanwhile permanently hardened the main vectors of division among Jewish liberal-Left.[54] Peace might somehow yet be negotiated with Vietnam, mainstream Jewish leaders assayed, but the American peace movement's calls for U.S. withdrawal from that bomb-blighted land signaled subversion. An elder historic (and family) opponent of the Jewish Communists, erstwhile Trotskyist leader Max Shachtman, personally wrote the speeches for George Meany demonizing antiwar demonstrators and attacking liberals leaning toward opposition. While Shachtman's former comrades of the Socialist Workers Party mobilized antiwar demonstrators, his own current organization, the Socialist Party/Social Democratic Federation, became a center of especially well-connected cold warriors, primed to send their own protégés into intelligence-related activities as they struck alliances with the hitherto WASPish military-industrial complex and put their socialistic ideas into a sort of full-speed reverse.[55]

These positions hardened into set pieces of the Jewish world in the 1970s–1980s, with former socialists turned neoliberal or neoconservative holding most of the cards against current progressives. The sheer savagery of charges and countercharges along specifically Jewish lines—with accusations on both sides of traitor to Jewish traditions—would seem familiar to any close observer. The fact that both critiques had roots in the socialist movement was hardly graspable by outsiders.

On one side of the internecine barricades, former SP/SDF and future Anti-Defamation League executives joined a long list of former socialists and other Jewish influentials around the Reagan administration and top AFL-CIO circles in the privatizating of neoconservative foreign policy measures beyond congressional restraint, from southern Africa to Central America; the savaging of Jesse Jackson's 1988 presidential bid (a bid ardently supported by their sister Second International Party, the Democratic Socialists of America); raising support for the Israeli Likud Party's "iron fist" policies against the Palestinians and beleaguered Lebanese by-standers; and making sure that Jews who criticized these positions were banished from the bounds of acceptable dissent.[56] Uncertain and, in some part, enraged at the prospect of Israeli peace negotiations a decade later, they threatened to fragment. Yet their institutional budgets remained enormous compared to anything on the Left side, their entré to centrist Democratic (and even conservative Republican) Party circles significant, and their faith in the disappearance of socialism's once fresh promise nearly absolute.

On the other side, a fresh Jewish Left and conscience liberals established a plethora of new groups, such as New Jewish Agenda, fought for community influence after the 1982 camp massacres in Lebanon, celebrated Israeli demonstrations against "Israel's Vietnam" and joined disaffiliated Jews in a wide variety of progressive campaigns. Outgunned, in several senses of the term, they held scattered weakened institutions, and occasional new entry of importance (*TIKKUN* magazine and its surrounding milieu) and above all, a rich tradition. Among the weakened Left, neither the DSA nor the ex-communist Committees of Correspondence nor even the tiny Communist Party would be imaginable without disproportionate Jewish participation. As they scanned the horizon, watching the capitalist experiment flounder in large parts of the former Eastern Bloc and also watching accelerating impoverishment of and environmental damage to the planet at large, they could safely look to a future, even if no one could say in what way that would be "Jewish."

At the end of the cold war, something central to the old passions seemed to give way, but that, too, would probably seem, in time, an illusion. The labor movement, in which Jews were now virtually absent save in leadership posts and the white-collar sector, slumped steadily downward, almost as if to be finished off by the mobility of capital in the world market. Manqué socialist rage sputtered mainly now toward questions of race and culture in the pages of *Commentary* or the *New Republic* and in the well-endowed think tanks. At what sometimes appeared the final round-up of a tradition, those once fixed upon the vision of socialism turned their harsh gaze toward the Popular Frontish elements of films and television, and upon the emerging neo-Popular Front currents of academic multiculturalism, as the hydra-headed foe.[57]

And they were not entirely wrong, in their own terms, to do so. Jewish memory repeatedly pulled upon forbidden zones of American socialist and even communist idealism, the past which they could bring back as their own exceptional democratic legacy. With the history of labor diminished, that past became more and more colored, so to speak, with the dream of multicultural democracy. Communists had not invented, but rather popularized and vulgarized the transracial notion of solidarity based upon their own Jewish identity as outsiders, nonvictors in white domination of the world by the West. As young Jewish record producers and journalists programmed and charted the hip-hop scene, leading Jewish entertainment creators, from Barbara Streisand to David Mamet, simultaneously recuperated moments of the past Jewish Left and depicted unending contradictions in which Jews found themselves victims, executioners, and above all bystanders to unending injustice of rich over poor and race over race. Jewish neoconservatives had nothing to compare to this vitality. When Allan Bloom exalted Plato and cursed black music as degenerate, he acutely identified both the continuing claims upon Western values and the curious hatred of the mass culture promoted by the marketplace of ideas that Jewish neoconservatives (some of the keenest of them formerly socialists) spent so much of energy defending against putative enemies.[58]

If the great error of Jewish Communists was the deification of the Soviet Union and a tendency to substitute domestic abstractions (like the "struggling masses") for American reality, the final irony of the mainstream reconstructed history of *Yiddishkayt* and Jewish radicalism by Ruth Wisse and Irving Howe among others is that in narrowing the field of Jewish variety and deepening the logic of political assimilation into a liberal or centrist American culture, terrible damage has been done to the saga of the Jewish relationship with that chaotic, always unpredictable culture. Critic Itche Goldberg, octogenerian editor of *Yiddishe Kultur* and the last of great Old Left Yiddish scholars, insists that the "two-fold alienation" of American Jewish life compelled in Yiddish writers both compassion and a critique inevitably turned inward.[59] The sources of alienation have not been stilled by generations of prosperity, nor by the orchestration of organized Jewish sentiment around national themes. It remains to be seen where the spirit will move next, when the opportunity arises.

Notes

1. Ruth Wisse, *A Little Love in Big Manhattan* (Cambridge, 1988), especially chapters 5, 7.

2. Irving Howe, *World of Our Fathers* (New York, 1976), 646.

3. These groups would include Lithuanians and Slovenes, where the first-generation community neatly divided between conservative-religious and progressive-secular; Finnish radical influence arguably lasted lasted longer, though with diminished power.

4. Abraham Cahan, *The Rise of David Levinsky* (New York, 1960 edition), especially 442–530. The last two volumes of Cahan's five-part autobiographical series, *Bleter fun Mayn Lebn* (New York, 1927) were devoted to the Leo Frank case, climaxing assimilationist Cahan's effort with an uncertainty about Jewish life even under the best of conditions.

5. J. Hoberman, *Bridge of Light: Yiddish Film between Two Worlds* (New York, 1992), 40.

6. Itche Goldberg, "Introduction" to Chaver Paver [Gershon Einbeinder], *Clinton Street and Other Stories*, trans. Henry Goodman (New York, 1974), vi.

7. Robert A. Gorman, "Michael Harrington," in *The American Radical* ed. Mari Jo Buhle, Paul Buhle and Harvey J. Kaye (New York, 1994) 341. The Christian socialist Harrington abandoned this organization to form the Democratic Socialist Organizing Committee, later Democratic Socialists of America, organizations no less Jewish in personnel but not dominated by Jewish labor and social personalities.

8. Among the many accounts of Yiddish culture's rise, Charles Madison, *Yiddish Literature* (New York, 1968) remains in many ways one of the most sensitive and perceptive. On American Yiddish theater's socialist origins and continuing radical threads, see Nathaniel Buchwald, *Teater* (New York, 1943), a sweeping treatise by a seasoned theatre critic at the *Morgn Freiheit*.

9. Kalmon Marmor, *Morris Vinchefsky, Zayn Lebn, Verk und Shofn*, which appears as vol. 1 of Morris Winchevsky, *Gezammelte Verk* (New York, 1927).

10. Aaron Lansky, "Artistic Values and Implicit Social Theory in the Early Yiddish Fiction of Mendele Mokher Sforim," (masters essay, McGill University, 1980), especially 28–40. Lansky went on to found the National Yiddish Book Center, a much-lauded (and heavily funded) project to save existing Yiddish volumes and to promote a rebirth of Yiddish culture.

11. Morris Winchevsky, *Gesammelte Verk*, III.

12. Later accounts of the origin of the Jewish labor and socialist movement tend to diminish or delete the role of German-American socialists. But see N. Goldberg, "Di Yidishe Sotsialistische Bevegung in di 80er Yorn," N. Goldberg, "Di Yiddishe Sotialistishe Bevegung euf di 80er Yorn," and Dr. Herman Frank, "Di Anheib fun der Trade Union-Bevegung," in A. Tsherikover, ed., *Geshikhte fun der Yidisher Arbeter-Bevegung in di Fareinikhte Shtotn*, II (New York, 1945), 276–96; 319–45; 346–94.

13. "Di Kunst un di Revolution," *New Yorker Yiddish Folkseitung*, April 15, 1886; also "Gedanken fur Pesakh," *ibid.*, April 8, 1987; S. Shnur, "Di Freie Velt," *ibid.*, August 13, 1887.

14. The philosophical implications in the opening statements of *der Naye Geist* (subtitled "Monatshift fur Visenshaft, Literatur un Kunst") I (October 1897), 1, alone are worth serious study. No English-language discussion has treated the *Naye Geist* or *Tsukunft* with any depth. Perhaps the most interesting memoir of the 1890s—like Winchevsky's reminiscence unreconciled to the self-justification of the winners—remains Leon Kobrin's *Mayne fufzige yor in Amerika* (New York, 1966), significantly published by the left-linked Yiddishe Kultur Farband, outside the Jewish establishment's grasp.

15. L. Budionov, "A Blondzhender Poet," and Leon Kobrin, "A Blondzhender Kritik," in *Der Naier Geist*, I (November, 1897), 104–07 and 168–72, respectively. Budionov would become Louis B. Boudin, the most prominent marxist economist in the U.S., while Kobrin remained an important dramatist in the Jewish world for decades.

16. Baruch Rivkin, *Di Gruntendentsin fun Yiddishe Literature* (New York, 1947). In a literature thick with volumes of criticism, this may be the finest.

17. See, e.g., Berndt Ostendorf, " 'The Diluted Second Generation' German-Americans in Music, 1870 to 1920," in *German Workers' Culture in the United States, 1850 to 1920* ed. Hartmut Keil (Washington, 1988), 261–288. Forty years after the fact, poet Moshe Nadir recreated the sights and sounds of the 1890s in *Rivington Stritt* (New York, 1931).

18. I wish to thank Lee Baxandall for providing documents from the island of Curacao, demonstrating the De Leon family's

Temple membership and Daniel De Leon's cessation of paying Temple fees in the middle 1880s (to his mother's evident dismay).

19. See Mari Jo Buhle, *Women and American Socialism* (Urbana, 1981), 176–79 for a profile of Malkiel, who went on to be a prominent figure in the Socialist Party and a leader of strike support for the Shirtwaist Strike of 1909.

20. Practically no close account exists of this story from the angle of De Leon loyalists. The most revealing is Henry Kuhn, "Socialist Labor Party, Part 1," in *The Socialist Labor Party, 1890–1930* (New York, 1931), 29–35. Compare, e.g., to the passing slander of De Leon in *World of Our Fathers*, 314, and to the closer and more eclectic (if demonstrably anti-De Leon) account in Winchevsky's biography, Kalmon Marmor, *Moris Vinchefsky*, Chapters 13–16.

21. The recollections of Leon Kobrin, *Futzige Yor im Amerike* on De Leon and the *Forward* milieu are again valuable in this regard, 201–31.

22. These conclusions emerge from an important dissertation by Matthew F. Jacobson, "Special Sorrows: Irish-, Polish-, and Yiddish-American Nationalism and the Disaporic Imagination," Brown University, 1992, Chapter 4.

23. Jacobson, "Special Sorrows," Chapter 5.

24. Sol Liptzin, trans. and ed., *Peretz* (New York, 1947), 326.

25. Little information exists on the topic, but it is likely that the Russian-language affiliate of the IWW, the Union of Russian Workers, was disproportionately Jewish, and that Emma Goldman's Yiddish-language followers divided their loyalties between the literature of the *Freie Arbeter Shtimme* and the appeal of the IWW's mass strikes. See Maria Woroby, "Russian Americans," in *Encyclopedia of the American Left*, 661–63, for the skimpy information available in this area. Yiddish sources are still best for *di yunge*, but see also the popular account in Irving Howe, *World of Our Fathers*, 429–34. Predictably, Howe discounts the political leanings of the youngsters and tends to diminish the life's work of those writers who later became communists.

26. I have tried to capture the atmosphere in "The Yiddish Poets of di Yunge: Inspiration of a Century," *Arsenal: Surrealist Subversion* ed., Franklin Rosemont (Chicago, 1989), 156–60.

27. Moshe Nadir, "A Few Observations," in *A Union for Shabbos*, trans. and ed. Max Rosenfeld, (Philadelphia, 1967) 198.

28. The most colorful account of ghetto reaction is in a trilogy by the mystic-revolutionary novelist, David Ignatov, *Euf Veite Vegn, III* (New York, 1932), 209–10.

29. Irving Howe, in *World of Our Fathers*, 317–20, offers an interesting mixture of explanations for antiwar attitudes in the Jewish population. But these tend to discredit the large degree of anticapitalist, internationalist idealism and to make too little of the Yiddish anarchist and Zionist leaders' impulses toward instinctive and almost uncritical support of U.S. intervention, a symptom of hardening attitudes in later decades.

30. Not surprisingly, the working class versions of Zionism peaked in the same years and fell into a similar relapse after the early morning of promise had dissolved into just another bad day. Communists had the crutch of Russia to fall back on. At that, David Ben-Gurion offered a socialistic explanation for support of the war, and then, contradictorily, responded enthusiastically to Russian events. After the Paris Peace Conference and the loss of hope for an early Jewish Middle Eastern state, U.S. labor Zionism slipped into the lower rung of what observers often called the most bourgeois Zionist movement in the world. It captured, however, a handful of the leading labor activists and Yiddish writers of the day—former SLPers who felt themselves outsiders to socialism and to communism. Mitchell Cohen, *Zion and State: Nation, Class and the Shaping of Modern Israel* (New York, 1987), chapter 5, carefully explores some of the key contradictions of labor Zionism in this period, but has little to say specifically about the U.S. wing.

31. This realistic portrait of popular revulsion for Cahan is, however, captured almost nowhere in the secondary literature, as if the stream of internal criticism against ghetto giant and against the bureaucratic labor movement he represented had been discrepancies best forgotten—a tendency all too common in the Jewish literary world, where the sins of Communism are retailed compulsively and continuously.

32. See Michael Rogin, "Blackface, White Noise: The Jewish Jazz Singer Finds His Voice," *Critical Inquiry* 18 (Spring 1992): 417–53.

33. Harold Meyerson and Ernie Harburg, *Who Put the Rainbow in the Wizard of Oz? Yip Harburg, Lyricist* (Ann Arbor, 1993), 28.

34. *Ibid.*, 55.

35. This is not to deny antiracist activities in other sectors of the Jewish or predominantly Jewish Left, but only to stress that in these other sectors (like the Socialist Party and the Workmen's Circle) the numbers of participants in these activities were always small and localized to New York, when compared with the race-oriented activists of the Popular Front milieu. See the essay by Paul Buhle and Robin D. G. Kelley, "Blacks and Jews in the Left" in the forthcoming anthology edited by Cornel West and Jack Salzman, *Black/Jewish Relations* (New York, 1995).

36. See Paul Buhle, "Jews and American Communism: The Cultural Question," *Radical History Review* 23 (Spring 1980): 9–36.

37. This phenomenon has hardly been examined. See interview with Anna Taffler, Oral History of the American Left archive, Tamiment Library, New York University.

38. For a newer look at a familiar topic heavily involving Jewish writers, see Barbara Foley, *Radical Representations: Politics and Forum in U.S. Proletarian Fiction, 1929–1941* (Durham, 1993).

39. See essays by Paul Buhle, "Lewis Mumford," and Norma Jenckes, "Clifford Odets," in *The American Radical*, 221–28 and 229–36, respectively. Also see, e.g. the politically nonpartisan account by Avram Kampf, *Jewish Experience in the Art of the Twentieth Century* (S. Hadley, Mass, 1984).

40. Nor was this exclusively limited to the Popular Front Camp, although realized the most substantially there. The staging of the musical "Pins and Needles" came mostly out of Local 22, ILGWU, a Lovestoneite redoubt where Charles (Sasha) Zimmerman achieved in the later 1930s a modus vivendi with communists; Dubinsky himself supplied funding for a series of important Yiddish-language films by Hollywood director Edgar Ulmer. See George Lipsitz, "The New York Intellectuals: Samuel Fuller and Edgar Ulmer," in *Time Passages: Colective Memory and American Popular Culture* (Minneapolis, 1990), 197–99.

41. See Avram Kampf, *Jewish Experience*, 50–87, with penetrating comments on artists who (although Kampf does not say so) were in many cases quite close to the Yiddish quarter of the Popular Front. Aside from the discussions on theatre and literature, see *Encyclopedia of the American Left* entries Popular Frontish art, mostly Jewish in origin, including choral work (Composers

Collective, Aaron Copland and Earl Robinson), painting (American Artists Congress, Max Weber and Louis Lozowick) and assorted other topics such as sports, comic strips, science fiction, etc.

42. Trotskyists were more accurate in suggesting that once in power, communist labor leaders became as bureaucratic as their non-Left counterparts, a behavior that the Popular Front model actively encouraged; black radicals similarly pointed out that the Popular Front lost interest in anticolonial struggles as soon as antifascism became dominant. See Paul Buhle, *Marxism in the United States* (London, 1991 edition). But neither of these criticisms are to the point here.

43. For small but vital groups of Trotskyists and for the aging Yiddish anarchists, international events had, if possible, even more significance than for communists. To the Trotskyists, Spain and the Moscow Trials became so absorbing that U.S. labor activities nearly lost their interest; for anarchists, Spain was simply the last great cause. Interview with Theodore Brise, 1980, about Yiddish anarchists, especially members of the Rudolf Rocker branch, Workmen's Circle, Los Angeles, in Oral History of the American Left file, Tamiment Library, New York University. Unfortunately, space does not allow for nor has there been sufficient preparatory exploration of Jewish Trotskyism, a subject hitherto examined only as a background to the political exodus of the New York intellectuals. Suffice it to say that Jewish Trotskyists considered themselves assimilationists (and their Yiddish-language newspaper lasted only a few months). But a strong personal current existed between Socialist Zionism and Trotskyism, representing different alternatives to Communist hegemony within the Left. More than a few individuals passed in each direction.

44. Alan Wald, *The New York Intellectuals: The Rise and Decline of the Anti-Stalinist Left from the 1930s to the 1980s* (Chapel Hill, 1987), chapter 11; also useful is Gary Dorrien, *The Neoconservative Mind* (Philadelphia, 1993), 68–13, a study of Irving Kristol, the protege of Irving Howe who became an editor of *Encounter* magazine during its CIA-funding of the 1950s and afterward a leading neoconservative corporate fund-raiser.

45. Andrew Ross, "Containing Culture in the Cold War," in his collection of essays, *No Respect: Intellectuals and Popular Culture* (London, 1989), 42–64.

46. Andrew Ross, "Reading the Rosenberg Letters," in *ibid.*, 15–41.

47. David Dubinsky and A.H. Raskin, *David Dubinsky: A Life With Labor* (New York, 1977), 259–61, seeks disingenuously to minimize Dubinsky's involvement with the Central Intelligence Agency by limiting his discussion to 1940s Europe rather than exploring the full range of AFL intelligence activities in Africa, Asia, the Pacific and Latin America. He also flatly denies human rights violations associated with the well-known involvement of French organized crime in brass-knuckle maneuvers to weaken the communist-led CGT. Irving Howe in *World of Our Fathers*, 353–55, adds a personally warm but similarly unconvincing account of Dubinsky's generally high-handed union activities, often to the detriment of his more democratic rival, Sidney Hillman; he also passes over Dubinsky's effort to undermine the CIO during the industrial union drive of the 1930s with an ILGWU-sponsored lily white autoworkers' union. Beth Sims also has a brief but useful account in *World of the World Undermined* (Boston, 1992), 38–40. The entry "Lovestoneites," in the *Encyclopedia of the American Left*, 435–37, describes Dubinsky's relation to the Jay Lovestone (or Right-communist) group, which supplied key figures Lovestone and Irving Brown to the labor movement's heavily funded international intelligence apparatus.

48. Robin D. G. Kelley has acutely shown how this construction of black identity by whites and middle-class blacks in the era of integration did not account for the social and economic situation of the poor community and thus ill prepared its supporters for the disillusion, rage, black nationalism and assorted activity in later decades. See Kelley's *Race Rebels: Culture, Politics and the Black Working Class* (New York, 1994).

49. Nancy Lynn Schwartz, *The Hollywood Writers' War* (New York, 1982) and Larry Ceplair and Steven Englund, *The Inquisition in Hollywood: Politics in the Film Community, 1930–1960* (Berkeley, 1983) cover much of the subject area. But I have been helped enormously by interviews with Robert Lees, Ring Lardner, Jr., Abraham Polonsky, Paul Jarrico, and others. Those taped interviews have been deposited at the Oral History of the American left, Tamiment Library, New York University.

50. See Paul Buhle and Thomas H. Roberts, "The Left in Hollywood," in *The Movie Book*, ed. G. Alberelli (New York, 1996).

51. Neal Gabler, *An Empire of Their Own: How the Jews Invented Hollywood* (New York, 1988), notes the often forgotten ADL role in the Hollywood red scare, 375–76.

52. William Chafe's biography, *Never Stop Running: Allard Lowenstein and the Struggle to Save American Liberalism* (New York, 1993) has a distinctly sympathetic treatment of this figure that many critics continue to dispute. Lowenstein's plan failed when he attempted to coerce members of the Mississippi Freedom Democratic Party to accept token representation within the segregationist Mississippi regulars. Chafe's volume raises many psychological issues touching on ethnic as well as personal identity, but fails to dispel memories of Lowenstein's cold war zeal, his visceral hatred toward distinctly Jewish radical sections of the antiwar movement favoring immediate U.S. withdrawal, and his many direct and indirect relations with CIA projects from his student days forward.

53. See Steve Gillon, *Politics and Vision: The ADA and American Liberalism, 1947–1985* (New York, 1987), chapter 8, for an interesting view of the conflict among long-standing liberals. While the older generation was committed to Johnson, the younger one sought to protect a larger cold war strategy by unloading the president. The AFL-CIO was in the extreme Right of this coalition; its favorite alternative candidate, Hubert Humphrey, was convinced that the Vietnamese revolution was a plot for red Chinese control of Asia, and AFL-CIO staffers were sufficiently dogmatic or simply ignorant about Asia to agree. Lowenstein, a Humphrey protege in African affairs, deserted his mentor to join the camp of Robert Kennedy during he 1968 campaign.

54. An excellent and balanced new study, Jerald E. Podair, " 'White' Values, 'Black' Values: The Ocean Hill-Brownsville Controversy and New York City Culture, 1965–1975," *Radical History Review* 59 (Spring 1994), 36–59, considers the various sides of this struggle and its implications for Jewish political life. At this moment Shanker, a Schachtman protege and reputedly Socialist Party/Social Democratic Federation member, turned sharply rightward toward an embrace of neoconservatism.

55. The only biography of this figure, Peter Drucker's *Max Shachtman and His Life: A Socialist's Odyssey Through the Twentieth Century* (Atlantic Highlands, 1993), chapter 9, unfortunately fails to describe the preparation of future Reagan foreign policy and security operatives in the Socialist Party/Social Democratic Federation, and makes far too little of Shachtman's role in articulating hardline AFL-CIO support of the U.S. war on Vietnam.

56. The political trail becomes more difficult to follow after the SDUSA abandoned its own formal publication, *New America*, to

sink its energy into the neoconservative Freedom House and related Freedom House publications from 1982 onward. For a good account of the rise of specific SDUSA leaders into intelligence-related activities connected to the AFL-CIO apparatus, see Sims, *Workers of the World Undermined*. A parallel account, by Daniel Cantor and Juliet Schor, *Tunnel Vision: Labor, the World Economy and Central America* (Boston, 1987) offers a still more detailed view of AFL-CIO intelligence-related activities in a hot spot of the 1970s–1980s. On the Anti-Defamation League's own intelligence and blacklisting campaign, see two important investigative reporting essays by Robert I. Friedman: "The Enemy From Within: How the Anti-Defamation League Turned the Notion of Human Right On Its Head, Spying on Progressives and Funneling Information to Law Enforcement," *Village Voice*, May 11, 1993; and "The Jewish Thought Police," *ibid.*, July 27, 1993.

57. A symposium, "The Left 40 Years Later," in *Dissent* 40 (Winter 1994) is especially revealing in this respect. See especially the contribution by Sean Wilentz, 16–17.

58. Bloom of course had never been on the Left, but he found his most important sponsor (and author of the book's Foreword) in manqué Marxist Saul Bellow, a Trotskyist in his formative years of the 1940s. Allan Bloom, *The Closing of the American Mind* (New York, 1987). During the early 1990s, Bellow tended to withdraw from provocative (and painfully racist) statements made earlier; yet he remained a literary weathervane of Jewish Left-turned-Right.

59. Itche Goldberg, "Introduction," to Chaver Paver [Gershon Einbeinder], *Clinton Street*, vi.

FOUR

The Italian-American Left: Transnationalism and the Quest for Unity

Michael Miller Topp

I. Introduction

In 1902 a feud erupted between two of the leaders of the Italian-American Left during a silk dyers' strike in Paterson, New Jersey. Luigi Galleani, the powerfully charismatic antiorganizational anarchist, had just arrived in the United States and was editing the local anarchist paper *La Questione Sociale*. Galleani was urging the strikers to confront their employers violently to win their demands. Giacomo Serrati, who had also just arrived in the country, was the founder of the Italian Socialist Federation (ISF), which would be the focal point of the Italian-American Left's energies in the years before World War I. He was also editing the ISF's weekly newspaper, *Il Proletario*. Serrati vehemently disagreed with Galleani over strike tactics, feeling that caution and restraint were needed, and the two men argued bitterly in pubic and through their respective newspapers.[1]

This seemingly harmless argument over strike strategy at the turn of the century—hardly unusual in labor disputes—in fact revealed a great deal about both the past and the future of the Italian-American and even the Italian Left. Galleani and Serrati were not strangers when they met during the strike in Paterson. Their animosity had its ideological roots back in Italy. Both men had come of age politically during the struggle waged between socialists and anarchists in 1892 over who would control the Italian Left. Serrati and Galleani had confronted each other then too, and though the socialists were able to win out over the anarchists, both men were left embittered towards each other.[2]

The rivalry between them continued and indeed grew even fiercer after the 1902 strike. In the course of the strike, Galleani had been wounded in the face and charged with inciting to riot. He had fled north and eventually settled in Barre, Vermont, home to group of Northern Italian marble workers who were dedicated anarchists. Galleani began publishing his *La Cronaca Sovversiva*, and was soon sending weekly issues of it from this small quarry town to Italians around the world. Within a few short years, he would have the well-deserved reputation of being the leading Italian-American anarchist in North America.

But Barre was also the home of a group of Serrati's followers, who by 1903 had just finished building a socialist meeting hall. Serrati's work in strengthening the ISF had been going extremely well. He had been delivering lectures and holding conferences almost daily, and drawing more and more socialist locals into the federation. Serrati must have been feeling confident when he accepted the socialists' invitation to be one of the first speakers at their hall in Galleani's stronghold in Barre.

He arrived in October 1903 to deliver a lecture on the "methods of the socialist struggle" and to face an inevitable confrontation with Galleani and the Galleanisti. Tensions between the two men had grown even worse in the months since the Paterson strike. Serrati had—inadvertently, he insisted—revealed Galleani's whereabouts to New Jersey authorities during an exchange with him in *Il Proletario*. Galleani, who had been publishing *La Cronaca Sovversiva* under the name George Pimpino, had vowed that Serrati's betrayal would not go unpunished.

Serrati's trip to Barre was a disaster. He missed the scheduled starting time for his lecture fighting off assaults by Galleanisti on his way to the hall. At the hall itself, a fight broke out between the socialists and the anarchists, and a socialist who had been stabbed in the neck shot and killed an anarchist. Although Serrati hadn't even been at the hall, he was accused of complicity in the crime. Galleani followed Serrati's trial faithfully in his paper, and wrote a series of articles titled "Giacomo Menotti Serrati: Spy and Assassin," recounting his accusations of Serrati's betrayal of him to the

New Jersey police and of his role in Corti's murder.[3] Although he was acquitted, Serrati was obviously shaken by his experience. Shortly after his trial ended in early 1904, Serrati left the United States, leaving the ISF and *Il Proletario* abruptly and in incapable hands. In many ways, the enmity between the Galleanisti and the ISF Serrati left behind would last for as long as the radical circles themselves did.[4]

The battle between Luigi Galleani and Giacomo Serrati created the context for internecine battles in not only the Italian-American but also the Italian Left. Though Serrati led a productive, even an exemplary life as a socialist after his return to Italy, even in the land of his birth his confrontation with Galleani continued to haunt him. The accusation against him resurfaced as late as 1914, when he became editor of *L'Avanti!*, the leading Italian socialist daily. He was replacing Benito Mussolini, who was taking his first step towards fascism by breaking with the socialists over the issue of whether Italy should intervene in World War I. Mussolini, who had met Serrati just after the incident in Barre, sought to discredit the new *L'Avanti!* editor by resurrecting the story.[5]

The dispute puts in sharp relief the transnational nature of Italian-American radicalism, the defining characteristic of the movement in the last two decades of the nineteenth century and the first two decades of the twentieth. Just as Serrati's confrontation with Galleani began in Italy and followed the socialist back there, so too did events in Italy and the evolution of the mindsets of allies and adversaries in the homeland have a profound impact on the thoughts and actions of Italian-American leftists. Among Italian-American radicals, the class war was truly an international phenomenon.

It also hints, more basically, at the enormous diversity of the Italian-American Left. This nationality group, to a far greater extent than other Europeans, covered the entire spectrum of class-based radicalism. There were, in Italian-American communities, as in Italy itself, anarchists, socialists, syndicalists, and eventually communists. Each group, moreover, had a considerable impact on their own immigrant community and on American society as a whole. Italian-American anarchists strived to present an alternative to capitalist culture; their message finally captured national and international attention when two Galleanisti, Nicola Sacco and Bartolomeo Vanzetti, were executed in 1927. Syndicalists in the Italian Socialist Federation sought to organize both unskilled and skilled workers into revolutionary unions, which would serve as the vehicles to overthrow capitalism. These syndicalists were at the forefront of efforts to organize Italian immigrants in the years before World War I, and were vaulted into prominence during the Lawrence strike in 1912. And a combination of socialists, syndicalists, and communists contributed to the "new unionism" of the postwar years through organizations like the Amalgamated Clothing Workers of America and the International Ladies' Garment Workers Union. This unified Italian-American Left also spearheaded the battle against fascism when Mussolini tried to broaden his sphere of influence to the United States.

This unity among these radical factions, however, took years to foster and proved extremely fragile. The nearly three decades of Italian-American radical activity before the war were characterized by virtually unceasing infighting. Italian-American radicals were almost always prepared to defend each other against persecution by external forces; but their positive accomplishments more often than not came despite one another rather than through cooperation. But it was not just because of this frequent infighting that this generation of Italian-American leftists found success only occasionally and ephemerally.

Especially in the years before the immigrant strike wave that began in 1909 and lasted until 1922, Italian immigrants were notoriously wary of union activity and difficult to organize.[6] They were an extremely mobile population. Not only were they apt to move throughout the country in search of employment, they were just as likely to return to Italy-return migration rates for southern Italians reached as high as fifty-six percent in some years. Southern Italians, who made up the bulk of the over four million Italians who immigrated to the United States between 1880 and 1920, were often unskilled, disenfranchised, and illiterate.[7] These Italian immigrants were thus subjected to the worst forms of exploitation, and usually ignored by the exclusive craft-oriented American Federation of Labor.

These conditions help explain why the anarchists, and especially the syndicalists in the ranks of the Italian-American Left, were able for a time to gain such prominent positions in their communities. The difficulties these radicals faced called for creative solutions, and for strategies that took into account the particular needs of their fellow immigrants. The successes they achieved with their fellow immigrant workers, especially during the immigrant strike wave, revealed enormous potential. Unfortunately, the postwar reaction and their own limitations overwhelmed them, and today, Italian-American radicals are better remembered for their martyrs than for their victories.

II. Italian and Italian-American Anarchists

The first Italian-American radical groups were organized by anarchists as the surge of Italian immigration began in the 1880s. They relied from the first on connections to their homeland for inspiration and guidance. When the first such circle was founded in New York City in 1885, its members named it after an Italian anarchist—they called it the *Gruppo Socialista Anarchico Rivoluzionario Carlo Cafiero*. The second Italian-American anarchist circle founded in the United States, this one in Chicago in the aftermath of the Haymarket affair in 1887, also took Cafiero as its namesake.[8]

Anarchist groups spread across the country during the 1890s, as virtually every leading anarchist in Italy came to the United States to help organize circles and found newspapers. Some stayed only a few months; some stayed for a number of years. All contributed to the growth of small but devoted gatherings of anarchists in cities and towns throughout the United States. The first to arrive was Francesco Saverio Merlino, a scholarly man from Naples who had been trained as a lawyer. He came to New York City in 1892, and, fluent in both Italian and English, founded and briefly edited both *Il Grido degli Oppressi* and the English-language paper *Solidarity*. He then embarked on a speaking tour of the United States, and after stopping briefly in Chicago, returned to Italy in 1893.

The powerfully charismatic Pietro Gori was the next to arrive, landing in New York in 1895. Like Merlino, Gori was trained as a lawyer; but he was also an extremely gifted speaker, playwright, and poet. He remained in the United States for a year, and during that time, he held between two hundred and four hundred meetings (estimates vary widely) from Boston to San Francisco. He would entice a crowd by playing the guitar and singing, and then exhort them to fight against the dual evils of the state and capitalism. Gori also founded *La Questione Sociale*, the paper that Galleani would eventually edit, in Paterson, New Jersey in 1895. The paper quickly emerged as one of the most influential and widely read anarchist papers in the country, and Paterson became a center of anarchist activity.

The most renowned Italian anarchist to visit the United States was Errico Malatesta. Malatesta had joined the anarchist movement at the age of eighteen in 1872, and would fight for his ideals until the day of his death in 1932. Already by the time of his visit he was revered by fellow anarchists in Italy. He arrived in the country in 1899, took up editorship of *La Questione Sociale*, and held numerous meetings in Spanish and Italian throughout the eastern U.S. He stayed for only a few months though. He returned to Italy after being shot and badly wounded by a rival in West Hoboken, New Jersey, an event that again revealed how fractious the Italian-American Left could be.[9]

As a result of the efforts of these visiting Italian anarchists, as well as the increasing number of Italian immigrants in general in the U.S., there were anarchist circles in major urban and industrial areas throughout the country by the end of the nineteenth century. There were anarchist groups in Boston, Philadelphia, Baltimore, Pittsburgh, Cleveland, Detroit, as far west as San Francisco, and as far south as the cigar-manufacturing community of Ybor City, Florida.[10]

Among the most ardent anarchist communities at the time was the remote quarry town of Barre, Vermont, where Luigi Galleani settled in 1903. Like the other visiting anarchists, Galleani was a well-educated man, trained as a lawyer in Turin. Galleani arrived in the United States in 1901, having just escaped after spending five years in internal exile on the island of Pantalleria. Unlike the other anarchist visitors, however, Galleani decided to settle in the United States.[11]

Until his deportation in 1919, Galleani was the leading Italian anarchist in the United States. Indeed, throughout his stay in this country, his influence on the anarchist movement was felt worldwide. He founded the *Cronaca Sovversiva* in Barre in June 1903, a newspaper which became a mouthpiece for Galleani's antiorganizational anarchist views. While the *Cronaca* never had a circulation of much more than four or five thousand, it was distributed and read across the United States and Europe, and in northern Africa, South America, and even Australia. In his paper, Galleani railed against all forms of government, against capitalism, even against virtually all labor unions, which he assumed—often with good reason—would soon become just as corrupt as the institutions they were seeking to change. The root of his unrelenting opposition to these coercive institutions, as well as to any efforts to reform these institutions, was a belief that only the wholesale destruction of the existing system would provide humanity with a chance to live in a just world. Thus he never hesitated to call for or defend violent acts if he felt they would enhance his revolutionary cause. He defended both Leon Czolgosz, who assassinated William McKinley in 1901, and Gaetano Bresci, who travelled from Paterson, New Jersey back to Italy in the same year to kill King Umberto. And he printed instructions on how to assemble and detonate dynamite bombs in the *Cronaca Sovversiva*.[12]

But Galleani and his followers' capacity for love of their fellow human beings was just as great as their hatred of capitalism and the state. Galleani was considered a model citizen in Barre during the nine years he lived there, until he moved his newspaper to Lynn, Massachusetts in 1912. Bartolomeo Vanzetti, who was so devoted to Galleani that he called him "our master," lived quietly in a Boston suburb in the years before his arrest, tending his garden and sharing his harvest with his neighbors. He befriended and even became a role model for the children of the family he boarded with in Plymouth. One of the children later commented, "Vanzetti was like a father to me. . . . He took an interest in everything I did and treated me with love and respect."[13] Galleani himself could hold an audience entranced for hours at a time with his vision of the future. A witness to one of his speeches reported, "I have never heard an orator more powerful than Luigi Galleani. . . . He has a marvelous facility with words, accompanied by the faculty—rare among popular tribunes—of precision and clarity of ideas."[14] It was this certainly, the force of his logic, that earned Galleani such devotion, but it was something more as well. It was the glimpse of a better world, and a way to live in dignity in this one that Galleani offered his fellow anarchists.

Anarchist groups and circles in cities and working-class towns whose members were inspired by Galleani did their best to spread the word of anarchism. Of five hundred anarchist newspapers published in the U.S. in a dozen or more languages between 1870 and 1940, Italian immigrants produced about one hundred. They produced newspapers and mountains of literature far beyond what one would have expected from their numbers. They reprinted and sold copies of classic anarchist texts by people like Johann Most, Elisee Reclus, and Peter Kropotkin.[15]

These anarchists invested an enormous amount of their energy in constructing alternatives to the capitalist institutions and values that they abhorred. The newspapers they edited and the literature they reproduced were efforts both to provide their own perspective on political and social events throughout the world and to argue for their own system of values. They established their own holidays and memorial days to replace nationalistic and religious holidays. Instead of celebrating Christmas or the Fourth of July, for example, they would commemorate May Day and November 11, the day the Haymarket anarchists were executed. They would often acknowledge these days with special editions of their papers, continuing a tradition that had its roots in Italy. They also established cooperative stores, which enabled them to sell and purchase goods more cheaply than they could if these goods were subject to market prices. Again in an attempt to present their own version of history, anarchists set up their own schools, many of them eventually named after Francisco Ferrer, a Spanish educator who was executed in Barcelona in 1909. Even the leisure activities of Italian-American anarchists frequently had political overtones. There were anarchist amateur dramatic societies virtually everywhere there were anarchist circles. And anarchist groups often used dances, festivals, and concert recitals not only to enjoy themselves, but also to raise money of their papers or for a comrade who was injured or in legal trouble.[16]

Despite—or perhaps because of—their ardency, the Galleanisti and other antiorganizational Italian-American anarchists were rarely at the forefront of labor struggles in the years before the war. Though their devotion to the cause of revolution was indisputable, their dreams of a violent resurrection and their adamant opposition to virtually all institutions, including labor unions, often led them to battle other revolutionaries almost as fiercely as they fought against the capitalist system. Galleani and his followers had little patience for syndicalism. Though syndicalists believed in the potential power of the general strike, as the Galleanisti did, their faith in unions—even revolutionary unions—alienated the anarchists. The antiorganizational anarchists had even less patience with socialists, who they perceived as hopelessly reformist. The fact that these anarchists were rarely willing even to acknowledge the sincerity of other radical factions restricted them to the role of merely offering—often unwanted—assistance in labor struggles led by others.

III. The ISF and the Brief Triumph
of the Syndicalists

In the first decade of the twentieth century, there was no single organization leading Italian-American workers. There were dozens of socialist circles and workers' organizations in the northeastern United States, which would become the center of the Italian Socialist Federation's activity. One of these groups, the *Partito*

Socialista della Pennsylvania, began publishing the future ISF weekly *Il Proletario* in 1896.[17] And there were socialist groupings scattered across the Midwest and as far west as San Francisco. The Italian Socialist Federation marked the first effort to draw these circles together and coordinate their activities and resources, but in its first years it was still struggling to find its identity. Throughout this early period, even as its members sought a place in the Italian-American community and in the American labor movement, the federation remained closely tied to and affected by allies and developments back in Italy. Virtually all of the early editors of the weekly *Il Proletario* were recent arrivals—or had in fact been sent for by the federation—from Italy. Giacomo Serrati had started writing articles for *Il Proletario* from Italy before he arrived, to accustom the paper's readers to his perspective.[18]

Seen in this light it was not surprising that Serrati sought to extract Italian-American leftists from the fractious world of the American Left soon after his arrival. He suggested the establishment of the Italian Socialist Federation so that his fellow immigrant leftists could concentrate on issues specific to Italian-Americans. Before he established the ISF in 1902, many of the locals that came to compose the federation had been affiliated with Daniel De Leon's Socialist Labor Party. But with the split between the doctrinaire and unyielding De Leon and the founders of the Social Democratic Party (later the Socialist Party of America), and with the increasing exploitation of incoming Italian immigrants, Serrati and those who joined him sought to chart their own course independent of the wrangling American leftist political parties and to concentrate on their own community.[19]

This was the plan that Carlo Tresca, himself a recent arrival from Abruzzi, followed when he assumed editorship of the paper in 1904. Rescuing the federation from a year of floundering, infighting, and economic scandal following Serrati's abrupt departure, Tresca refocused the ISF's energies on fighting the elite of the Italian immigrant community—the *padroni,* the colonial press, and the priests. Though Tresca was a young man when he arrived in the United States, he already had a long history of agitation in his native town of Sulmona in the region of Calabria. He had been editor of a socialist paper, *La Germinal,* and had already faced libel charges leveled by local priests; he also had been sentenced to jail for his involvement in a railroad strike in Calabria. Once he was settled in Philadelphia, to which the paper had moved from New York, Tresca did much to reinvigorate the ISF—old sections that had wandered off now reaffiliated, and new sections began to join.[20]

Tresca's greatest contribution to the ISF was the introduction of syndicalist ideas and an early embrace of the Industrial Workers of the World. Tresca had arrived in Philadelphia a determined industrial unionist. Under his editorship, *Il Proletario* ignored electoral efforts and concentrated on efforts to unionize workers and to win strikes. When the IWW was established in 1905, no one from the ISF was present at the founding convention, but Tresca embraced the new organization in the pages of *Il Proletario* immediately and without reservation. Tresca recognized that the IWW was an ideal organization for ISF members. The IWW, like the majority of federation members, advocated revolutionary industrial unionism and rejected the reformism of the Socialist Party and the American Federation of Labor. Best of all, it allowed federation members a potential entry way into the American labor movement without having to deal with the still nagging question of political party affiliation.[21]

But the ISF, which still had a reformist minority in its ranks, did not embrace syndicalism wholeheartedly for another six years. This was due at least in part to Tresca's departure; he left *Il Proletario* and the federation in June 1906. Tresca was a fiercely independent man, and by the end of his tenure he felt that ISF members were placing too many restrictions on his editorship and his actions. Though in the future he would ally himself with the ISF and the IWW during strikes, he never again belonged to a radical organization. He moved closer to the mining towns in western Pennsylvania, where he published his own newspapers—*La Plebe* beginning in 1906 and *L'Avvenire* beginning in 1909—before settling in New York where he began publishing *Il Martello* at the end of 1917. Federation members, for their part, criticized Tresca for his "libertarian tendencies" in explaining his departure. So weary were they, in fact, of Tresca's tactics and his temperament, that they sent to Italy for a much more temperate man, a mathematician named Guiseppe Bertelli, to replace Tresca.[22]

Once again political battles in Italy had a ripple effect, which reached the federation. When Bertelli left Italy, socialists and syndicalists there were embroiled in an ideological battle that would soon result in the departure of the syndicalists from the Italian Socialist Party. Though his beliefs had seemed compatible with those in the ISF when he was in Italy, once in the United States Bertelli quickly embraced reformist socialism and brought the discord between the syndicalist and reformist elements in the federation to a boil. According to Italian historian and ex-*Il Proletario* editor and ISF member Mario De Ciampis, Bertelli realized soon after he arrived that he was out of place in the federation. Rather than leave immediately, however, Bertelli attempted to guide the federation into one of the two American Left parties— first the SLP, and then the Socialist Party. He believed that the ISF, despite its members' growing affinity for the IWW, was too isolated from the American Left. His efforts were ultimately unsuccessful, and by the beginning of 1908 he had left the federation angry and bitter about his experience, taking the reformist elements with him. He settled in Chicago, where in 1909 he started his own reformist paper, *La Parola dei Socialisti*. He affiliated his group with the Socialist Party, and to spite his former organization, took its name, calling his group the Italian Socialist Federation of the Socialist Party (ISFSP). The departure of the reformists from the ISF left the federation entirely in the hands of the syndicalists.[23]

It was through the syndicalist Italian Socialist Federation that he Italian-American Left would briefly assume leadership of the Italian-American community and would have its greatest impact on the American labor movement in the pre-World War I years. The ideology of syndicalism emerged in Europe and in the United States in the first decade of this century, a product of the frustration that many leftists felt with the gradualism and the balloteering of the socialists. Syndicalists preached direct action at the point of production—strikes waged by both unskilled and skilled workers directly against their employers, organized by revolutionary unions. It was an ideology that borrowed heavily from anarchism—syndicalists not only derided the electoral process as hopelessly corrupt and ineffectual, they sought to abolish the state entirely and to replace it with a vaguely defined system of unions organized to produce and distribute good equitably.

Despite the haziness of their vision of a future society, the syndicalists' methods and ideological bent were particularly well-suited for the Italian-American working-class population at the turn of the century. They recognized that these immigrants were among the most downtrodden and exploited workers in the country. Talented, charismatic syndicalists like Carlo Tresca and Arturo Giovannitti, by offering these men and women help in wrestling from their employers a modicum of control over their own lives, gave them a sense of dignity and a glimpse of a brighter future.[24]

At the ISF's convention in Utica, New York in 1911, its members officially declared the federation a syndicalist organization, and even made membership in the IWW mandatory. The ISF, now unified and having achieved an unprecedented level of ideological coherence, set out immediately to end the isolation its years of infighting had produced and to earn a place for itself in the Italian-American community. But, despite its new ties to the IWW, the ISF's first concerted effort to earn recognition and respect among Italian-Americans reflected both their and their community's ongoing connection to their homeland. The timing of the Utica convention was crucial—it coincided with the launching of Italy's imperialist war against Tripoli.

Federation members were firmly united by their antimilitarism, and when the prime minister of Italy made the decision to invade the African coastal city, they reacted quickly. Edmondo Rossoni had just arrived in the United States, chased out of Italy, France, and then Brazil for labor organizing and spreading antimilitarist propaganda. Though he had been appointed as a union organizer by the ISF shortly after his arrival and had already impressed federation members with his success among garment workers in New York, he was sent out on a nationwide tour to speak against Italy's war.[25] He and other federation members held meetings in Italian-American communities to protest against the war, and invaded the meetings of the patriotic Italians who approved of Italy's imperialist undertaking. And the ISF attacked the war unrelentingly in the pages of *Il Proletario*. However, these activities, as earnest as they were, had little significance in and of themselves. There was no way that the Italian Socialist Federation could stop the war from thousands of miles away.

What the ISF was able to do, though, was to use the war to articulate their opposition not just to the specific conflict but to the entire notion of Western civilization poised on the brink of world war under capitalism. Federation members argued that Italy was attempting to join the ranks of the other imperialist nations, and to use land conquests, as all of them did, to avoid the failures of capitalism in their own lands.[26]

Its opposition to the war enabled the ISF to present its ideology to its fellow immigrants; the opportunity to put its ideology into practice came soon after, in Lawrence, Massachusetts. The Lawrence strike of 1912 was part of the massive strike wave waged by unskilled immigrants, primarily in the textile, garment, steel, and mining industries, beginning in 1909. In the years before the United States entered the war, hundreds of strikes were led by the IWW and the Socialist Party—in, for example, the steel town of McKee's Rock, Pennsylvania in 1909, the garment centers of New

York and Chicago in 1909 and 1910, and the mining towns of the Mesabi Range in Minnesota in 1916. Italian immigrants participated in strikes with increasing enthusiasm as time went on— hesitantly in the shirtwaist strike in New York in 1909, more enthusiastically in the cloakmakers' strike in New York and the cigarmakers' strike in Ybor City, Florida in 1910, more enthusiastically still in Mesabi. More than any other, though, the strike in Lawrence inspired Italian-American workers and radicals.[27]

The Lawrence strike was the greatest triumph of the Italian Socialist Federation and of the Italian-American Left as a whole. It was the federation's first significant opportunity to participate in the strike wave and to earn a place for itself in the American labor movement. From the beginning of this strike waged by nearly 25,000 workers, many of them Italian (but composed of nearly two dozen nationality groups), the ISF worked side by side with the Industrial Workers of the World.[28]

The federation sustained the Italian immigrants' determination to stay out by drawing on their past experience in labor struggles in Italy. When food supplies dwindled and incidences of violence against the strikers increased, the ISF drew on a strategy long familiar to labor organizers in Italy to assuage the strikers' concerns about their children. They organized a "children's exodus"— arranging for the children of the workers to be sent out of town, and out of harm's way, to the homes of sympathizers from Vermont to Pennsylvania for the duration of the strike.[29] After virtually all of the striker's demands were met, the ISF turned its attention to freeing the two strike leaders who had been arrested early in the strike.

The arrest of ISF leader Arturo Giovannitti along with IWW organizer Joseph Ettor on trumped-up murder charges brought Giovannitti and the ISF to national attention for the first time. Rallies were held and funds collected in cities across the country. And Giovannitti's poem "The Walker," written during his stay in prison, earned him the title of "the poet of the working class." In the Italian-American community, Giovannitti became a folk hero, and the ISF was vaulted into a position of leadership. There were demonstrations for Ettor and Giovannitti everywhere there was a collection of Italian-American workers. The entire Italian-American press, much of which had previously been staunchly antilabor, supported the strikers and the prisoners, keeping news from Lawrence on the front pages for nine months.[30]

In its attempt to free the two prisoners, the ISF turned the trial into an international issue by alerting their allies in Italy and seeking their assistance. Italian unionists and radicals were quick to respond. Every major city in Italy had a defense fund for the arrested leaders. Giovannitti was even nominated for parliament by workers in Modena. And when the date of the trial approached, the ISF turned again to their friends in Italy, who produced a series of blistering articles in *Il Proletario*, which helped to promote an enormous demonstration on behalf of the prisoners. The demonstration, led by an emboldened ISF and by Carlo Tresca, was something strikingly new in labor struggles. It was a demand, directed against the state itself, that Ettor and Giovannitti be released. It attracted thousands of workers back into the streets of Lawrence months after the strike had been won.[31] Soon after the march the men were acquitted, due largely to the weakness of the case against them, but also at least in part because of the massive outpouring of support they received.

Despite the enormity of the ISF's success in Lawrence, the strike and the protests against the trial revealed certain limitations of the federation and its philosophy. Their anarchistic opposition to the state, manifested in their eleventh-hour demonstration for the prisoners, and the skepticism with which they met the Socialist Party's efforts to assist the strike widened the breach between federation members and both Italian-American and American socialists. Certain socialists denounced the syndicalists' tactics, and one Italian-American socialist, Frank Bellanca, dismissed Giovannitti as the "buffoon of Lawrence."[32] The ISF itself angrily denounced the Socialist Party months before it moved to expel IWW leader William Haywood from its ranks; federation members were already certain, long before Haywood himself was, that the socialists would be unable to tolerate the syndicalists' presence in the party for much longer. And less than a year later, when Giovannitti and two other syndicalists met with ISFSP members Frank and Augusto Bellanca to try to work out their differences, the meeting ended in a fistfight.

The strike also revealed an ISF that—despite its obvious success at inspiring them—was nonetheless in some ways alienated from the people it was trying to organize. One aspect of this alienation was rooted in regional differences between the strikers and the leaders of the ISF; the *Risorgimento*—the reunification of Italy—five decades earlier had left northern Italy far richer and stronger industrially than southern Italy, and many northern Italians looked down on southern Italians. The Italian-American working class was largely southern Italian, and southern Italian strike leaders like Giovannitti and Tresca won the adoration of the strikers. But northern Italian federation members like Rossoni, and especially the anarchists and syndicalists contributing to *Il Proletario* from cities in northern Italy, were often condescending and even contemptuous when they addressed the strikers.[33]

The other source of alienation was rooted in the pervasive maleness of the Italian Socialist Federation, and indeed of the Italian-American Left in general. Especially in the textile and garment industries, a large proportion of the workforce was composed of women. At Lawrence, over half of the strikers had been women. Nonetheless, no one on the federation so much as mentioned the distinctive contributions that women workers were making to the strike.[34] Nor was this silence about women's place in the workforce and in strikes and unions particular to the ISF. In an article in *La Cronaca Sovversiva*, Luigi Galleani (offering his unsolicited assistance) urged the strikers at Lawrence on by telling them to abandon "their eunuch-like slackness" and thus ignored the presence of women in the strike altogether.[35] Men in the Italian-American Left, and especially the federation syndicalists, would not overcome their unwillingness to recognize the importance of women in their union organizing efforts until after the war.

Even in the face of these shortcomings, though, there was no mistaking the magnitude of what the ISF had helped the Lawrence strikers accomplish. They had helped these unskilled workers realize that they could command the attention and respect, not just of their employers, but of the entire nation. If the victorious strike and the successful effort to free the prisoners in Lawrence foreshadowed problems that the ISF would face, they first and foremost revealed the enormous potential of the federation and of the ideology of syndicalism.

After the Lawrence strike, however, the promise of the ISF was short-lived. Just before World War I began, syndicalists experienced two crushing defeats. The first was in 1913 in Paterson, New Jersey where the ISF and the IWW unsuccessfully attempted to build on their dramatic victory in Lawrence. The second setback for syndicalism was the collapse of the potentially revolutionary series of strikes in Italy in June 1914 known as "Red Week." During the strikes in Italy, workers had shown signs of being ready for a revolution, but the syndicalists themselves had been caught unprepared and embarrassed.[36]

Still reeling from these defeats, the ISF became mired in a debilitating debate on Italian intervention in World War I soon after the war began in August 1914. The debate within the federation on possible responses to the war—either an education campaign directed to Italian immigrants to convince them to oppose the war or an embrace of the war with an eye to the advantages that the chaos it produced would bring the syndicalist movement—quickly produced what was for many an irreparable split in the movement. The debate devastated the ISF because it revealed serious divisions between federation members on issues concerning ideology and even identity. Soon after the debate began it was no longer about whether Italy should enter the war; it was about how the federation defined the ideology of syndicalism. The neutralists in the federation, who opposed Italy's entrance into the war, were led by Flavio Venanzi, a talented but unassuming scholar and writer originally from Rome, and by Giuseppe Cannata, a chemist and autodidact from Sicily who was far more comfortable as an orator than Venanzi. They argued that federation members who supported the war were violating their class principles—were in other words, violating the principles of syndicalism. According to the interventionists, those who favored Italy's entrance into the war, however, syndicalism was an extremely malleable ideology. The interventionists were led by Edmondo Rossoni, who managed to maintain his position as editor of *Il Proletario* throughout the ten-month debate, and Alceste de Ambris, a close friend of Rossoni's who contributed regularly to the paper from his home in Milan. Rossoni and de Ambris argued the syndicalism was malleable enough to embrace their change of heart, from vehement antimilitarism in the prewar days to equally vehement enthusiasm for the war once the fighting began.[37]

The debate soon devolved even further, to the point where conflicting definitions of masculinity were being contested in the federation. Masculinity and courage in the Italian Socialist Federation had long been measured in terms of members' willingness to face imprisonment and occasional violence for their beliefs. This was the standard that the neutralists held to, arguing, justifiably as it turned out, that they would endure enormous wrath for their opposition to the war. The interventionists, however, began to argue that the blood spilled and the passions aroused by the war were just the sparks that were needed to arouse the working class from its stupor. They attacked the neutralists' masculinity, using violent and sexually laden imagery to argue that those who favored the war were the only ones in the federation who were truly courageous.[38]

In issuing this assault, they were consciously drawing on similar arguments that were being conducted in Italy, by Benito

Mussolini, among others, about the failures of the Left in *that* country. (Mussolini was the editor of *L'Avanti!*, the leading socialist daily in Italy, when the intervention debate erupted.) The interventionists in the federation were well aware of developments on the Left in Italy. Rossoni had kept in close contact with his Milanese friend de Ambris, and he himself had been back and forth between Italy and the United States several times in the three years before he assumed the editorship of *Il Proletario* in early 1914.[39]

Ultimately the wartime debate in the federation not only irreparably damaged the organization, but also contributed to the rise of the fascist movement in Italy. After the exhausting debate in the ISF, Rossoni was finally expelled from the organization. He began a vehemently nationalistic newspaper in Brooklyn called *L'Italia Nostra* (Our Italy). Shortly afterward, he left the United States and returned to Italy, where he joined the Italian army and finally headed up Mussolini's fascist union movement.[40] While the number of adherents he took with him is difficult to calculate, he left behind an organization that never recovered from the crisis. The ISF never regained its prominence in the Italian-American community. It committed itself completely to the IWW, despite the fact that the Wobblies were shifting their focus westward, away from the federation's locus of strength on the East Coast. Thus the ISF, already battered by the intervention debate, sealed its fate. By 1917, both the federation and the IWW were faced with an onslaught of wartime arrests and deportations equalled only by the persecution of the Union of Russian Workers. ISF members were forced to change the name of their newspaper twice and to hide its mailing lists to avoid deportation. Even these efforts were ultimately unsuccessful—several ISF members were arrested and deported to Italy.

IV. The Quest for Unity: "New Unionism" and the Postwar Reaction

At the same time that the fortunes of the syndicalist Italian Socialist Federation began to decline, Italian-American socialists finally began to achieve lasting successes after years of unionizing efforts among their fellow immigrants in the garment industry. Since their defection from the ISF in 1907 and the founding of the ISFSP in 1908, Italian-American socialists had had little impact on labor struggles in their communities. Giuseppe Bertelli, who had led the socialists out of the federation, had struggled just to maintain membership in his organization at five hundred—the number needed to earn the right to a secretary-translator paid for by the Socialist Party. He had spent all of his time keeping his debt-ridden *La Parola dei Socialisti* in print; apparently in the ten years following his departure from the ISF, he never personally partici-pated in a major strike.[41] But others who had left the federation with him, like Arturo Caroti, or who had arrived after the bitter split, like Frank and Augusto Bellanca, were leading tens of thou-sands of Italian-American garment workers into "new unions" like the International Ladies' Garment Workers Union and the Amalgamated Clothing Workers of America by the start of World War I.

The Bellanca brothers were instrumental in the establishment of the ACWA, one of these new unions that carried the energy of the immigrant strike wave through the war by striking a middle ground between the revolutionary IWW and cautious, conserva-tive, and often exclusive unions like the American Federation of Labor. Like the IWW, their conventions and their newspaper, *Il Lavoro*, edited by Frank Bellanca, were often characterized by radical rhetoric. They also sought to carry on the syndicalist tradition of building industrial unions composed of skilled and unskilled workers alike. Unlike the IWW, however, they made concerted efforts to build stable treasuries and lasting locals.[42]

The new unions, and Italian-American participation in them, represented something strikingly new for these immigrant radicals in three other ways as well. First, these unions were multi-ethnic; both the ILGWU and the ACWA boasted large Jewish and Italian memberships. Although this produced considerable tension at times, it also helped break down the insularity and isolation of Italian-American leftists and workers. For many of them, these unions marked the first time they had shared membership in an enduring organization with people of other nationalities.

Second, these unions gave serious—and especially in the Ital-ian-American community, long needed—attention to the capabili-ties and needs of women workers. Arturo Caroti was first hired by the ILGWU during the shirtwaist strike in New York in 1909 specifically to try to organize Italian women workers. After the strike ended, he was hired in 1910 by the Women's Trade Union League to continue his efforts. Although he had little success, it was not for a lack of trying; he established two different organiza-tions in an attempt to draw more Italian-American women into the labor movement. He brought this mentality with him when he assumed editorship of *La Lotta di Classe*, one of the two Italian-language ILGWU newspapers (the other one was *L'Operaia*).[43]

Third, the new unions were vehicles for unprecedented cooperation between Italian-American socialists and certain syndicalists. Because the ILGWU and the ACWA advocated syndicalist strategies and principles like industrial unionism, the overthrow of the capitalist system, and even the general strike—and because they were still viable unions despite the onslaught of wartime suppression and the ensuing red scare—disaffected federation members found a comfortable home in these organizations. Thus Arturo Giovannitti, who since the Lawrence strike in 1912 had been living in New York and editing a political and artistic journal called *Il Fuoco*, began assisting ILGWU- and ACWA-led strikes in 1916. By 1922 he accepted a position as head of the ILGWU's educational department. Carlo Tresca too became disillusioned with his former allies in the ISF and the IWW. Soon after the war he was throwing his energies into helping the new unions, and endorsing them in his newspaper *Il Martello*. He and Giovannitti were able to lend their support to the workers in Lawrence, the site of their triumph seven years earlier, during a strike led by the ACWA-inspired Amalgamated Textile Workers of America in 1919. Their presence was not universally hailed; there were some in the ACWA who were wary of their participation, despite the enthusiasm they generated among Italian-American workers. Nonetheless, socialists, Italian-American Communists like Anthony Capraro, and Giovannitti, Tresca, and other ex-federation syndicalists were able to forge a fragile sense of unity and once again help the workers in Lawrence win their demands.[44]

The Lawrence strike of 1919 was not the only, or even the most significant unified effort by the Italian-American leftists. That same year they helped establish the Italian Chamber of Labor of New York City, an institution that had long been the dream of a variety of Italian-American radicals. Various Italian-American radicals had in fact tried to establish such a chamber on five previous occasions over the last fifteen years. The Italian Chamber of Labor was again composed of Italian-American syndicalists, socialists, communists, and union organizers; the Italian Socialist Federation and, of course, the Galleanisti did not participate.[45]

The Italian Chamber of Labor was to be a federation of all of the Italian labor organizations in New York and the surrounding area. There were two main reasons why this attempt to found the chamber was successful, when all the other attempts had been ruined by factionalism. The first reason was the overwhelming success that chambers of labor in Italy—on which the immigrants' chamber was originally based—were enjoying in the old country. After the war, when Italy was poised briefly on the brink of revolution, there were chambers of labor in every major city in the country, with a total membership of over two million workers. They functioned as social and educational centers, provided job placement, and coordinated strikes; in some rural areas they were powerful enough even to dictate what crops would be planted. So one motive for founding a chamber of labor in New York City was rooted firmly in the immigrants' awareness of the growing success of the institution in their country of origin.[46]

The second reason was the realization shared by Italian-American leftists and unionists that it was time to begin a more structured and organized effort to help fellow Italian immigrant workers integrate themselves more fully into the broader American labor movement. This may well have been motivated in part by their observations of the success the United Hebrew Trades had been able to achieve—Italians and Jews had just begun to cooperate regularly in unions such as the Amalgamated Clothing Workers of America.[47] It was also rooted in their conclusion that they had to put aside their past differences with each other if they were going to build on their success in Lawrence and continue to offer any realistic help to Italian workers. They realized they had to soften their political stances to be able to fulfill what they saw as the need of the hour—dealing with the problems specific to Italian workers as they sought a more lasting and influential place in the American working-class movement.

In the Chamber of Labor there was a specifically and overtly ethnic dimension to Italian-American leftists' efforts that had rarely been apparent previously. Chamber members tried to make their organization an educational and financial resource center for Italian immigrant workers. Any Italian who visited the Chamber of Labor's offices and showed his or her union card was entitled to use any of the chamber's services free of charge. The chamber assisted its member unions and even outside unions by committing whatever resources it had to strikes involving Italians all over the East Coast. It also sent its speakers, including chamber secretary Arturo Giovannitti, free of charge to any union that requested them.[48]

Unfortunately, chamber members' dreams of an organization as powerful as its models in Italy, or even one that would unite all of the Italian-led unions and locals in the New York area, went unfulfilled. The chamber was established just as the immigrant strike wave that had begun in 1909 was nearing its end, when the postwar reaction—the red scare and the panicked movement to "Americanize" immigrants—was at its height. Thus chamber members ending up spending most of their time defending existing unions against advocates of the "open shop" movement and fending off Americanizers' efforts to intimidate immigrant workers into docility.

But if in one sense the chamber—and the unity of the Italian-American Left that it represented—came too late, in another sense they could not have been established at a more crucial moment. Though this new organization could not achieve its original goals, it provided a base from which a unified Italian-American Left could defend itself at the moment when it was finally submerged by the worldwide reaction against radicals and labor. It provided these immigrant radicals with a chance to battle, albeit unsuccessfully, against the rise of fascism in Italy and in the United States and against the culmination of the red scare and nativism in the United States—the assassinations of Sacco and Vanzetti.

Mussolini's rise to power in 1922 compelled the members of the chamber to abandon permanently their hopes for a working-class revolution. Given their limited resources, they decided they had to fight against fascism rather than for the working class. Chamber members led the way in establishing the first antifascist organization in the United States; the Anti-Fascist Alliance of North America was launched during emergency meetings held by the chamber in 1922 and early 1923. Most of the early leadership of the Anti-Fascist Alliance was composed of chamber leaders. Virtually all of the leaders of the chamber would dedicate the rest of their lives—or at least the next two decades—to fighting against fascism.[49]

Their vantage point from across the ocean gave Italian-American radicals a unique vantage point and important opportunities in their battle against the fascists. In the first years of his regime, Mussolini made a concerted attempt to create enthusiasm for fascism in Italian-American communities. In fact, in the early days the center of fascism in the United States was in New York City—the home of the Italian Chamber of Labor and the AFANA. As far as these first antifascists were concerned, they weren't fighting an evil ideology from across an ocean—they were fighting it in their own neighborhood. Thus they used the pages of union newspapers to print exposes on Mussolini and his regime and to discourage Italian immigrants from supporting the dictatorship and from sending their money to Italian banks. Carlo Tresca, who was the first person in the Italian-American community (and, indeed, in the United States) to realize the threat that fascism posed, did the same in *Il Martello*. For a time after Mussolini suppressed all opposition papers in Italy, in fact, the AFANA's *Il Nuovo Mondo*, established in 1927, was the only antifascist daily in the world.[50] The Left-led antifascists held countless rallies against Mussolini's supporters, broke up fascist meetings, and battled the fascists in the streets of New York City. Carlo Tresca and his allies took after fascist supporters with baseball bats on more than one occasion. Their efforts were not entirely unsuccessful. Mussolini complained by the early 1930s that contributions from Italian-Americans had fallen a billion lire short of his expectations. And Tresca's effectiveness was reflected in Mussolini's ongoing efforts to silence or even kill him.[51]

Unfortunately, despite Tresca's and the AFANA's efforts, he fascist movement gained considerable support among Italian-Americans in the United States. And the laboriously constructed unity of the Italian-American Left fell apart by the end of the 1920s, when disputes between communists and socialists in the AFANA split the organization.[52] But what was in many ways the final blow to the Italian-American Left occurred even before the antifascist coalition fell apart.

Nothing symbolized the end of an era of Italian-American radicalism more clearly than the trial and executions of Nicola Sacco and Bartolomeo Vanzetti in 1927.[53] Their deaths showed not only the international breadth of the postwar reaction, but also how dangerous—how life-threatening—it had become to be an immigrant radical in the United States. In 1912, a national and international liberal and Left coalition had been able to save Arturo Giovannitti and Joseph Ettor when they were on trial for their lives during the Lawrence strike. After the war, an even more broadly based coalition could not save Sacco and Vanzetti.

Though few outside of their radical circle had ever heard of the two Galleanisti, their fellow Italian-American leftists realized the implications of their arrest in 1920. Galleani had been hounded relentlessly by Federal authorities for his wrathful condemnations of the war; he was finally deported in 1919. His *La Cronaca Sovversiva* had been denied mailing privileges, and though his supporters attempted to keep the paper alive by delivering it to subscribers by motorcycle, Galleani finally decided to move the paper back to Italy with him. Before he left, Galleani had asked his fellow anarchists to seek revenge. By the time of Sacco and Vanzetti's arrest, federal prosecutors were rounding up as many Galleanisti as they could, suspecting that they were responsible for the bombs that were mailed to leading antiradicals and that exploded on Wall Street in 1919 and 1920.[54]

Tresca was the first to call attention to the arrests in the immigrant radical community. In mid-June, he announced in *Il Martello,* "The innocence of these two men must be brought out. Sacco as well as Vanzetti are well-known veterans of the movement for freedom . . . who may be guilty of political heresy, but not of a common crime.[55] Tresca contacted Giovannitti and union leaders in the Italian Chamber of Labor to help him alert the Italian-American community. They responded quickly, drawing attention to the arrests in labor newspapers and holding rallies.

As the trial began in the waning days of the red scare, it was not difficult for these immigrant leftists to convince labor leaders and native-born radicals that the Massachusetts court was incapable of rendering a fair verdict. They secured the support of the American Civil Liberties Union, the ACWA, the ILGWU and the Socialist Party. Eugene Debs' first act after his release from prison in December 1921 was to send five dollars—his prison pay—to the Sacco-Vanzetti Defense Committee.[56] Even the notoriously cautious American Federation of Labor and several Boston Brahmin women were convinced that Sacco and Vanzetti had been unjustly convicted.

As motion after motion for a new trial was denied, support for Sacco and Vanzetti grew, until by the eve of their execution they had become, in the words of a *New Republic* writer, the "two most famous prisoners in all the world."[57] This was no idle claim; rarely if ever before (or since) has a trial provoked such an outburst of worldwide indignation. At a time when Italian-Americans were as divided as they had ever been, when fascists and antifascists were battling each other in the streets, the trial produced unprecedented unity in this immigrant community. The fascist-led Sons of Italy joined the Italian-American Left in calling for Sacco and Vanzetti's release. Even Benito Mussolini protested the unfairness of the verdict.[58] American intellectuals, poets, and artists like Jane Addams, John Dewey, Dorothy Parker, and Edna St. Vincent Millay put together petitions and were arrested as mass meetings.[59] In a last-ditch effort to save the two anarchists, John Dos Passos put together a pamphlet titled "Facing the Chair" in 1927. The pamphlet was a detailed analysis of the seven-year history of the flawed trial, and included appeals for Sacco and Vanzetti from Debs, the AFL, and French intellectual Anatole France. Rallies were held for the prisoners in cities across the globe; workers demonstrated in London, Paris, Belfast, Moscow, Berlin, Vienna, Budapest, Bucharest, Rome, and Madrid. There were protests in Norway, Sweden, Denmark, Switzerland, Holland, Japan, and China, as well as in North and South Africa, and Central and South America.[60]

None of it was enough to save the two men. And though for many American intellectuals, the death of the Sacco and Vanzetti case was a radicalizing moment that would redefine their political mindset for at least the next decade. For the prisoners themselves and for Italian-American radicals as a whole the executions marked the end of a road rather than the beginning of one.

Notes

1. For example, Giacinto Menotti Serrati, "A Signor Galleani," *Il Proletario*, July 15, 1901; G. M. Serrati, "A *La Questione Sociale*," *Il Proletario*, October 4, 1902

2. Paolo Valera, *Giacinto Menotti Serrati, direttore dell'Avanti!* (Case Editrice La Folla, Milan, 1920), 37–38; "Galleani, Luigi," Casellario Politico Centrale (CPC), Busta 2241, Archivio Centrale dello Stato, Rome; "Serrati, Giacinto Menotti," CPC, Busta 4769. CPC files were kept by the police on all Italian radicals in Italy and abroad.

3. For example, El Vecchio, "L'Assassino di Elia Corti al Socialist Block la sera di sabato," *La Cronaca Sovversiva*, October 10, 1903; *La Cronaca Sovversiva,*, "L'Assassinio di Elia Corti," *La Cronaca Sovversiva*, November 21, 1903; El Vecchio, "L'Assassinio di Elia Corti" *La Cronaca Sovversiva*, January 2, 1904; The Anarchists of the United States, "Giacinto Menotti Serrati: spia ed assassino," *La Cronaca Sovversiva*, January 2, 1904, two-page supplement. "El Vecchio" (the old one) was one of Galleani's pen names.

4. An account of this encounter is included in Mario de Ciampis, "Storia del movimento socialista rivoluzionario italiano," *La Parola del Popolo, Cinquantesimo Anniversario, 1908–1958*, (December 1958-January 1959), 136–163. See also Valera, 37–38.

5. Ugo Fedeli, *Luigi Galleani: Quarant'anni di lotte rivoluzionarie 1891–1931*. Edizioni "L'Antistato," (Cesena, 1956), 130.

6. See David Montgomery, *Workers' Control in America: Studies in the History of Work, Technology, and Labor Struggles* (Cambridge:

Cambridge University Press, 1979), especially "The 'New Unionism' and the Transformation of Workers' Consciousness in America, 1909–1922," 91–112.

7. John Bodnar, *The Transplanted: A History of Immigrants in Urban America* (Bloomington: Indiana University Press, 1985), 53.

8. Paul Avrich, *Sacco and Vanzetti: The Anarchist Background* (Princeton: Princeton University Press, 1991), 45.

9. Rudolph Vecoli, " 'Primo Maggio' in the United States: An Invented Tradition of the Italian Anarchists" in Andrea Panaccione, *May Day Celebration, Quaderni della Fondazione G. Brodolini* (Venice: Marsilio Editori, 1988), 59–62; Avrich 46–48.

10. Avrich, 46; see also Gary Mormino and George Pozzetta, *The Immigrant World of Ybor City: Italians and Their Latin Neighbors in Tampa, 1885–1985* (Urbana: University of Illinois Press, 1987).

11. Galleani, Luigi," CPC Busta 2241.

12. See Rudolph Vecoli, "Luigi Galleani," in *Encyclopedia of the American Left*, ed. Mari Jo Buhle, Paul Buhle, and Dan Georgakas, (New York: Garland Publishing Co., 1990), 251–53; Avrich 48–52.

13. Avrich, 42.

14. *Ibid*, 49.

15. *Ibid*, 54.

16. Vecoli, especially 70–74; Avrich 54–56.

17. Bruno Ramirez, "Immigration, Ethnicity, and Political Militance: The Italian-American Left's Experience," unpublished paper (Montreal, 1987), 5; de Ciampis, 138.

18. de Ciampis, 140–41. For a history of the Italian Socialist Federation, see Elisabetta Vezzosi, "La Federazione Socialista Italiana del Nord America tra autonomia e scioglimento nel sindacato industriale, 1911–1921, "*Studi Emigrazione*, XXI, 73 (March 1984): 81–110.

19. *Ibid*, 141–42; "Serrati, Giacinto Menotti," CPC Busta 4769.

20. "Tresca, Carlo," CPC Busta 5208; Dorothy Gallagher, *All the Right Enemies: The Life and Murder of Carlo Tresca* (New Brunswick: Rutgers University Press, 1988), 23–24; de Ciampis, 143–44.

21. Vezzosi, 87–88; Ramirez, 11–14.

22. Nunzio Pernicone, "Carlo Tresca" in *Encyclopedia of the American Left*, 780–82; "Tresca, Carlo," CPC Busta 5208.

23. "Bertelli, Giuseppe," CPC Busta 554; de Ciampis, 146–47; Vezzosi, 89–90.

24. For a history of the syndicalist ISF, see Michael Miller Topp, "Immigrant Culture and the Politics of Identity: Italian-American Syndicalists in the U.S., 1911–1927" (Ph.D. diss., Brown University, 1993). For more on Arturo Giovannitti, see Wallace Sillanpoa, "The Poetry and Politics of Arturo Giovannitti" in *The Melting Pot and Beyond: Italian Americans in the Year 2000*, ed. Jerome Krase and William Egelman (Staten Island: The American Italian Historical Association, 1987), 175–89.

25. "Rossoni, Edmondo," CPC Busta 4466.

26. Richard Bosworth, *Italy and the Approach of the First World War* (New York: St, Martin's Press, 1983), 77–120; Claudio Segri, *Fourth Shore: The Italian Colonization of Libya* (Chicago: University of Chicago Press, 1974), 3–19, 22–32; for an analysis of the ISF's reaction to the war, see Topp, 25–61.

27. Edwin Fenton, *Immigrants and Unions, A Case Study: Italians and American Labor, 1870–1920* (New York: Arno Press, 1975), 320–66; Montgomery, 93–95.

28. Philip Foner, *The Industrial Workers of the World, 1905–1917* (New York: International Publishers, 1965), 306–50; Melvyn Dubofsky, *We Shall Be All: A History of the IWW* (Chicago: Quadrangle Books, 1969), 228–58.

29. Foner, 324–26; Ardis Cameron, *Radicals of the Worst Sort: Laboring Women in Lawrence, Massachusetts, 1860–1912* (Urbana: University of Illinois Press, 1993), 142–43, 154.

30. Elizabeth Gurley Flynn. *The Rebel Girl, An Autobiography: My First Life (1906–1926)* (New York: International Publishers Co., 1955), 149; Fenton, 514–15.

31. Foner, 343; Flynn, 148.

32. Fenton, 145.

33. Topp, 102–03.

34. Cameron, especially 135–69. Cameron does an excellent job of showing how women's networks constructed before the strike proved crucial to maintaining the infrastructure of the strike.

35. L'Eretico, "Lo Sciopero a Lawrence," *La Cronaca Sovversiva*, March 16, 1912.

36. See, for example, Steve Golin, *The Fragile Bridge: Paterson Silk Strike, 1913* (Philadelphia: Temple University Press, 1988); Anne Huber Tripp, *The IWW and the Paterson Silk Strike of 1913.* (Urbana: University of Illinois Press, 1987); Spencer Di Scala, " 'Red Week' 1914: Prelude to War and Revolution" in *Studies in Modern Italian History: From the Risorgimento to the Republic*, ed. Frank Coppa, (New York: Peter Lang, 1986), 123–33.

37. Rudolph Vecoli, "The War and Italian American Syndicalists," University of Minnesota, unpublished paper; de Ciampis, 160–61.

38. Topp, 136–42.

39. "Rossoni, Edmondo," CPC Busta 4466.

40. *Ibid.*

41. Elisabetta Vezzosi, *Il Socialismo Indifferente: Immigrati italiani e Socialist Party negli Stati Uniti del Primo Novecento* (Rome: Edizioni lavoro, 1991), 148.

42. Steven Fraser, *Labor Will Rule: Sidney Hillman and the Rise of American Labor* (New York: The Free Press, 1991), 94, 105; Fenton, 532–36, 545–46.

43. Fenton, 500–03, 508.

44. David J. Goldberg, *A Tale of Three Cities: Labor Organization and Protest in Paterson, Passaic, and Lawrence, 1916–1921* (New Brunswick: Rutgers University Press, 1989), 123–27; Rudolph Vecoli, "Anthony Capraro and the Lawrence Strike of 1919" in *Pane e Lavoro*, ed. George Pozzetta (Ontario: Multicultural History Society of Ontario, 1980), 3–27. Vecoli's essay is also available in *Labor Divided: Race and Ethnicity in United States Labor Struggles 1835–1960*, ed. Robert Asher and Charles Stephenson (Albany: State University of New York Press, 1990), 167–82.

45. Fenton, 547–50, 554–58; Ramirez, 22–23.

46. Martin Clark, *Modern Italy: 1871–1982* (New York: Longman Group Limited, 1984), 206–07.

47. See Robert Asher, "Union Nativism and the Immigrant Response," *Labor History* 23, no.3 (Summer 1982): 325–48.

48. Arturo Giovannitti, "Secondo Congresso Annuale: Rias-

sunto Morale dalla Segr. Generale della Camera di Lavoro Italiano"
Il Lavoro, March 5, 1921; Ramirez, 23.

49. Arturo Giovannitti, "La Camera di Lavoro di New York per
impedire l'avanzata del fascismo in America" *La Giustizia,* March
31, 1923; "La Camera di Lavoro e l'agitazione antifascista" *Il Lavoro,*
April 21, 1923.

50. Leonardo Frisina, "Our Italian Labor Institutions" *Pro-
meteo,* May 1, 1927, p.10, from the Elizabeth Gurley Flynn Papers
at the Immigrant History Research Center, microfilm P1400. See
also John Diggins, *Mussolini and Fascism: The View from the United
States* (Princeton: Princeton University Press, 1972).

51. Gallagher, 105–08, 129–30. Tresca was gunned down in
New York City in 1943. He was also an outspoken opponent of
Soviet communism as well by this time, so the identity of his
assassins remains shrouded in mystery.

52. Diggins, 114.

53. There is an extensive body of work on Sacco and Vanzetti
and their trial in addition to Avrich's work. See for example Robert
D'Attilio, "Sacco-Vanzetti Case" in *Encyclopedia of the American Left,*
667–70; Robert D'Attilio and Jane Manthorn, eds., *Sacco-Vanzetti:
Developments and Reconsiderations, 1979* (Boston: Boston Public Li-
brary, 1979); Herbert B. Ehrmann, *The Case That Will Not Die*
(Boston: Beacon Press, 1969); Roberta Strauss Feuerlicht, *Justice
Crucified: The Story of Sacco and Vanzetti* (New York: McGraw-Hill
Book Company, 1977); Brian Jackson, *The Black Flag: A Look Back at
the Strange Case of Nicola Sacco and Bartolomeo Vanzetti* (Boston:
Routledge & Kegan Paul, 1981); Nunzio Pernicone, "Carlo Tresca
and the Sacco-Vanzetti Case," *The Journal of American History* 66
(December 1979): 535–47; William Young and David E. Kaiser,
Postmortem: New Evidence in the Case of Sacco and Vanzetti (Amherst:
The University of Massachusetts Press, 1985). See also John Dos
Passos, *Facing the Chair: Story of the Americanization of Two Foreign-
born Workingmen* (Boston: Sacco-Vanzetti Defense Committee,
1927); and Marion Denman Frankfurter and Gardner Jackson, eds,
The Letters of Sacco and Vanzetti (New York: The Viking Press, 1928).

54. Avrich, 158, 205–07. Avrich argues that Galleanisti may
well have been involved in these bombings.

55. Gallagher, 79. When Tresca referred to Sacco and Vanzetti
as "well known," he was speaking about their reputations in

the Italian-American radical community. Even within this world, however, they seemed to be relatively obscure figures until their trial.

56. Gallagher, 81; *Documentary History of the Amalgamated Clothing Workers of America:* Proceedings of the Fifth Biennial Convention of the ACWA Held in Chicago, Illinois, May 8 to 13, 1922, pp. 345–47; Nick Salvatore *Eugene V. Debs: Citizen and Socialist* (Urbana: University of Illinois Press, 1982), p. 328.

57. Bruce Bliven, "In Dedham Jail," *New Republic,* June 22, 1927.

58. Jackson, 76.

59. Feuerlicht, 389–90.

60. *Ibid* 393.

FIVE

The Polish-American Left

Mary E. Cygan

Introduction

In 1919 the national secretary of the Socialist Party, Adolph Germer, called attention to the fact that the party's foreign language
federations had grown to account for 53 percent of the party's total
membership. He warned that this new majority was dangerous for
the party because, in his opinion, the federations were not able to
rise above "nativistic and nationalist prejudices."[1] Germer's report
influenced the way the incumbent executive board would view the
political challenge to its leadership in 1919. The challenge was
real enough, but Germer's analysis had obscured its nature. The
political faction that mounted the attack on the incumbents was
not exclusively foreign-born, nor did all the foreign-born members
support the attack. Alarmist rhetoric, which lumped together all
the foreign-born into an imaginary majority bloc, played a part in
the party's decision to suspend seven of the foreign-language
federations, all of them Eastern European, at the 1919 convention.

  It is easy to see how Germer's thesis would persuade his
fellow incumbents, reflecting as it did the "nativistic prejudices,"
which some of them had openly expressed for the past decade.
Germer, himself, had favored immigration restriction during the
party's debate on that matter in 1910. But, it is more surprising to

see the shadow that Germer's thesis has cast on historical scholarship since then. There has hardly been an account of the disintegration of the Socialist Party that has not invoked the infamous 53 percent, and rarely has the Polish Left been mentioned in any other context.

Historians such as Theodore Draper, Daniel Bell, James Weinstein, Christopher Lasch, and Warren Susman have portrayed the foreign language federations in terms similar to Germer's: as alien and unsympathetic to American concerns, not as victims of American nativism themselves. In their scholarship, the federations appear, at best, as "much closer in spirit to the socialist parties of the countries of their national origin than to the American Socialist party,"[2] and, at worst, nothing more than, "small national socialist parties attached to the American organization."[3] Historians have been most severe in their judgments of the East European federations, declaring that they persisted in "retaining close ties to the Eastern European homelands, with little knowledge of the mood or traditions of American-born workers.[4] Regardless of the number of foreign-born in the American industrial workforce, some historians conclude that there was, "a greater appeal in a socialism under the leadership of a man like Eugene V. Debs, for example, who . . . gave the appearance of 'native' American radicalism in his person, rhetoric and even conduct than in the growing power of foreign language federations on the Left of the American socialist movement."[5] Generally, they agree that "the foreign language federations, in their preoccupation with European events . . . showed nothing but ignorance of American conditions."[6]

Polish-language sources suggest a very different picture of the Polish-American Left. They reveal a complex socialist movement, embracing a range of experiences, perspectives, and forms of organization.

Activity Among Artisans and Laborers in the Midwest: 1880s

On May 5, 1886, Leo Krzycki, who would become a leading figure in the American Socialist Party, the Amalgamated Clothing Workers of America, and the Congress of Industrial Organizations, witnessed a scene that would remain with him for the rest of his life. The five-year-old Krzycki watched as distraught Poles surged into his father's tavern to identify the dead and the wounded who had been brought there after the Milwaukee Bay View Massacre. For three days, the Polish laborers, who had been left out of the agreements made that spring between Milwaukee's industrialists and skilled workers, took to the streets to demand a general strike. On May 5, they confronted the state militia, which included the Kosciuszko Guard, a unit made up of middle-class Poles, outside a Bay View rolling mill on Milwaukee's south side. The militia fired into the crowd, killing five instantly and injuring many others.

Many of the Poles who marched had recently been organized into the Knights of Labor—some into factory assemblies, some into a separate Polonia assembly. In marching that day, they had defied their own officers in the Knights of Labor who had tried to deflect the call for a general strike. They had also defied their pastor by using St. Stanislaus Roman Catholic parish as the point of departure for their marches each day. While they benefitted from the networks the union and the parish had created, they acted independently.

Leo Krzycki would grow up to bridge the gap between the Polish-American rank-and-file and their would-be leaders in a career that would span over fifty years. American-born but fluent in Polish, he would work with Poles from the various waves of immigration that proceeded from distinct regions in Poland, with first-, second- and third-generation Polish-Americans from these regions, and with those who were steeped in Polish Roman Catholic traditions and idioms as well as those who based their identities on a strident anticlerical position. The influence of socialism in the Polish-American community would depend on the ability of leaders like Krzycki to learn to work with such a varied constituency.[7]

For a time, the leadership itself would be divided into a complex array of parties and organizations. This complexity stemmed not so much from abstract debate over ideological principles as from differing premigration experiences. In the late-eighteenth century, the three imperial powers bordering Poland carved it up among themselves and for the next 120 years, Russia, Prussia, and Austria controlled the government, economy, and culture of their respective parts of Poland. Developments such as the emancipation of the Polish serfs, parliamentary government, industrialization, and urbanization occurred under three different regimes with different policies, at different tempos, and marked by different forms of political and cultural repression.[8]

The Prussian partition sent the first wave of economic emigrants to the United States, where they settled on the Atlantic seaboard and in the Great Lakes cities. We know, for example that at the time of the Bay View strike, some Polish carpenters and tinsmiths in Chicago were referring to themselves as anarchists. They were most likely associated with the anarchist International Working People's Association, which was also attracting Chicago's Czech and German workers before the Haymarket Square Riot in May 1886.[9]

Poles in the Socialist Labor Party: 1888–1900

In the 1880s, Polish political emigrés in New York began organizing the nucleus for a future Polish-American socialist party. They began by establishing a mutual benefit society, *Ognisko*, [The Forge]. Like similar emigré circles in Geneva, Paris, Brussels, and London, the *Ognisko* group embraced an eclectic set of exiled critics, writers, artists, and activists who shared information and raised funds to aid colleagues in the partitions in prison or underground. Their newspaper, also called *Ognisko*, gives us an insight into their perspective, one that drew on utopian and romantic populist traditions. They believed in placing property in the hands of the commune or *gmina* (an old Polish word related to the German *gemein*). Though this group spent much of its time in "Mother Budzinska's" restaurant or involved in escapades escaping creditors, some of the young talents who started out in it would play a larger role later, such as the socialist journalist and publisher, Leon Wild.[10]

Some of the members of *Ognisko*, led by Adam Moren and Władysław Fiszler, formed a Marxist political group, *Równość* [Equality]. In 1888 *Równość* became an emigré affiliate of Proletariat, the first Marxist group to operate in Polish territory, and in 1890 it formed the first Polish local of the Socialist Labor Party with 33 members. Impatient with the bohemian coffee house ethos of *Ognisko*, the *Równość* group agreed that the key to the future of Poland lay in the small industrial working class and resolved to address Polish workers in American cities.[11]

They were able to claim some results when over the next few years more Polish-language locals joined the Socialist Labor Party. In 1894, Moren and Fiszler helped four of them to form the Alliance of Polish Locals of the Socialist Labor Party or ZOP (*Związek Oddziałłów Polskich*). Soon after, the number of ZOP locals (averaging about twenty-five to thirty members each) rose to eight, including groups in Manhattan, Brooklyn, Newark, Philadelphia, and Buffalo. The ZOP organized lecture tours, distributed socialist literature and began pressing the leading Polish fraternal organization of the day, the Polish National Alliance, to reverse its 1889 decision to expel socialist members. By January 1896 a mass rally in Buffalo featuring ZOP speakers along with dramatic readings and revolutionary tableaux drew a crowd of one thousand.[12]

An open letter to Polish socialists in the Prussian partition written from Buffalo in 1896 gives us an insight into the membership of the ZOP, which seemed to reflect the profile of the first wave of Polish economic emigrants. Ten of the eighteen who signed the letter listed their hometowns: two were from Poznan and six others were from cities within fifteen miles of Poznan, an area dotted by sugar refineries, breweries, and machine shops. A ninth listed himself as from Kujawy, a region northeast of Poznan.

It is worth noting that this letter appeared in the Berlin *Gazeta Robotnicza* and that American agents for this newspaper made up an important network for the Polish-American Left. They handled subscriptions for their local groups, forwarded correspondence, and wrote articles on local activities. Thus the curious situation developed in which Polish-American immigrant readers could follow the Polish socialist movement in other parts of the United States by reading this Polish-language newspaper published in Berlin.[13]

Unlike the bulk of the membership, the officers of the ZOP were not economic immigrants from the Prussian partition but political emigrés from other partitions. As emigrés from a colonized nation, they grappled with choices that have faced many marxist anticolonial movements since then, especially how to balance the fight for national independence with class-based forms of consciousness and organization. Their debate, in the meetings of *Równość* in New York, echoed arguments going on within the Proletariat in Warsaw with Fiszler supporting the struggle for national independence and Moren arguing against it.[14]

When the Second International was formed in 1889, the immediate problem facing Polish socialists was whether to form a Polish party transcending the boundaries of the three partitions, or to work within the socialist parties of Austria, Prussia, and Russia. At the 1891 convention, the pro-independence Poles won the right to organize separate Polish parties in each of the partitions, and immediately formed a coordinating body: the London-based *Zwiazek Zagraniczny Socjalistów Polskich* [Alliance of Polish Socialists Abroad] or ZZSP. Within the next two years the ZZSP helped form a Polish Socialist party [PPS] in the Russian partition, a Polish Social Democratic Party [PPSD] in Galicia, and a Polish Socialist

Party [PPS] in the Prussian partition. Though all these parties shared the goal of an independent Polish socialist state, they developed different strategies for working within the legal and economic conditions of their respective partitions, and each expected to cooperate with the socialist parties of the three partitioning powers.[15]

From New York, Władysław Fiszler from Galicia maintained close contacts with the London ZZSP, which helped to enhance his authority in his arguments with Moren. Adam Moren, on the other hand, agreed with Rosa Luxemburg's forceful arguments against expending any effort for the political autonomy of Poland, and tried, from New York, to attack the credentials of some of the pro-independence Poles to the 1891 Socialist International Convention. In America he found some allies in the immigrants from the eastern reaches of the old prepartition Polish republic who felt little interest in being part of a revived Polish state—such as the Polish-speaking Lithuanians and Estonians who had been attracted to ZOP locals in Pennsylvania and New Jersey. By relying on ties with supporters of the Social Democracy of the Kingdom of Poland and Lithuania [SDKPiL] and with De Leon, Moren based himself on a shrinking minority in the Polish-American leftist community. His circle shrunk even further as he attacked his former supporters, getting De Leon to expel some of them from the SLP.[16]

New Immigration from the Russian Partition

In the meantime, Poles from the Russian partition began arriving in large numbers. Unlike the earlier immigrants from the Prussian partition who often came as families intending to settle in the United States, the new immigrant from Russian Poland was more likely to be a young male hoping to work for a few years and then to return home. One historian has estimated that by 1900, emigrants from the Russian partition made up 64 percent of Pennsylvania's Polish population, and of these, 75 percent were male, mostly fourteen to forty-five years old. A new strategy that included more vigorous recruitment in the industries where these men worked, greater attention to youth-oriented social organizations, and a stronger presence in Polish ethnic organizations would drastically change the profile of the organized Polish-American Left.[17]

Political activists from the Russian partition arrived along with the new economic immigrants. Bolesław Miklaszewski, for example, began his political career as a student activist in Warsaw, earned a doctorate in chemical engineering in Switzerland, and gained experience organizing Polish coal miners in Silesia before the London-based ZZSP, taking note of his several arrests and deportations from both the Russian and Prussian partitions, sent him to America for seven months in 1896. In that short tour, Miklaszewski established new locals in the Pennsylvania anthracite fields and cities like Chicago, Toledo, Cleveland, Detroit, Pittsburgh, Syracuse, and Trenton—approximately twenty in all. Miklaszewski was a powerful advocate for the ZZSP's pro-independence position, and these new locals would further weight the balance against Moren's faction.[18]

While Miklaszewski was working with the United Mine Workers and recruiting young Polish men into pro-independence ZOP locals, other socialists recognized the potential of working with the sports programs and paramilitary drill teams sponsored by the *Sokół* [Polish Falcons] and the *Związek Młodzieży* [Polish Youth Alliance]. These groups—ostensibly preparing a cadre of physically fit, well-drilled young men who would one day serve the cause of Polish independence—offered a good forum for political discussion. Clerical condemnation, among other evidence, suggests that the Left had some influence in locals in Pennsylvania, Massachusetts, and New Jersey.[19]

Pressure from the growing numbers of immigrants from the Russian partition brought changes to the Polish National Alliance, the leading Polish-American secular fraternal organization. As early as 1895, the alliance revoked its previous ban on socialists. The resulting influx prompted the fraternal's weekly, *Zgoda* [Harmony], to run a defensive reply to claims from both the Right and Left that a jump in membership of approximately 3,500 in 1895 had occurred, "thanks to the socialists." In that same year, Dr. Teodor Kodis, a physician with ties to the Russian populists and the Proletariat Party, was elected national vice president of the fraternal and director of its education department.[20]

On May 1, 1990, Poles affiliated with the pro-independence ZZSP established a new newspaper in Chicago, *Robotnik* [The Worker]. By October 1900, no one was surprised when the pro-independence locals dominated the ZOP convention and voted to form a new group, the *Związek Socjalistów Polskich* [Alliance of Polish Socialists]. The new ZSP voted to assess its members 5 cents a month for the PPS in Europe, named *Robotnik* as its organ, and set up its headquarters in Chicago. The ZSP also committed itself to supporting the new American Social Democratic Party and that autumn, three Poles active in the ZSP in Chicago ran for city office on the social democratic ticket.[21]

The steps taken by the new ZSP paralleled changes in the larger politics of the American Left whose center of gravity was also shifting away from the Socialist Labor Party headquartered in the East and toward the Social Democratic Party (the precursor of the Socialist Party of America), which would make its headquarters in Chicago. The former ZOP had already largely disintegrated when Leon Czolgosz, a Polish anarchist loosely associated with it, assassinated President William McKinley in 1901. Though Buffalo's Polish socialists condemned Czolgosz's action, the wave of federal agents that swept through that community after the assassination effectively suppressed what remained of its socialist movement.[22]

The Leadership of the Polish Socialist Alliance (ZSP)

The immigrant activists from the Russian partition who led the ZSP actually represented two distinct generations, each with its own historical perspective and programs. Aleksander Dębski was typical of the older generation of activists who had been born to gentry families in the Russian partition in the late 1850s and early 1860s. Many of them had childhood memories of the 1863 uprising against the tsar; they idolized the resistance fighters and acquired an enduring hatred of the tsarist troops. It was these memories that inspired their classroom demonstrations against secondary school teachers who carried out the program of forced russification.

In their twenties, in Russian universities, they joined conspiratorial groups in which they debated the future of Poland and read Polish political thought, history, and literature. Dębski and his Polish friends fell in with Russian populists and discovered the Russian and western European radical literature of the period as well. But their association with Russian populism was a difficult one marked by instances of betrayal. They came away disillusioned and suspicious of a movement that seemed riddled by corruption and double agents. They also came away sharing the populists' disappointment in the revolutionary potential of the people after their disastrous attempts to organize Russian peasants in the 1870s. Like the Russian populists, they concluded that the revolutionary movement against tsarist absolutism would have to rely on conspiracy and terrorist actions and that a mass movement was something in the vague future. At the University of St. Petersburg Dębski had attempted to enroll in the Institute of Roads and Communication which, as must have occurred to him, was a good place to learn about explosives.[23]

By the 1880s many of the radicalized Polish students had left the Russian universities for an underground existence in Polish cities. Once there they worked with Warynski's Proletariat until, after arrests and prison terms or Siberian exile, they made their way to the emigré centers in Western Europe. It was just such a path that Débski followed before becoming a delegate to the Second International, where he persuasively argued the case for Polish autonomy at the 1891 and 1896 conventions.[24]

These experiences underlay the program the older generation would promote in Europe and the United States. They would support conspiratorial action to effect an eventual armed uprising against the tsar. Much of their American activity would be geared toward raising funds and training volunteers for revolutionary militias in Europe. Though they accepted an obligation to cooperate with Marxist parties internationally, their deepest attachment was to Poland, an attachment which predated their exposure to Marxism. Still, they sharply rejected the conservative nationalist position, and committed themselves to establishing a socialist Polish state.

The leading voices of the younger generation came to maturity over twenty years after the 1863 uprising—in a Poland that had turned away from the insurrectionary tradition, that had begun to urbanize and industrialize, that had no role for the gentry class or its idealistic impulse, whether of a Right or Left stamp. New classes came to the fore of the movement as leaders emerged from the factories and workshops of the Russian partition. Others from the last wave of Polish immigration, from the Austrian partition, joined them. Finally, the PPS sent a few left-wing intellectuals to the United States to argue its program and aid in organizing the recruitment.

Available biographies for the younger generation confirm the varied origins of this leadership. Jan Borkowski, a weaver, came to the United States in 1897 after having organized construction workers in Budapest. By 1900 he was living in Chicago and editing the ZSP organ, *Robotnik* in return for free room and board. In 1902 and 1903, when Borkowski was active with the anthracite strike in Pennsylvania, the Milwaukee tanners' strike, and campaigning for socialist candidates in Milwaukee's municipal elections, Feliks

Cienciara, a former typesetter, took over the editing of *Robotnik*. Zygmunt Piotrowski, son of a Galician shoemaker, would be another prominent activist in this camp. He arrived in 1912 after working his way through law school and helping found a socialist educational center in the Tatra Mountains for railroad workers.[25] In contrast to the working-class origins of this group of activists were the careers of the young intellectuals sent by the PPS for one- to two-year tours. Marjan Bielecki, for example, attended the Riga Polytechnic before organizing workers in Riga and Kowno. After prison terms in Warsaw's infamous Pawiak Prison and Siberia he lent his journalistic and oratorical talents to the Polish-American movement in 1911 and 1912.[26]

The program of this generation reflected its historical experience. From their work organizing strikes in the Russian partition and organizing and tutoring an electorate in the Austrian partition, these younger leftists had developed a strategy based on mass education and mobilization. In the great Pennsylvania anthracite strike of 1902, the younger generation organized approximately 25 Polish socialist locals and led at least two UMW locals.

In the meantime, the older generation built a presence within the Polish National Alliance. Dębski's experience in the parliamentary maneuvering at the Second International probably helped him to increase the impact of the twelve ZSP delegates (among 378 delegates) at the 1903 PNA convention, which was held, fortunately for Dębski, in Wilkes-Barre where feelings generated by the strike still ran high. Dębski checked the increasingly powerful right-wing National Democrats to gain funds from the financially successful fraternal insurance society for socialist concerns such as aiding political prisoners in the Russian partition and caring for political refugees.

In 1905, revolutionary ferment rocked the entire Russian empire, including the Russian partition of Poland. The ZSP, with its links to activists in Europe, was perfectly positioned to provide information about the exciting events in the homeland, and its rallies attracted huge crowds. The conservatives within the Polish National Alliance were on the defensive, and as one of them admitted later, "there was a moment, in which it seemed to the broad mass of fraternal members, that the [conservative] executive committee had indeed made a mistake in backing the [rightist] National League."[27] By the following year, the ZSP had lost some of the momentum it had gained in 1905 as the intense interest generated in that year began to fade. However, the ZSP would remain a vocal minority within the Polish National Alliance where it would engage in the debate about Poland's future.

The Polish Section of the Socialist Party

In November 1906, the PPS in the Russian partition split along the fault lines of the two generations, and at the same time the ZSP in the United States began to do the same. The older generation would accept the leadership of Jozef Pilsudski whose semimilitary cadre instigated street fighting during the 1905 revolution and afterwards continued to mount terrorist actions against tsarist officials. In the Russian partition, this group would be known as the PPS-*Fracja Rewolucyjna* [Revolutionary Faction]. The younger generation, stressing the mass mobilization of the working class, called itself the PPS-*Lewica* [Left]. In Chicago, in 1907, the younger generation began publishing its own paper, the *Dziennik Ludowy* [People's Daily] alongside *Robotnik*. By 1908, the younger generation left the ZSP to form itself into the Polish Section of the Socialist Party, becoming one of the first foreign-language federations accepted by the American Socialist Party.

What remained of the ZSP, a group about half the size of the new Polish Section, moved *Robotnik* to New York and concentrated almost exclusively on the struggle in Poland. *Robotnik* carried little American news. Its editors were given to messianic rhetoric about the role of the Polish worker not only in the liberation of Poland, but in the salvation of Western civilization from selfish individualism.[28]

In contrast, the new Polish Section's paper, *Dziennik Ludowy*, offered broad coverage of international and national news. Correspondents sent in regular reports of conditions in mining and manufacturing centers where Poles worked, e.g. factory closings, layoffs, accidents, and fires in places like McKeesport, Newark, Grand Rapids, and Kenosha. The editors urged Poles to work with the Socialist Party rather than confine themselves to support for Polish parties in the homeland, arguing that "the majority of the emigrants are staying here for a long time if not permanently," and that "we need to protect ourselves from the despicable actions of strikebreakers and from the exploitation of American capitalism."

The *Dziennik Ludowy* introduced its readers to the idea of industrial unionism—holding up the American Railway Union and the Industrial Workers of the World (at least until 1913) as models.

At the same time, the editors explained their qualified support for the AFL and the strategy of "working from within," [*zreformowania od wewnątrz*] as opposed to the dual unionism of the Socialist Labor Party. They held that the essence of socialism called for the social ownership of "fields, factories, and workshops" and complete social equality, "regardless of skin color or language."[29]

American historians have, by and large, portrayed the foreign-language federations of the Socialist party as problematic examples of separatist tendencies within American socialism. Yet, when viewed from the perspective of the Polish community, the significance of the Polish Section is just the opposite. Those Polish-born socialists who joined the Polish Section were expressing their commitment to the American movement, because they could always have chosen the alternative of working within the ZSP. The point was not lost on the ZSP, which more than once accused the Polish Section of succumbing to Americanization.

The secretary-translator of the Polish Section included some statistics about its membership in his report to the 1913 National Convention of the Socialist Party. He claimed 1,870 dues-paying members in 148 locals at the end of 1912. Almost half of the members (49 percent) belonged to labor unions, and 29 percent had been socialists in the old country. Women made up nine percent of the membership, mostly in seven women's locals. All but sixteen of the members were born in Europe, reminding us that Americans of Polish descent (and probably some Polish immigrants) who joined English-speaking locals are not reflected in these figures for the Polish Section.[30]

Circulation figures for the *Dziennik Ludowy* show that the readership was not confined to members of the Polish Section. In 1913 the *Dziennik Ludowy* reported a circulation of eight thousand. Comparing this Polish language daily with two others published in Chicago at the same time reveals that the socialist daily achieved about half the circulation of the daily paper controlled by the Polish Roman Catholic Union, *Dziennik Chicagoski* (15,837) and about a third of the circulation of the Polish National Alliance daily, *Dziennik Związkowy* (26,600). The *Dziennik Ludowy* increased its readership steadily, reaching eighteen thousand in 1918 (which would have ranked it eleventh for that year out of some three hundred English and foreign-language socialist periodicals published in the United States). A satirical and anticlerical socialist weekly also published in Chicago, *Bicz Boży* [God's Scourge], topped even this with a circulation of twenty thousand in 1916, though an anticlerical monthly edited by activists from the Polish

Section, *Wolna Myśl* [Free Thought] seemed to disappear after a year. Also in Chicago, Polish Wobblies briefly published *Solidarność* [Solidarity].[31]

Outside Chicago, on the eve of World War I, Polish socialists put out four other newspapers: the ZSP's *Robotnik* in New York, the *Telegram Codzienny* [Daily Telegram] also in New York, the *Naprzód* [Forward] in Milwaukee, and the *Górnik Polski* [Polish Miner] in Pittsburgh. In addition, other major Polish papers sometimes reported favorably on the Left such as the *Ameryka-Echo* [America-Echo] in Toledo, the *Kuryer* [Courier] in Milwaukee, and *Dziennik dla Wszystkich* [Everybody's Daily] in Buffalo.[32]

Thus, while the actual numbers of Polish-American socialist activists remained in the thousands, a socialist subculture infused a large part of the literate, secular Polish-American community during the first two decades of the twentieth century. Biographical interviews and available memoirs suggest that many of those attracted to the Left had spent some time in manufacturing or urban centers before emigrating. Some were raised in such environments; others spent less than a year, but just enough to introduce them to a politicized artisan subculture. One Pole who arrived before World War I, for example, had worked in a sugar refinery near Warsaw before emigrating and explained that "anyone who could read," at the refinery was a socialist.[33] Another Pole who migrated to Warsaw from a poor village was befriended there by a socialist before emigrating. As a result of this friendship, he began attending evening lectures, read natural science and classic Polish literature, gave up alcohol and cigarettes, and began to question his old religious beliefs. Like others who underwent a similar process, he felt alienated from the worldview of his rural past, and on a visit to his family, he concluded, "there was no one to talk to about what I was feeling," in his home town. Thus the pattern was set. He would seek out other alienated young people like himself but would find it hard to contain the contempt he felt for the tradition-bound villagers, whom he saw as static, superstitious, and passive—a mindset that would shape, and limit, the recruitment efforts of the Polish-American Left.[34]

One other avenue for politicization was contact with the teacher's seminaries established in rural Galicia by public education activists. One graduate who later emigrated to Chicago was surprised to find that other Poles in Chicago took him for a socialist due to the opinions he readily expressed, so he, "became a regular reader of the . . . *Dziennik Ludowy*."[35]

The Poles who filled the ranks of the Polish Section had

experienced a great transformation in their own identity, and so believed it was possible to change the mentality of others. They tried to convince themselves that the socialist movement would become a strong political force once a majority could be brought to question the "existing order of things," and activists from the Polish Section initiated a variety of popular culture and education programs. The *Polski Uniwersytet Ludowy* [Polish People's University], for example, offered lectures and organized courses on history, literature, economics, natural science, and technical drawing. Some of the organizers, such as Zygmunt Piotrowski, had helped establish similar organizations in Galicia before emigrating. An editor of *Dziennik Ludowy*, Michal Sokołowski, directed the *Nowe Życie* [New Life] choir, which won awards in citywide choral competitions. A drama group, which grew out of this choir, launched the careers of several talented actors who went on to make a living in the Polish-American commercial theater. Socialists in Milwaukee, Buffalo, Pittsburgh, and elsewhere sponsored similar projects.[36]

Many of these courses and programs were designed to instill confidence and pride in the talents of the Polish people. History courses stressed Polish peasant and national revolts, and literature courses taught that the Polish language, though sometimes the source of embarrassment in America, was the same language in which the great bards cast their profound vision of the Polish nation. From the outside, such programs might seem to encourage a separatist mentality, but the impulse behind them would have been familiar to Eugene Debs, who understood that before workers could be organized, they had to believe in their own self-worth and ability to act. Debs aimed to awaken feelings of pride in his listeners, in part by evoking and reinterpreting Protestant symbols and themes familiar to his native-born audience. Leaders like Piotrowski and Sokołowski also aimed to restore to Polish-born workers a greater self-awareness, including a keener sense of their own past and its connection to the future they could make for themselves.[37]

The Polish Section could reach those who were predisposed toward a critical stance. However, it would ultimately alienate those who might respond to workplace agitation, new economic or scientific ideas, or historical arguments, yet still consider themselves Catholic. The editors of *Dziennik Ludowy* pointed to this problem when they declared, "He is a bad socialist who can only ridicule [religious] prejudices and not offer a hand toward the uprooted."[38] But as long as many of their readers felt embarrassed by Polish religious traditions, their impact on the larger immigration coming directly from the countryside would be limited.

Three Main Branches of the Polish-American Left on the Eve of WWI

By 1912, the Polish-American Left consisted of three main branches. The largest was the Polish Section of the Socialist Party, which organized Poles on behalf of the American party and which supported the Polish independence movement as a means toward the end of a socialist Poland. Smaller, and drawing primarily on older political refugees still arriving from the Russian partition, was the ZSP, which shared many of the aims of the Polish Section but assigned the independence movement the greatest priority. Finally, a few small groups affiliated with Rosa Luxemburg's SDKPiL opposed the independence movement in principle but could not yet point to much success in organizing along pure class-based lines. These last groups came closest to exemplifying the Eurocentric attitude attributed by historians of American socialism to the foreign-language federations.

In December 1912, with the Balkan conflict opening the possibility of a war between Austria and Russia, the ZSP set out to mobilize the Polish-American community to support the idea of war against the tsar. Through the Falcons, the popular young men's athletic organization, they invited representatives from the broad spectrum of Polish-American organizations to form the *Komitet Obrony Narodowy* [Committee for National Defense]. As in 1905, the ZSP captured the interest of the larger community, which had been stirred by sketchy news of events in the homeland, and most of the invited organizations responded to the appeal from the Falcons. At the founding convention of the KON, these organizations endorsed a statement of purpose, which pledged to "support by all possible means, the movement for an uprising against Russia, the greatest enemy of Poland, the embodiment of oppression, cultural imperialism, barbarity and ignorance, and the eternal guardian of European absolutism."

The actual purpose of the KON was to support Pilsudski's PPS-Revolutionary Faction and the part of the European Falcon movement, which had become militarized. Pilsudski had already secured Austrian approval to organize and train a corps of Polish riflemen in Galicia. Dębski and others in the ZSP hoped to send funds, and ultimately, Polish men trained in Falcon units in

America to Galicia. The ZSP understood this as a plan to play off the superpowers: first, by taking advantage of Austrian tolerance and self-interest to initiate an uprising in the Russian partition, and later—with the help of the United States, which Pilsudski predicted would enter the war—to reclaim Polish territory held by Austria and Prussia. The KON would repeatedly stress that the goal was not to recreate the old monarchical republic, but a *polska ludowa* or People's Poland, but this did not relieve the younger generation's distrust of the older generation's continued emphasis on a military solution to the problem of Polish independence.[39]

An editorial in the Polish Section's *Dziennik Ludowy* warned that the focus on mounting an armed uprising in the Russian partition "completely ignored the daily matters of workers' struggles which should be the basis of a socialist movement." The editors argued that the ZSP was stretching the definition of socialism to embrace almost any pro-independence position, even those advocated by centrist or rightist groups. They recommended greater support for industrial unions, socialist workers' insurance societies, cooperatives, and popular education.[40]

Yet, the Polish Section had to contend with the fact that for Polish-Americans thinking of comrades and families back home, the choice was not so much whether Poles would participate in the expected war but on what terms. There was no question that much of the war would be fought on Polish territory. Pilsudski's Polish army-information—dedicated to establishing a people's republic—presented a better alternative than Poles drafted into the armies of the partitioning powers killing each other to preserve one or the other empire. Its solution was to propose that the Polish Section and the ZSP merge to form a single organization within the American Socialist Party. At a joint meeting in March 1913, the ZSP and the Polish Section created the new *Związek Polski Socjalistycznej Partji* or Polish Federation of the Socialist Party—the new official Polish-language section of the Socialist Party.[41] By October 1913, a few locals would pull out of the new Polish Federation to reform the old ZSP and publish *Robotnik*, but most locals stayed in the new organization.

Like the earlier Polish Section of the Socialist Party, the new hybrid Polish Federation promoted a broad range of activism. For example, the *Dziennik Ludowy* gave detailed coverage to the Western Federation of Miners strike in Michigan and encouraged its readers to attend rallies supporting the strikers. Some Polish Federation locals opened building funds for community centers, and the Polish Federation launched a campaign to recruit Polish women into the Socialist Party.[42] Former ZSP officials now in the Polish Federation promoted the Socialist Party with surprising diligence. Bronislaw Kulakowski, a major figure in the KON, visited dozens of Polish settlements in late 1913 and early 1914 to talk on the role of the Socialist Party in the international labor movement. At the same time, his cohort, Henryk Anielewski worked with the Polish Women's Alliance on the problem of adult illiteracy and spoke, along with Jane Addams, at a protest meeting on public school issues.[43]

The range of Polish Federation activities in these years suggests that were it not for World War I, the Polish Federation might have continued to recruit new members, which the Socialist Party would not otherwise have been able to reach. The Polish Federation activists had the talent, the language skills, and the ties to a Polish leftist tradition that enabled them to do much more than translate. They could "interpret" in the broadest sense of the word, linguistically and culturally, and agitate around special problems of immediate interest to the ethnic community. In addition to promoting Socialist Party perspectives on class, electoral, and labor issues, the Polish Federation tried to articulate a progressive analysis of community matters. Failing to address these issues would have meant leaving a vacuum for conservatives to exploit. In particular, to abandon the debate over the means and end of the Polish independence movement would have conceded a great deal to the Right in the Polish-American community, and to the radical internationalist Left as well. The fact that the Socialist Party did not comprehend either of these challenges facing the Polish Federation at the beginning of the war would help to seal its own fate when the ruinous breakup of the party came in 1919.

In January 1913, the clerically controlled Polish Roman Catholic Union became the first Polish organization to withdraw from the KON. In response the KON tried to hold onto other Polish-American organizations by defining the supporters of Roman Dmowski's National Democrats as the extreme right wing within Polonia and the KON as the mainstream. Thanks to the ZSP's longtime presence in the larger Polish National Alliance, that fraternal remained in the KON until the summer of 1914 when the backers of the conservative National Democrats finally forced it to pull out. They won success, in part, by portraying the KON as Austrophiles.[44]

A major study of the KON argues that with these defections, the KON actually grew stronger. Freed from the need to compromise with centrist groups, it reemerged as a "vigorous, centralized leftist organization." It openly recruited men in America for Pil-sudski's Polish Legions, technically under Austrian command, but retaining their own uniform and cultivating an egalitarian ethos. Its soldiers addressed each other as "citizen" and used the Polish eagle without the royal crown as its symbol. From the beginning of the war to 1916, the KON had about five thousand young men drilling in small units in Polish-American settlements, and in 1915 it opened a training camp at Congers, New York, staffed by former officers of the Austrian and Russian armies. The membership of the KON's 250 locals was somewhere between six thousand and ten thousand—not including the Youth Alliance or other groups affiliated with it. From 1915 through 1917, it raised, on average, seventy thousand dollars per year.[45]

Aware of this recruitment and fund-raising, the clerical Right and other Polish-Americans who supported Roman Dmowski's ethnocentric National Democrats (who were allied with the other superpower, Russia) launched a counter attack, which missed its mark at first. Its demand that federal authorities investigate the camp at Congers backfired when the investigation, finding nothing illegal, cleared the KON, and its initial attempts to organize a competing armed force with the French Foreign Legion ended in disaster. But in this period, the Right built a case for charging the KON with being a tool of Austria once the United States entered the war.[46]

In the meantime, the internationalist Left also began challeng-ing the Polish Federation and its affiliation with the KON. A few internationalists had remained with the Socialist Labor Party after the majority of Polish-American socialists abandoned it in 1901. A small influx of SDKPiL activists arriving after 1905 made contact with them and decided to remain outside the Socialist Party. In 1908, they formed the American Section of the SDKPiL, which folded within the next two years. Some of them entered the Polish Section at this point to agitate against its support for the independence movement.[47]

Beginning in 1914, several newly arrived and talented SDKPiL activists would open a much more aggressive program. Wincenty Dmowski, a Warsaw machinist with ties to the SDKPiL (and no known relation to Roman Dmowski the right-wing nationalist), joined the Polish Federation editors of Pittsburgh's *Górnik Polski* [Polish Miner], and after a struggle over the independence issue, gained control of the paper in 1916. In 1915, the Polish Federation sponsored a lecture tour by Daniel Elbaum, a chemical engineer who had been active with the SDKPiL in Europe, but recalled him when it learned that he had been ridiculing Polish Federation officers in his lectures. In that same year, the Polish Federation executive committee suspended Hipolit Głuski, another SDKPiL supporter, from his paid position as secretary-translator of the Polish Federation for refusing to handle Polish Federation business pertaining to the pro-independence KON, characterizing it as, among other things, pro-German (the charge made by the Right). A referendum of the Polish Federation general membership (following several months of debate in the pages of the *Dziennik Ludowy*) showed that 77 percent of those voting accepted the Polish Federation affiliation with the KON and that 67 percent thought Głuski should lose his post if he failed to reflect this position in his capacity as secretary-translator.[48]

Within the next year, approximately half a dozen locals supporting the SDKPiL activists (three in Chicago, one in Detroit, and several in Pennsylvania) petitioned the Socialist Party to expel the Polish Federation. In July 1916, as some prominent American socialists began to question the party's antiwar position publicly, the national executive committee reaffirmed the Socialist Party's opposition to the war, and gave the Polish Federation an ultimatum: either cease all support for the KON and the Pilsudski Legions or leave the Socialist Party. The Polish Federation refused to abandon the independence movement and so found itself outside the party it had worked to promote among Polish-Americans. The internationalists then organized themselves into a new Polish Section and reentered the Socialist Party as the official Polish-language federation. The expelled Polish Federation locals, representing the bulk of Polish-American socialists, returned to their roots, and reformed the ZSP one last time. This final version of the ZSP, like the one of 1900, encompassed the whole spectrum of the pro-independence Polish-American Left.[49]

From the point of view of the expelled Polish Federation locals, the struggle that forced them out of the party had not recently developed around the war, but grew out of the long-standing divisions of the Polish Left. The American Socialist Party seemed to them naively unaware of the range of European positions and, in particular, uninterested in the backgrounds of Wincenty Dmowski and Daniel Elbaum, the leaders of the new Polish Section.[50] Dmowski and Elbaum had sided with a minority even within the antiwar SDKPiL to call for a Third International in 1915.[51] In 1919, they would join the challenge to the old guard of the Socialist Party and would help form the first Polish-American communist group, affiliated with the Communist Party of

America. It might be said that in 1916 the Polish Federation went through the sort of split that would affect the whole American Socialist Party in 1919—and that in 1916, the executive committee of the Socialist Party sided with the Polish faction that would challenge it in 1919.

Whether or not keeping the larger Polish Federation in the Socialist Party in 1919 would have helped it to avert the fragmentation of the socialist movement at the end of the war (or, at least, bring a more theoretically sophisticated perspective to the debate than labeling all opposition to the executive committee as "foreign" or "European") cannot be proven.[52] But the fact that government surveillance, prosecutions, and deportations would affect all of the factions in the next few years is inescapable.

By the time the United States entered the war in the spring of 1917, the tsar had been overthrown and Pilsudski's Legions were in Warsaw. So, the KON felt free to support the American war effort against the central powers. It also tried to sway the Wilson administration to back the provisional government in Warsaw, which it hoped would achieve "land reform, nationalization of industry, social security, secularization of culture, and the democratization of society."[53] Competing for Wilson's attention, was the protogovernment that Roman Dmowski's National Democrats had established in Paris. Alarmed, the KON persuaded several prominent progressives to lobby on KON's behalf, including John Dewey who wrote an eighty-page confidential report to the Military Intelligence Bureau characterizing the Paris group as reactionary, aristocratic, imperialistic, priest-ridden, and anti-Semitic. Dewey argued that the KON, on the other hand, had much in common with Wilsonian democratic principles.[54]

But Wilson, who had been relying on the advice of the celebrated pianist, Ignacy Paderewski, on Polish issues since 1915, remained unimpressed. Paderewski helped several Polish-Americans (some of them Republicans) who supported Dmowski's Paris government gain access to the White House. They portrayed the KON as a collection of Bolsheviks and German agents, and advocated the arrest of KON activists under the Espionage and Sedition Acts. The federal government made a few arrests on these grounds and initiated extensive surveillance of newspapers, organizations, and individuals supporting the KON.[55]

In October 1917, the Wilson administration approved plans to recruit Polish immigrants for a Polish army to serve under French operational command. Prominent Polish-Americans accepted the new army, even those who had grave doubts about Dmowski and his followers in Paris. They convinced themselves and others that the army was a nonpartisan force. The KON, fearing the new army would make Dmowski's group look more like a de facto government, urged Poles to enlist in the United States army instead of the new force. In June 1918, the KON received a federal ultimatum: cease all opposition to the Polish army in France or disband. Thus the curious situation arose that a Democratic administration, upon the urging of Republican ethnic leaders, censured an organization for advocating enlistment in the United States army rather than in a separate military force under foreign command.

The KON remained on the defensive and lost credibility with the larger community, which would regard the Polish army in France (also known as the Blue Army or as General Haller's army) as heroes. A few years after the war, Tomasz Kozak, a socialist journalist, analyzed the decline of the Polish-American Left. He argued that from 1913 to 1916 the Left had led the politicization of the Polish-American community, and that after 1917, it was caught up in an exhausting battle with the right wing, which won a "miserable autocracy thanks to the terror of exceptional wartime laws."[56]

The Polish-American Left
Regroups After WW I

At the end of the war, the ZSP tried to recover from the losses it had sustained. Lecture tours by Polish-Americans and by visiting Poles—including women speakers for the first time on a significant scale—brought a temporary "flood of new memberships." The *Dziennik Ludowy* increased its readership until its circulation peaked at 24,188 in 1921.[57]

The younger generation had always been somewhat uncomfortable with their association with the KON. As one of them said, "We are in the KON because we cannot not be, yet we can display our class position [as socialists] in all our actions."[58] Throughout the war, the *Dziennik Ludowy* gave front-page coverage to strikes by machinists, refinery workers, and other war production workers. The editors, from the younger generation, ridiculed the "capitalist press," which attributed these strikes to Prussian agents and explained them as the result of "shortages and poverty." After the war, Polish-American leftists from this generation helped organize the massive steel, meatpacking, and coal strikes of 1919–1922.

Polish speakers and editorials in Polish socialist papers enthused about industrial unions replacing dozens of separate craft unions and schooling workers in class-consciousness so that they feel, "for the first time as a massive united social class acting against another, smaller though ruling class."[59] Other activists, such as Zygmunt Piotrowski helped mobilize Polish-Americans in key strikes in the tanning, garment, railroad, refining, meatpacking, and farm equipment industries in this period.[60]

Socialists from the older generation resettled in Poland at the same time. Some of them created the *Stowarzyszenie Mechanikow Polskich* [Society of Polish Mechanics] an organized reemigration scheme, which aimed to create model, worker-managed factories and vocational institutes in Poland. About twenty thousand Polish-Americans invested in the enterprises sending about one thousand (presumably skilled) reemigrants to settle among the various SMP sites to provide technical expertise in the early 1920s. The organizers proclaimed that "our dividends will be a People's Poland," but investment never reached projected levels, and though some of plants were still in production after World War II, the project fell short of its founders goals.[61]

Through the 1920s, Polish-American socialists saw their newspapers and organizations shrink, fold, or merge.[62] They identified several causes: government repression and the discouraging results of the postwar strikes, the gains of the Polish-American conservatives during the war years, the confusion in the community over the socialists' position on the war itself, the strong pressures to assimilate (during the Americanization and immigration restriction movements of the 1920s), the lure of postwar investment opportunities in America and Europe (which, as they warned, often as not turned out to be too good to be true), and a desire to focus on private, family concerns and enjoy new consumer goods after the exhausting war years.

There was at least one attempt to form a national coalition of the former socialists along with the new populists supporting rural reform in the interwar Polish state, labor organizations, and other progressive, Polish-American secular groups in the 1920s. Though nothing permanent emerged, a loosely defined *lewica* [left] remained a powerful minority in the Polish National Alliance up to 1930. The *lewica* took up a diverse range of issues, such as promoting more technical education for Polish-American youth and exposing the diversion of war relief funds raised in America to right-wing political parties in Poland.[63]

With Pilsudski's 1926 coup, the *lewica* enjoyed a surge of

popularity due to its ties to the new chief of state. Expectations of land reform and other concessions to the Left at the time of the coup ran high. But Pilsudski disappointed many of his supporters by courting the large landowners instead and putting power into the hands of a group known as "the colonels." In the 1930s, his government unleashed a campaign of *sanacja*, or anticommunist purification, jailing thousands of socialists and populists.[64] In the United States a new group of emigrés, equating support for the colonels with Polish patriotism, began to coalesce. An extreme, anticommunist minority, they were regarded with suspicion by the Left, as well as the moderates and the clerically oriented conservatives at this time.

A New Leadership Emerges in the 1930s

In the meantime a new generation of leftist leaders was emerging out of the socialist subculture of the teens and early twenties. Politicized in Polish-American settlements rather than in Europe, this generation was able to transcend the cultural conflicts that limited the influence of the earlier leaders with the larger community. Stanley Nowak, born in Galicia in 1903, arrived in Chicago's stockyard district as a boy. As a youth, Nowak earned money distributing flyers for a Polish-language theater. Enthused by the plays he had seen, he began reading Polish novels. Within a short time he was attending lectures at the People's University and conducting tours of the Field Museum of National History for other Poles. In the 1920s, he worked in a Chicago garment shop organized by the ACWA and held his first union office at nineteen.[65]

Bolesław Gebert left the Russian partition for the Pennsylvania coalfields where his horizons would broaden as he began reading Polish literature, and then the *Dziennik Ludowy*. In 1913, at the age of eighteen, he was elected to a UMW grievance committee in Nanticoke, and within a year formed a Polish socialist local and a Polish amateur theater group there. By 1915, he was working with Daniel Elbaum and the internationalists who were gaining control of Pittsburgh's *Górnik Polski*.[66]

In late 1916, having won control of *Górnik Polski* and the Polish Section of the Socialist Party, the internationalists transferred their headquarters and editorial offices from Pittsburgh to Detroit, renaming their paper the *Głos Robotniczy* (Worker's Voice). In moving to Detroit, Dmowski and Elbaum were anticipating a major migration pattern, which would bring to that city Poles and other East Europeans from Pennsylvania, Ohio, and West Virginia. From 1914 to 1930 the Polish population of Detroit would grow 66 percent. The fact that the vast majority of these Poles would work in large factories employing thousands meant that the future Polish Bureau of the Communist Party would be based in, "Detroit's Polonia [which] became one of the most proletarian of any of the major cities in the United States."[67]

After Dmowski and Elbaum were deported, Gebert stayed with *Głos Robotniczy*, touring Polish-American settlements to raise subscriptions. By 1924, Gebert would be secretary of the Polish Bureau of the Communist Party and editor, with Tadeusz Radwanski (a seasoned SDKPiL activist sent from Poland), of its organ the *Trybuna Robotnicza* (Worker's Tribune)—known after 1936 as *Głos Ludowy* [People's Voice].[68]

Coming of age within the Polish-American community, shaped by the Polish Left and the American labor movement, both Nowak and Gebert were prepared to appreciate the organizing potential of popular culture and ethnic networks long before the opening of the Popular Front. Thanks to such networks, both had already met Leo Krzycki in the 1920s. In fact, Gebert and Krzycki would continue to meet in secret to compare notes about their strategies to organize Poles, though their respective Communist and Socialist Parties would have disapproved had they known at that time.

Thus it was not serendipity that brought together key organizers of the United Auto Workers on the eve of the dramatic Detroit sit-down strikes. Nowak joined the UAW organizing staff after Leo Krzycki introduced him to Homer Martin, president of the UAW at a *Trybuna Robotnicza* picnic in May 1936. Soon after, Nowak designed a campaign to appeal to the whole Detroit area Polish community, not only to workers on the shop floor. For example, he had the UAW purchase time on a popular Polish-American radio comedy program for talks by himself or Krzycki; and the host of the program, an actor Nowak knew from his youth, would include songs and humorous monologues ridiculing employers and supporting the union in the rest of the program. Nowak also established a Polish Trade Union Committee with activists from different plants around Detroit who cultivated contacts with ethnic organizations (including parish-based societies) that socialists and communists had ignored for decades. Thanks to these contacts, the PTUC was able to meet in ethnic halls, which enhanced the legitimacy of the union and allowed freer discussion than would have been possible at the plant.[69]

Krzycki and other Polish leftists had learned the lessons of the 1886 Bay View strike. They learned to leaflet churchgoers instead of deride them. They learned to have confidence in the radical tendencies already present in the community. Nowak would make Mary Zuk, a Polish homemaker who had helped lead a citywide meat boycott protesting high prices, an officer of the PTUC. The networks these women built would help feed strikers in the future.[70] Though some CIO organizers were as shaken by the spontaneous sit-down strikes as the Knights of Labor officials had been by the seemingly leaderless Polish strikers of 1886, Krzycki would boast, "The sit-down strikes came from the people, not from the leaders. I was a leader and I know."[71]

In 1936, as Krzycki and Nowak were unfolding their plan to engage the whole Detroit Polish community, Bolesław Gebert was back in Pittsburgh, participating in a conference of 447 delegates from ethnic fraternals representing the workforce in the steel industry.[72] And at about the same time, Stella Nowicki, a Polish labor organizer recruited by a Chicago-based Croatian-American Communist with the CIO Packinghouse Workers Organizing Committee, was joining a Polish parish sodality and other local youth groups.[73] By the end of the decade, the CIO would recruit an estimated six-hundred thousand Polish workers nationwide in key industries, especially the auto, steel, meatpacking, rubber, and agricultural equipment industries.[74]

World War II and the Cold War

In World War II, Polish-American leftists took up foreign policy positions that would eventually undermine the momentum they had gained by championing economic issues during the depression. And, as in World War I, an organized right wing successfully used these foreign policy issues to increase its influence at the expense of the Left and take control of Polish ethnic organizations.

Just as the leftists in the KON took the lead in organizing a wide range of Polish-American organizations under an umbrella group on the eve of World War I, so the Polish Left tried to shape Polish-American opinion after the Nazi attack on the Soviet Union in June 1941. In January 1942, the Polish Section of the International Workers Order sent Stanley Nowak and Bolesław Gebert on a three-month tour to speak to numerous East European ethnic organizations, church groups, and union locals to encourage support for an American-Soviet alliance. Thanks to this groundwork, about 2,500 delegates from twelve East European groups met in Pittsburgh in April 1942 to create the American Slav Congess.[75] The ASC elected Leo Krzycki president and Blair Gunther, a Pittsburgh judge active with the Polish National Alliance, chair. At the beginning, the whole spectrum of the Polish-American community welcomed the ASC, even the Polish Roman Catholic Union.

But by 1943, new concerns shook the Left-led coalition. Statements by ASC leaders, such as the University of Chicago economist, Oskar Lange, raised fears about possible postwar Soviet claims to territory it seized between 1939 and 1941. In April 1943, the Nazis announced the discovery of a mass grave with the bodies of four thousand Polish officers who had been captured by the Soviets in 1939. Stalin claimed the Nazis had executed the officers and broke off relations with the Polish government-in-exile in London when it asked the International Red Cross to investigate the site. This, and other Soviet actions in 1943, suggested to many that Stalin intended to create a rival Polish government.[76] In this context, visits to the Soviet Union in the spring of 1944 by Oskar Lange and Rev. Stanislaus Orlemanski, both affiliated with the ASC, received negative publicity in the ethnic and American press. Though there is evidence that the Roosevelt administration secretly facilitated the trips, they were portrayed as dangerously naive. Rev. Orlemanski's claim that he had persuaded Stalin to restore complete religious freedom to Roman Catholics in the Soviet Union reinforced this impression.[77]

Polish-American organizations alarmed by these events left the American Slav Congress, and only a few leftist organizations attended the second congress in 1944. At this point, the anti-Soviet right wing took the lead in reorganizing the Polish-American community into a new coalition. When the KNAPP [National Committee of Americans of Polish Descent] established itself in 1942, other Polish organizations kept their distance, viewing it as an extremist group, which condemned even the Polish government-in-exile in London as soft on communism. At first its political base was confined to right-wing emigrés with ties to the interwar *sanacja* government. However, the discovery of the mass graves at Katyn greatly enhanced its credibility, because it had been claiming that the Soviet Union was guilty of such mass executions. In the spring of 1944, the Polish American Congress, strongly influenced by KNAPP, was founded as a new umbrella group embracing many of the organizations that had left the ASC. The Roosevelt administration, which had previously cooperated with the ASC, courted the new Polish American Congress and won its endorsement in the 1944 elections.

After the war, Polish-American leftists who tried to oppose the anti-Soviet foreign policy of the Polish American Congress discovered that the Polish-American community was deeply hostile to the post-WWII Polish Communist regime. Some of the leftists blamed the new influence the right wing had achieved in Polish-American organizations. Certainly, those who had supported the ASC after 1944 were red-baited in the Polish-language press and radio. But some of the leftists reluctantly admitted that the widespread anti-Soviet sentiment was not completely engineered by the PAC, but was partly informed by contact with relatives and friends living in the new People's Republic of Poland.[78]

After 1944 the Left never regained the influence it had enjoyed several times in the past in the organized Polish community. Though Polish leftists lost their voice in such organizations, this does not mean that the grass roots of the community blindly followed the would-be leaders of the right wing. Polish-Americans ignored the PAC's endorsement of Thomas Dewey in 1948 and voted consistently and overwhelmingly for Harry Truman and other Democratic candidates in the postwar years. A study of voting behavior concluded that into the 1970s Polish-Americans continued, "to vote for national and local Democratic party candidates identified with the party's progressive wing even when those candidates paid little attention to them."[79]

Conclusion

To portray Polish-American socialists as merely concerned with homeland issues and marginal to the American Left is to distort their understanding of themselves and their work. Most of them were actively engaged with the American socialist movement, but understood the American working class as a multi-ethnic proletariat—and addressed the Polish immigrant as part of it. They expected that American socialists should have shown the same sort of interest in the movement of the Polish proletariat in Europe that Polish socialist papers like the *Dziennik Ludowy* showed in the organization of workers in Belgium, Britain, Argentina, South Africa, and elsewhere. They also believed they had a special responsibility to address the issues that the Polish-American right wing used to build a base in the Polish-American community.

The choices they faced were not unlike those faced by anticolonial and neocolonial resistance movements since then. Like Filipino, Salvadoran, Korean, Irish, or South African emigrants, they saw the United States as a safe haven and, at the same time, as implicated in the subjugation of their homeland. While mobilizing their compatriots in America to aid a resistance movement at home, they recognized that those same compatriots were vulnerable to exploitation in the United States. Rather than being nativist themselves, as Germer charged in 1919, they challenged the American Left to broaden its understanding of American concerns.

Notes

1. James Oneal, *American Communism: A Critical Analysis of its Origins, Development and Programs* (New York: Rand, 1927), 53–54.

2. Theodore Draper, *The Roots of American Communism* (New York: Viking, 1957), 32–33.

3. Daniel Bell, *Marxian Socialism in the United States* (Princeton: Princeton University Press, 1967), 79.

4. James Weinstein, *The Decline of Socialism in America* (New York: Monthly Review Press, 1967), 183.

5. Warren I. Susman, *Culture As History* (New York: Pantheon, 1984), 77.

6. Christopher Lasch, *The Agony of the American Left* (New York: Vintage, 1969), 39.

7. Eugene Miller, "Leo Krzycki—Polish American Labor Leader," in *Polish American Studies* 33, no. 2 (Autumn 1976): 52–64. Leon Fink, *Workingmen's Democracy* (Urbana: University of Illinois, 1983), 178–94, 197–98. Roger D. Simon, "The Bay View Incident and the People's Party in Milwaukee," unpublished seminar paper, University of Wisconsin-Milwaukee, 1967 (in UWM Golda Meir Library Special Collections), 3–11, 16–18. Philip S. Foner, "The Polish-American Martyrs of the First May Day," in David Roediger and Franklin Rosemont, *A Haymarket Scrapbook*, (Chicago: Charles H. Kerr, 1986), 88–92.

8. For background on nineteenth-century Polish history, espe-

cially the partitions and resistance movements see, Piotr Wandycz, *The Lands of Partitioned Poland, 1795–1918* (Seattle: University of Washington Press); R. F. Leslie, *The History of Poland Since 1863*, (Cambridge: Cambridge University Press, 1980), and R. F. Leslie, *Reform and Insurrection in Russian Poland, 1856–1865*, (London: University of London, 1963).

9. For an overview of Polish-American immigration see, Andrzej Brożek, *Polish Americans, 1854–1939*, (Warsaw: Interpress, 1985), and John Bukowczyk, *And My Children Did Not Know Me: A History of the Polish Americans* (Bloomington: Indiana University Press, 1987). On the IWPA and anarchist immigrants in this period see Bruce Nelson, *Beyond Martyrs: A Social History of Chicago's Anarchists, 1870–1900*, (New Brunswick: Rutgers University Press, 1988).

10. Stanislaw Osada, *Historya Związku Narodowego Polskiego* [History of the Polish National Alliance] (Chicago: Polish National Alliance, 1905), 277–96. Henryk Nagiel, *Dziennikarstwo Polskie w Ameryce* [Polish Journalism in America] (Chicago, 1894), 87 and "Pamietnik Nr 29," [Memoir No. 29] in *Pamiętniki Emigrantów: Stany Zjednoczone* [Emigrant Memoirs: United States], vol. 2, (Warsaw: Ksiazka i Wiedza, 1977), 118. Jan Wepsięc, *Polish American Serial Publications, 1842–1966*, nos. 541, 594 (Chicago, 1968).

11. Krzysztof Groniowski, "Socjalistyczna Emigracja Polska w Stanach Zjednoczonych, 1883–1914," [Polish Socialist Emigration in the United States, 1883-1914] in *Z Pola Walki* no. 1, (1977):4–5. Ten years ago Groniowski opened up the possibility of retrieving the history of early Polish American socialism by patiently culling out correspondence from Poles in the United States printed in socialist newspapers in Europe, thus discovering a wealth of information about newspapers and groups for which no known American sources exist. In this thirty-one page article he summarizes hundreds of entries from these papers supplementing them with citations to unpublished correspondence in party archives in Poland.

12. Groniowski, 8–9. Correspondence from Jozef Rutkowski to the Berlin *Gazeta Robotnicza*, February 22, 1896 in Danuta Piatkowska, ed., *Korespondencja z Ameryki w Prasie Polskiej na Ślasku, 1868–1900* [Correspondence from America in the Polish Press in Silesia, 1868–1900] (Wroclaw: Ossolineum, 1980), 159–60.

13. Letter appearing in Berlin's *Gazeta Robotnicza*, June 12, 1897, reprinted in Piatkowska, 168.

14. On the Warsaw Proletariat see Lucjan Blit, *The Origins of Polish Socialism*, (Cambridge: Cambridge University Press, 1971) and Norman Naimark, *The History of the 'Proletariat': The Emergence of Marxism in the Kingdom of Poland, 1870–1887* (Boulder: East European Monographs, 1979).

15. Two helpful surveys in English, which expand on these European developments, are Piotr S. Wandycz, *The Lands of Partitioned Poland, 1795–1918* (Seattle: University of Washington Press, 1984) and R. F. Leslie, *The History of Poland Since 1863* (Cambridge: Cambridge University Press, 1980).

16. Groniowski, 4–5. See Wandycz, 295–96, for a summary of arguments advanced by pro-independence Polish socialists. For a summary of the debate between Luxemburg and Lenin on the question of Poland's independence see Leszek Kolakowski, *Main Currents of Marxism*, vol. 2 (Oxford: Oxford University, 1978), 88–97 and J. P. Nettl, *Rosa Luxemburg* (Oxford: Oxford University Press, 1969).

17. Victor Greene, *Slavic Community on Strike, Immigrant Labor in Pennsylvania Anthracite* (South Bend: Notre Dame University, 1968), 16–17.

18. Stanislaw Konarski, "Bolesław Grzegorz Miklaszewski," [1871–1941] in *Polski Słownik Biograficzny* [Polish Biographical Dictionary] (hereafter cited as PSB). (Krakow-Warszawa-Wroclaw: Polish Academy of Sciences, 1935–), vol. 21, 58–61. Feliks Cienciara, *Wspomnienie* [Memoirs], ms. in the archives of the Polish Museum of America. Groniowski, 10–11.

19. Brożek, 120, 214, 221–22, 225. The antitsarist Youth Alliance declared its sympathy with the Japanese in the Russo-Japanese war and asked their European contacts for instructions about action to take in the event of armed insurrection in Poland. Stanislaw Lempicki, *Historia Związku Mlodzieży Polskiej w Amerjce* [History of the Polish Youth Alliance in America]. (Chicago: Wydawnictwo ZMP, 1905), 15–23, 38–40, 102–07. Also see Wandycz, 210–11, 288–90 on similar developments in Europe.

20. Membership in the Polish National Alliance in 1890 was 3,426 and in 1900, 28,358. Donald Pienkos, *PNA: A Centennial History of the Polish National Alliance of the United States of North America*. (Boulder: East European Monographs, 1984), 74, 329. The increase in 1895 was 3,562; the average annual increase in the preceding decade had been 722. Osada, 443. Delegates to the PNA

convention included two members of *Ognisko* and one each from *Rowność*, the Knights of Labor and a Chicago anarchist. Osada, 626–627, 767. Janusz Krajewski, "Teodor Kodis," [1861–1917], PSB, vol. 13, 245–56.

21. Groniowski, 16–18. Wepsięc, no. 922.

22. William Falkowski, "Class Formation in Buffalo Polonia, 1873–1901," (Ph.D. diss., SUNY–Buffalo, 1991), chapter 11. Cienciara, 6.

23. Norbert Barlicki, *Aleksander Debski, Życie i Dzialanosc, 1857–1935* [Aledsznder Dębski, Life and Work, 1857–1936], (Warsaw: Wydawnictow Stowarzyszenia B. Wiezniow Polityczynych, 1935). Wladyslaw Pobog-Malinowski, "Aleksander Dębski," [1857–1935], PSB, vol. 5, 145–49. For citations to other activists of this generation who fit this biographical pattern see Cygan, 164–65.

24. Barlicki, 97–98.

25. On Borkowski, see Groniowski, 13–15, 19–21; Cienciara, 3; and Miroslaw Francic, *Komitet Obrony Narodowej w Ameryce, 1912–1918* [The Committee for National Defense in America, 1912–1918], (Wroclaw: Ossolineum, 1983), 25. On Cienciara see Brozek, 113–14; Groniowski, 14–15, 18–20; and Cienciara. On Piotrowski see 'Leon Ziaja "Zygmunt Kazimierz Piotrowski" [1891–1940?]. PSB. vol. 26, 521–523; Zygmunt Piotrowski, "Polski Rucah Socjalistyczny w Ameryce" [Polish Socialist Movement in America], in *Księga Pamiątkowa P.P.S.* [P.P.S. Memorial Album] (Warsaw: Robotnik, 1923); and Adam Ciołkosz, *Ludzie P.P.S.* [People of the P.P.S.] (London: Central Committee of the Socialist Party, 1981),96–99.

26. Leon Wasilewski, "Marjan Bielecki" [1879–1912], PSB, vol. 2, 42. *Kalendarz Ludowe* [People's Almanac], 1913, 126.

27. Osada, 591. The National League was the precursor of the National Democratic Party.

28. On the split in the PPS in Europe see Wandycz, 310–13, 320–21; and Leslie, 79–81, 103–04. On the split in the United States see Piotrowski, 259–60; Groniowski, 25. Examples of this sort of prose could be found in any issue of *Robotnik* in these years, but see especially, December 5, 1907; January 3, 1908; January 11, 1912.

29. See, especially, *Dziennik Ludowy*, October 21, 22, 23, 1907;

December 16, 1907; March 19, 1908. The quote is from November 14, 1907.

30. "Report of Polish Translator-Secretary," in the minutes for the Meeting of the National Committee of the Socialist Party, May 1913.

31. Circulation figures from N. W. Ayer and Sons, *Directory of Newspapers and Periodicals* for years cited. Information on other papers is from Wepsięc.

32. N. W. Ayer and Wepsięc.

33. Izydor Brudzinski, interview with the author, Cypress, California, June 1983.

34. Marceli Siedlecki, "Moj Pierwszy Pamietnik 1878–1936" [My First Memoir, 1878–1936] in *Pamietniki Emigrantow 1878–1958* [Emigrant Memoirs 1878–1958], (Warsaw: Czytelnik, 1960), 479, 490–93. For examples of other biographies see Cygan, 56–57, 168–69.

35. Tadeusz Kantor, "W Ameryce Na Wozie i Pod Wozem" [In America On the Wagon and Under the Wagon] in *Pamiętniki Emigrantów 1878–1958* [Emigrant Memoirs 1878–1958] (Warsaw: Czytelnik, 1960), 603, 612, 620–21.

36. *Dwudziestolecie Towarzystwa Spiewu i Dramatu Nowe Życie, 1907–1927* [Twentieth Anniversary of the New Life Singing and Drama Society, 1907–1927] (Chicago, 1927).

37. Nick Salvatore, *Eugene V. Debs, Citizen and Socialist*, (Urbana: University of Illinois 1982), 228, 342–43.

38. *Dziennik Ludowy*, November 26, 1907.

39. On the origins of the KON see Francic, 14, 21, 25–26. On related European events see Wandycz, 328, or Leslie, 59–60. On the KON's activity among the young men's athletic and military organizations, see M. B. Biskupski, "The United States and the Rebirth of Poland, 1914–1918," 2 vols. (Ph.D. diss., Yale University, 1981), 20–21.

40. *Dziennik Ludowy*, November 6, 1913.

41. Roman Mazurkiewicz, "Jeden Lud Pracujacy—Jedna Jego Partja," [One Working People—Its One Party], in *Kalendarz Ludowy* [People's Almanac], (Chicago, 1913), 19–21. Groniowski, 26–27, 30.

42. On the copper strike, *Dziennik Ludowy* throughout 1913 and 1914. On community centers, *Dziennik Ludowy*, February 12, 1914. On efforts to recruit women: *Dziennik Ludowy* November 25, 1913; December 4, 1913; February 2, 1914 and *Kalendarz Ludowy* 1912, 34, 138. It is difficult to determine the relationship between the Poles in the Socialist Party and the Industrial Workers of the World in this crucial decade, and especially the Poles' reaction to the antisabotage amendment to the SP constitution in 1912 and the expulsion of Bill Haywood from the National Executive Committee in 1913 over that issue. Those Poles who had been most interested in techniques of sabotage (the older generation in the ZSP) had turned their attention to recruiting and training for Pilsudski's Legions by this time. The younger generation had no tradition of sabotage and their attitude seems to have been summed up by Bronisław Kułakowski in a speech in Wallingford, Connecticut, where he noted that the IWW had all but disappeared from Lawrence after the great textile strike and observed that, "the IWW has no interest in winning political rights because that is a field requiring organization, and they have none." *Dziennik Ludowy*, February 17, 1914. Still, the *Dziennik Ludowy* continued to run notices of meetings for two Polish locals of the IWW in the Chicago area, nos. 85 and 500.

43. Halina Kiepuski, "Bronisław Kułakowski" [1865–1924], PSB, vol. 16, 170–71; *Dziennik Ludowy*, February 17, 1914; December 17, 1913.

44. Louis J. Zake, "The National Department and the Polish American Community 1916–1923," *Polish American Studies* 38, no. 2 (Autumn 1981), 18–25.

45. On the KON, see Francic, 30, 108–12, 123–28, 220. On events in Poland, see Wandycz, 338. On recruitment of Polish-Americans, see Biskupski, 65–67 and Joseph T. Hapak, "Recruiting a Polish Army in the United States, 1917–1919," (Ph.D. diss., University of Kansas, 1985), 149.

46. Biskupski, 74–81, 131.

47. Groniowski, 24, 25, 30.

48. Groniowski, p. 24, 30, 31, 32. Bolesław Gebert, *Z Tykocina za Ocean*, [From Tykocin Across the Ocean], (Warsaw: Czytelnik, 1982), 32, 37. Piotrowski, 261. *Dziennik Ludowy*, July 1, 3, 7, 12, 1915.

49. *Dziennik Ludowy*, January 6, 1916; February 9, 1916. Piotrowski, 261.

50. Gebert, 53–55, 98. Both Elbaum and Dmowski would be deported and settle in the Soviet Union.

51. One of the SDKPiL representatives at the 1915 Zimmerwald Conference which called for a Third International, Paweł Lewinson [Łapinski], had been in the United States in 1907 and played a key role in the split of the older and younger generations into separate organizations. At that time he had taken a hard line against Pilsudski's faction. In 1918 he joined the Bolsheviks, became an editor of *Izvestia* and later a correspondent during the Spanish Civil War. He committed suicide in prison after being arrested in Moscow in 1937 during Stalin's purge of Polish communists. Janina Kasprzakowa, "Paweł Lewinson [Łapinski], PSB, vol. 17, 238–41. *Dziennik Ludowy*, February 9, 1916.

52. Those of the younger generation who differed with the SDKPiL perspective did not dismiss it. In their discussion about the direction the ZSP and KON should take after the war, they reminded the older generation that, "whether or not one agreed with the Bolshevik program, it was necessary to recognize the great sociopolitical significance that movement had for the whole world." Francic, 192–93.

53. Wandycz, 353. Also see Joseph Rothschild, *East Central Europe Between the Two World Wars*, (Seattle: University of Washington Press, 1974), 45–46.

54. John Dewey, "Confidential Report of Conditions Among the Poles in the United States," (Washington, 1918). Also see John Dewey, "Autocracy Under Cover," *New Republic*, August 24, 1918, 103–06; and [John Dewey], "America and Polish Politics," *New Republic*, November 9, 1918, 38–40.

55. I would like to thank M. B. Biskupski for sharing with me his notes from his research into collections documenting federal surveillance of the KON: Federal Bureau of Investigation, Record Group 65; Dept. of Justice, Record Group 60; Post Office Department, Record Group 28; War Dept. General Staff: Military Intelligence Division, Record Group 165. Paderewski greatly exaggerated his constituency in the Polish-American community and tended to take credit for fund-raising and organization efforts by others. See Francic, 110 and M. B. Biskupski, "Paderewski as Leader of

American Polonia, 1914–1918," *Polish American Studies* 43, no. 1 (Spring 1986): 37–56.

56. On the creation of the Haller Army, see, Hapak, 151–53. On the ultimatum to KON, see Francic, 191, 194–97.

57. Among the women who undertook speaking tours were Zofia Praussowa of the Central Executive Committee of the PPS, Dorota Kluszynski, Helen Dłuska (all visiting from Europe) and Stanisława Kucharska, editor of the organ for the Polish locals of the Amalgamated Clothing Workers of America, *Przemysłowa Demokracja* [Industrial Democracy], 1918–1925, and of the satirical weekly *Bicz Boży* [God's Scourge] in 1918. Piotrowski, 262. Wepsiec, no. 42, no. 871. N. W. Ayer, 1921. The ZSP counted 79 locals at its 1921 convention, double the number twenty months before. Piotrowski, 262. *Dziennik Ludowy*, January 2, 1920.

58. *Dziennik Ludowy*, February 8, 1916.

59. *Dziennik Ludowy*, July 27, 1915; January 8, 1920.

60. Ziaja, 521–23. Adam Ciołkosz, *Ludie P.P.S.* [People of the P.P.S.], (London: Central Committee of the Polish Socialist Party, 1981), 98.

61. Adam Walaszek, "Stowarzyszenie Mechaników Polskich w Ameryce, 1919–1945," [The Society of Polish Mechanics, 1919–1945], *Przeglad Polonijny* 12, no. 2 (1986): 26.

62. *Bicz Boży* shut down in 1918, and attempts to revive it in 1927 and 1934 failed. Dębski, who had acquired the *Telegram Codzienny* in 1916 sold it in 1922. The *Dziennik Ludowy* and *Robotnik* shared editors from 1922 to 1926 when the *Dziennik Ludowy* folded. *Robotnik*'s circulation remained at about 27,000 through the 1920s. *Robotnik* (which published into the 1960s) actually gained readers during the sit-down strikes of the mid-1930s to reach a circulation of 36,200 in 1936. Information on closings and circulation are from Wepsiec and N. W. Ayers, 1921–1926.

63. On plans for such a coalition see, for example, Buffalo's *Dziennik dla Wszystkich* [Everybody's Daily] March 6, 1922. On monitoring fundraising see *Dziennik dla Wszystikich*, March 27, 1922. On populist parties see Olga Narkiewicz, *The Green Flag: Polish Populist Politics, 1867–1970*, (London: Croom Helm, 1976). On the role of the *lewica* in the Polish National Alliance, see Pienkos, 160–61.

64. On Pilsudski's coup see Leslie, 133–38, 172–75, 180–81. Zygmunt Piotrowski, the former ZZSP activist still active with the PPS in Poland was among those beaten by state police in 1933. Ziaja, PSB, vol. 26, 523.

65. Stanley Nowak published his memoirs in serial form in the *Głos Ludowy* in the 1970s. Information about his interest in Polish literature and theater appears in *Głos Ludowy*, April 20, 27, 1974. Some, but not all, of this material appears in English in Martha Collingwood Nowak, *Two Who Were There* (Detroit: Wayne State University, 1989).

66. Gebert, 36–37, 70.

67. Thaddeus Radzilowski, "Patterns of Slavic Secondary Migrations as Reflected in Fraternal Records, 1895–1905," delivered at the Symposium on a Century of European Migration, Immigration History Research Center, St. Paul, 1986; and Thaddeus Radzilowski, "Klasowosc, Etnicznosc, a Spolecznosc Lokalna: Polonia w Detroit i Jej Wklad w Organizacje CIO," [Class, Ethnicity and Local Community: Polonia in Detroit and its Contribution to the Organization of the CIO], *Przegląd Polonijny* 12, no. 2 (1987): 55–67.

68. Gebert, 73–77. Wepsięc, no. 76, 204.

69. Nowak, *Two Who Were There*, 75–84.

70. George Schrode, "Mary Zuk and the Detroit Meat Strike of 1935," *Polish American Studies* 43, no. 2 (Autumn 1986): 5–39; see also comments by Thaddeus Radzilowski, in "Communications," *Polish American Studies* 44, no. 1 (Spring 1987): 96–97.

71. Miller, 57.

72. Gebert, 104–08.

73. Stella Nowicki, "Back of the Yards," in Alice and Staughton Lynd, *Rank and File*, (Princeton: Princeton University Press, 1981), 85.

74. Bolesław Gebert, "Policy w Amerykanskich Zwiazkach Zawodowych: Notatki i Wspomnienia," [Poles in American Labor Unions: Notes and Reminiscences], *Przeglad Polonijny* 2, no. 1 (1976): 151.

75. The twelve ethnic groups were: Bulgarians, Carpatho-Ruthenians, Croations, Czechs, Macedonians, Montenegrins, Poles, Russians, Serbs, Slovaks, Slovenians, and Ukrainians. The

office of Strategic Services concluded at this time that the American Slav Congress, 'Was not excessively pro-Soviet." Peter H. Irons, "The Test is Poland,': Polish Americans and the Origins of the Cold War," *Polish American Studies* 30, no. 2 (Autumn 1973): 17. For other sources on the ASC see, Mary Cygan, "American Slav Congress," in *Encyclopedia of the American Left* ed. Mari Jo Buhle, Paul Buhle and Dan Georgakas, (New York: Garland Publishing, 1990), 28–29.

76. Charles Sadler, " 'Pro-Soviet Polish Americans,': Oskar Lange and Russia's Friends in the Polonia, 1941–1945," *Polish Review* 22, no. 4 (1977): 26. Robert Szymczak, "The Unquiet Dead: The Katyn Forest Massacre as an issue in American Diplomacy and Politics," (Ph.D. diss., Pittsburgh: Carnegie-Mellon University, 1980). Though approximately four thousand bodies were discovered at Katyn between eight thousand and ten thousand, officers had been missing since 1939. In 1992, Mikhail Gorbachev officially acknowledged Soviet responsibility for the Katyn massacre and opened Soviet archives to scholars from abroad.

77. Sadler, 25–39. On federal involvement in the trips, see Martin Weil, *A Pretty Good Club: The Founding Fathers of the U. S. Foreign Service*, (New York: W. W. Norton, 1978), 163–77.

78. Irons, 18, 35–36. Richard C. Lukas, *The Strange Allies: The United States and Poland, 1941–45*, (Knoxville: University of Tennessee, 1978).

79. Stanislaus Blejwas, "Old and New Polonias," *Polish American Studies* 38, no. 2 (Autumn 1981): 62–71. On voting behavior see, Thaddeus Radzilowski, "Introduction," in Nowak, 13–27.

SIX

The Ukrainian Immigrant Left in the United States, 1880–1950

Maria Woroby

Ukrainian Immigration: Background and Statistics (1880–1950)

Ukrainian migration to the United States began on a large scale in the late 1880s and peaked during the decade preceding World War I, with a total of 67,009 individuals entering the U. S. in 1914. Migration declined sharply during the war years. Although this trend was reversed slightly in the early 1920s, implementation of the Immigration Act in 1924 virtually put an end to mass Ukrainian emigration to the United States. Despite the 1924 quota restrictions, statistics reveal that approximately fifteen thousand to twenty thousand immigrants settled in America during the 1920s and 1930s.[1]

The majority of Ukrainian immigrants were males from the ages of 14 to 44. The majority of male migrants were unmarried at the time of migration; if married, males tended to migrate alone, either leaving their spouses and families behind with the intention of returning or sending for them at a later date. Most Ukrainian immigrant women were married. Unmarried women usually emigrated as part of an extended family. The number of single Ukrainian women migrating to the U. S. specifically in search of employment cannot be determined or approximated from immigration records. Individual accounts, diaries, and written memoirs acknowledge that there were many unmarried immigrant women and recount their experiences in America from a singularly unique perspective.[2]

The majority of Ukrainian immigrants arriving prior to World War I were recruited almost exclusively from the impoverished peasant class. Originally attracted to America by agents from the coal-mining companies of Pennsylvania and by other immigrants, more than half of the Ukrainians who emigrated before 1914 found employment in the anthracite coal-mining communities of Shenandoah, Shamokin, Mt. Carmel, Olyphant, and Scranton. Besides coal mining, unskilled Ukrainian migrants found employment in iron and steel production, the meat-processing industry, and automobile production. Unmarried Ukrainian women were employed primarily in the textile industry, light manufacturing (cigar and leather goods factories), as well as by domestic and personal services. Although a majority of Ukrainian immigrant women did not work outside of the home (66 percent according to immigration records for 1899–1910), their economic responsibilities were significant. Besides caring for their own families, Ukrainian immigrant women often took in boarders or piecework.

While Ukrainian immigrants were clustered by industry, they were scattered geographically. Their primary areas of settlement, as previously noted, were in Pennsylvania and other urban-industrial states of the Northeast—New York, New Jersey, and Ohio. Tertiary areas of settlement developed in the urban centers of Chicago, Minneapolis, and Detroit, while some immigrants chose the rural farmlands of North Dakota, Wisconsin, Virginia, and Texas to establish their communities.

World War II precipitated a third wave of Ukrainian immigration to the U.S. (1947–1955). During the German occupation of western Ukraine and parts of the Ukrainian SSR, hundreds of Ukrainians were brought to work as forced laborers in the German war industries. Others fled their homeland with the advance of Soviet troops in late 1944. By the end of the war, thousands of Ukrainians resided in displaced persons camps in the western zones of Germany and Austria. Ukrainian-American relief organizations, principally the United Ukrainian American Relief Committee (UUARC), sponsored thousands of displaced persons. This effort raised the total number of Ukrainian immigrants in the U.S. after the war to approximately 85,000 persons.

Many of the Ukrainians who arrived in the U.S. after 1947 had a different socioeconomic background than their predecessors. For example, a 1948 survey of Ukrainians living in displaced persons camps in Germany revealed that 12.3 percent were professionals, administrators, or entrepreneurs; 26.6 percent were skilled laborers; and 61 percent were unskilled or farm laborers. The advantages of education and professional or occupational training helped to secure the economic and social positions of post-World War II Ukrainian immigrants and served to increase the number of Ukrainian professionals in the U.S.

The post-World War II Ukrainian emigrés had a profound influence on Ukrainian immigrant politics and organizational life. Their politically conservative and nationalist sentiments strengthened existing nationalist organizations and led to formation of new groups. The passionate anti-Soviet stance of the majority of post-WWII Ukrainian immigrants also fueled the fires of existing anti-Soviet views among Ukrainian-Americans, resulting in the creation of a strong, vocal lobbying group bent on altering the U.S. government's foreign policy toward the USSR.

The church was the focal point of organizational activity and group identity for the majority of the early Ukrainian immigrants. Because the Ukrainian migrants did not find in America a church organization of their own (the Uniate Church to which most of the immigrants belonged was peculiar to western Ukraine), they had to organize their religious activities from a bare foundation. Many immigrants devoted themselves and their material resources to this end.

Among the first secular organizations created were fraternal benefit societies or mutual aid societies. The role of these cooperative insurance organizations became increasingly important as the tolls of the industrial workplace—accidents, sickness, and death—became a major concern to Ukrainian working men and women. The need to insure oneself and to protect one's family was urgent for an immigrant without property or savings. The first Ukrainian aid society, the St. Nikolas Brotherhood, was established by Rev. Ivan Voliansky in 1885. Within two years, there were seven "brotherhoods" in Pennsylvania that eventually merged into the Union (*Spoluchennia*) of Ruthenian Fraternal Organizations.

Ukrainian Social Democratic Movement in the United States (1905–1915)[3]

Whether fleeing tsarist persecution or emigrating with the expressed purpose of organizing the Ukrainian immigrant masses, the Ukrainian socialists who arrived in America were youthful, educated, and, often, seasoned veterans of organized left-wing political activity or the trade union movement in Europe. They were accustomed to cooperating with Polish, Jewish, and Russian socialist groups in the homeland and continued to form alliances— personal rather than organizational—with similar groups in the U.S. This was especially true of the radicals who emigrated from the Ukrainian territories in the Russian empire and identified with the dominant Russian culture. Many of these socialists joined existing Russian-American social democratic organizations and remained active exclusively in Russian emigré politics. On the other hand, Ukrainian immigrant socialists from Galicia formed ties with the Polish, Lithuanian, and to some extent, German-Austrian socialist elements in the U.S., publishing articles in the Polish-American radical press, or cosponsoring cultural or social activities. Nonetheless, critical ideological differences between Ukrainian immigrant socialists and their Slav-American counterparts especially over Ukrainian national autonomy often preempted any serious, sustained political cooperation. There are no published sources describing the demographic character of the immigrant membership of Ukrainian socialist organizations. Records of socialist organizations, publishing houses, and the like were either destroyed during U.S. government raids (1918–1921) or remain privately held.

Although Ukrainian proponents of socialism were present in the U.S. during the early years of the twentieth century most often in the capacity of "correspondents" for the Galician radical press, only after the 1905 revolution in Russia was any attempt made to establish formal socialist organizations within the immigrant community. An influx of new emigrés, especially key members of the Revolutionary Ukrainian Party (RUP) and the Ukrainian Social Democratic Party (USDP) of Galicia, helped provide a source of leadership that the immigrant socialist movement sorely lacked. This leadership was also strengthened by new emigrés from Germany who participated in the German social democratic movement. This group included such men as T. Pochynok and T. Lata, who later played important roles in the founding of the Ukrainian Federation of the Socialist Party of America (UFSP).

The first explicitly Ukrainian-American socialist organization established in the United States was *Haidamaky*. Founded in 1907 in New York City, *Haidamaky* was a branch of *Sich*, a gymnastic organization originated in 1900 in Galacia. The term *Haidamaky* means restless or rebellious people and has Turkish derivatives. A. Petriv, a founding member, wrote of the group:

> Among a group of young Ukrainians in New York City an organization was founded in 1907 named "Haidamaky"—an athletic organization as well as an educational one. The following year the organization's monthly *Haidamaky* began to appear. This was a small, unpretentious newspaper without a clear working class position but a paper that, nevertheless, expressed an understanding that the worker's fate was not the same as that of priests and lords.[4]

In 1909, the group changed its name to the Ukrainian Progressive Worker's Organization—*Haidamaky* and approached the SP to begin the process of formal affiliation. A subsequent decision of the *Haidamaky* leadership to change the organization into a worker's fraternal order c. 1911 had dire consequences. Shortly after the change took place, the organization's left-wing members withdrew and went on to establish the Ukrainian Federation of the Socialist Party of America. *Haidamaky* remained insecure financially, and the flu epidemic of 1918 wiped out all of the organization's capital assets, leaving it bankrupt. At its height, during the years 1916–1917, *Haidamaky* had a membership of three thousand individuals throughout the U.S.

Concomitant to the founding of *Haidamaky*, members of two different *Sich* branches met and adopted a platform calling for a Ukrainian-American socialist organization that supported the Ukrainian Radical Party in Galicia c. 1909–1910. Dubbed the Ukrainian Workers Party in America (*Ukrainska Robitnyche Partiia v Amerytsi*), the new organization rejected an affiliation with the SP on the grounds that the SP "was not progressive enough." The group adopted *Khlopsky Paragraf* (Peasant's Paragraph), a newspaper published by a group of Ukrainian immigrant "radicals" in Salem, Massachusetts as its organ. Torn by internal squabbling over allegations that members of the editorial staff of *Khlopsky Paragraf* had ties with the Presbyterian Church and arguments over the "national question," the Ukrainian Workers Party disbanded after only a year.

The platform adopted by the Ukrainian Workers Party brought the issues of "social patriotism" and "internationalism" to the forefront for the first time in America. Supporters of the Ukrainian Workers Party were accused by other, more militant Ukrainian socialists, of being "half-socialists" (*napiv-sotsiialisty*) because of the

Party's insistence upon upholding the Galician Ukrainian Radical Party's position on Ukrainian self-determination as well as its rejection of any cooperation with the SP. Ironically, the social democratic elements of the Ukrainian immigrant Left repudiated the "national socialism" espoused by the Ukrainian Workers Party only to fall victim to similar accusations by Bolshevik supporters a few years later.

There was little if any national coordination among the early Ukrainian immigrant socialist organizations. The *Haidamaky*, headquartered in New York City, drew its members primarily from the city and surrounding communities. This was also true of the short-lived Ukrainian Workers Party. The Ukrainian immigrant socialists who were associated with the "new" Rusyn National Association[5] and its organ *Narodna Volia*, were involved primarily in fraternal politics and activities. However, the Ukrainian Workingmen's Association did have close, but informal, ties with the *Haidamaky* during the fraternity's early years.

In an attempt to remedy the situation, Ukrainian immigrant socialists in Detroit, led by two Ukrainian emigrés from Germany— T. Pochynok and T. Lata—began publishing *Proletar* in 1911. The newspaper was designed from the outset to be more than just a local/regional paper by providing a mechanism to facilitate the establishment of a national network of Ukrainian socialists. The following year, another Ukrainian immigrant radical newspaper—*Robitnyk* (The Worker)—made its debut in Cleveland. A battle developed over which paper would become the official organ of the Ukrainian immigrant socialist movement in America. The struggle occurred at a time when the Ukrainian immigrant Left had just begun to take on organizational shape and establish formal alliances with the SP. In 1912, several Ukrainian branches of the SP were founded, including branches in Detroit, Cleveland, Philadelphia, and New York City. Competition for leadership and control of the movement eventually boiled down to two cities, Cleveland and Detroit. This leadership conflict tore apart the fledgling Ukrainian socialist movement. Local organizations collapsed, and by the end of 1913, only the Detroit branch of the SP was still active; both *Proletar* and *Robitnyk* had ceased publication. For a short time, the only outlet for socialist thought and agitation were the pages of *Haidamaky* and *Narodna Volia*.

By 1914, the leadership of the Detroit Ukrainian socialists managed to regroup and began publishing a new edition of *Robitnyk*. The appearance of this newspaper revitalized the moribund Ukrainian immigrant Left, and local socialist organizations were resurrected. The onset of World War I also contributed to the growth of new SP branches in Ukrainian communities where none had existed in the past.

In 1915, the Detroit Ukrainian socialists set up a provisional committee with the expressed task of organizing a Ukrainian foreign-language federation of the SP. Elected to the provisional committee were T. Pochynok, Fediushko, I. Hundiak, E. Kruk, Zavoiko, and Savruk. The Ukrainian immigrant socialists in Cleveland appointed a similar "provisional committee" and also began publishing a newspaper, this time called *Proletar*. The two factions appeared ready to resume their old feud. Sensing that a renewed battle would undermine recent gains in the movement, the leadership of *Haidamaky* decided to intervene. They were able to get the Detroit and Cleveland groups to formally join forces and merge their respective newspapers. Cleveland was selected as the publishing site for *Robitnyk* because of superior typographic and printing equipment. Renewed organizational efforts resulted in formal alliance with the SP in June 1915. At the time of its admittance, the Ukrainian Federation had twenty locals, representing one thousand members.

Ukrainian Federation of the Socialist Party of America (UFSP) (1915–1919)

The UFSP was an umbrella organization representing a hodgepodge of socialist and quasi-socialist sentiments. Among its membership were Ukrainian immigrant pacifists and anticlerics, supporters and opponents of Ukrainian national autonomy, pro-Austrian Galician nationalists, and pro-Russian federalists. During the opening years of World War I, the opposing voices of "social patriots" and "internationalists" added to the organizational and ideologial chaos. This general state of confusion characterized the UFSP's first convention which was held November 28–30, 1915. Attending were twelve delegates representing twenty locals, four members of the UFSP's Provisional Organizing Committee, representatives of the *Haidamaky* and two guests, Myroslav Sichynskyi and Andrii Dmytryshyn, an organizer for the Ukrainian Federation of the Socialist Party of Canada (UFSPC). Representing the SP at the convention was Charles Ruthenberg.

Controversy racked the convention. At the center of the polemical storm was Myroslav Sichynskyi. In 1908, Sichynskyi, a young Galician student, assassinated Count Potocki and the Polish governor of Galicia. With the help of friends in Galicia who succeeded in bribing Polish guards with money sent by Ukrainian-Americans, Sichynskyi escaped from prison on November 3, 1911. Before arriving to a hero's welcome in America in October 1914, Sichynskyi lived for a time in Norway, Denmark, and Sweden. Once in the U.S., Sichynskyi made formal alliances with the UFSP, garnering substantial support from the "social patriots" within the organization. Shortly before the UFSP convention, Sichynskyi and his supporters helped establish the Federation of Ukrainians in the United States at an all-Ukrainian congress held in New York City in October. Nationalist in political orientation, the federation was bent on uniting the immigrant community in support of autonomy for Russian and Austrian Ukrainian territories. Sichynskyi's influence and that of the "social patriots" were reflected in the nationalistic resolutions adopted by the convention.

Although Ruthenberg can be credited for toning down these nationalist sentiments and for trying to interject the SP's position on some of these issues, his attempts to steer the convention delegates away from pledging UFSP support for Sichynskyi's Federation of Ukrainians failed. Sichynskyi's popularity among UFSP delegates was so great that he was even elected editor of *Robitnyk*, the UFSP organ! Sichynskyi was somehow able to convince his UFSP delegates that his editorship of *Robitnyk* would not conflict with his leadership role in the Federation of Ukrainians. Only one "internationalist" was elected to the UFSP executive committee—Y. Fediushko.

During the period between the first and second UFSP convention, held in May 1917, the Ukrainian immigrant socialist embarked upon an aggressive organizing campaign. These efforts were particularly successful in Michigan thanks to a handful of Ukrainian-Canadian socialists who had recently emigrated. Led by Andrii Dmytryshyn and George Tkatchuk the "Canadian contingency" formed the backbone of the UFSP's newly formed "agitation committee." The "Canadians" were also credited with strengthening support for the internationalist camp within the UFSP. By the second UFSP convention, Detroit had emerged as both the organizational center of the UFSP and the center of internationalist (later Bolshevik) support within the federation.

When UFSP delegates gathered in Rochester, New York for the federation's second convention, Sichynskyi's popularity had waned considerably, due in part to his lack of participation in UFSP activities. But events in the homeland were the principal factors that weakened the influence of the "social patriots." The nationalist elements within the Ukrainian immigrant community, supported by the heirarchy of the Ukrainian Catholic (Uniate) Church in America, had supported Austria because they believed that Austria would support Ukrainian demands for an independent state.

When the U.S. entered the war in 1917, the picture suddenly changed. Ukrainian immigrant political leaders who had made their pro-Austrian views public were held suspect by the U.S. government, and a considerable number of them were detained.

The Ukrainian immigrant Left articulated its position on the war at the Rochester convention. Delegates represented some 46 locals with approximately two thousand members. The gains made by the federation's "internationalists" were reflected in the resolutions adopted at the convention:

1. As long as capitalistic rule exists, there will be slavery, nations will oppose nations, and class will fight class. Imperialism, the capture of colonies and their subsequent annexation and incorporation into large nations, is a necessary by-product of capitalism;
2. Capitalism can be destroyed only through class warfare. The day capitalism is destroyed all other slavery will be destroyed;
3. Anyone who follows a different path is not striving for national freedom for his people. He has only painted the yoke a different color while the form remains the same;
4. Until socialism is achieved as the new order which will bring downtrodden nations, including the Ukrainians, full freedom, the obligation of the Ukrainian proletariat is to energetically fight the class war against nationalism and strive for full freedom and rights in the struggle to achieve true democracy."[5]

The convention's delegates agreed to sever all ties with organizations that did not "follow the path of class warfare." The UFSP also adopted the SP's stance on the war. Since Sichynskyi had not shown up at the convention, he had forfeited his position as editor by default. Evhen Kruk was elected as *Robitnyk*'s new editor. The new executive committee consisted of A. Dmytryshyn, D. Mois, N. Korzh, I. Bychyk, N. Kobrinskyi, T. Pochynok, and Evhen Kruk. With the exception of Pochynok, all were in the internationalist camp.

Once the UFSP adopted a formal antiwar position, a barrage

of antiwar articles hit the front pages of *Robitnyk*. U.S. "bourgeoise capitalists" were accused of ignoring the bloodbath that had taken place in Belgium and Galicia and then entering the war when it appeared as if U.S. hegemony in Europe was a diplomatic reality. *Robitnyk* urged the Ukrainian immigrant working class to unite with workers of all lands in a massive antiwar effort. To this end, UFSP locals sponsored numerous antiwar meetings throughout the country and participated in demonstrations sponsored by other socialist and labor organizations.

When the February Revolution broke out in Russia in 1917, the Ukrainian immigrant Left welcomed the events with reserved enthusiasm. Recognizing the February Revolution as the "beginning of liberation for the oppressed proletariat and peasantry of Russia and the world," and thus a time for "rejoicing," the UFSP was, once again, faced with the "national question" and its implications for European Ukrainian national autonomy. The leadership of the UFSP, having just purged its ranks of "Second Internationalist social patriots," did not have enough time to put together a new platform addressing the "national question" as it pertained to the revolutionary events in Russia.

The Ukrainian immigrant response to the February Revolution varied according to political outlook. For the rank-and-file Left, the end of tsarism signalled the beginning of the proletarian/peasant revolution. The nationalists, on the other hand, hoped that the revolution would weaken Allied forces to the advantage of Austria/ Germany. Other Ukrainian immigrants believed that the February Revolution would hasten the end of the war, and all camps realized that the revolutionary events in Russia spelled changes for the Ukrainian territories of the former empire—if not complete Ukrainian independence then some sort of democratic autonomy within a federated Russia. The subsequent takeover by the Bolsheviks in October 1917 drew the final line between the Ukrainian immigrant Right and Left, leaving the radical Left as the only segment of the immigrant population optimistic about the new turn of events in Russia.

Bolshevik support within the UFSP had been growing steadily since the UFSP's second convention. After the October Revolution, the "internationalist" leadership of the UFSP (Andrii Dmytryshyn, George Tkatchuk, S. Soroka, among others) proclaimed its alliance with the Bolshevik position and established close ties with the left wing of the SP and the Bolshevik contingency within the Russian Federation of the SP.

Within their own ranks, however, the left wing of the UFSP

was challenged by none other than Evhen Kruk, a wholehearted supporter of Volodymyr Vynnychenko, the writer-revolutionary head of the Ukrainian Social Democratic Labor Party (USDLP). Vynnychenko and his party were playing a leadership role in the *Radao*, a confederation of progressive and socialist organizations that had emerged as the full-fledged government of an independent Ukrainian People's Republic in October 1917. Kruk increasingly underscored the tension between the Bolshevik government in Moscow and an independent Ukraine. In an April 27, 1918 article in *Robitnyk*, he placed the blame for these tensions on the Bolsheviks.

Dozens of letters from readers critical of Kruk poured into *Robitnyk*. More often than not they remained unpublished. The polemics between the social democrats and the Bolsheviks took on the same tone as socialist vs. nationalist arguments. Many regular readers cancelled their subscriptions to *Robitnyk*. Others such as the Cleveland UFSP local instituted official boycotts. The crisis was financial as well as editorial. The UFSP executive committee, in an open letter to its membership published in the May 9, 1918 issue of *Robitnyk*, disclaimed any responsibility for Kruk's editorial views and announced that the problem would be dealt with at a special meeting of the UFSP council, May 13–15, 1918 in Cleveland, Ohio.

On May 16, the day after the UFSP council meeting, *Robitnyk* announced that responsibility for its editorial policy would now belong to an editorial committee of four "comrades." Replacing Kruk were H. Lehun, P. Ladan, D. Mois, and I. Selskyi. The participants at the council meeting also decided to let the membership of the UFSP vote on the future editorial policy of *Robitnyk*. As stated in the report of the council's proceedings:

> *Robitnyk* must be edited with a neutral stance on events in Russia and the Ukraine. Its readers must have an equal voice no matter what their views or if their views oppose the editor. There should be room for all viewpoints—and each author will be responsible for explaining his position, not the editor.

Even though Kruk was retained by the UFSP as an "assistant," he did not return to *Robitnyk*. On May 22, 1918, *Robitnyk* noted that Kruk had become ill and had left Cleveland for Detroit where he planned to rest and recover from his ailments.

Shortly after the reorganization of *Robitnyk*, the UFSP leadership decided to send its top organizers (Dmytryshyn, Tkatchuk and Soroka) into the field to strengthen the left wing's position

among the federations' membership, but *Robitnyk*'s troubles were
not over. Caught up in the red scare and patriotic hysteria that
gripped the U.S. during the remaining years of the war, the
UFSP and *Robitnyk* were added to the federal government's list of
undesirables. On June 1, 1918, the editorial offices of *Robitnyk* were
raided by federal authorities and staff members present at the time
were arrested. Among those jailed were M. Andreichuk, P. Ladan,
V. Savchyn, F. Pshybylskyi, M. Turkevjch, S. Korpan, and an
innocent bystander who happened to be watching the raid through
a window. The day after the raid, one Cleveland newspaper
headlined: "Federal Authorities Close Austrian Newspaper—
Bolshevik Plot Halted by Raid!" The UFSP's Detroit offices were
also raided, a move that resulted in the arrest of George Tkatchuk,
who was detained until the end of the war.

Robitnyk resumed publication on June 10, 1918. In that issue, a
staff writer, I. S. Svitenkyi, published a lengthy article detailing
the anti-German position of *Robitnyk* and the UFSP. Svitenkyi
denied allegations that the UFSP had connections with the Industrial Workers of the World (IWW) and other American radical
groups. Svitenkyi's repudiation of the IWW raised speculation
in the Ukrainian immigrant mainstream press about the "true
intentions of the UFSP and its involvement in American radical
politics." The incident sparked renewed efforts by Ukrainian immigrant nationalist and religious institutions to discredit the Ukrainian immigrant Left. Some members of the UFSP attempted to
unseat the federation's left-wing leadership. Several members of
Detroit's "social patriot" camp (T. Pochynok, T. Lata, Y. Fediushko,
D. Borysko) called for a meeting of all Ukrainian immigrant socialists opposed to bolshevism. Backed by *Narodna Volia*, the group
called for disbanding the UFSP and establishing a new socialist
organization. Organizers were not able to generate enough support for their proposals, and subsequently the national committee
of the SP expelled them.

In July 1918, *Robitnyk* offices were raided again and staff
members arrested. P. Ladan, I. S. Svitenkyi, and V. Savchyn spent
months in jail, since it was impossible for Cleveland's UFSP local
to raise the necessary fifteen thousand dollars in bail. UFSP leadership, with the help of SP officials, instituted a national defense
fund to aid the increasing number of its membership who suddenly found themselves in American jails.

The decision was made to move both *Robitnyk* and its headquarters to New York City. Shortly thereafter, federal authorities
raided the press for a third time while the newspaper's equipment

and documents were in transit. Authorities delayed the train that was carrying *Robitnyk* materials just outside of Cleveland for several days. During the raid, nearly all of the press and UFSP documents on board (some nineteen thousand items!) were destroyed and press equipment damaged. *Robitnyk* did not resume publication until December 12, 1918.

In spite of the U.S. government's intentions to shut down the UFSP, the federation survived and grew. Headquartered in New York City, the UFSP's leadership witnessed a tremendous rise in membership—from nearly two thousand members in 1917 to over six thousand members in 1919. The left wing of the UFSP was in full control. At its third convention in April 1919, the UFSP voted to formally recognize the Third International and to support the American left wing in challenging the right-wing leadership of the SP. In June, representatives of the UFSP met with other federations in New York City in an effort to form a Communist Party of America. Throughout the summer months, *Robitnyk* chronicled the Ukrainian immigrant Left's participation in the reorganization effort, and on September 13, 1919, *Robitnyk* proclaimed that as of September 1, ". . . our Ukrainian Federation became . . . the Ukrainian Federation of the Communist Party in America."

The activities of the Ukrainian immigrant socialists were not confined to the political arena during this period. They created a vital social and cultural life that appealed to many working-class Ukrainians. Their support for fraternal activities within the Ukrainian immigrant community meant close cooperation with the Ukrainian Workingmen's Association during the association's early years (c. 1911–1917). Dedicated to furthering education among the immigrants, the Left founded numerous "Ukrainian Workers Schools" that offered adult education classes in a variety of subjects. Although most of the courses were taught in Ukrainian, socialist locals also organized English-language classes for the immigrant workers. Children's "Saturday schools" were another common feature of this education activity. Other programs for children—games, choirs, athletics—were sonsored by socialist "workers clubs" in conjunction with adult programs.

Most of the larger Ukrainian immigrant communities supported at least one of these "workers clubs." The clubs were advertised in the Ukrainian socialist press as places to relax and enjoy the company of fellow Ukrainians—places where workers could speak their own langauge, read Ukrainian newspapers, and periodicals, or borrow Ukrainian-language books from small club libraries. The "workers club" was often the setting for lectures sponsored by local socialist groups as well as a dance hall, bar, and a place to play cards and billiards. There was even a socialist-run "Ukrainian Workers Restaurant" in New York City (437 East 5th Street), where, as a 1919 advertisement in *Robitnyk* claimed, immigrant workers could get "real" Ukrainian food. Concern for the health of immigrant workers manifested itself in a strong antidrinking campaign. Discussions about the evils of alcohol appeared often in the radical press.

During any given year, the immigrant Left sponsored a host of balls, dances, masquerades, concerts, and dramatic events. A typical evening might consist of a concert (opera solos, declamations, choral performances) followed by a dance. More often than not, these events were also fund-raisers for a wide array of causes—the operating budget of *Robitnyk*, defense funds for jailed Ukrainian socialists, socialist "reading rooms," etc. In addition, many UFSP locals had their own amateur "drama circles" that staged a variety of Ukrainian-language plays, ranging from such traditional musicals as *Natalka Poltavka* to plays with class-conscious themes such as *The American Nobleman* or *Galician Strike*. *Robitnyk* even ran articles offering instructions on how to establish a drama troupe and where to get costumes.[6]

During the summer months, UFSP locals sponsored numerous picnics and "excursions," and daylong trips to a park, the ocean, or a farm. Many of these events were cosponsored with other ethnic socialist organizations, such as the Russian Socialist Federation, the Lithuanian Socialist Federation, or Polish labor groups. The Ukrainian immigrant Left continued to support social/cultural activities well into the 1930s.

Ukrainian Immigrant Left and the Communist Party of America (1919–1950)

The final break with the SP and establishment of an American Communist movement during the summer of 1919 drove the Ukrainian radical Left to new heights of revolutionary fervor and solidarity. So sweeping was the enthusiasm of the newly created Ukrainian Federation of the Communist Party (UFCP) that its leadership was compelled to declare that the victory of the proletariat in America was just around the corner and that "in a few more days, weeks, months not a trace of the old order will be found. . . . A new life is brewing among the Ukrainian immigrants in America. The Ukrainian worker is tearing away all threads to the past and is preparing to build a new world. . . ."[7] The controversies that divided the new movement into two major factions—the Communist Party of America (CP) and the Communist Labor Party (CLP)—were largely avoided as the Ukrainian Federation solidly backed the CP. However, during this period of discord, the minority Bolshevik opposition within the Ukrainian Federation, headed by Evhen Kruk, broke with the federation and joined the rival CLP. Duirng the early years of the 1920s, the Ukrainians within the CLP managed to publish four different newspapers *Komunist* (Communist, 1920), *Nash Shliakh* (Our Path, 1920), *Chervona Zoria* (Red Star, 1921), and *Robitnycha Pravda* (Workers Truth, 1922). All were edited by Kruk. Following unification of the two parties in 1921, Kruk and the majority of his supporters returned to the ranks of the CP.

Just as the Ukrainian immigrant Communists began to solidify their theoretical/organizational base, the entire American Communist movement fell victim to renewed government repression. Hundreds of Ukrainian immigrants, whether radicals or not, were caught up in the infamous raids of 1919 and 1920. *Robitnyk* was shut down by federal authorities in January 1920. Dozens of UFCP members were arrested and detained. Some Ukrainian immigrant radicals were deported, but there appears to be no available data on the actual number of deportees or the countries of destination. The U.S. government crackdown on radical activities came at an inopportune time. The postwar recession, the brutal treatment of striking workers, the xenophobic American reaction to "foreigners," and the loss of prestige suffered by the Ukrainian nationalist camp at Versailles contributed toward amplifying immigrant support for the Communist Left. Even *Svoboda*, the organ of the Ukrainian National Association, for a brief moment in its history seemed prepared to take another look at the Bolshevik platform. Late in 1920, *Svoboda* noted:

> Our newspaper always has been and is now in favor of the principle that the Ukrainian people will win by means of revolution—while counterrevolution will result in defeat— and for that reason we have always supported revolutionary politics in Ukraine. Today, the only true defenders of revolution—defenders with weapons in their hands—are the Bolsheviks and the parties which support them. Then our newspaper says that Ukrainians should join the one revolutionary front of the Bolsheviks.[8]

Despite this new receptiveness, the Ukrainian Communists, like their American counterparts, went underground. UFCP lead-

ership felt that it was better to go underground than to be
"smashed" by the U.S. government's "pogroms" against the Communist movement. Unlike the leadership of the Russian Federation
of the CP, which was totally disbanded by arrests and deportations
during the Palmer period, key members of the UFCP managed to
escape arrest and continue "party" work even though there was
no "official" party. *Robitnyk* was replaced three weeks after its
demise by the *Ukrainskyi Shchodennyi Visti* (the *Ukrainian Daily
News*), which began publication on January 31, 1920.

From its inception until the 1904s, the *Ukrainian Daily News*
remained the voice of Ukrainian immigrant Communists, but, it
never appeared as the official organ of the UFCP. In its first issue,
the *Ukrainian Daily News* proclaimed itself to be simply "a daily
newspaper for Ukrainian working people in the United States."
Not until 1932 did it become affiliated formally with ORDEN, the
Ukrainian Section of the International Worker's Order (IWO). By
the late 1940s, references to that particular affiliation were dropped
from the masthead.

Although the UFCP had "disappeared" in legal terms, the
immigrant Communists continued to be active. During the 1920–
1923 period, they made a decision to focus inward on the Ukrainian immigrant working-class community and its cultural,
educational, and material needs. While perfunctory articles and
editorials covering CP affairs appeared in the *Ukrainian Daily
News* (eulogies in the event of a party official's death, reports
of conventions, reprints of the CP's party platform, etc.), the
overwhelming majority of its pages were devoted to Ukrainian
immigrant concerns, followed by events in Soviet Ukraine and
Russia, international news, and U.S. national news. Whether or
not the CP's move to "Bolshevise" and "Americanize" the party
during the 1920s exacerbated the inward focus of the Ukrainian
immigrant Communists is not clear. The changes instituted by the
CP—the abolition of the foreign-language federations, and the
emphasis on shop and factory nucleii—were simply ignored.

The immigrant Communist leadership was well aware of the
Ukrainian immigrants' growing disaffection with established political organizations (both on the Right and Left), and viewed the
situation as an opportune time for advancing its revolutionary
platform. The Ukrainian immigrant Communists were also concerned about the changes affecting the demographic character
of the Ukrainian immigrant community. Children of immigrant
workers were growing up in a capitalist country that was not
concerned about their welfare or their cultural heritage, and the

Left perceived the situation as critical if their movement had any future at all.

These sentiments were the driving force behind the Left's decision in 1923 to call for a "Ukrainian Labor Congress" and to invite all Ukrainian immigrant organizations to participate. The Congress was advertised as follows:

> The Ukrainian Labor Congress does not pretend to know "high politics." It is not intended in the building of national homes or in the collection of hundreds and thousands of dollars for projects of a similar nature. The Congress presents for itself a humble, straight and clear task: to analyze all of the shortcomings of our present reality, to determine all of our most dire needs, cultural—educational as well as political—economic, and to find a way to satisfy them. . . .
>
> Here we are being exploited not only by the American nobleman ["pan"] but also by our own nobility in the role of priests and so-called intellectuals.
>
> We came here seeking a better life and the truth and they have followed us in order to keep us in ignorance, to live off of our bloody labor, and to make us faithful servants of the American nobleman, just as in the past they kept us faithful servants of the Austrian and Russian noblemen. . . .
>
> "Give, give, give" that is all we have heard from our noblemen during the past few years. Let's say enough to all of this, enough of being taken care of by people without a conscience. . . . We must take our destiny into our own calloused hands. . . .[9]

The Left's proposal received an overwhelmingly positive response from the immigrant community, but nationalist organizations declined to attend after first agreeing to do so. When the congress convened in New York City on April 23, 1924, there were 191 delegates representing an array of organizations from Pennsylvania, New York, New Jersey, Ohio, Illinois, Wisconsin, Connecticut, Rhode Island, Massachusetts, and Michigan. The Ukrainian immigrant Communists played a critical leadership role at the congress, and the Left was instrumental in convincing the delegates to establish the Union of Ukrainian Workers' Organizations (SURO). The leadership of the Union consisted of a 25-member national committee, which subsequently elected a seven-person executive committee. Many familiar names from the immigrant Left were associated with the Union's leadership including Dmytryshyn, Borysko, Tarnovsky, Tkatchuk, and Ladan.

The resolutions adopted by the delegates called for establishing courses for illiterates, special classes for children and youth, a publishing house, teacher-preparatory courses, choirs, drama troupes, and dance ensembles. The congress pledged full support for the Ukrainian Soviet Republic and the Bolshevik government of Ukraine, and it called for unification of all Ukrainian lands under the Soviet Ukrainian banner. The congress also pledged full support of the American working class in its fight aagainst capitalist exploitation.

From 1924 until the mid-1930s, the Ukrainian immigrant Communists were active participants in SURO. The organization grew from thirteen hundred adult members in 1926 to nearly eleven thousand adult, youth, and child members in 112 branches. By its fifth convention, which took place in New York City on January 24–26, 1932, SURO operations included the sponsorship of 12 Young Pioneer branches (with some three hundred children), 36 cultural schools, 64 reading rooms, 35 drama groups, 17 choirs, and 12 bandura orchestras, all of which were housed in 23 separate "Workers' Homes," either owned or rented by SURO.

The Ukrainian immigrant Communist movement created *Ukrainska Sektsia Mishnarodnoho Ordenu* (ORDEN) as the Ukrainian Section of the International Workers Order (IWO). Membership grew at a rapid pace, from twelve hundred members in 1932 to fifteen thousand adult and child members in 1938. Similar to the other foreign-language sections of the IWO, ORDEN sponsored lectures, classes, summer camps for adults and children, and a variety of social events. ORDEN published its own almanac and a journal titled *The New Order*. Political funds were also organized, and with the outbreak of the Spanish Civil War, ORDEN, in cooperation with SURO, raised one thousand dollars for the American Lincoln Brigade fighting on the side of the Loyalists. A number of SURO members joined the Lincoln Brigade during this period, and at least two Ukrainians—Maichael Zayats of Brooklyn and Dmytro Semeniuk of Philadelphia—were killed in action.[10]

During the Popular Front movement of the 1930s, SURO and ORDEN helped launch a Ukrainian National Front at a congress convened in New York City on September 5–6, 1936. A total of 353 delegates, representing some twenty thousand Ukrainian-Americans participated. Even a few delegates from the Ukrainian National Association, the Ukrainian Workingmen's Association, and the Greek Catholic Union (a Carpatho-Rusyn fraternal organization) came to the congress.

Throughout the late 1920s and 1930s, the Ukrainian immigrant Communists displayed undaunted devotion to the Soviet Union, the Ukrainian Soviet Republic and the dictates of the Comintern. The accomplishments of Soviet Ukraine were emphasized in nearly every issue of the *Ukrainian Daily News*, and Ukrainian immigrants in America were encouraged to support their Soviet homeland both ideologically and materially. Although there are no recorded statistics on the number of Ukrainians who returned to Soviet Ukraine during this period, there is evidence that Ukrainian-Americans participated in technical training courses that were designed to provide skilled labor for Ukrainian Soviet factories and agricultural collectives. The immigrant Communists were equally supportive of the Communist effort in Galicia, particularly the Communist Party of Western Ukraine (KPZU), until the Comintern's dissolution of the KPZU in 1938.

In many respects, the Ukrainian immigrant Communists' unqualified commitment to the Soviet Republic and the Soviet political machine contributed to their declining influence in the immigrant community in the 1940s. The Ukrainian Communists never quite recovered from the loss of face during the 1932–1933 famine in the UKSSR and the political uncertainty following the Hitler-Stalin Pact. The Moscow Trials and the eventual repudiation of the Stalin years at the Twentieth Soviet Communist Party Congress in 1956 would further undermine the movement.

Ukrainian Left and Ukrainian Community and Organizational Life: A Summary

For many Ukrainian immigrants, the Left provided the only secular political alternative that addressed both their economic and cultural needs. To what extent the Left successfully met these needs is another question; nevertheless, Ukrainian immigrant radicals were instrumental in initiating programmatic changes within existing immigrant institutions—changes that offered relief in the workplace yet preserved ethnic solidarity. The Ukrainian immigrant Left's ties with the immigrant community were fluid. During periods when the immigrant community was particularly receptive to the Left, such as the post-WWI years and the 1930s, Ukrainian immigrant radicals often emerged in leadership roles within existing fraternal, cultural, and, on occasion, political institutions.

However the published research on Ukrainian immigration to date either ignores or downplays the role of the Ukrainian Left, making it difficult to gauge the extent of the Left's involvement in immigrant-based institutions beyond a few key personalities and what impact radical political ideology had in shaping the goals and priorities of Ukrainian immigrant secular organizations.

The Ukrainian immigrant Left's involvement with organizing trade unions among Ukrainian immigrant workers demonstrated a commitment for improving the economic well-being of the Ukrainian-American working class, whose economic interests were generally ignored by religious institutions and the more conservative fraternal orders. Although the Ukrainian Catholic Church and the Orthodox Church supported the labor movement duirng the early 1900s (led by the so-called "radical priests"), their position shifted dramatically when the church leadership began to perceive an organized labor force as a threat to both faith and church participation. These sentiments extended to religious-based fraternals such as the Greek Catholic Union, Providence (*Providinnia*) Association of Ukrainian Catholics and the Ukrainian National Aid Society. Religious institutional alliances along with the entrepreneurial/ nationalist elements of the Ukrainian community contributed to the church's anti-union stance. Thus, the immigrant Left was able to take the lead in unionization efforts.

By the 1920s, there were "Ukrainian" branches among a host of trade unions, including the Garment Workers' Union, Boot and Shoe Workers' Union, Fur Workers Union, United Mine Workers, and others. The UFSP was heavily involved in organizing restaurant workers (the majority of whom were women) in the New York City area (c. 1919). The Left press published announcements, reports, and articles related to Ukrainian immigrant labor organizations from 1911 to well into the 1940s. Both *Robitnyk* and the *Ukrainian Daily News* ran regular columns ("On the Labor Front" or "From the Labor Movement in America") that focused on trade union activities, strikes, or Ukrainian immigrant union members.

The Ukrainian socialists formed a close alliance with the Ukrainian Workingmen's Association (UWA) from its founding in 1911 until 1917–1918 when the fraternal became an outspoken critic of bolshevism. The relationship was renewed to a certain extent with the Workingmen's Association's participation in SURO during the late 1920s and 1930s. But the alliance with SURO was not formal. It appears that individual branches of the UWA joined SURO at the membership's discretion, rather than with a full organizational endorsement of SURO activities. The same relationship existed between the UWA and ORDEN.

The early years of the UWA provide the best example of the Ukrainian Left's involvement with a secular immigrant organization in the interest of the Ukrainian immigrant working class. Although Ukrainian socialists did not hold executive positions within the UWA, they dominated many of its branches. The branches might be named after saints, Ukrainian poets, or Karl Marx! The pages of *Narodna Volia* offered a curious mixture of church-related news, labor news, socialist tracts, and polemical correspondence among various Ukrainian socialist factions. In 1915, when the UFSP was formally admitted to the SP, *Narodna Volia* encouraged its readers to join local branches of the UFSP or establish new locals if one did not exist in their community.

The rallying cause that would, on occasion, bring Ukrainian socialists, labor groups, fraternals, and other secular organizations together was the "cause of Ukraine"—its struggle against foreign rule and quest for national self-determination. Although the Ukrainian Left refused to participate in nationalist-sponsored organizations and fund-raisers (the only exception being the Federation of Ukrainians in the United States, which received support from the social patriots within the ranks of the Left), the Left did support a variety of "nonpartisan" causes from as early as 1906 through the 1930s.

By far the most successful relationship between the Ukrainian immigrant Left and immigrant-based organizations was developed under the auspices of SURO. The roster of delegates that participated in SURO conventions throughout the late 1920s and 1930s represented nearly all segments of the Ukrainian immigrant community, except for the religious/nationalist elements. During these years, SURO's "Popular Front" activities amplified Ukrainian immigrants' concerns for the Ukrainian homeland in the Front's attack against fascism. What is amazing is how quickly the tide turned in the late 1930s and 1940s when the Ukrainian immigrant community once again embraced nationalism, and nationalist-inspired organizations experienced a tremendous growth in support. The war revived the Ukrainian immigrant community's long-held aspirations for Ukrainian independence, and groups representing monarchial, nationalist, and republican political persuasions were founded during the war years. Nationalist sentiments came to dominate Ukrainian immigrant organizational life thereafter.

Notes

1. Vasyl Halich, *Ukrainians in the United States* (Chicago: University of Chicago Press, 1937). See generally chapters 1 and 2.

2. Julian Bachynsky, *Ukrainska Immigratssia v Zyednenych Derzhavach Ameryky* (Lvov, 1914) contains vivid descriptions of Ukrainian immigrant women.

3. Any systematic account of Ukrainian immigrant radicalism in the U.S. is hampered by the lack of available resources. Primary and even secondary resources are scarce. The organizational records of the Ukrainian sections of the Socialist Party and Communist Party have not survived. The only secondary source that focuses exclusively on the Ukrainian Left is written in Ukrainian, Mykhailo Nastisivskyi, *Ukrainska Imigratsia v Spoluchenykh Derzhavakh* (New York: Union of Ukrainian Labor Organizations, 1934). This invaluable work is written by an "insider" and resembles a memoir more than a historical chronology. A few other Ukrainian-language works offer brief glimpses of radicalism with the context of the general development of the immigrant community. The Ukrainian immigrant Left is discussed briefly in an unpublished Ph.D. dissertation, Myron Kuropas, "The Making of the Ukrainian American, 1884–1939—a Study in Ethno-National Education," University of Chicago, 1974. No other English language research has been published to date. I have also been able to read copies of *Robitnyk* (1917–1919) which were available at the Immigration History Research Center, University of Minnesota.

4. Quoted in Nastisivskyi, *Ukgrainska Imigratssia*, 75–76.

5. Ibid., 78.

6. P. Beztalanyi, *Robitnyk*, March 17, 1919, 2:4, for example, deals with SP theater groups.

7. *Robitnyk*, September 16, 1919.

8. *Svoboda*, September 9, 1918.

9. Protocol of the 1926 Convention of the Union of Ukrainian Labor Organizations, New York, 1927.

10. "Ukrainskyi Biytsi v Ispaniyi (Ukrainian Fighters in Spain)," *Narodni Kalendar na Rik 1939*, ORDEN, 1940, 115–16.

SEVEN

Greek-American Radicalism: The Twentieth Century

Dan Georgakas

Greek immigration to the United States is primarily a twentieth century phenomenon. As late as 1880, there were only five hundred Greek immigrants in America. Some eighteen thousand would arrive in the last two decades of the nineteeth century, fully sixteen thousand arriving in the 1890s. The numbers swelled tenfold to 167,000 in the first decade of the new century and would total approximately half a million by 1940, the cultural nucleus of contemporary Greek America.

The initial wave of Greek immigration was overwhelmingly male, reaching over 95 percent in the western states, and overwhelmingly unskilled and uneducated. Contrary to early historians who depicted the newcomers as apolitical, the immigrants were immediately drawn into a variety of reform and revolutionary movements.[1] Greeks were enrolled in the Industrial Workers of the World (IWW) less than a year after its formation in 1905 and in 1919 were among the founders of what became the Communist Party-USA (CP). In addition, the Socialist Labor Party (SLP) had made sufficient headway with Greek workers in New England that in 1916 it was able to launch a Greek-language newspaper, *Organosis* (The Organization).

Much of the history of the Greek working class, which was the dominant component of Greek America through to the 1940s, has been lost. One factor blurring this record is that Greeks were usually such a small minority in any given location that non-Greek organizers rarely thought them important enough to single out for specific agitation. Labor historians have generally followed suit by lumping Greeks into the "and other immigrants" category. With a few notable exceptions, ethnic historians have virtually ignored the Greek working class to concentrate on other aspects of Greek America.[2] The standard ethnic history, Theodore Saloutos's *The Greeks in the United States*, does not devote even one chapter to labor and the usually dependable Saloutos incorrectly and irresponsibly declares, "Marxism made no appreciable progress among Greek Americans. The rank and file were bitterly opposed to it and could be counted upon to fight it with all the power at their command."[3] Saloutos's view was largely accepted as a given until the 1980s. During that decade a new wave of younger historians began to look more closely at primary documents, sought out period materials that had been in private hands, and took oral histories. Coupled with in-depth work done on the Intermountain West, a previously hidden history of Greek-American radicalism began to emerge.[4] During the first decades of the century, that radicalism was often associated with the IWW, and from World War I through the 1950s, with the CP. In both periods the most radical layer of Greek-American society was its working class.

The Industrial Workers of the World

Early Greek immigrants often congregated in the industrial towns of New England. By 1913 the third highest concentration of Greeks in the United States after New York and Chicago was in Lowell, Massachusetts, where Greeks also made up the third largest ethnic group working in the textile mills. Greek workers had organized an independent labor union, partly to overcome the hostility of earlier immigrant groups. The union's main organizational focus, however, was on employers. From 1900 on, there was rarely a year in which Greeks did not strike at one or another Lowell mill.

In the wake of its great victory at Lawrence, Massachusetts in 1912, the IWW organized strikes throughout New England. Lowell shaped up as an easy follow-up victory if the Greeks agreed to participate. Elizabeth Gurley Flynn was sent by the IWW to address the Greek workers. Years later she wrote of her warm reception and recounted that the Greeks became "the backbone" of a successful strike.[5] Months before, one of the IWW marching songs in neighboring Lawrence had celebrated the enthusiastic participation of Greek workers.[6]

A question that has long hung over these IWW successes is how much enduring impact they left. For Greeks there is circumstantial evidence that the IWW memory persisted for a considerable time. Demosthenes Nicas, an IWW who went on to become an organizer for the CP and the Congress of Industrial Organizations (CIO) created Greek worker clubs throughout New England in the early 1930s.[7] Many of these clubs were in just those centers where the IWW had been most active. The same pattern is found among Greek organizers for the Fur and Leather Workers in the late 1930s and in local campaigns by workers not nationally affiliated. One can also argue that the IWW past contributed to the activist liberal tradition that produced a string of post-World War II liberal Democrats: Governor Michael Dukakis, Senator Paul Tsongas, CIO Massachusetts State Director James Ellis, Congressman Nicholas Mavroulis, and numerous lesser known local officials and trade unionists.

Massachusetts organizers often tried to mobilize the entire community in the old IWW style. In 1933 during a strike of mostly Greek workers at Peabody, 220 Greek merchants and civic leaders were persuaded to issue a public letter backing the strikers and labeling strike-breaking "the most inhumane practice in the civilized world."[8] The class source of this statement is remarkable enough, but all the more so as the owner of the struck shoe factory was Greek.

Institutions central to the lives of Greek male workers were the *kafenia* (coffeehouses). These often had political or regional constituencies that avidly read and discussed political literature. Primarily, however, *kafenia* were places where males gathered to get the news of the day, play cards, receive mail, hire translators, and consult letter writers. *Kafenia* also occasionally sponsored shadow puppet shows (the Greek *karagiozis*), lectures, and musical evenings. During the first decades of mass immigration, the *kafenia* rather than the churches served as de facto community living rooms. This began to change with the steady arrival of Greek women, but the *kafenia* remained important centers as late as the 1940s.

Labor radical John Poulos has provided an insider's view of the *kafenia* ambiance of the early 1930s.[9] His father, a vice president of an antimonarchist organization, owned a *kafenion* in Lynn,

Massachusetts. Poulos found that political recruitment was usually somewhat secretive and one-on-one. The process generated structures more akin to affinity groups than formal parties. Political discussion was incessant with individuals recounting personal experiences within ideologial or ethnic frameworks. Among the Lynn *kafenion* regulars were former members of the SLP and IWW. Militant supporters of Sacco and Vanzetti made a particularly strong impression on John Poulos and his younger brother Constantine. Mostly as a result of this political exposure, the brothers devoured all the radical literature they could get hold of. Both soon became prominent community activists. We can assume that other Greek organizers who have not left a public record of their ideological formation had similar political baptisms in other *kafenia*.

John Poulos's first major political activity was to organize some two thousand predominantly Greek workers into a food workers local of the American Federation of Labor (AFL). In due course he led his group into the newly formed CIO, then in its most radical phase. Poulos was a delegate at the founding convention of the CIO and was named CIO director of the North Shore area, where he oversaw the organizing of tens of thousands of workers in cities such as Lynn, Peabody, and Salem. Poulos was also drawn into the Trotskyist movement and at various times was a member of the Communist League of America, the Socialist Workers Party, and the Workers Party. While this orientation was kept discreet from his direct CIO work, his radical views were not concealed and had no adverse effect on his influence with rank-and-file workers.

Constantine Poulos became editor of the monthly magazine of the American Hellenic Educational Progressive Association (AHEPA), the largest and most influential Greek fraternal order. During his editorship the magazine had a strong leftist tilt most obvious in its strong antifascism and defense of the foreign-born.[10] With the onset of World War II, Poulos became a correspondent for the Overseas News Agency, and in 1943 he became the first American reporter to enter occupied Greece. He immediatley established cordial contacts with the Communist-led guerilas of the National Liberation Front and his upbeat reports were carried in major American dailies, *The Nation*, and the Greek-language press. At war's end even though Poulos did not even consider himself a Marxist, he was expelled from Greece for "pro-Communist" sympathies. He suffered a period of graylisting and ended up as owner/editor of a small-town newspaper where his work eventually earned him a Pulitzer Prize.[11]

At the same time that the IWW was leading strikes of textile workers in Massachusetts, it was deeply involved in strikes by food workers employed by New York City hotels. Formal IWW units and unions with IWW stalwarts continued to be at the core of various food worker locals well into the 1920s. Successor AFL and CIO locals would be noted for their radical ideology and direct action tactics. Hundreds of Greek workers were involved in these organizations and many actions took place in the immediate vicinity of the largest Greek community in Manhattan. Activists like Haris Claron who organized food workers at Columbia University for one of these unions in the late teens were still active forty years later in the anti-junta movement of 1967–1974. Claron and other militants also established the Spartakos Workers Club, which was destined to play a major role in the Communist movement launched in 1919. The Spartakos Club was located in the west twenties, which put it adjacent to the fur district where some two thousand Greeks were employed, the flower district, which was dominated by Greeks, and the vibrant Greek taverna scene of Eighth Avenue.[12]

Even more Greek workers were exposed to IWW influence in the West. By 1910 there were some forty thousand Greek males in that region working as miners, railroad workers, lumbermen, and construction workers. Greeks were peripherally involved in numerous IWW actions, but the best documented interaction involved a 1912 saw mill strike in Grays Harbor, Washington.[13] Greeks were the largest ethnic component of the striking workforce and the action was known locally as the IWW-Greek strike. Physical violence by the police was used against the strikers and the Greek section was physically cleared as a prelude to the forced expulsion of all Greeks by ship and train. This civic deportation occurred at a time when Greeks would often go hundreds of miles to support strikers from the same villages or region in the homeland. When the nearly two hundred Greek workers expelled from Grays Harbor scattered throughout the region, their experiences were rehashed at every *kafenion*, whether seen as being primarily an ethnic or class insult. The Greek Consul, then residing in Tacoma, was outraged and registered a formal complaint.[14]

That same year Greek workers participated in a strike led by the radical Western Federation of Miners (WFM) at Bingham, a copper-mining suburb of Salt Lake City, Utah. Elimination of the local Greek labor boss, the most powerful in the West, was a prime ethnic issue, but the Greek miners were fully aware of the broader class questions involved. Well before the strike, the WFM constitution and WFM political literature had been printed in Greek

. translations. When would-be scabs escorted by National Guards-men and company police tried to enter the mine, they were fired upon by workers. Leading this armed defense were Cretans who had recently waged guerilla war against the Ottoman Turks on their home island. They seized the high ground around the mine entrances and could not be dislodged. Even when the company agreed to dismiss the Greek labor boss, the Greeks voted to continue the strike. The final settlement did not include recognition of the WFM, but labor bosses were eliminated, wages raised, and safety standards established. The Greeks had worked closely with Italian and Japanese costrikers, and their reputation as steadfast militants had been enhanced.[15]

Historians have debated how much of the Greek motivation at Bingham was a matter of *philotimo* (honor) and how much reflected class-consciousness.[16] All agree that the ten thousand Greeks in the Intermountain West had been at sites heavily propagandized by the IWW, WFM, and other radical organizations. Some Greeks lived in towns run by Socialist Party (SP) administrations and one Seattle carpenter is on record as judging the Socialists as far too conservative.[17] The one Greek organizer for the IWW known by name is Louis Theos (Theodropoulos) who was in Utah and Colorado organizing clandestinely in 1912. The undercover approach was typical of many IWW organizers at the time and blended with the Greek tradition of secret revolutionary societies of the kind that had led the national liberation movement against the Turkish empire. Despite these traditions, Greek names are found in IWW and WFM branches at Bingham as early as 1906.[18]

Less direct indication of IWW influence is the rhetoric used by Greeks in some of their public letters. One Colorado newspaper quoted a Greek worker as saying, "The miners union is greater than the U.S. government and when the union gives the word to fire upon soldiers, we will obey that order."[19] IWW slogans such as "An injury to one is an injury to all" easily fused with the concept of *philotimo*. Public letters by Greeks also contain a greeting translatable as "fellow worker," the IWW equivalent of comrade. Finally, the idea of an industrial army to address ethnic and class injustices was certainly congenial to men with a recent revolutionary tradition and a cultural ethic in which ownership of a gun was considered a sign of national and individual independence.

In the year following the gunplay at Bingham, Greeks were involved in the Ludlow strike in Colorado. The leader of the Greeks was Louis Tikas. His immediate support group was composed of some fifty Cretans, some of whom were Bingham veterans. Historian Zeese Papanikolas has spent years trying to establish Tikas' background and ideology.[20] Amid the many gray areas that have emerged from that analysis are many radical elements.

Before becoming an organizer for the United Mine Workers (UMW), the job which took him to Ludlow, Tikas owned a *kafenion* in Denver, Colorado that was directly across the street from the IWW hall. The *kafenion* served a Greek working-class district that was largely confluent with the major area of IWW activity. Given the Greek passion for politics and the IWW gift for publicity, it is impossible that Greeks passing through Denver would not have been exposed to the IWW perspective. At one point Tikas tried to join the Denver Police Department and was rejected on the grounds that he was an IWW.[21] Whether true or false, that such an assertion seemed credible to the Denver police says a great deal about Tikas' political reputation.

Although *philotimo* clearly motivated Tikas and other Greeks during the Ludlow strike, they marched with celebrated radicals such as Mother Jones and had cordial relations with other ethnic groups. In fact, Tikas was not killed defending Greeks but trying to bring non-Greek families to safety during a machine gun assault by the company on the strikers' colony. Even more than Grays Harbor and Bingham, the martyrdom of Tikas and the near civil war over what became known as the Ludlow Massacre surely stirred Greek miners and *kafenia* regulars throughout the West.

Thirteen years after the Ludlow Massacre, Colorado miners again felt strong enough to strike. The union officially involved was the same UMW that had employed Tikas as an organizer, but the actual strike leaders were IWWs, a fact featured in one newspaper headline after another. A score of strikers were killed during a long struggle that saw the Rockefeller interests using machine guns and aircraft against the strikers. In the southern coal fields, the area where Tikas had been active, Greeks were among those killed, were frequently cited as leading agitators in local newspaper stories, and composed the majority of those involved in an IWW-organized lawsuit against the company. This considerable Greek involvement in the 1928 strike is determined almost exclusively from distinctly Greek names on records and thus constitutes a minimal record.[22]

Details about such events and their impact on the permanent Greek communities that eventually formed have remained blurred. Few of the participants were ever interviewed by professional scholars, and many spent their declining years in the rundown areas of industrial centers, a phenomenon that may account for their frequent appearance in the hardboiled school of fiction associated with Dashiell Hammett. The Greektown bachelors were not at ease with the increasingly church-oriented Greek communities and do not appear in most local parish histories.[23] Others in the first generation married non-Greeks and produced offspring without significant Greek identity. Only occasionally are flashes of the old passions visible. In Salt Lake City, a plaque before the major Greek Orthodox Church lists all the local Greeks killed in foreign wars or mine disasters, a striking and unusual coupling of national and class pride. By and large, however, the tens of thousands of Greek workers who labored west of the Mississippi make up a lost epoch of Greek-American history.[24]

An insight on how the IWW ambiance affected individual Greeks in this region is offered by L. S. Stavrianos. Best known as a historian of the Balkans, Stavrianos worked at the Greek desk of the Office of Strategic Services (OSS) during World War II. In 1952 he published *Greece: American Dilemma and Opportunity*, a landmark critique of American policy in Greece, which the government tried to suppress.[25] In the 1930s, while still a young man, Stavrianos had spent his summer vacation in Vancouver, Canada. He worked in a dingy Greek diner in a Skid Row area adjacent to Vancouver's version of Hyde Park. IWWs who gave speeches in the park frequented the diner for coffee and doughnuts. In a book summing up his life's learning, he writes that he felt "overwhelmed by what they told me."[26] Their analysis of the world did not ultimately satisfy him, but they spurred him to ask questions and to challenge conventional solutions: "The IWWs left an imprint far deeper and more enduring than anything I ever learned in a classroom or textbooks."[27]

The cultural arc linking the antimonarchist *kafenion* in Lynn, the Spartakos Workers Club in New York City, the Tikas *kafenion* in Denver, and the Skid Row diner in Vancouver is not the classic orbit of ideological agitation. It does not indicate that IWW anarcho-syndicalism prevailed among Greeks in some subterranean or homeopathic manner. But it does suggest that some IWW views and attitudes became woven into the Greek ethnic tapestry to become part of ongoing labor, intellectual, and community traditions.

The Communist Party

In 1919 John Reed, the celebrated author of *Ten Days that Shook the World*, led a left-wing split from the Socialist Party (SP) to launch an American Communist party on the Russian model. Four other communist parties were begun at approximately the same time. A decade of bitter infighting would ensue before the groups coalesced into what became the Communist Party-USA (CP). Although there had been no distinct Greek-language federation in the SP, Greek radicals rallied to Reed's organization. New York's Spartakos Club soon became the organizing hub of what emerged as the largest and most important radical current in Greek America.

The revolutionary debates among Greeks were as intense as elsewhere in the American movement. The IWW, badly mauled by persecution during World War I and destined to implode at its 1924 convention, issued three of its standard pamphlets in Greek for the first time: "The Revolutionary IWW," "The Economic Interpretation of the Job," and "What is the IWW?"[28] These indicate a Greek presence at the Chicago IWW printing headquarters and some expectations of recruitable Greek workers. Another presentation of socialist alternatives originating in Chicago was George Katsiolis' *The Crimes of Civilization*, a Greek-language book that appears to have been self-published.[29]

Joining in the debate was the SLP, which published at least ten pamphlets in Greek from 1917–1933 while continuing to irregularly publish the newspaper *Organosis*.[30] All but one of the pamphlets were written by SLP founder Daniel De Leon or his successor Arnold Petersen. The exception was a 1920 pamphlet titled "The Condition of Greek Worker Federations in America."[31] The addresses on the pamphlets for contacting Greek-speaking SLPers included a post office box office in Cincinnati, Ohio, and street addresses in Detroit, Michigan, and Brooklyn, New York. The Brooklyn address was on Atlantic Avenue in a district heavily populated by Greek waiters,[32] and the Detroit address was on a major artery in that city's growing Greektown. The cover matter urged Greek workers to adhere to the Detroit IWW, a SLP organization that had broken from the formal IWW in 1908. The SLP pamphlets were usually printed at party headquarters in New York, but some were made by Greek printers such as the D. C. Divry firm in New York—famous for its Greek dictionaries and school books. The 1917 translation of De Leon's "Reform and Revolution" apparently sold well enough to be reprinted with new typesetting in 1930.

The fledgling Communists had two major advantages over their IWW and SLP rivals. They were associated with a successful workers revolution and they had working relations with a homeland party that provided them with agitational literature. Among the imported titles were standard revolutionary texts such as a Greek translation of Lenin's *State and Revolution* and Greek-oriented titles such as I. K. Kordatou's *An Economic Interpretation of the Greek Revolution of 1821*.[33] This literature, usually printed in Athens, bore a stamp with an American address and directions on how to order more literature. Such links with the homeland party became a permanent feature of the Greek-language Communist movement in America.

Easily the most effective outreach developed by the Greek Communists was a succession of newspapers published daily, twice a week, and weekly at various times: *Phone tou Ergatou* (Voice of the Worker), 1918–1923; *Empros* (Forward), 1923–1938; *Eleftheria* (Freedom), 1938–1941; and *Helleno-Amerikaniko Vema (Greek-American Tribune)*, 1941–1959.[34] The earlier titles had a revolutionary tone and featured hammer and sickle insignias on their mastheads; the later two reflected the less abrasive style and rhetoric of the Popular Front. From the mid-1920s through the late 1930s, the papers carried reports from the USSR written by Greek Communists living in Rostov. Damon Eristeas (D. Kanonidis), a poet and author, was particularly active in this regard.[35] Peak circulation of the Communist press came in the 1940s when *Vema* would hit ten thousand for special events and ran 8,500 regularly. This compares decently with the claimed thirteen thousand circulation of the liberal *Keryx* (The Herald) or the sixteen thousand claimed circulation of the conservative *Atlantis*, the two national Greek-language dailies.[36] Because *Vema* had multiple readers at the workers clubs that served as its distribution centers, its impact on Greek-speaking workers was comparable to that of the dailies, which went to individual homes and institutions.

From the onset the Greek Communists directed their energies almost exclusively to the working class. The region of greatest agitation was bound on the east and west by New York and Chicago and on the north and south by Boston and Baltimore. Rather than trying to recruit the workers in this industrial belt directly into the CP, the organizers were satisfied if their contacts accepted party literature and frequented a workers club. Serving as political *kafenia*, these workers clubs were utilized to distribute CP literature, promote special campaigns, and generally serve as a conduit to community activists.

A breakthrough organizing success for the Communists came in the mid-1920s. The Fur Workers Union had recently come under the leadership of Communist Ben Gold who understood the mainly Jewish union would not be secure until some three hundred Greek-owned fur shops employing some fifteen hundred Greek workers at any given moment were also organized. The Greek workers had never been approached by fur union organizers who spoke Greek. Gold addressed this problem by hiring four organizers from the ranks of the Spartakos Club. By August 1925, hundreds of Greeks were attending organizational meetings. That October a ten-day strike organized all of the Greek shops and brought Greek wages and conditions up to the higher standards of the unionized shops.[37]

For the next decade the Fur Workers Union, perhaps the most radical union in New York City, would be under constant attack from gangsters hired by the employers and anticommunist politicians. The conservative Greek press, shamelessly anti-Semitic at times, took Greek workers to task for believing they had more in common with Jewish workers than Greek bosses. Workers were further berated for belonging to a union that gave full rights to blacks. Much was made of the fact that hundreds of Greek women worked in these shops. Such attacks had little effect. The Greek furriers were known as extremely loyal and militant trade unionists. The New York Greek unit grew strong enough to support organizing drives in other states. Tom Galanos, a Greek organizer known for his militancy, became the major leader of all the furriers in Newark, New Jersey. John Vafiades, leader of the New York furriers, took part in an organizing drive in Massachusetts aimed at leather workers, which culminated in an expanded Fur and Leather Workers Union. The general success of the union was extraordinary. By 1940 it had achieved one hundred percent representation in fur and leather.

The fur workers were the bedrock of the Greek Left. They supported a whole plethora of activities associated with progressive trade unions: summer camps, theatrical nights, musical events, lectures, and the like. The fur workers were also key to the success of the Communist press and played a role in creating the Greek lodges of the International Worker's Order, which hit a peak of thirty Greek lodges with some fifteen hundred members.[38]

Given the proportionally small number of Greeks in any given work site, Greek Communists usually worked in a multi-ethnic context. This is evidenced in the work of Demosthenes Nicas who was a CIO organizer in a belt roughly extending from Akron, Ohio to Pittsburgh, Pennsylvania. Nicas used *kafenia* patrons and *Empros* subscribers to make contacts in each new town. When full-blown strikes were on the agenda, every effort was made to engage the

Greek community as a whole. During a key organizing drive in Akron, for example, both Greek churches were open to the strikers for organizational needs and both parishes were supportive in other ways as well. Panayotis Kajalias, one of the Akron leaders was a Communist whose roots went back to the SLP. Nicas was often in contact with such persons as he engaged in the broad task of building the CIO.[39]

Other radicals had both deeper and lesser contacts with the Greek community per se. Charles Rivers, a Greek Communist who worked as an organizer for the radical United Electrical Workers (UE) in campaigns that organized over a hundred thousand workers, had only nominal Greek contacts until his later involvement with the anti-junta movement.[40] In contrast, writer Theano Papazoglou-Margaris, who worked closely with Nicas in the late 1930s to keep the Communist workers club in Chicago afloat, became a beloved weekly columnist for *Keryx*. Papazoglou-Margaris who wrote in Greek and often featured Greek women in her writing also has the distinction of being the first Greek woman to contribute to a Communist newspaper, the pioneering *Phone tou Ergatou*.[41]

Individual biographies of some representative 1930s Communists and sympathizers illustrate their geographic spread and community impact. In 1930 food worker Steve Katovis was killed by New York City police during a strike. The circumstances were such that Katovis was mourned as a labor martyr. More than twenty thousand workers of all ethnic backgrounds viewed his corpse at a workers center on Union Square and some fifty thousand demonstrated in his name. A 31-page biography issued shortly thereafter provides insights into the life of a rank-and-file Communist militant.[42] Before joining the CP, the Greek-born Katovis had been an IWW who worked on both coasts as a taxi driver, mechanic, and dock worker. As part of his CP duties, he went to Jersey City every other week to organize restaurant workers with his brother. He also belonged to an informal group of six Greeks who attended night school to study engineering. Once trained, they planned to go to the USSR "to build socialism."

A second labor martyr of that era was Nick Bordoise (Condorakis). He and another worker were killed by police during the famous San Francisco General Strike of 1934. Their joint funeral was turned into a major labor parade led by Harry Bridges, the legendary longshoremen's leader. Three trucks were needed to carry the mourning flowers as thousands of longshoremen marched in the funeral cortege and thousands more lined the streets. Scores of Greek relatives and friends, singing the "International" with raised fists clenched in the communist salute, marched directly behind Bordoise's coffin. Sam Darcy, the local Communist leader, eulogized Bordoise, calling him one of the party's most active members. Commentators have further noted that Bordoise's wife and brother were also militants.[43]

The activities of other Greek radicals in the Bay Area indicate that Bordoise did not operate in an ethnic vacuum. In 1933 poet Takis George published a collection of his work which contained poems praising Lenin, Stalin, the prototypical worker, and a USSR heralded as "the mecca of humankind."[44] George had previously published *Modern Greek Proverbs* as one of the Haldeman-Julius Blue Book series of socialist-inclined literature. What is most significant about George is that he was not only a respected member of the Greek community but that he was a teacher at the local Greek school. Among his students were Jim Dilles who later wrote *The Good Thief*,[45] one of the few proletarian novels by a Greek-American author, and Tom Nicolopulos, who became a labor mediator identified with progressive causes. In his later years Nicolopulos contributed regularly to the biweekly newspaper *Hellenic Journal*. His journalism recounted the 1930s in South City, a smokestack suburb some ten miles south of San Francisco. Nicolopulos deals at length with the radical literature familiar to the hundred or so Greeks living in South City boarding houses. He notes their support of Upton Sinclair in the 1934 governor's race, their broad acquaintance with political issues of all kinds, and their interaction with other ethnic groups.[46] Also involved in San Franciso radical circles was Alex Georgiadis who was an activist in two militant unions, the San Francisco Newspaper Guild and the Pile Driver's Union. He became coorganizer of the California CIO Political Action Committee of 1948 and in the late 1960s was involved in the formation of the Venceremos Brigades which sent volunteer workers to Castro's Cuba.[47]

The multifaceted nature of 1930s radicalism is personified in Alexander Karanikas. As a student in the 1930s he was active in the antifascist movement and wrote poetry for publications as varied as the *Harvard Advocate* and the *Hellenic World*. During the war years he wrote a biweekly column for the *CIO News* (Allegheny-Kiski Valley edition) that was often reprinted in *Vema*. Karanikas also wrote pro-labor commentary for local radio stations in New Hampshire and Pennsylvania. In 1948 he ran for Congress as a candidate of the Progressive Party in his native New Hampshire. Blacklisted as the decade ended, he went back to college from which he emerged as an expert on how modern Greeks had been depicted in American literature. His *Hellenes & Hellions* has become the standard work in that field. Karanikas further contributed to Greek-American history as an advisor to two television films about the Greeks in America shown on public television's American Playhouse: King of America and My Palikar.[48]

Another gauge of leftist ideology is that some two hundred Greeks living in America volunteered to fight for the Loyalists in the Spanish Civil War. Most served with the American brigade but a few enrolled in the multinational Dimitrov Brigade. The names and brief identifications of these volunteers have been preserved in a memorial chapbook. A number of individuals are photographed holding copies of *Empros* and most appear to have working-class origins.[49]

The Greek Communists tried to harness the strong antifascist sentiment of the community through the creation of The Greek Workers Federation (1935–1937), later renamed The Greek American Union for Democracy. One of its major successes was in joining forces with liberals associated with *Keryx* to thwart efforts of General Metaxas, the pro-German Greek dictator, to set up American support groups similar to the German Bund. This coalition with liberals blossomed with the coming of World War II as both groups fought for aid to Greek guerillas and general Greek war relief. Rallies, war bond drives, and social events of all kinds marked an alliance whose dominance of the community was duly noted in OSS documents.[50]

Greek labor showed its formal power by creating the Greek-American Labor Committee. Twenty-two AFL and CIO locals with a combined membership of over one hundred thousand were directly represented and there were observers from twelve other unions. The committee was an effective pressure group within the Democratic Party, the CIO, and the Roosevelt administration in general. At the end of the war, the committee appeared at hearings in Washington D.C. in an unsuccessful bid to alter American policy in Greece.

The ties between Greek Communists in America and homeland Communists had deepened during the war years. Playing a significant role in that process was the Greek Maritime Union, which until 1941 had been named the Greek Seaman's Union. Its six hundred members were all Greek nationals. When the Nazis occupied Greece, union headquarters were split between New York and London. The New York leaders established close ties with the Spartakos group, the fur workers, and Greek-Americans in the National Maritime Union. As fervent radicals devoted to the

Popular Front, the Greek seamen volunteered to man ships that carried munitions from America to Murmansk, the most dangerous of all the North Atlantic runs. Their heroism was so outstanding that the union was separately decorated by Stalin, Roosevelt, and Churchill. While fully participating in this invaluable war effort, the union simultaneously struggled with Greek shipowners in a successful effort to upgrade conditions and wages to American standards. Through the 1940s, the New York local published its own newsletter and was involved in the social life of the Greek-American Left. Not a few marriages were one by-product. The Greek-born head of the Greek Maritime Union, for example, wed an American-born fur worker.[51]

The heady rise and community visibility of the Communists in the 1940s was to be followed by an abrupt decline into cultural oblivion. The Greek Communists were doubly vulnerable to McCarthyism. Like all Communists deeply invovled in labor unions, they bore the full brunt of the antiCommunist provisions of the Taft-Hartley Act. Most of the unions with which they were affiliated were either purged from the CIO or purged Communists from their ranks. The Greeks also endured negative fallout from the bitter civil war in Greece in which the U.S. backed a monarchist/liberal coalition fighting guerillas backed by Yugoslavia and the eastern bloc nations. As all Greek-American organizations not in the CP orbit enthusiastically supported the American policy in Greece, any vocal dissenters faced immediate ostracism from the community. This atmosphere quickly evaporated the alliance with liberals. When scores of Greek radicals went to court to fight deportation, there was no community support of the kind that had been mounted in the late 1930s to defend the foreign-born.

Among those who would be deported were leaders of the Greek Maritime Union and the Fur and Leather Workers Union. More typical targets were rank-and-file militants like Gus Polites, a retired Detroit restaurant worker who had organized auto workers in the 1930s and had been active in the workers club in Greektown. The purpose in prosecuting such a man was less to combat contemporary Communist influence than to send a message to the community about the long-term perils of being an avowed radical. A number of Greeks facing deportation were so infirm that they died before their cases were legally resolved. The deportation policy, however, was entirely effective in breaking the back of the Communist movement among Greeks. Sympathizers ran for the sidelines while known reds formally or informally dropped out of sight.[52]

Some of the organizational policies of the Greek Communists contributed to the totality of their debacle. *Vema* continued to print almost entirely in Greek, a practice that had inevitably cut it off from American-born Greeks who usually did not read Greek well, if at all. *Kafenion* culture, which had been central to Communist organizing had declined with the gradual demise of Greektowns, the rising influence of the Greek Orthodox Church, and growing ethnic affluence based on assimilation. The strong and open bond with Greece's Communists and the USSR, a boon in the 1940s, became an ideological albatross with the deepening of the cold war. The Greek Communists refused to distance themselves from their homeland comrades. Working mainly with American progressives such as activists in the American Labor Party and readers of the *National Guardian*, they attempted to win better treatment, if not outright release of Greek political prisoners.[53] Support in the Greek-American community for such efforts was nil. *Vema* folded in 1959 as the direct support group fell to less than a hundred and fewer and fewer sympathizers were willing to risk having a Communist paper seen in their home or workplace. The era of Communist influence in Greek America was over, and a convenient cultural amnesia soon took hold that wiped out even its memory.

The NonCommunist Left

The only significant radical opposition the Greek Communists ever faced in organized labor was a 1934 New York City hotel workers strike that was under Trotskyist influence. Among the strike leaders was Aristodemos Kaldis, later to become a prominent painter. In 1906 a seventeen-year-old Kaldis had arrived in Boston where he quickly became active as a journalist and labor agitator. He was drawn to the communist movement and in the late 1920s he aligned with Trotsky. After taking up residence in New York City, Kaldis became editor of *The Communist*, a monthly Greek-language newspaper launched in 1930 that lasted for only a handful of issues. His first editorial was addressed to comrades in the Spartakos Club whom he urged to fulfill the original mandate of the Bolshevik revolution by breaking with Stalin.[54]

Such appeals to activists proved ineffective. With the onset of the 1934 strike, which was highlighted by street rallies that attracted thousands of workers, the Trotskyists hoped to directly recruit a mass base. Kaldis was part of a multi-ethnic leadership that formed a' new union affiliated with the AFL. Although the immediate strike was won, the organizers soon quarreled amongst themselves and the new union disintegrated. During this same period, Kaldis had met his future wife, Laurie Eglington, editor of the influential *Art News*. Although Kaldis never disavowed his radical politics, he was never again organizationally affiliated and devoted himself to painting. In 1937 he befriended Diego Rivera, then working on his Rockefeller Center mural. A few years later Kaldis attracted considerable attention in the art world with twelve lectures at Carnegie Hall passionately espousing the principles of modern art.[55]

Many other influential artists and intellectuals were involved in the radicalism of the 1930s. Theodore Stamos, eventually to become a famous abstract expressionist, was a member of the original John Reed Club, but broke with the CP over the Hitler-Stalin Pact. He continued to think of himself as a democratic socialist but was not politically active.[56] Critic Nicholas Calas arrived in New York City in 1940 and presented his anarcho-surrealistic perspectives in major art publications. Although another unaffiliated leftist, he remained in direct contact with the most famous of all Greek Trotskyists, Michael Raptis (better known as Pablo).[57] Kimon Friar, who became the most prolific translator of contemporary Greek poets, including Communist Yannis Ritsos, was active on behalf of Loyalist Spain.[58] Broadway gossip columnist Paul Denis, a militant in the Newspaper Guild, headed "Greeks for Norman Thomas" in 1936.[59] Dean Alfange, a former national officer in AHEPA, ran for governor of New York on the American Labor Party ticket in 1940. Later he joined other social democrats who bolted the ALP, which they felt had fallen under Commmunist influence, to found the Liberal Party.[60] By far the most famous of the antiCommunist radicals was actor/director Elia Kazan who broke with the CP in 1935 and became infamous as a government "friendly witness" in the 1950s.[61]

Specific antiCommunism, however, was not the rule in Greek America until after World War II. More typical was the casual fusion of art, politics, and community found in the life of Helen Christophorides Nicas. Her father, Demetrius Christophorides, was always a liberal, but in 1936, he left a reporter's job at *Keryx* to become editor of *Eleftheria* and then *Vema*. Her husband, Demosthenes Nicas, a paid CIO organizer from 1937–1939, had joined the IWW in 1916 shortly after his arrival in America and had switched to John Reed's Communist Labor Party in 1919. Before her marriage to Nicas in 1942, Helen Christophorides had frequented an informal social circle centered on sculptor Michael Lekakis, a group she has characterized as very progressive but not political. Her sister, in turn, belonged to a dance troupe of young Greek-American women organized by Maria Theresa Bourgeois, a former student of Isadora Duncan. Half of their repertoire consisted of traditional folk dances and the other half of modern dances inspired by Duncan. The troupe performed in ethnic auditoriums and in professional venues such as Carnegie Hall. In the mid-1930s Helen Christophorides had also been a founding member of the Artemis Club, the first organization of Greek women at Hunter College and probably anywhere in the city university system. Her strictly political activism had been limited to helping her father edit the English-language sections of *Eleftheria* and *Vema* and serving as de facto circulation clerk.[62] These individual experiences reflect the general leftist climate of the era. Nothing remotely similar would recur until the 1960s, and the impact in ethnic communities would not be nearly as intense or pervasive.

The Anti-Junta Movement

The Greek military dictatorship of 1967–1974 sparked a protest movement that was a somewhat anemic reprise of the radical/liberal alliance of World War II. This political force consisted of from ten to twenty local committees at any given time. Each committee sponsored lectures, rallies, and other public events. A number of them issued newsletters and both the New York and Boston committees had radio programs. The committee membership was largely composed of liberals outraged by dictatorship in Greece, New Left activists seeking a community base, stranded Greek nationals of leftist persuasion, and veterans of the Communist Left. The movement drew thousands to its events but its hard core remained in the hundreds. The independently organized groups were often in contact with one another but attempts to form a national umbrella organization ultimately proved futile. Contacts with anti-junta organizations in countries other than Canada were episodic.

For the greater part of the junta's existence, the Greek-American community remained neutral or thought the junta an unpleasant but necessary component of the cold war. That view was bolstered by the enthusiastic support the junta received from then Vice President Spiro Agnew and an industrial group headed by oil magnate Tom Pappas. Only as the fascistic nature of the regime became absolutely clear through its use of torture and other brutalities did Greek-American sentiment turn negative. The anti-junta movement most certainly played some role in that process of education. Of greater long-term consequence was that anti-junta activists, vindicated by their fierce defense of democratic values, would become community leaders in the decades that followed.

Leading anti-junta liberal academics such as Adamantia Pollis were founders of the Modern Greek Studies Association, which has become the premier scholarly organization of its kind. The *Journal of the Hellenic Diaspora*, begun by radicals as an anti-junta organ, evolved into a prestigious academic journal without losing its leftist edge. Other anti-junta activists became prominent in Greek-language theater, Greek Orthodox television production, and the Greek press, most prominently at *Proini* (The Morning), a Greek-language daily founded in 1976. Movement alumni remained united in the determination that never again could dictatorship arise in Greece without Greek-Americans considering it absolutely indefensible on any grounds.

Complicating the legacy of the anti-junta movement was that one of its strongest currents was made up of supporters of socialist Andreas Papandreou. When Papandreou was elected prime minister in 1980, many individuals who had been active in the American anti-junta movement entered government service in Greece or staffed Greek agencies in the United States. Some Greek-Americans concluded that much anti-junta activity had just been an overseas extension of homeland politics rather than a bona fide indigenous movement. On the positive side, Papandreou's election legitimatized socialism as a political ideology. Papandreou's conservative predecessor had already decriminalized the Greek Communist Party (KKE), an act seen as informally closing the era of the civil war.

Despite these developments, a left-leaning immigrant flow, and the fact that half of the Greek population consistently voted left of center, the Greek-American Left did not revive. The immigrant impact proved short-lived and was mainly confined to overseas branches of homeland movements that were largely irrelevant to most Greek Americans. Some new cultural organizations and radio programs had radical sponsorship, but they avoided ideological identification, much less proselytizing. Other initiatives, such as the Greek American Labor Council founded by trade unionists in 1990 to work within the AFL-CIO and to promote working-class issues in the community, were essentially reformist in nature. Most radicals primarily operated as individuals in various scholarly and artistic fields. While the impact of all these activities and those noted earlier was not negligible, it did not constitute a coherent political movement. Mitigating against a new radicalism was the affluence of Greek Americans and their increasing comfort with assimilation into mainstream culture.

Conclusion

Although the existence of a Greek-American Left had been denied by almost all historians writing before the 1980s, Greek radicals have played a significant role in Greek-American life at various times and places. During the early decades of the twentieth century, the Greek Left consisted primarily of unskilled workers operating in affinity groups that struggled for basic civil rights and labor reform. In the 1920s the Communist Party succeeded in building a hard core of Greek cadre that gained considerable community influence in the working-class and antifascist movements of the 1930s and 1940s. Concurrent with that development a variegated nonCommunist Left was active in various cultural spheres.

McCarthyism and the cold war closed the era of the Communist Left, wiping out not only its memory but the memory of its predecessors. An anti-junta movement, now greatly admired but not initially popular, put reform and even radicalism back on the ethnic agenda in the 1960s. One long-term consequence was a new wave of scholarship that added labor, feminist, and radical currents to existing ethnic histories, which had largely been restricted to religious life, fraternal organizations, and prominent individuals. As the century ended, the Greek-American Left lacked organizational expression, existing primarily as an informal network of mutual interests.

The course of Greek-American radicalism and its belated appearance in ethnic histories probably contains elements to be found in other immigrant experiences that have not been examined for this kind of hidden history. The merger of ethnic and class interests in the early period of immigration is likely a common phenomenon with conventional historians inclined to a strictly ethnic interpretation of social struggles. The fate of ethnic Communist movements is almost inevitably linked to the experience of Communism in the homeland and the nature of the bonds between homeland and overseas Communists. Noncommunist radicalism may exhibit a similar paradigm. In the Greek case, the lack of radical alternatives to Communism in America surely reflects the circumstance that Greece had no viable socialist or anarchist movements prior to the 1960s. The relative isolation of radical artists and intellectuals not organizationally affiliated is yet another probable constant.

The entire ethnic trajectory may finally prove to be more closely related to basic American patterns than ethnic specialists care to admit. The Communist movement among Greek Americans, despite many unique aspects, largely parallels the general course of American Communism. For all immigrants of the Great Migration, there is also a predictable decline in all forms of radicalism as the group moves toward assimilation and is culturally diluted by outmarriage. When the cultural center of any given group is the fourth and fifth generations, cohorts without the experience of even one foreign-born grandparent, political patterns in that community are like to converge even more strongly with that of the dominant American culture.

Notes

1. Typical of two early and highly influential commentators who struck this note are: Henry Pratt Fairchild, *Greek Immigration to the United States* (New Haven: Yale University Press, 1911), 209–10 states, "Socialism finds no followers among the people of this race in the United States." He goes on to say Greeks are not inclined to join trade unions. Thomas Burgess, *Greeks in America* (Boston: Sherman, French, and Co., 1913) 154 opines, "[The Greeks] care naught for labor nor the I.W.W."

2. The great exception to this rule is the monumental work on the Intermountain West by Helen Zeese Papanikolas. Particularly insightful are her "Greek Workers in the Intermountain West: The Early Twentieth Century," *Byzantine and Modern Greek Studies* 5 (1979): 187–215 and her *Emily-George* (Salt Lake City: University of Utah Press, 1987). Also sensitive to working-class issues is Bobbi Malafouris, *Ellines Tis Amerikis, 1528–1948* (Greeks in America) (New York: Isaac Goldman printer, 1948).

3. Theodore Saloutos, *The Greeks in the United States* (Cambridge: Harvard University Press, 1964), 332. Saloutos' comment is all the more odd in that unlike the early historians who were mostly Protestant missionaries who had a Greek political agenda, Saloutos was a professional historian with liberal politics. He

often took controversial positions regarding Greek Orthodoxy in America and was highly skillful in handling the politics of the Greek press and fraternal organizations. His occasional notes on labor show no bias. One can only speculate this particular comment reflects the atmosphere of the cold war and its impact on ethnic self-images.

4. The outstanding debate on this issue with direct reference to the Saloutos tradition is Dan Georgakas, "The Greeks in America"; Charles C. Moskos, "Georgakas on Greek Americans: A Response"; Dan Georgakas, "Response to Charles C. Moskos"; and Alexandros Kitroeff, "The Moskos-Georgakas Debate: A Rejoinder"; *Journal of the Hellenic Diaspora* 14, nos. 1 & 2 (Spring-Summer 1987): 5–77.

5. Elizabeth Gurley Flynn, *The Rebel Girl: An Autobiography—My First Life, 1906–1926* (New York: International Publishers, 1955), 145.

6. Joyce L. Kornblush, ed., *Rebel Voices: An IWW Anthology* (Ann Arbor: University of Michigan Press, 1964), 180.

7. Dan Georgakas, "Demosthenes Nicas: Labor Radical" in Dan Georgakas and Charles C. Moskos, eds., *New Directions in Greek American Studies* (New York: Pella Publishing, 1991), 95–110. The most detailed account of a Greek-American Communist now in print. Original taped interviews of 1987–1989 on deposit with Oral History of the American Left, Tamiment Library, New York University.

8. Philip S. Foner, *The Fur and Leather Workers Union: A Story of Dramatic Struggles and Achievements* (Newark: Nordan Press, 1950), 540.

9. John Poulos Collection, Tamiment Library, New York University. This collecton provides an archive for the personal papers of Constantine Poulos and an archive of Greek Trotskyism. Poulos collected any and all materials on Greek radicalism. The resulting collection contains material from non-Trotskyist sources such as *Vema*, anti-junta material (1967–1974), and extensive material on the Greek resistance in World War II. The collection is augmented by forty books and pamphlets, most in English.

10. Copies in Poulos Collection.

11. In addition to material in Poulos Collection, author's interview with Eric Poulos, son of John Poulos, summer of 1986.

12. Author's interview with Haris Claron, 1971.

13. A good account of the strike is found in Philip S. Foner, *The Industrial Workers of the World: 1905–1917* (New York: International Publishers, 1965), 221–224. This text offers some instances of Greek involvement in IWW strikes.

14. Ibid., 223.

15. Gunther Peck, "Crisis in the Family: Padrones and Radicals in Utah, 1908–1912," in Georgakas and Moskos, *New Directions*, 73–94.

16. Ibid. summarizes some of this debate.

17. Spiro Orfens, a Seattle carpenter carried on a correspondence with erstwhile friend Jack London on London's heated denial of continuity between ancient and modern Greeks. Earl Labor, Roger C. Leitz III, and I. Milo Shephard, eds., *The Letters of Jack London, 1896–1905*, 3 vols. (Stanford: Stanford University Press, 1988), 1101, 1533–1534, 1545–1548, 1551, 1575.

18. Data from Phil Mellinger, researcher of the Bingham WFM, Joe Hill Conference, Salt Lake City, Utah, November 1990.

19. Cited by Papanikolas, "Greek Workers," 201.

20. Zeese Papanikolas, *Buried Unsung: Louis Tikas and the Ludlow Massacre* (Salt Lake City: University of Utah Press, 1982). Author has established a regular correspondence with Papanikolas regarding subsequent research.

21. Author interview with Z. Papanikolas, October 1993.

22. IWW Clippings Collection, Walter Reuther Library, Wayne State University, Detroit, Michigan. Also Foner, "IWW," 262 & 492 and Papanikolas, "Greek Workers," 287.

23. James Patterson, "The Unassimilated Greeks of Denver," *Anthropological Quarterly* 4 (1970): 243–253 deals well with this issue.

24. Dan Georgakas, "Towards Greek American Studies," *Journal of the Hellenic Diaspora* 16, nos. 1–4, (1989), takes up this issue. Dan Georgakas, *Greek Americans at Work* (New York: Labor Resource Center Queens College, 1993) offers a broad popular survey of Greek workers in America.

25. Department of State memorandum on meeting with spe-

cific editors published in *The Nation*, January 24, 1987, 70 after discovery by Elias Vlanton through Freedom of Information Act.

26. L. S. Stavrianos, *Lifelines from Our Past* (New York: Pantheon, 1989) 4.

27. Ibid., 5.

28. Author has a copy of the first title. The other two are available in IWW Pamphlets, Walter Reuther Collection, Wayne State University, Detroit, Michigan. These have incorrectly been cited previously as being issued prior to World War I.

29. Privately printed in 1922. Copy in Poulos Collection.

30. No copies are known to have survived.

31. Author has six of these pamphlets in personal collection. Four others are advertised in these, including the one expressly written for Greeks. To be donated to Tamiment Library.

32. Brooklyn had such a high concentration of Greeks that when immigrants returned to Greece one of the standard nicknames given them was "Brooklis." One of the IWO clubs of the 1930s was composed entirely of Greek waiters living in Brooklyn. Another example of Greek concentration was that the prestigious Michel's Restaurant off Grand Army Plaza was staffed by Greeks who lived in a nearby apartment house called the Acropolis. Enough Greek males remained in this area, now known as Park Slope, to maintian a *kafenion* on Flatbush Avenue near Seventh Avenue until the early 1980s.

33. Author has copies in personal collection. To be donated to Tamiment.

34. Very few of these issues have survived. Most of what is known about their contents are from extensive reports on them by various federal agencies. A full run of them is supposedly in Third International files in the former Leningrad, Russia; but there is no record of anyone ever using them. The New York Public Library has the following on microfilm: scattered numbers of *Phone* from 1922 and 1923, scattered copies of *Empros* from 1926 and 1927, and a complete *Empros* for 1937–1938. These were collected by George Tselos, Demosthenes Nicas, and Dan Georgakas.

35. Correspondence in 1991 with A. Kaprozilos who has worked for years on Greeks of the Soviet Union and has consulted *Komunistis*, a newspaper published in Rostov.

36. Constantine G. Yavis, Foreign Agents Registration Section, War Division, Department of Justice, "Propaganda in the Greek American Community, April 21, 1994, 1–8. Copy in Poulos Collection. Of related interest, Elias Vlanton, comp., "Documents: The O.S.S. and Greek Americans," *Journal of the Hellenic Diaspora* 9 nos. 1–3, 1982.

37. Foner, *Fur and Leather*, 161.

38. Poulos Collection.

39. Georgakas, "Nicas," 107. The transnational aspects of the movement are illustrated by an incident in Nicas's political life. In 1932 he was taken by Greek sailors to organize workers clubs in the ports of Argentina. Police trouble ensued and attempts to repatriate Nicas to a Greek jail were thwarted only by the intervention of Greek Communists active in Great Britain, pp. 102–103.

40. Charles Rivers tapes, Oral History of the American Left, Tamiment Library, New York University. Accompanied by four books of photographs and press clippings. Author interview, August 1993.

41. Chicago activities in Georgakas, "Nicas," 104. *Phone* article cited by Alexander Karanikas, *Hellenes & Hellions* (Urbana: University of Illinois Press, 1981), 92. Also see Theano Papazoglou-Margaris, *Duo Kosmi* [Two Worlds], (New York: Pella, 1993). A collection of short stories published in cooperation with the Hellenic Cultural Organization of Chicago and the Theano Papazoglou-Margaris Memorial Fund Committee.

42. A. B. Magil and Joseph North, *Steven Katovis: Life and Death of a Worker* (New York: International Publishers, 1930). Available at Tamiment.

43. Author interview with Tom Nicolopulos, October 1993. Obituary in *Western Worker*, June 25, 1934. Frederic Caire Chiles, "War on the Waterfront: The Struggles of San Francisco Longshoremen, 1931–1934." (Ph.D. diss., University of California—Santa Barbara, 1981), 202–296. Other materials available at Labor Archives & Research Center, San Francisco State University.

44. Photocopies of poems and title page of collection provided by Tom Nicolopulos to author.

45. Published in New York: Thomas Y. Crowell, 1959.

46. Author interview, October 1993. Tom Nicolopulos,

"Boardinghouse Days in South San Francisco," *The Hellenic Journal*, October 21, 1993, pp. 6–8.

47. Obituary. *Oakland Tribune*, February 8, 1991, p. C5.

48. Full resume provided author by Karanikas, 1993.

49. Stefanos Tsermengas and Lefteris Tsirmirakis, *No Psaran— Ellines antifasistes ethelontes stin Ispania* [They Shall Not Pass—Greek antifascist volunteers in Spain], (Athens: Synchroni Epochi, 1987).

50. Vlanton, "OSS."

51. Author interview, August 1985, Havana, Cuba.

52. Author interview with Nicas. Author consulted files of George Crockett, a lawyer in Detroit who defended Greek radicals in the 1950s, August 1985.

53. See account of campaign to collect twenty tons of clothing for Greek prisoners in *Daily Worker*, October 24, 1950, p. 4 and rally announcemnet in *National Gaurdian*, March 8, 1954, p. 2.

54. Available in Poulos Collection.

55. Kaldis File, Poulos Collection. Also see George Vlamavanos, "A Greek Tribute to Kaldis," *Journal of the Hellenic Diaspora* 6, no.2 (Summer 1979): 89–93.

56. Marina Kasdaglis and Peter Pappas, "A Discussion with Theodore Stamos," *Journal of the Hellenic Diaspora* 9, no. 4 (Winter 1982): 45–52.

57. Poulos Collection. Memorial meeting on his death, January 26, 1988.

58. Author interview, summer 1986.

59. Author interview, autumn 1986.

60. News item, *The GreekAmerican*, February 14, 1987, p. 6; obituary, *New York Times*, October 27, 1989; and interview with former colleagues, autumn 1993.

61. Elia Kazan, *A Life* (New York: Alfred A. Knopf, 1988) contains numerous passages on Kazan's politics, CP membership, resignation, anti-CP testimony, etc.

62. Interview with Helen Christophorides Nicas, 1987–1989. Partly contained on Nicas tapes at Tamiment.

EIGHT

The Arab-American Left

Michael W. Suleiman

The Arab-American community is composed of all the Arabic-speaking peoples who immigrated to the United States from regions or countries that are collectively referred to as the Arab world and are presently members of the League of Arab States. Their numbers are disputable but are generally thought to be about 2.5 million.[1] Most Arab-Americans as well as most students of the Arab community in the United States would be surprised to read about any leftist leanings among Arab-Americans, if leftism is defined as revolutionary radicalism. Such a political orientation is almost entirely confined to organizations that are U.S. branches or support groups of overseas organizations such as Marxist-oriented Palestinian groups or the Iraqi communist party. On the other hand, given a wider definition of leftism including issues such as consumers' rights, health care reform, women's rights, and religious diversity, a tradition of left liberalism in Arab America has often had an impact beyond that of the ethnic community itself.[2] Arab-American organizations have also been in the forefront of opposition to U.S. policy in the contemporary Middle East. In advancing their views, such organizations often use leftist rhetoric and project themselves as anti-imperialist rather than simply nationalist.

The Arab-American community is generally perceived as fairly conservative, if not passive, and uninterested in political issues. The apolitical character of early Arab immigrants was described by M.M. Maloof in a 1917 Boston newspaper, "The Syrian is not a conspicuous member of the body politic."[3] This appraisal was confirmed in the earliest scholarly study of Arabs in America by Philip Hitti who wrote, "Syrians cut no figure in the political life of this nation. Very few of them interest themselves in politics or aspire to office."[4]

By and large, Arab-Americans have retained the feeling that political participation is futile and that they are unable to change well-entrenched American policies concerning the Arab world, whether Republicans or Democrats win the national elections.[5] Nevertheless, over the years, different attempts have been made to get Arabs to participate more actively in politics. Most recently, the Arab American Institute (AAI) was founded in 1985 to combat political apathy by organizing the Arab community to enter American politics. The AAI has worked mainly in the left wing of the Democratic Party and uses the liberal rhetoric associated with the civil rights movement.

Whether politically active or not, Arab-Americans are generally written of as conservative in politics and Republican in party affiliation.[6] In the article previously cited, Maloof wrote: "In politics Syrians are predominantly Republicans. They are never associated with any radical movements and there is no such thing as a Socialist or Anarchist among them."[7] Reading such a statement, one must bear in mind that in 1917, the urban Republicans were reformers, and progressive Republicans of the era launched third-party movements for Theodore Roosevelt and Robert La Follette. New immigrants were often excluded from the Democratic Party by Irish and German political bosses. In New York City, liberal Fiorello La Guardia and radical Vito Marcantonio both won their first offices as Republicans. Maloof's remarks on Arab-American politics are most likely an overstatement and it is very typical of immigrant writers to project their group as respectable and loyal to the new nation. In any case, hardly any writings on the subject exist. Research for this study, therefore, is based on early Arab-American newspapers/journals; essays, novels and autobiographies written by Arabs in America; on the few public opinion surveys administered specifically to gauge the views of Arabs in America; and on my role as an Arab-American participant observer. I will detail Arab-American views on generic leftist issues: anti-imperialism, racial tolerance, male/female equality, the labor movement, consumer advocacy, and health care.

Anti-Imperialism

Economic gain was the main reason for the early Arab immigration to America. This often meant that immigrants did not consider political activity in the United States as necessary, appropriate, or fruitful. Nonetheless, throughout the history of Arab immigration to the United States, there have been journalists, writers, and intellectuals who fled tyranny at home. Such individuals thrived in the atmosphere of freedom in the new homeland—and used their safe haven to launch attacks on real or imagined abuses wherever they were found, especially in the countries they left behind. Early Arab-American immigrants literally viewed the United States (and the West generally) as a relative paradise not only in economic terms but also in its political freedom and anti-imperialist stands.[8] Their attacks against imperialism and political oppression were directed at the Ottoman empire, which occupied their homelands and oppressed their people. Among the earliest and loudest voices against imperialism was that of Joseph Maloof whose newspaper *Al-Ayam (al-Ayyam)* was almost completely devoted to that cause.[9] Another rabid anti-Ottomanist was Selim Sarkis whose journal, *Al-Musheer (al-Mushir)*, was shut down in Egypt only to be briefly resurrected in New York City.[10]

The attacks against Ottoman imperialist control gained momentum early in the century and culminated in an all-out campaign by almost all Arab-American writers throughout the WWI years. Such attacks (and diatribes) are extensive in the writings of N. Mokarzel, Amin Rihani, Abraham Rihbani, Kahlil Gibral, Elia D. Madey, F.M. Al Akl and many others.[11] Often, as in the case of N. Mokarzel, their anti-imperialism was tainted in that they wanted to replace one imperialist power (Turkey) with another (France), which was viewed as their protector and supporter.[12] Of all these writers, the most anti-imperialist was Amin Rihani who waged major speaking and writing campaigns for Arab independence.[13]

The post-World War II period had a much different perspective. The United States, now a superpower with major international interests, joined the European imperialist powers in protecting and advancing a status quo in the Middle East that was unacceptable to large numbers of Arab-American intellectuals. Anti-imperialist attacks, therefore, began to target U.S. policy in the Middle East as much as, if not more than, European domination of that region. Especially after the establishment of Israel with much and continuing American support, Arab-Americans strongly condemned such activities as the epitome of imperialist/colonialist enterprise. In general, the most active and most intense in their attacks against Zionism/Israel and their supporters were newly arrived Arab-American immigrants. While imperialism was denounced as the perpetrator of injustice against Palestinians, it was not until the mid-1960s that anti-imperialist campaigns became intelligently developed, and effectively articulated. These anti-imperialist campaigns were clearly situated in an overall leftist ideology. Among Arab-American promoters of these ideas, the most articulate have been Ibrahim Abu-Lughod, Fawaz Turki, Naseer Aruri, Abdeen Jabara, Edward Said, and the former senator from South Dakota James Abourezk.[14] Among national Arab-American organizations, two stand out as consistently anti-imperialist in their pronouncements, publications, and the rhetoric of their conference speakers. These are the Association of Arab-American University Graduates (AAUG, founded in 1967) and the American-Arab Anti-Discrimination Committee (ADC, founded in 1980).

The introduction to the AAUG publication *The First Decade, 1967–1977* states that the history of AAUG is "a chapter out of the historical struggle for the human rights of all people and not just some people. It is a history of the unity of humane and rational peoples of all origins putting forth once more a commitment to the promise of the human species: a life of liberty, equality, and fraternity for all."[15] More generally, any review of the conference participants, the speeches, and the publications of the AAUG would clearly show an anti-imperialist bent.[16] Obviously, it is not the case that the entire membership is consciously or actively anti-imperialist. However, the guiding spirit and much of the leadership have been. This is particularly true of the speakers at the Sunday breakfast sessions of AAUG conferences.

As its name indicates, the ADC is concerned about the discrimination Arab-Americans face due to the predominantly negative image of Arabs in the mass media. This concern was particularly evident during the 1990–1991 conflict with Iraq. Much of ADC's efforts are directed at influencing newspaper publishers, television producers, and movie makers through lobbying or public pressure. Some specific campaigns have been quite successful. In 1993, for example, the Walt Disney organization was persuaded to partially alter an anti-Arab song for its home video release of *Aladdin*.[17] The ADC has also been active in trying to keep the congressional playing field between Palestinian and Israeli inter-

ests as level as possible. Nearly every national convention high-
lights this effort and ADC officials are frequent visitors to the
Middle East where they confer with leading political figures.[18]

Of the post-World War II Arab-American leftists, the person
who has written most to expose the imperialist paradigm has been
Edward Said. In *Orientalism* (1978) and more recently in *Culture
and Imperialism* (1993), he argues that the imperialist West, including the United States, has divided the world into the Orient and
the Occident. The former is distinctly different from the latter and
cannot (and should not be allowed to) represent itself. Orientalism
is, in Said's words, "the corporate institution for dealing with the
Orient . . . a Western style for dominating, restructuring, and
having authority over the Orient."[19] In aspiring to, and working
toward, global dominance, the U.S. says and does the same things
that other imperial powers have said and done: "There is always
the appeal to power and national interest in running the affairs of
lesser peoples; there is the same destructive zeal when the going
gets a little rough, or when the natives rise up and reject a
compliant and unpopular ruler who was ensnared and kept in
place by the imperial power."[20] This is done with the collaboration,
often passive, of "intellectuals, artists, journalists whose positions
at home are progressive and full of admirable sentiments, but the
opposite when it comes to what is done abroad in their name."[21]

Racial/Ethnic Tolerance

Anti-imperialist sentiment implies tolerance of different cultures
and peoples, an idea that also translates into an appreciation of
diversity and multiculturalism at home. While Arab-Americans
have been subjected to much prejudice and some discrimination,
their reaction to such treatment has varied. The earlier arrivals paid
little attention to anti-Arab bias and discrimination, manifesting a
willingness to put up with such practices since their residence in
America was temporary and for the specific purpose of economic
gain.[22] As they struck roots and desired to stay, they were shocked
by the discovery that some judges considered them "non-white"
and therefore ineligible for U.S. citizenship. The Arab community,
by its own choice as much as the consequence of discrimination,
had isolated and insulated itself from the rest of American society.
While these Arabs thought of themselves as white and aspired to
high social/economic status, they had neither philosophical nor
sociological/anthropological bases for racial/ethnic gradations or

prejudice. Their intellectuals frequently preached the equality and brotherhood of all races in their editorials, poetry and fiction. But they certainly wanted the right to become American citizens. Their main response to the argument that they were non-white was to provide proof that they most definitely belonged to the white "race."[23]

It was not until after WWII and the rise of the civil rights movement that some Arab-American individuals and groups began to address the racial/ethnic issue. Essentially, the anti-imperialist Arab-Americans were also the ones who advocated ethnic/religious tolerance and better treatment for the oppressed minorities—including Arab-Americans. Thus, in the 1960s and 1970s, Abdeen Jabara, Allen Amen, and the Arab Community Center for Economic and Social Services (ACCESS) led a fight against a proposed urban renewal project in the city of Dearborn, Michigan, which would have gravely affected a lower-income group of Arab-Americans, mostly Yemenis.[24] Jabara and others also became actively involved in the defense of Yemeni workers in the auto factories in Detroit as well as in the organizing drives of the United Farm Workers in California.[25] At that time, Jabara was part of a law collective deeply involved in all aspects of Detroit's vibrant radical movement. In a memorandum of December 1, 1970, Lt. Dennis Mulaney of the Detroit Police Department's Red Squad wrote: 'There is hardly an underground newspaper, black liberation, or left wing group of any kind in Detroit that at one time or another was not represented by [Jabara's] law firm."[26]

While Jabara and other Arab-American leftists abhorred prejudice and discrimination against any racial or ethnic group, it soon became clear to them that *activism* on this issue should not be restricted to their own group. The notion of building coalitions with other oppressed racial/ethnic groups was advanced, and formal and informal cooperation started.[27] The culmination of this process was the close cooperation and active involvement of relatively large numbers of Arab-Americans in the Rainbow Coalition and the presidential campaign of the Rev. Jesse Jackson.[28] In fact, Jackson's sympathetic remarks concerning Palestine and the Palestinians mobilized many erstwhile passive Arab-Americans into political activity. A survey conducted in 1989 among politically active Arab-Americans found that 44 percent of the sample had either never participated in politics before the 1988 election year or had done only volunteer work. These developments ushered in a substantial increase in membership (28 percent) for both the

Democratic and Republican parties, but especially for the Democrats.[29]

The Arab-American most clearly associated with the cause of racial/ethnic minorities is James Abourezk, who founded the American-Arab Anti-Discrimination Committee (ADC) in 1980 as a defense against anti-Arab prejudice, harassment, and discrimination. This was done after his stint in the U.S. Senate, during which he became sensitized to the concerns and needs of Arabs and Arab-Americans.[30] Abourezk's main commitment for most of his political career had been to American Indians. As he wrote in 1989: "In America there are millions of examples of injustice, of the unfair treatment of people who have no power or no money. Treatment of Indian people in the United States provides us with a clear illustration of inequitable justice for the poor."[31] His sympathy was translated into practical measures designed to help alleviate some of their difficulties and the discrimination against them. Specifically, as chairman of the Indian Affairs Subcommittee of the Senate Interior Committee, Abourezk succeeded in getting the Senate to pass "two worthwhile bills." The first was the Indian Freedom of Religion Act, a nonbinding Congressional Resolution, which nevertheless enables Indians to protest government activity deemed offensive to their religious beliefs and practices. The second was the Indian Child Welfare Act, which, among other things, requires that a tribal court (not the welfare agency) decides where the child of an alcoholic or otherwise delinquent mother is placed.[32]

Religious Freedom/Tolerance

Some Arab-Americans, especially among the early arrivals, have stated emphatically that they left their homeland because of Ottoman government-inspired and -supported harassment/oppression of religious minorities, especially Christian Arabs.[33] Nevertheless religious and sectarian conflict has been common among all religious groups in the new homeland. This rivalry was so strong among early Arab-American immigrants that each sect had its own newspaper, which was often used to defend its constituents and attack all others—while simultaneously accusing the opposition of religious bigotry![34] It is this, especially intra-Christian, sectarian conflict that many Arab-American leftist intellectuals openly and vociferously decried.

The conflict took on aspects of a life and death struggle

among rival "nations." In particular, the fierce rivalry between the Maronite Catholics and the Protestant missionaries was carried into the New World, as some prominent Maronites either abandoned their sect or their faith.[35] Gibran, for instance, found himself in disfavor with the Maronite hierarchy for his *Nymphs of the Valley* and later for *Jesus, the Son of Man*.[36] Conversely, at one time or another, almost all the Arab-American newspapers attacked church control of the political and social life of its people in the old *and* the new country. Some popular fiction also openly attacked religious institutions, especially the Maronite church, and corruption of some of its clergy.[37] Abraham Rihbany, a Unitarian minister who converted from the Orthodox church, expressed well the freedom and tolerance he admired in America: "I have journeyed from the religion of 'authority for truth' to the religion of 'truth for authority'—a religion which teaches me the fatherhood of God, the brotherhood of man and the friendliness of the universe, and makes me heir to all the prayers, songs, and sermons of the ages."[38]

While Gibran Kahlil Gibran, Abraham Rihbany, Abdel-Massih Haddad, and F.M. Al Akl spoke out against intolerance, bigotry, and conflict, by far the strongest advocate of religious tolerance and the freedom of religion was Amin Rihani. Rihani stands out in this area because of his eloquence, the forcefulness of his arguments, his respectful and reverential treatment of different religions and, most importantly, his practicing and living his beliefs on a daily basis. When he wrote excoriating Arabic newspapers for their many ills, including sectarian intolerance, he was very effective because he was believable and above reproach.[39]

Since WWII, the general atmosphere in America has been secular, and most Arab immigrants during this more recent period have adopted this approach. In other words, most Arab-American intellectuals, including Muslim Arabs, now unconditionally endorse the notion of religious diversity and tolerance.[40]

Male-Female Relations and the Feminist Movement

The male-female dynamics among Arab-Americans have been the subject of a great deal of discussion, debate, and some controversy. Almost from the beginning of Arab-American immigration, there have been strong advocates of female emancipation, among both men and women. What "emancipation" meant has differed over the years and according to the orientations of those advocates. By and large, however, there is much more "freedom" for women today in terms of general community acceptance, stronger commitment to gender equality, and greater tolerance of "deviant" behavior.

Long before formal calls for emancipation were heard, and often *without* the explicit consent of male relatives, Arab women began to immigrate to the U.S., frequently traveling alone or with other female relatives. Even more important, Arab-American women were able to earn a living by working alone outside their household as peddlers, often spending one or more nights on the road, away from home and family.[41] Another "emancipating" practice was that of many ambitious or strong-willed Arab-American women whose husbands either were nonsupportive, irresponsible, or unambitious. They simply ignored, abandoned, or circumvented their husbands in order to raise the family unaided, improve their economic/social status, or simply to go on with their own lives in pursuit of self-fulfilling careers.[42]

Among the better-known examples of those women who "emancipated" themselves are Shukrie Thabit, Laila Abou-Saif, and the mothers of Gibran Kahlil Gibran and William Peter Blatty. Whereas Gibran expressed his appreciation to his mother primarily through love and affection, Blatty sang his mother's praises, often in a humorous fashion, in two books. Blatty's mother was an indomitable character who overcame poverty, prejudice, discrimination and adversity in her successful struggle to nurture and protect her family. And she wished not to be forgotten! Her son obliged her by writing about her and about his own upbringing noting, as the title of the second book indicates, *I'll Tell Them I Remember You*.[43]

Of the seven Arab-American women who have written autobiographies, two have been active in government and journalism and two have found their "freedom" in religion. It is nevertheless worthy of note that although Layyah Barakat and Rahme Haidar were certainly not leftists, religious zeal and missionary activity liberated them from the prevailing tradition and allowed them a forum for their own self-development.[44]

Laila Abou-Saif, self-styled variously as liberal, leftist, and revolutionary, has written about her struggle for gender equality and personal self-development. She was raised in a wealthy upper-class Christian (Copt) family in Egypt but rebelled against a stultifying tradition and a strong-willed mother who dictated "respectable" behavior. Eventually, Abou-Saif got married, reluctantly became pregnant, had an abortion ("I would have died as a person, as myself, with that baby's birth"), had an affair, divorced her husband, did not wish to remarry ("I wanted to earn my own money. I knew this was the secret to a woman's independence"), embarked on her own career, joined the women's liberation movement, and eventually settled in the United States.[45]

Over a period of some one hundred years in America, Arab-Americans of the liberal Left have sought different things at different times in their call for the emancipation of women. At the turn of the century, for instance, advocates of female liberation called for better education, jobs, cultural refinement, good breeding— and conservative and proper behavior. Today, some Arab-American women call for total equality, freedom to do whatever is necessary for self-development, and general acceptance of their sexual preferences.[46] In this they are representative, albeit in smaller numbers, of the American population as a whole.

Activism in the Workplace

The first documented case of Arab-American trade unionism concerns the role played by Farris Marad in the 1912 Lawrence strike. The Syrian/Arab immigrants of Lawrence, like the new arrivals from southeastern Europe, were living in extremely poor, overcrowded, segregated neighborhoods, huddled in dismal tenements in a city with high crime rates. The majority of the Arab workers were employed in the textile mills when the Industrial Workers of the World (IWW) led a series of strikes in support of better work conditions and higher wages. The strike leaders planned and oriented the "union, strike committee, and relief group along ethnic lines."[47] Donald B. Cole, an exhaustive chronicler/analyst of the Lawrence strike, found that three Syrian/Arab strike leaders played an important, if secondary, role. Dr. Hajjar, an Arab physician, was a strong supporter of the strike, urging confrontation with the soldiers. Furthermore, "Farris Marad and the Syrian Drum Corps led the Thursday parade," and the Arab strikers helped "stop the machines at the Wood Mill." And at least one of the strike-organizing meetings was held in the basement of the Syrian Church.[48]

The role of the Arab community in Lawrence is typical of the pattern of ethnic groups that participated in the massive strike wave of 1912–1913. Although often a small portion of the total workforce, the portion of Arabs who were working class was large.

For example, the silk factories of Paterson and West Hoboken, New Jersey, also hit by IWW strikes, employed about 80 percent of the Arabs in those cities.[49] Arabs were part of the itinerant army of unskilled workers characteristic of that era and were present at various labor disputes. Jenks and Lauck reported in 1913 that fully one-fourth of the seasonal agricultural workers in and around Oneida, New York were Arabs.[50] Large numbers of Arabs also congregated in Pittsburgh steel mills and Detroit auto plants.[51]

By far the most prominent labor activist to emerge from Arab America was George Addes, a leader in the founding of the United Auto Workers during the 1930s. Addes first came to public view during a historic strike in Toledo, Ohio that was under the influence of A.J. Muste's radical American Workers Party. Although a Roman Catholic, Addes remained identified with the most radical elements of the UAW, a faction dominated by Communists. After years of bitter struggle with the social democratic faction led by Walter Reuther, Addes and other leftists allied with the Communists were expelled from the UAW in 1947.[52] No work has ever been done to determine if Addes had a significant following among the Arab auto workers in Detroit and Toledo, a region that had the largest concentration of Arabs in America at that time. Nor has there ever been a study of his political perspectives.

The most recent display of Arab military militancy in the auto industry came in the aftermath of the 1973 Arab-Israeli War. Some two thousand workers, constituted as the Arab Workers Caucus, staged wildcat strikes, slowdowns, boycotts, and rallies to protest the UAW's purchase of Israeli bonds. A few years earlier, these Arabs had honored wildcat strikes in the auto industry called by the League of Revolutionary Black Workers as a challenge to UAW leadership. The Arab upsurge was contained by retaliations and minor concessions, and by 1980 was a spent force.[53]

Consumer Advocacy

Among Arab-Americans who have been active in promoting the rights of ordinary citizens is Anthony "Toby" Moffett, who was director (1971–1974) of the Connecticut Citizen Action Group, worked with Nader's Raiders, and later became a U.S. Congressman (1975–1983).[54] Along similar lines, Senator James Abourezk worked hard to break up the major oil companies that were overcharging their consumers. He introduced bills that would have forced horizontal and vertical divestiture of oil companies.

Easily, the consummate consumer advocate and public citizen number one is Ralph Nader, an American of Lebanese background. His education on this issue began early, at home, where his parents encouraged all their children to be concerned and active citizens who should fight for what is right.[56] When he found his legal education at Harvard primarily designed to service big business, he educated himself on how to use the law to serve the public, especially on social issues. His first major battle with big business was over car safety. His book, *Unsafe at Any Speed*,[57] and numerous articles and interviews earned him the wrath and enmity of General Motors and its leaders who proceeded to investigate and harass him. In particular, they viewed his Arab heritage as a weakness they could use against him, falsely accusing him of anti-Semitism. Eventually, General Motors was forced to apologize, and settled Nader's lawsuit against the company out of court.[58] He used the settlement money, $425,000, to open in 1969 a public interest law firm, the Center for the Study of Responsive Law, a think tank for the development of policies designed to protect the public from big business. He later started another consumer advocacy law firm, the Public Interest Research Group, which mushroomed into many branches and organizations that attracted talented, hardworking students, and professionals willing to volunteer much time and effort in defense of the public interest.

In time, numerous Nader's Raiders groups were established all over the country. Their main function was to draw attention to products and business practices harmful to the public and to propose ways to ameliorate the situation. No major area of business, economy, environment, or politics has escaped their scrutiny. In fact, as a result of Nader's crusading on behalf of the general public, significant legislation has been passed by the U.S. Congress, including the Traffic and Motor Vehicle Safety Act (1966) and the Occupational Health and Safety Act (1970). The Nader groups continue to produce numerous investigative reports, which are often used as a basis for corrective legislation.[59]

Health Care

Arab-Americans have been in the forefront in advocating and developing health care systems that are affordable and available to all who need them. The very first successful cooperative medicine program and "the first co-operative hospital in the United States" were introduced and established by Dr. Michael Shadid in Elk City, Oklahoma in the late 1920s.[60] In doing so, he had to overcome the strenuous opposition of the American Medical Association (AMA). The battle went on from 1929 to the early 1950s when an out-of-court settlement of the conflict was effected. In the end, it was a victory for Dr. Shadid, his staff, and supporters. In showing how the settlement did not alter the cooperative medicine program in place, Shadid wrote:

> We will still publish our monthly bulletin; our doctors are still on salary, not on a fee basis; we still have our own prepayment plan; we are still a cooperative association; our Board of Directors is elected by the members and both the medical director and the business manager are responsible to them. Our constitution and by-laws are still as they were, a cooperative constitution and standard coop by-laws.[61]

Especially after Dr. Shadid's victory over what he called the American Meddler's Association, he devoted more of his time and effort to helping other doctors and groups throughout the country who were interested in addressing the medical needs of their communities, including preventive medicine, at prices people could afford.

Another Arab-American doctor, F.M. Al Akl, was also very concerned about providing adequate health care for all who needed it—and there was great need for it during the depression of the 1930s! Concerned about the general welfare of people in all their activities, he viewed war as senseless. In striving for a better world, Al Akl advocated combatting the poverty and squalor that undermine health. He saw hunger as physically and mentally incapacitating—areas that must be remedies if proper health is to be restored and maintained. He concluded that a national health policy was essential.[62]

During the same period, still another Arab-American doctor decided that it was more important to improve the health conditions for the general public than to make a lot of money in private practice. George Hatem was born in 1910 in Buffalo, New York and moved to North Carolina at an early age. He finished his medical studies at the American University of Beirut and the University of Geneva in Switzerland before going to China in 1933. While he retained his American citizenship, he made China his adopted home until his death in 1988.

Known in China as *Ma Haide/ Ma Hai-teh,* meaning "Virtue

from Overseas," Hatem became an internationally recognized figure in medicine. This great humanitarian devoted his whole life to
the improvement of health conditions in China, often working
with the zeal of a missionary. He is credited with "directing the
campaign that eliminated venereal disease as a health problem" in
China,[63] and "his efforts have reduced the incidence of leprosy in
China by more than 80 percent."[64] These phenomenal achievements earned him numerous honors and awards. In the United
States, the citation for the prestigious Albert Lasker Public Service
Award reads, in part: "Dr. Ma's contributions can be compared in
importance to the eradication of yellow fever and the bubonic
plague, and, as a model for the public health control of venereal
diseases, they stand alone."[65]

Dr. Hatem used social science in conjunction with natural
science, employing large numbers of volunteers to inform the
masses and to gather data for use in preventive measures. His
humanitarian spirit and strong idealism inspired medical service
and public health advances, especially among the people of
China.[66]

Dr. Nicholas Assali came to the United States via Brazil and
distinguished himself in research and writing in the area of gyne-
cology and obstetrics. The great costs of medical care began to
worry him and he became convinced that "continually rising
medical costs were an enormous burden on the American people."[67] He became disillusioned with the AMA when it opposed
President Harry Truman's proposal to set up a federally supported
health care system. When President John F. Kennedy proposed a
federal program of health care for the elderly, Assali and others
formed the "Doctor's Organization in Favor of Health Care for the
Aged," in support of the Medicare bill. As a result, he had to
suffer the full wrath of the AMA and its subsidiaries—and the
ostracism of his medical colleagues.[68]

Arab-American involvement with health care reform achieved
its most public face when entertainer Danny Thomas founded St.
Jude's Children's Hospital in 1962.[69] The hospital cares for children
with so-called incurable diseases free of charge and is engaged in
research to find treatments and cures. In order to depersonalize
this effort and make it a true community project, Thomas formed
the American Lebanese Syrian Associated Charities (ALSAC) to
carry on fund-raising for the maintenance and expansion of the
hospital.[70] Since Thomas' death, his actress daughter Marlo
Thomas, a noted feminist, has inherited leadership of the project.

Summary and Conclusion

We can distinguish between two groups of Arab-American leftists. One group included individuals and organizations that have focused on international issues and causes, especially justice for the Palestinians. In the case of George Hatem, this international humanitarianism actually meant a physical transfer to another country. The other group has more often focused on American domestic issues and the American political process. Obviously, these orientations are not mutually exclusive, but they do reflect a tangible difference in emphasis.

The most viable leftist tradition among Arab-Americans is that of reform and liberalism. In contrast to many other immigrant groups, there is no tradition of anarchist, socialist, or communist organizations. Worker activism has remained episodic and localized. This low volume of political activism is characteristic of a community that has been politically passive for most of its history in America. Only since the 1960s have organizations such as the AAUG, ADC, and AAI begun to mobilize the community to address political and ideological concerns. The new organizations strive to influence American policy in the Middle East and to challenge negative Arab stereotypes in American popular culture.

Other reformist traditions within the community relate to women's liberation and religious diversity. But the issues that have been closest to the hearts of Arab-Americans are consumer advocacy and health care. These have garnered the greatest and most enthusiastic community support. In part, this reflects a cultural tradition that emphasizes and encourages care for the needy and the helpless.[71] This sentiment has been expressed well by one of the Arab-American doctor/activists, Al Akl, who wrote:

> It is not simply because I am a physician that I have such a profound veneration for medicine. Perhaps my respect for the noble art of healing is a tradition with me. For the Arabs call their doctor *hakeem*, which means the sage.[72]

Notes

1. See Sameer Y. and Nabeel Abraham, eds., *The Arab World and Arab Americans: Understanding a Neglected Minority;* and *Arabs in the New World: Studies on Arab-American Communities* (Detroit, Mich.: Center for Urban Studies, Wayne State University, 1981,

1983 respectively); and John A. Zogby, *Arab America Today: A Demographic Profile of Arab Americans* (Washington, D.C.: Arab American Institute, 1990).

2. For a general discussion of leftists and the Left see Edwin M. Coulter, *Principles of Politics and Government* (Dubuque, Iowa: Wm. C. Brown, 1991), 126, 158, 166–67.

3. M.M. Maloof, "From Beersheba to Berlin, via Boston," *Boston Evening Transcript,* 22 Aug. 1917, part 2, p. 5.

4. Philip K. Hitti, *The Syrians in America* (New York: George H. Doran, 1924), 89. In this study, all Arabic-speaking immigrants, including early arrivals to the United States who were known as "Syrians" at the time, will be referred to as Arab Americans.

5. See Michael W. Suleiman, "Early Arab-Americans: The Search for Identity." In *Crossing the Waters: Arabic-Speaking Immigrants to the United States Before 1940,* ed. Eric J. Hooglund (Washington, D.C.: Smithsonian Institution Press, 1987), 50.

6. See Hitti, *op. cit.,* 90; and Alixa Naff, *Becoming American: The Early Arab Immigrant Experience* (Carbondale, Ill.: Southern Illinois University Press, 1985), 328.

7. Maloof, *op. cit.*

8. See, for instance, Salom Rizk, *Syrian Yankee* (Garden City, N.Y.: Doubleday, Doran & Co., 1943).

9. *Al-Ayam (al-Ayyam)* (Jan. 13, 1898 to May 17, 1900) is on microfilm, a copy of which is at the Library of Congress.

10. *Al-Musheer (al-Mushir)* was published in the United States in 1899–1900. Despite his attacks against Ottoman oppression and his calls for liberty and equality, Sarkis was a supporter of the British regime in Egypt—a stance that certainly tarnishes if it does not negate his "revolutionary" rhetoric.

11. N. Mokarzel spread his ideas through speeches and the columns of his newspaper, *Al-Hoda.* Elia D. Madey (Ilya Abu-Madi) expressed his views in poetry and in his journal/newspaper, *Al-Sameer (al-Samir).*

12. In addition to his editorials in *Al-Hoda,* see also *Al-Hoda, 1898–1968: The Story of Lebanon and Its Emigrants Taken From the Newspaper Al-Hoda* (New York: Al-Hoda Press, 1968).

13. Rihani was a prolific writer in both Arabic and English on

numerous topics, including the championing of Palestinian and Arab causes. For a complete list of his publications, see Albert Rihani, comp., *Amin Rihani.* (In Arabic). (Beirut: Rihani Press, 1941).

14. Among Ibrahim Abu-Lughod's publications are the following edited works: *The Arab-Israeli Confrontation of June 1967: An Arab Perspective* (Evanston, Ill.: Northwestern University Press, 1970); *The Invasion of Lebanon,* coeditor with Eqbal Ahmed (London: Institute of Race Relations, 1983); *Palestinian Rights: Affirmation and Denial* (Wilmette, Ill.: Medina Press, 1982); and *Settler Regimes in Africa and the Arab World,* coeditor with Baha Abu-Laban (Wilmette, Ill.: Medina Press, 1974). See also his "America's Palestine Policy," *Arab Studies Quarterly* 12, nos. 1 & 2 (Winter/Spring 1990): 191–201. Among Fawaz Turki's publications are: *The Disinherited: Journal of a Palestinian Exile* (New York: Monthly Review Press, 1972); *Poems from Exile* (Washington, D.C.: Free Palestine Press, 1975); *Tel Zaatar Was the Hill of Thyme* (Washington, D.C.: Free Palestine Press, 1978); and *Soul in Exile: Lives of a Palestinian Revolutionary* (New York: Monthly Review Press, 1988). Among Naseer Aruri's publications are the following edited works: *Middle East Crucible* (Wilmette, Ill.: Medina University Press International, 1975); and *Occupation: Israel over Palestine* (Belmont, Mass.: AAUG, 1983 and 1989). All three individuals have been frequent speakers on university campuses.

15. (Detroit: AAUG, 1977), 2.

16. *Ibid.* This monograph provides a general overview of publications, resolutions, and conferences of the AAUG up to 1977. See also, *Publications Catalog* (Belmont, Mass.: AAUG Press, n.d. [1987]).

17. See "Disney Alters Lyrics for 'Aladdin,' ADC Wins Partial Victory," *ADC Times* 14, no. 4 (July–August 1993): 1, 8–9.

18. For views of the membership of ADC on various issues, see Baha Abu-Laban, *Social and Political Attitudes of Arab-Americans: What the 1989 ADC Survey Reveals.* ADC Issue Paper No. 24 (Washington, D.C.: ADC, 1990).

19. *Orientalism* (New York: Vintage Books, 1978), 3.

20. *Culture and Imperialism* (New York: Alfred A. Knopf, 1993), xxiii.

21. *Ibid.*

22. Oral history interviews clearly show that Arab-Americans did not remember much prejudice or discrimination against them as a group. See Naff, *op. cit.*, 247–59.

23. See Kalil A. Brishara, *The Origin of the Modern Syrian* (New York: Al-Hoda Publishing House, 1914); Joseph W. Ferris, "Syrian Naturalization Question in the United States," parts 1 & 2, *Syrian World* 2, nos. 8, 9 (February & March 1928), 3–11, 18–24; and Suleiman, *op. cit.*

24. See Barbara C. Aswad, "The Southeast Dearborn Arab Community Struggles for Survival Against Urban 'Renewal.' " In *Arabic Speaking Communities in American Cities*, ed. Barbara C. Aswad (New York: Center for Migration Studies and AAUG, 1974), 53–83; Dan Georgakas, "Arab Workers in Detroit," *MERIP Reports*, no. 34 (January 1975): 13–17; and Nabeel Abraham, "Detroit's Yemeni Workers," *MERIP Reports*, no. 57 (May 1977): 3–9, 13.

25. Abdeen Jabara's activism on behalf of the Arab rights in the United States is of long-standing. See Abdeen M. Jabara and Noel J. Saleh, "Chaldeans and Blacks: From Conflict to Cooperation," *The Detroit Free Press*, 28 October 1983, p. A11; Abdeen Jabara, "Anti-Arab Racism in the Auto Plants: The Case of Nagi Mohamed," *Al-Jaliyah* 1, no. 2 (February 1979): 2–3; "Operation Arab: The Nixon Administration's Measures in the United States After Munich," "IRS Proposes to Revoke AAUG Tax Exemption: Another Form of Political Harassment?" In *The Civil Rights of Arab-Americans; "The Special Measures,"* ed. M.C. Bassiouni. Information papers no. 10 (North Dartmouth, Mass.: AAUG, 1974), 1–15; 49–54; "Workers, Community Mobilized in Detroit," *AAUG Newsletter* 7, no. 2 (June 1974): 10.

26. Detroit Police Department, Red Squad File. Cited in Michael Steven Smith, *Notebook of a Sixties Lawyer* (Brooklyn: Smyrna Press, 1992), back jacket cover.

27. See Abdeen Jabara, "A Strategy for Political Effectiveness." In *Arab Americans: Continuity and Change*, ed. Baha Abu-Laban and Michael W. Suleiman (Belmont, Mass.: AAUG Press, 1989), 201–5.

28. See Helen Hatab Samhan, "Arab Americans and the Elections of 1988: A Constituency Come of Age." In Abu-Laban and Suleiman, *op. cit.*, 227–50.

29. Michael W. Suleiman, "Arab Americans and the Political Process." In *The Development of Arab-American Identity*, ed. Ernest

McCarus (Ann Arbor, Mich.: University of Michigan Press, 1994). Forthcoming.

30. See, in particular, James Abourezk, *On Democracy and Dissent* (Washington, D.C.: Middle East Affairs Council, 1977). This is the text of a speech Abourezk delivered at a Jefferson-Jackson Day Dinner—after attempts to *disinvite* him because of his "pro-Arab" views were stymied.

31. James G. Abourezk, *Advise and Dissent: Memoirs of South Dakota and the U.S. Senate* (Chicago: Lawrence Hill Books, 1989), 214.

32. *Ibid.,* 199–223.

33. This is a common theme in almost all autobiographies of the early arrivals—although they also state that they came to make money and attain a better life. See the "composite" biography of an Arab-American entitled "The Life Story of a Syrian." In *The Life Stories of Undistinguished Americans as Told by Themselves,* ed. Hamilton Hold (New York: Routledge, 1990), 147–58. This is a reprint of the 1906 edition.

34. Even a quick glance at the early Arabic press in America will show the continued bickering/sniping, which went on among the editors/owners of those newspapers. For a quick review, see Henry H. Melki, "Arab-American Journalism and Its Relation to Arab-American Literature," (Ph.D. diss., Georgetown University, 1972).

35. See, for instance, Charles Whitehead, *Sketch of Antonio Bashallany; A Syrian of Mount Lebanon* (New York: The American Tract Society, 1856).

36. Alfred A. Knopf published the English versions of these two works in 1948 and 1928. See also any of the major biographies of Gibran, e.g. Khalil S. Hawi, *Kahlil Gibran* (Beirut: The Arab Institute for Research and Publishing, 1972); and Mikhail Niamy, *Kahlil Gibran: A Biography* (New York: Philosophical Library, 1950).

37. In addition to Gibran, see Amin Rihani, *al-Makkari wa-al-kahin* (The Muleteer and the Priest). (In Arabic). (Beirut: Dar Rihani, 1969). Reprint of 1904 New York edition; and Yusuf Shadid Abi-Lamh, *Riwayat fatat al-ghab* (The Girl of the Forest). (In Arabic). (New York: Al-Hoda Publishing House, 1905).

38. Abraham Mitrie Rihbany, *A Far Journey* (Boston: Houghton Mifflin, 1914), 345–46.

39. See Amin Rihani, "We and Our Newspapers," published in Arabic in 1901, reprinted in Melki, *op. cit.*, pp. 176–90. Abdel-Massih Haddad wrote often against religious intolerance and bigotry through editorials in his newspaper *Al-Sayeh (al-Sáih)*.

40. For surveys of Islam and Muslims in the United States, see Yvonne Y. Haddad and Adair T. Lummis, *Islamic Values in the United States* (New York: Oxford University Press, 1987); and Yvonne Y. Haddad, ed., *The Muslims of America* (New York: Oxford University Press, 1991).

41. Such activities took place frequently enough to generate much discussion/debate in the Arabic press concerning personal safety for the women involved, as well as the propriety of such behavior. See, for instance, the following articles, all of which appeared in *Al-Hoda* newspaper: "Our view of the Druze Woman," 6 February 1909, p. 4; "A Look at Druze Emigration," 6 February 1909, p. 4; "The Syrian Woman in the United States," 5 March 1899, pp. 15–17; "Immigration and the Woman," 3 July 1908, p. 1.

42. See Shukrie Thabit, *My Favorite Furnished Room Stories* (Brooklyn: Thabit Management Co., 1975). These are not really stories but anecdotes from Thabit's life history.

43. William Peter Blatty (N.Y.: W.W. Norton, 1973). See also, by the same author, *Which Way to Mecca, Jack?* (New York: Bernard Geis Associates, 1960).

44. In addition to Shukrie Thabit, already cited, see Helen Thomas, *Dateline: White House* (New York: Macmillan, 1975); and Selwa "Lucky" Roosevelt, *Keeper of the Gate* (New York: Simon and Schuster, 1990). The missionary women were: Layyah A. Barakat, *A Message from Mount Lebanon* (Philadelphia: The Sunday School Times Co., 1912); and Princess Rahme Haidar, *Under Syrian Stars* (New York: Fleming H. Revell, 1929)—a book that is less biographical and more descriptive of the people and the country. See also the interesting and heart-warming account of Delia Ann Tinory's life history as told to, and recorded by, her son: Eugene P. Tinory, *Journey from Ammeah* (Brattleboro, Vt.: Amana Books, 1986).

45. Laila Abou-Saif, *A Bridge Through Time: The Story of an Arab Woman Who Defied Centuries of Tradition* (Brooklyn: Lawrence Hill Books, 1993). Other than the added foreword by Gloria Steinem and a change in the subtitle, the book appeared earlier under a pseudonym (Laila Said) published by Summit Books (New York, 1985). The quotes are from pages 47 and 67.

46. See, for instance, Joanna Kadi's essays and the edited anthology tentatively entitled: *Food for Our Grandmothers: Writings by Arab-American and Arab-Canadian Feminists* (Boston: South End Press, 1994).

47. Donald B. Cole, *Immigrant City, Lawrence, Massachusetts, 1845–1921* (Chapel Hill: University of North Carolina Press, 1980), 180. Even Arab-Americans involved in such activity are likely to deny it in later years because they feel it might taint them as radical or revolutionary—terms that are anathema to most Arab-Americans. See, for instance, Marad's denial, in later years, that he had an influential role in the 1912 Lawrence strike. *Ibid.*, 188.

48. *Ibid.*, 180–89. One of the two fatalities in the strike was an Arab boy, John Ramey (Rami, Ramie), who was bayonetted by a militiaman. See U.S. Congress. House. The Committee on Rules, *Hearings on House Resolutions 409 and 43: The Strike at Lawrence, Mass.* (Washington, D.C.: Government Printing Office, March 1912), 415. See also Justus Ebert, *The Trial of a New Society* (Cleveland: I.W.W. Publishing Bureau, 1913).

49. Nabeel Abraham, "Arab Americans." In *Encyclopedia of the American Left*, ed., Mari Jo Buhle, Paul Buhle and Dan Georgakas (New York: Garland, 1990), 53.

50. Jeremiah W. Jenks and W. Jett Lauck, *The Immigration Problem* (New York: Funk and Wagnalls, 1913), 96.

51. For early reports on Arab-Americans working in factories, see (in addition to Jenks and Lauck) Prescott F. Hall, *Immigration and Its Effects upon the United States* (New York: Henry Holt & Co., 1906), 126; and Louise Seymour Houghton, "Syrians in the United States: Business Activities," *The Survey* 26 (August 1911): 647–65, especially 651.

52. Information about Addes was culled from Jean Gould and Lorena Hickok, *Walter Reuther, Labor's Rugged Individualist* (New York: Dodd, Mead & Co., 1972).

53. See Dan Georgakas and Marvin Surkin, *Detroit: I Do Mind Dying* (New York: St. Martin's Press, 1975), *passim.*

54. See Toby Moffett, *The Participation Put-On: Reflections of a Disenchanted Washington Youth Expert* (New York: Delacorte Press, 1971); and *Nobody's Business: The Political Intruder's Guide to Everyone's State Legislature.* Introd. by Ralph Nader (Riverside, Conn.: Chatham Press, 1973).

55. Abourezk, *Advise and Dissent*, 122–25.

56. See Rose B. Nader and Nathra Nader, *It Happened in the Kitchen: Recipes for Food and Thought* (Washington, D.C.: Center for Study of Responsive Law, 1991).

57. (New York: Grossman, 1965).

58. See Michael W. Suleiman, "Arab-Americans: A Community Profile," *Journal: Institute of Muslim Minority Affairs* 5, no. 1 (1983), 29–35.

59. Several books have been written about Ralph Nader, most of them laudatory, some critical. See Robert F. Buckhorn, *Nader: The People's Lawyer* (Englewood Cliffs, N.J.: Prentice Hall, 1972); Hays Gorey, *Nader and the Power of Everyman* (New York: Grosset & Dunlap, 1975); Kelley Griffin, *Ralph Nader Presents More Action for a Change* (New York: December, 1987); Richard Curtis, *Ralph Nader's Crusade* (Philadelphia: Macrae Smith, 1972); and Charles McCarry, *Citizen Nader* (New York: Saturday Review Press, 1972).

60. See Michael A. Shadid, *A Doctor for the People* (New York: The Vanguard Press, 1939), 15.

61. Michael A. Shadid, *Crusading Doctor: My Fight for Cooperative Medicine* (Boston: Meador Publishing Co., 1956), 279.

62. F.M. Al Akl, *Until Summer Comes* (Springfield, Mass.: The Pond-Ekberg Co., 1945). In particular, see pp. 322, 324, 354–55.

63. Stuart Auerbach, "Home from China; Doctor Who Gained Fame in China Pays Long-Delayed Visit to Carolina Home: Carolina Doctor Gained Fame in 46-Year Mainland Career," *Washington Post*, 30 April 1978, p. A1.

64. "U.S. College Honors American-Born Doctor in China," *Chicago Tribune*, 23 September 1987, p. 4C.

65. Walter Sullivan, "Dr. George Hatem Is Dead at 78; Leader in Public Health in China," *New York Times*, 6 October 1988, p. 15B.

66. In addition to the innumerable reports and journalistic accounts that have been published about Hatem's work in China, see E. Grey Dimond, *Inside China Today: A Western View* (New York: W.W. Norton, 1983); and Sidney Shapiro, *Ma Haide: The Saga of American Doctor George Hatem in China* (San Francisco: Cypress Press, 1993).

67. Nicholas S. Assali, *A Doctor's Life* (New York: Harcourt, Brace, Jovanovich, 1979), 208.

68. *Ibid.*, 207–15.

69. Danny Thomas, with Bill Davidson, *Make Room for Danny* (New York: G.P. Putnam's Sons, 1991), 314.

70. See also the interview with Danny Thomas in Gregory Orfalea, *Before the Flames: A Quest for the History of Arab Americans* (Austin: University of Texas Press, 1988), 108–16.

71. See, for instance, the values contained in stories in Arabic primers in Egypt and Iraq and reflected in responses to a survey of students in Morocco in Michael W. Suleiman, "Values and Societal Development; Education and Change in Nasser's Egypt." In *Political Behavior in the Arab States*, ed., Tawfic E. Farah (Boulder: Westview Press, 1983), 93–106; 'Education and Change in Iraq: Values Expressed in Children's Readers." In *Man and Society in the Arab Gulf*, vol. 3 (Basrah, Iraq: Center for Arab Gulf Studies, Basrah University, 1979), 429–52; and "Attitudes, Values and the Political Process in Morocco." In *The Political Economy of Morocco*, ed. I. William Zartman (Boulder: Westview Press, 1987), 98–116.

72. Al Akl, *op. cit.*, 320.

NINE

The Hidden World of Asian Immigrant Radicalism

Robert G. Lee

I. The Invisibility of Asian-Americans in the Historiography of American Radicalism

In the great celebratory photograph of the driving of the "golden spike" at Promontory Point, Utah in 1869 joining the Central Pacific Railroad to the Union Pacific Railroad and spanning the continent, not one of the more than ten thousand Chinese workers who had carved the Central Pacific roadbed through the Sierras and through the desert was pictured. The speeches of the day praising the dynamism of American capital, the skill of American technology, and the strength and tenacity of American labor made no mention of the Chinese, over a thousand of whom had died building the railroad. This moment captured in this photo is the supreme metaphor for the erasure of Asian-Americans from American history.

Historians of immigration, with only a few exceptions, have tended either to treat immigration from Asia as an event unrelated to immigration from Europe or, more commonly, to ignore it altogether.[1] Discounting the prehistoric migrations over the Alaskan land bridge or the less well-documented transpacific migrations to Mesoamerica, the various Asian migrations to the Americas have been a critical aspect of the development of the world capitalist system. Asian settlement in the Americas began in the 1700s when Filipino sailors established communities in what is now Louisiana and Texas. So-called Manilamen had sailed aboard the Spanish galleons that plied the silver trade between Manila and Mexico City. The Chinese who arrived in California in 1848 were part of a continuous succession of Asian immigrants. Coming to the United States as, in Ronald Takaki's phrase, "a yellow proletariat," immediately and unavoidably brought Chinese, Japanese, Korean, Indian, and Filipino immigrants directly into the complex and interrelated processes of class and racial formation in America.[2]

Although Asian immigrants to the United States have and continue to be overwhelmingly working people, their experience of struggle has been made almost totally invisible in the master narrative of American labor and radical history. This essay begins with an examination of the erasure of the Asian immigrant experience from the historiography of the American working class. The hostility, violence, and disenfranchisement meted out to successive waves of Asian immigrants in the United States shaped a transnational politics that involved Asian immigrants and exiles in nationalist and socialist movements on both sides of the Pacific. The second and third parts of this essay examine the development of these political struggles. The fourth section examines the role of the Asian immigrant Left in its heyday during the late 1930s and early 1940s. The essay concludes with a brief history of Asian immigrant labor in Hawaii, an alternative narrative of immigration, labor, and struggle.

The well-known hostility of the mainstream of the U.S. labor movement towards successive groups of Asian immigrants to the United States, shaped not only the experience of Asian immigrants in the United States but also significantly shaped the historiography of Asians in America. The first studies of Asian immigration to America responded to the questions that the opponents of Asian immigration had raised about Asian assimilation into American society. Mary Coolidge's *Chinese Immigration* (1909)[3] was a defense of Chinese immigrants, which blamed the anti-Chinese movement in nineteenth-century California squarely on Irish ruffians. The Chinese, she argued, were neither coolie labor as Denis Kearny's Workingmen's Party had claimed, nor were they socially unassimilable.

Paul Siu, the son of a Chinese laundryman and a doctoral

student of Chicago sociologist Robert Park, was the first to study the Chinese immigrant experience from the inside. His dissertation *The Chinese Laundryman: a Study in Social Isolation* (1938)[4] was concerned with the process by which immigrants assimilated into mainstream American society. In explaining the relative social isolation of Chinese laundrymen in Chicago, Siu was the first to use the term sojourner. Sojourners, in Siu's view, worked in one locale but maintained a cultural loyalty to their distant homeland. Siu argued that American racial prejudice and legal restrictions were at the heart of producing this phenomena. Nevertheless, since Siu's study the sojourner thesis has more often been used to explain away than to explain the social experience of Asians in the United States.

Perhaps the most important study of the Chinese to have misused the sojourner thesis was *Bitter Strength: A History of the Chinese in the United States from 1850–1870*[5] by Gunther Barth, a student of Oscar Handlin. Barth argued that the white working class was only defending its vision of liberty when it attacked the Chinese whose sojourner mentality made them unfit for settlement in America. Barth compounded the error when he argued that the credit ticket system by which most Chinese workers after 1860 paid for their passage to California was a thinly disguised version of the notorious coolie trade. There is little or no evidence that this was so. Even the most vociferous crusaders against the coolie trade, which was often plied on American ships to the Caribbean and to Chile and Peru, found no cause to believe that immigration to California fell into this category of bound labor.[6]

Unfortunately, Barth's thesis continued to influence a number of other important studies of Chinese immigrantation. Most important among these was Alexander Saxton's *The Indispensable Enemy: Labor and the Anti-Chinese Movement in California*,[7] which analyzed the politics of the anti-Chinese movement in terms of its class basis. Saxton demonstrated how the interests of Democratic Party politicians and trade union leaders were joined through the movement to expel Chinese workers from the California labor market. Despite the precision of his work on the politics of the labor movement, Saxton relies uncritically on Barth's account of the Chinese and subsequently pays insufficient attention to the development of race as central to working-class ideology. Stuart Creighton Miller, in *The Unwelcome Immigrant: The Image of the Chinese In America*,[8] challenges Barth only to the extent that he finds the basis for negative attitudes towards Chinese immigrantation in the earlier writings of missionaries, businessmen, and diplomats about China itself. Roger Daniels, studying the development of the anti-Japanese movement, which followed on the heels of the passage of the Chinese Exclusion Acts in *The Politics of Prejudice, The Anti-Japanese Movement in California and the Struggle for Anti-Japanese Exclusion,*[9] argued that exclusionists had operated on a mistaken assumption: since the Japanese immigrants were unlike the Chinese laborers, they could not be considered sojourners.

None of these studies critically questioned the Barth thesis that nineteenth-century Chinese labor in California was coerced labor. Neither did these earlier studies seek to assign any agency or subjectivity to Asian immigrants themselves. As a result, the view of helplessly victimized Chinese immigrants as faceless, docile, and unassimilable into a presumably colorblind working class has remained the dominant image and has been projected onto successive Asian immigrant groups. This image of a people without historical weight, happy to work at lower wages than other Americans and culturally indisposed to political activism or protest is still very much alive in the contemporary myth of Asian-Americans as the so-called model minority.

One of the lasting achievements of the Asian-American student revolution of the late 1960s was the establishment of Asian-American Studies in the academy. By seeking to examine the Asian-American past through the perspective of Asian immigrants themselves, scholars in Asian-American studies have begun to sketch out a new theoretical model in which immigration from Asia to the United States might be analyzed. In *Labor Immigration Under Capitalism: Asian Workers in the United States Before World War II,*[10] Lucie Cheng and Edna Bonacich have brought together important essays on Chinese, Japanese, Filipino, Korean, and Asian-Indian immigration. In her introductory and theoretical essays, Edna Bonacich argues that the processes of immigration can best be understood in terms of the development of global capitalism. She argues that, in the broad context of imperialism, the economic dislocation and creation of populations of workers available for emigration from Asia can be related to the capitalist development of the United States generally and the high demand for cheap labor on the West Coast in particular. The essays in this volume provide considerable detail on both the economic contexts, which led to emigration, and the labor contexts in which Asian immigrants found themselves once in the United States. The essays show the specific historical moments and particular mechanisms of this system differed from place to place, but the pattern of displacement and absorption of Asian workers into the American labor market in Hawaii and on the West Coast is a general one that establishes a common economic terrain for the Asian experience in America.

Ping Chiu in his pioneering and detailed economic study of the nineteenth century, *Chinese Labor in California*,[11] argued that Chinese labor was not bound labor and that in only one arena of the California economy, cigarmaking, did the Chinese compete directly with white labor. It may be noted that it was from the CigarMakers Union that Samuel Gompers, the most rock-ribbed foe of Asian immigration and Asian membership in the American labor movement, rose to power in the AFL. In *This Bittersweet Soil: The Chinese in California Agriculture, 1860–1910*, Sucheng Chan documents the critical role that Chinese played as agricultural laborers, skilled workers, tenant farmers, and in some cases, farm owners.

While Chinese workers in the United States had not come to the United States as coerced labor, once in the United States they quickly became more fully proletarianized than their white counterparts. While white workers could attempt to use the family as a means of resisting complete proletarianization, the Chinese working-class immigrant, prohibited by immigration law from constructing familial relations in the United States, had with few exceptions no such means of resistance. Capitalists saw Asian workers as a cheap and easily manageable workforce, which could also be deployed as a reserve army of labor to fight the growing militancy of labor unions and to instill discipline amongst its labor force. The journals of manufacturing associations and newspapers that supported employers were quick to praise the Asian workers for their industriousness, quick learning, and sobriety. But would-be employers were soon to find out that Asian workers were not at all the docile labor force they had imagined. Despite their virtual exclusion from the American working-class movement, Asian workers organized their own strikes and engaged in various forms of resistance against white employers, Asian employers, and labor contractors.

As early as the summer of 1867, between five and seven thousand Chinese workers building the transpacific railway in the High Sierras struck the Central Pacific. At the time there were approximately eight thousand Chinese workers working on the Central Pacific, mostly Chinese who had immigrated earlier to seek their fortunes in the gold fields but who had been driven out of the mining districts. The Central Pacific paid these Chinese workers from $30 to $35 dollars a month without board while it paid white workers $35 with board worth about $.70 a day. The Chinese workers struck demanding pay parity with white workers, a wage of $40 to $45 a month, better working conditions, and an eight-hour day. The strikers' slogan was "Eight hours a day good for white men, all the same good for Chinamen." Their strike collapsed after a week, when the Central Pacific owners cut off food to the Chinese camps and took "Other such coercive measures."[12] While the strike itself failed, the prior threat of this strike was thought to have prompted the Central Pacific to increase Chinese pay to $35 a month. Although this early strike is mentioned in passing in a number of works, little has been written about it. The brief account of it in Ping Chiu is the most detailed. Indeed it is sadly ironic that although the role of the Chinese in building the transcontinental railroad is the one universally cited contribution of Asian immigrants to American history, there is no full-length study of the experience.

Shortly after the Civil War, Southern plantation owners planned to bring in Chinese workers to supplement black labor in the South. Lucy M. Cohen, in *The Chinese in the Post-Civil War South: A People Without A History*[13] provides the most detailed account of this episode. In 1869, some 250 Chinese workers were recruited to work on the Houston and Texas Central Railroad, one thousand to work for the Alabama and Chattanooga Railroad, and six hundred to work on sugar and cotton plantations in Arkansas, Louisiana, and Mississippi. Within the year, the Chinese working on the Houston and Texas had filed suit against the railroad for breach of contract. A year later when the Alabama and Chattanooga went bankrupt, hundreds of Chinese were among the workers who were owed back wages and who seized the company's cars and equipment. Chinese plantation labor was likewise a disappointment to the plantation owners who were used to and had been led to expect a compliant labor force. Chinese plantation crews demanded strict adherence to their contracts and would not yield to arbitrary work rules. Mistreatment of Chinese workers by overseers was met by mass protest, work stoppages, and, on occasion, violence. Few renewed their contracts.

In 1870, Calvin Sampson brought a crew of 75 Chinese workers to North Adams, Massachusetts to replace striking Irish and French-Canadian workers in the soling room of his shoe factory. For a time, this seemed to be an ideal strategy to undermine the growing strength of the Order of St. Crispins, a semisecret guild union. The national debate that Sampson's experience touched off has been given much attention by historians, yet little has been written about the experience of the Chinese workers themselves. On the one hand, a number of the mostly teenaged Chinese workers seemed to have been adopted by families in North Adams. On the other, after Sampson brought a second crew of Chinese workers in 1873, 43 of the Chinese workers were summarily dismissed after rioting and attempting to murder their Chinese foreman for having attempted to hold their pay in escrow.[14] In the same year, Chinese workers were brought to Belleville, New Jersey to replace striking Irish female workers in the Passaic Steam Laundry plant. Within a year or two, however, the frustrated owner reported that the Chinese workers were themselves engaging in strikes and many had left the plant. By 1885, all the Chinese workers had been dismissed.[15]

A strike by a "large force" of Chinese hop pickers in Kern County, California in 1884 was described in a report to the Knights of Labor as "militant" and a positive indication that the Chinese could be successfully organized.[16] Three years later, Chinese assemblies were organized in New York by District 49 of the Knights of Labor only to be dissolved into larger mixed assemblies on order of Terence Powderly, the national leader of the Knights of Labor, who had gone on record as not only opposing Asian labor but declaring that Asians were unfit to reside in the United States. Nevertheless, Powderly had conceded that there were indeed a few Chinese Knights of Labor.[17]

The hostility of the AFL leadership towards Chinese workers extended to include Japanese and ultimately all Asian immigrants. In 1903, when Japanese and Mexican workers in the sugar beet fields of Oxnard, California organized the first multiracial union, the Japanese and Mexican Agricultural Workers Association (JMAWA), they were met with hostility on the part of the AFL headquarters. Tomas Almaguer has analyzed the JMAWA's attempt at interracial solidarity in the face of the AFL's policy of racial intolerance.[18] The JMAWA struck in June of 1903 and appealed to the AFL for a charter, with the support of the California Central Labor Committee. Samuel Gompers, however, was adamant that the AFL retain as a central principle opposition to not only the importation of Asian labor but to the exclusion from the American labor movement of any Asian workers already in the United States. Gompers demanded as a price for an AFL charter that the Mexican members oust their Japanese partners from JMAWA. The Mexican immigrant workers refused Gompers' offer.

The hostility of organized labor towards Asian immigrant workers was formalized in a series of laws and regulations, which, from the mid-1850s to the mid-1940s, systematically disenfranchised Asian immigrants. Beginning in 1870, increasingly severe restrictions were put on immigration. Special taxes and regulations were introduced to limit the growth of Asian-operated businesses. Laws were passed prohibiting Asian immigrants from owning farmland. Marriage between Asians and whites was prohibited in many states. In other words every aspect of Asian life in America was strictly controlled and encumbered by the state.

While earlier studies such as Elmer Sandemeyer's *The Anti-Chinese Movement* and Roger Daniels's *The Politics of Prejudice* dealt extensively with the political history of legislation against Chinese and Japanese immigration,[19] it has only been recently that studies of how that legislation specifically affected the lives of Asian immigrants have been published. Most notably, the essays in *Entry Denied* (1991), edited by Sucheng Chan, have shed light both on the effects of the Exclusion Acts on the Chinese community and on the various ways in which Chinese in America resisted those restrictions.[20]

In addition to evasion, illegal entry, and tactics such as putting property in the hands of American-born children, Asian immigrants resisted exclusionary and discriminatory laws through thousands of challenges in the courts. Among the Chinese alone, Sucheng Chan has counted over one thousand cases recorded in the *Federal Reporter* and over 150 cases heard before the United States Supreme Court.[21] Chan estimates that this represents less than ten percent of the cases filed and heard.

Another factor shaping Asian immigrant politics was the open violence against Asian immigrants. Chinese gold miners were repeatedly harassed, robbed, and murdered in the mining districts from the 1850s onwards. Among the riots against Asians that attracted some attention were the massacres of Chinese residents in Los Angeles in 1871; in Rock Springs, Wyoming, Eureka, California, and Seattle and Tacoma, Washington in 1885; and along the Snake River in Oregon in 1887. Asian Indians were expelled from Bellingham and Everett, Washington in 1907 and from Live Oak, California in 1908. Japanese farm laborers were driven out of various places in California, including Turlock and Livingston in 1921; Delano, Porterville, and Los Angeles in 1922; Hopland and again Los Angeles in 1924; and Woodlake in 1926. Japanese farm workers were similarly expelled from Toledo, Oregon in 1925. Filipinos were attacked by California mobs in Stockton in 1926, Dinuba in 1928, Exeter in 1929, and Watsonville in 1930. Some of the more notorious incidents such as the Rock Springs Massacre or the Tacoma Riots have been studied in isolation. Roger Daniels, Yuji Ichioka, Howard A. Dewitt, and Joan Jensen have reported on the violence against Chinese, Filipinos, and Indians as separate groups.[22] There is yet no study of anti-Asian violence as a part of the social and cultural history of the U.S., but Carlos Bulosan's fictionalized autobiography, *America is in the Heart*, gives a vivid sense of its intensity and its dailiness for Filipino workers on the Pacific Coast.[23]

II. Nationalism in a Transnational Community

Facing the hostility of a racially defined working class, exploitation in a racially and ethnically segmented labor market, and almost complete political and social disenfranchisement in the United States, Asian immigrants were a stateless proletariat. Unprotected by citizenship rights within the country in which they lived, not protected by their countries of origin, which, with the exception of Japan, were either colonial possessions or apolitical invalids. Even the Japanese government, which had been able to slow the anti-Japanese movement in the United States through its diplomatic efforts, was ultimately forced to accept the Gentlemen's Agreement of 1908, the Alien Land Law of 1917, and the exclusion of Japanese immigrants altogether in the Immigration Act of 1924.

The various anticolonialist and nationalist movements that emerged in China, Korea, and India were therefore given widespread moral and material support in Asian communities in the United States. Such support for the building of a strong nation state in one's land of origin was not nostalgia but a critical necessity for the improvement of conditions in the United States. A strong diplomatic presence on the part of Asian countries would be one of the few sources of protection for immigrants who had been declared ineligible for citizenship. The question of nationalism was, however, never simple. Various movements had to compete vigorously for the loyalty and not insubstantial material support of the overseas Asian communities.

Asian immigrant politics took on a transnational character as Asian immigrants engaged in resistance to racial discrimination and class exploitation in the United States and in nation building in the lands of their origins. From the turn of the century, there was tremendous movement of political activists back and forth across the Pacific. Katayama Sen, for example, would become a Christian Socialist as a student in Iowa and return to Japan to help found the Social Democratic Party. A decade later, he would return to the United States and eventually become a founding member of the U.S. Communist Party. Revolutionary newspapers like *Ghadar* (Urdu for revolution), which were published in places like Seattle and Oakland, were circulated and read in Calcutta and Bombay. The newspapers injected issues of racial discrimination and mistreatments in the United States into the political agenda of nationalist movements in Asia as the *Komagata Maru* Incident of 1914 mobilized Indian patriots on four continents. Finally, the outcomes of national crises in the Asian countries often had repercussions for class politics within the Asian immigrant community, such as the 1905 Chinese boycott of American goods.

Eve Armentrout Ma has shown in her *Revolutionaries, Monarchists and Chinatowns*[24] that during the first decades of this century, racial exclusion, nationalism, and class politics were inextricably linked. As many Chinese workers had come to the United States illegally, they were vulnerable to threats of deportation. Their isolation from potential class allies often, but not always, led them to rely on ethnic solidarity to protect themselves. As a result, Chinese-American communities tend to be dominated by merchant elites, often through social and political organizations that laid claim to a homeland tradition. In fact, far from being traditional, the Chinatown organizations were hybrids, adopting Chinese forms and titles to a completely different set of social demands and meanings.[25] By the turn of the century, the entry of radical intellectuals and professional revolutionaries into those communities brought class contradictions into open conflict.

Although they made up only one-fifth of the Chinese population, the merchants from the Sam Yup region, Canton, and its environs, dominated the political and economic life of Chinatowns throughout the country through their control over the Chinese Consolidated Benevolent Association (CCBA). The CCBA was also known as the Chinese Six Companies, and its political authority to regulate community affairs and represent the Chinese community was recognized by the Qing government and American authorities alike. Although the Sam Yup merchants had been the first to settle in California, the great majority of the Chinese community who had arrived since the late 1860s were people from the Sze Yup region, the poorer rural districts away from Canton. The Sze Yup people were completed excluded from the leadership of the Chinese Six Companies and were principally organized in surname associations and secret societies.

The passage of the Geary Act in 1892 provided the impetus for a shift in the political balance between these two factions. The act provided that all Chinese residents in the United States register with an appropriate authority or risk deportation. The Chinese community saw this law as a prelude to the forced repatriation of all Chinese immigrants and was rightly alarmed. The Chinese Six Companies called for a mass boycott of the registration provisions of the Geary Act and threw its support behind a legal challenge to the law.

In 1893, in *Fong Yue Ting v. US*, the U.S. Supreme Court held that the registration provisions of the Geary Act were a constitutionally allowable extension of the government's right to exclude and expel aliens. The Chinese, even though they might otherwise be legal residents, had no right to resist the demand for registration. The *Fong Yue Ting* defeat jeopardized all who had refused to register and was a serious blow to the prestige of the Chinese Six Companies. This led the Sze Yup to boycott Sam Yup businesses. The struggle resulted in the legendary tong wars of the late nineteenth and early twentieth century. The ensuing warfare led the Sze Yup associations and the Secret Society known as the *Zhigongtong* or Chinese Freemasons to rival the Chinese Six Companies in power and prestige.

In the meantime, two nationalist political parties, the *Xingonghui* (Revive China Society) and the *Baohuanghue* (Protect the Emperor Society), had been founded, respectively, in Hawaii in 1895 and in Vancouver in 1899. The first was organized by Sun Yatsen to promote a revolutionary overthrow of the Qing dynasty while the second was organized by advocates of reform. Each vied for the support of the Chinese camps in America. Initially, both parties were successful in appealing for support from the *Zhigongtong*, while the Chinese Six Companies supported the reform party. The struggle between the nationalist parties became sharper in 1904 when the Chinese Exclusion Acts came up for renewal. The reformist *Baohuanghui*, and its supporters in the Chinese Six Companies, favored a modification of the law, which would have allowed for the continued exclusion of Chinese laborers. The revolutionary *Xinzhonghui*, the *Zhigongtong*, and the Sze Yup associations favored complete repeal. Thousands of Chinese merchants in the United States and China began a massive boycott of American goods to protest the renewal,[26] but the exclusion acts were extended indefinitely. This extension exposed the complete inability of the crumbling Qing government to wrest even the smallest concession from the United States.

The boycott movement was, from its inception, highly factionalized with reformers and revolutionaries each trying to define the movement's goals and strategies to meet their own agendas. When the movement collapsed in the face of American intransigeance, each side blamed the other for the defeat. The result was a Chinese-American community, unified in support of Chinese nationalism as a general principle but increasingly polarized along class and regional lines over the specific meaning of that nationalism. These camps were to shape the political terrain of Chinese America for the increasingly sharp class politics of the 1920s and 1930s.

Korean immigration to the United States before the 1960s was a trickle compared to Japanese or Chinese immigration. Ironically it was not American exclusion laws that limited Korean immigration but rather Japanese government restrictions that put a halt to Korean immigration.

Beginning in 1904 some seven thousand Koreans were brought to work in the cane fields of Hawaii. They had been recruited by the Rev. Horace Allen, the U.S. minister to the Korean court, on behalf of the Hawaii Sugar Planters Association (HSPA), which had sought to undercut the growing power of the Japanese, who, by 1885, made up two-thirds of the plantation workforce. A much smaller workforce, numbering in the hundreds, went to the U.S. mainland.

In 1905, as soon as it gained a position of preeminence on the Korean peninsula as a result of its victory over Russia, the Japanese government, seeking to protect the position of Japanese workers in Hawaii, put pressure on the Korean government to halt emigration to the United States. In 1907, the United States government declared that it would consider Korean immigrants only if they had been issued Japanese passports. This recognition of Japanese hegemony effectively stopped the immigration of Korean workers, but Korean women continued to immigrate under the terms of the Gentlemen's Agreement, which allowed "picture brides" to enter with the intention of marrying immigrants already resident in the United States. Students and ministers were also exempted as nonlaborers. By the time that Japan formally annexed Korea in 1910, thousands of Korean nationalists, intellectuals, students, and others had fled. Some five hundred entered the United States as political refugees. Although Chong-sik Lee has studied the nationalist movement in *The Politics of Korean Nationalism*[27] in the context of Korea, a detailed study of how the nationalist movements mobilized the Korean communities in America has yet to be written. Nevertheless, articles by Kingsley Lyu, Linda Shin, and the chapter on the independence movement in H. Brett Melendy's *Asians in America* provide the outlines of the movement in the U.S.[28]

Since Horace Allen had first gone to Korea as a missionary, he favored Christian converts as applicants for immigration. Korean Christian churches therefore played a significant role in shaping the nationalist movement among Koreans in America. Of the three principle nationalist leaders who arrived in the first years of the century, Ahn Chang-ho, Park Yong-man, and Syngman Rhee, two were devout Christians.

Ahn, a Christian intellectual who believed that moral regeneration and individual transformation were the keys to a successful Korean struggle for independence organized the *Hung Sa Dan* (Young Korean Academy) to train an intellectual elite that could return to govern Korea. By contrast, Park Yong-man believed that Korea's independence could only be secured through military means. After graduation from the University of Nebraska where he had studied political science and military science, Park established a Korean Youth Military Academy in Nebraska and went on to set up four other military academies in California, Missouri, and Wyoming.

Syngman Rhee entered the U.S. as a divinity student at Harvard and became the first Korean to earn a doctorate in the United States, (from Princeton in politics). After serving as YMCA secretary in Seoul, Rhee returned to the United States in 1911 to become principal of a Korean community school in Hawaii at Park's request. Soon after his arrival, however, Rhee split with Park over the strategy for achieving independence. Rejecting armed struggle, Rhee advocated lobbying the international community, especially Washington, where he had cultivated friends.

Meanwhile in 1909, members of the San Francisco-based Korean Mutual Aid Society and the Southern California-based Korean Restoration Society assassinated Durham Stephans, an American who had just been appointed as the foreign affairs advisor to the Japanese protectorate government in Korea. After Stephans' assassination, the various Korean nationalist groups came together as the Korean National Association and set up military training centers in Hawaii. In 1912, Park went to Hawaii and consolidated the various cadet groups into the three hundred-man Korean National Brigade.

Ahn, Park, and Rhee served in a short-lived Korean provisional government established in Shanghai in 1919 after the suppression of the March 1st movement in Korea. After the collapse of the provisional government, the divisions between the Ahn and Park group and Rhee became irreconcilable. Ahn and Park remained in China while Rhee returned to the U.S. Ahn would be executed by the Japanese for his involvement in blowing up Japanese buildings in China and Park would be assassinated in 1928 while organizing Korean military units in North China.

Breaking with the Korean National Society, Rhee established the *Donji-hoe* (Comrade Society) in 1921 and his own Korean Christian Church. The *Donji-hoe* drew the majority of its support from the substantial Korean community in Hawaii but was unable to maintain mainland branches. The rival *Hung Sa Dan* continued to attract nationalist activists in California and elsewhere in the U.S. into the late 1940s. The rivalry was so severe that Melendy reports that *Hung Sa Dan* activists feared to travel to Korea when Rhee was president for fear of being persecuted as communists.

In the late 1930s, the Sino-Korean Peoples League was organized in Hawaii to oppose the conservative *Donji-hoe*. Little has been written about the Sino-Korean Peoples League and it is unclear what sort of support it was able to mobilize in the Korean communities, but its stated goal was to "unite Koreans in the United States, Hawaii, China and Korea." Its name and goals suggest that it followed the Chinese Communist Party's (CCP) call for a broad united front against Japanese imperialism. Even though the Shanghai provisional government had quickly collapsed, China had remained a primary base of operations for Korean nationalists. Korean radicals had been involved with the CCP from its inception and by the 1930s, a strong contingent of Korean revolutionaries was operating with the CCP in Yenan. Korean guerrillas units, including one commanded by Kim Il Sung, were also in action against the Japanese in Manchuria and North China.[29]

The Sino-Korean Peoples League was instrumental in organizing a federation of Korean political parties to support the war effort against Japan in 1941, but it left the federation when a leader was refused the position of liaison with the U.S. government. Syngman Rhee became an elder statesman of the independence movement and returned to an independent Korea in 1945 as president of a fragile coalition that included both the Korean partisans who had fought a bitter war against the Japanese and nationalists who had spent decades in exile. Rhee remained president of South Korea under American aegis until ousted by mass protests in 1960.

270 The Immigrant Left in the United States

III. Towards Social Revolution: Anarchism
and Socialism

By the end of the first decade of the twentieth century, nationalism
in Asia was infused with radical social ideologies. Asian radicals
avidly studied the writings of the whole panoply of European
and American revolutionary thinkers from the Fabians, Edward
Bellamy and Henry George, to Marx, Bakunin, and Kropotkin.
Their works and the writings of scores of less well-known social
theorists were all intensively debated in Bombay, Beijing, and
Tokyo. Due to its own foreign policy interests, the Japanese government found it advantageous to offer a refuge for radical students and political exiles from China, India, and the Philippines.
The University of Tokyo soon became a magnet and haven for
Asian activists. As Martin Bernal has observed in the case of
the Chinese intellectuals, many of the first works on socialism,
anarchism, and Marxism were first read in Japanese translation.[30]

Since students and intellectuals were among the few Asians
allowed entry into the United States, Asian communities in the
United States became havens for political activists seeking refuge
from repression in their home countries. Despite the well-known
racial prejudice against Asians on the part of the mainstream of
the American labor movement, including many of those who
considered themselves socialists, many Asian radicals were nevertheless drawn to the United States in their search for revolutionary models.

As in the case of the early nationalist movement in the Chinese-American community, the struggle against British rule over
India was deeply connected to the struggle against the exclusion
and discrimination against Indian immigrants in the United States
and Canada. As Joan Jensen has shown in *Passage from India; Indian
Pioneers in America,*[31] the mobilization of Indians both in India and
on the North American continent involved issues of class, religion,
and region. Although the early nationalist movements among the
Chinese or Koreans in the United States had no close ties to
American political movements, such was not the case with the
Indian independence movement. Opposition to British colonialism
was a cause many Americans espoused, from anti-imperialist
liberals to Irish immigrant activists fighting for Ireland's independence. In addition, the Socialist Labor Party (SLP) and the newly
founded (1905) Industrial Workers of the World (IWW) both actively welcomed Asian immigrants as members, opening up new
political space for Asian-American radicalism.

Between 1907 and 1914, some six thousand Indians immigrated to the United States either from India, the Philippines, or Canada. The majority were Sikhs. Most were farmers who had left the plague-stricken and economically depressed Punjab; others were veterans of the British forces that had suppressed the Boxer Rebellion in China in 1900.[32] A smaller number were students, mainly Bengali, many of whom had already become involved in the nationalist movement. The British partition of Bengal and its mishandling of the devastating plague in the Punjab fueled nationalist anger at the same time that the Japanese victory over Russia in 1905 and the Chinese boycott of American goods in the same year served as inspiration. The British response to this upsurge of political activism in Indian colleges and universities was to have student activists expelled, whereupon hundreds of young nationalists went to universities in Japan, Europe, and the United States.

The Indian nationalist movement in the United States was to coalesce around the activities of the *Ghadar* Party. The *Ghadar* Party was established in Seattle in 1913 by the young Indian activists, Taraknath Das and Har Dayal. Das had left college in India in 1905 to become a political agitator. Fleeing arrest in India, he spent a short time in Tokyo before coming to the U.S. in 1906. In 1907, Das was turned down for U.S. citizenship, but became a translator for the U.S. Immigration Service in Vancouver where he began to publish the *Free Hindustan*, a newspaper advocating independence for India. Das was fired for refusing to stop publishing his paper and went to Seattle where he continued to publish *Free Hindustan* with the help of local socialists and Indian students. In 1909, Das enrolled in Norwich University, a well-known military college in Vermont. He immediately attracted attention by advocating Indian independence and persuaded ten more Indian students to apply before he himself was expelled for his political activities. Das continued to travel around the country organizing students and making contact with other anti-imperialists such as the editor of the *Gaelic-American*.

Har Dayal came to California in 1911.[33] Unlike Das, who had come from a poor background, Dayal was from a high-caste, well-to-do family. Dayal taught Indian philosophy at Stanford University without pay (the university would later deny he had ever been on its faculty) but spent most of his time in political activity. He read Marx, Bakunin, and Kropotkin. He became secretary of the Radical Socialist Club in San Francisco; later founded the Bakunin Club, an anarchist study group; and was a speaker at a number of IWW meetings and rallies.

Das and Dayal organized the *Ghadar* Party under the auspices of the Hindu Association of the Pacific Coast and the Sikh *Kalhsa Diwan*, the major Sikh organization in California. The party thus brought together the two streams of Indian immigrants in America, Bengali Hindus, primarily students and intellectuals, and Punjabi Sikhs, mainly agriculturists and lumber men. They announced the publication of the party's new paper *Ghadar* with Dayal as its first editor.

Apart from independence from Britain, the party had broad if vaguely articulated revolutionary goals.[34] The *Ghadarites* had the support of the IWW, the SLP, and Irish-American nationalists. The anarchist influence on Har Dayal could be seen in the *Ghadar* Party's faith in spontaneous mass uprisings. The *Ghadar* Party generally advocated a strategy of direct action and immediate agitation similar to the strategies adopted by the IWW. In 1914, Har Dayal was arrested and ordered deported as an anarchist. He fled to Switzerland and Ram Chandra, a cofounder of the party, replaced him as editor of *Ghadar* and head of the movement. The party's newspaper was widely distributed throughout the Indian diaspora: in the United States, Canada, Japan, Hong Kong, the Phillipines, British Malaya, Trinidad, Guinea and Honduras, South and East Africa, and of course, India.

In the Pacific Northwest and British Columbia, hundreds of Sikhs had found work in the lumbering industry, while thousands of others found work in agriculture in the Central Valley of California. Indian immigrants had also settled in British Columbia. The Asian Indian population on both sides of the border became the target of agitation and mob violence. In Bellingham, Washington, hundreds of Indians were driven from the town in 1907. Violence against Indian workers also occurred in British Columbia, Alaska, and California.

As World War I began, Indians everywhere were galvanized by the *Komagata Maru* Incident in May of 1914. Hundreds of Indians aboard a chartered Japanese freighter, the *Komagata Maru*, attempted to land in Vancouver. They were stopped by Canadian officials enforcing Canada's Continuous Voyage Laws, aimed at curbing non-white immigration. The standoff lasted two months during which time virtually the entire Asian Indian population of the West Coast was mobilized in support of the would-be immigrants. After the Indian appeal to the British crown went unheeded and their food and water were on the verge of running out, the *Komagata Maru* returned to Yokohama. Much as the failure of the 1905 boycott had made clear to Chinese in America, the *Komagata Maru* Incident served to underscore the helpless of the Indian community in the Americas and to enhance the attractiveness of the *Ghadar* call for revolution.[35]

The onset of World War I led to over a thousand *Ghadar* members to make their way back to India to attempt to foment the spontaneous uprising that would drive out the British. The party, always loosely organized and quite open in its appeal to revolt, had long been under close surveillance and infiltrated by the British government. Immediately upon their return to India, the *Ghadarites* were arrested, hundreds imprisoned, and dozens hung. After America's entry into the war, Taraknath Das and other leaders of the *Ghadar* Party were arrested and threatened with deportation for their political activities against British imperialism in India. Defending the *Ghadarites* still in the United States from deportation became a civil rights issue for anti-imperialists and the Left in general. The IWW, the SP, and an assortment of liberals came together to organize the Friends of Freedom for India. Agnes Smedley, a longtime supporter of the movement was elected its secretary.[36] The Friends of Freedom for India lobbied for the protection of the right of aliens to engage in political activity in the United States. The FFI was even able to persuade Samuel Gompers, no friend to any Asian worker, to allow the AFL to champion these rights. Nevertheless in 1914, Congress passed a bill that made aliens who advocated political change in any country liable to deportation. The *Ghadar* Party, its hopes for a popular uprising smashed, its leadership dispersed and under heavy persecution, and its organization infiltrated, collapsed as a revolutionary threat to British rule in India after Ram Chandra was assassinated in 1918.

When the Japanese *Shakai Minshuto* (Social Democratic Party) was established in 1901, Japan had already undergone forty years of capitalist transformation under the rule of the conservative nationalist Meiji oligarchy. Japanese intellectuals who were searching for more democratic and egalitarian models continued to look to the West for inspiration. John Crump, in *The Origins of Socialist Thought in Japan*, details the significance of European and American socialist and anarchist ideologies on the early Japanese socialist movement.[37] Crump observes that five of six founders of the SDP were Christians and that two of them had studied in the United States.

Katayama Sen, spent eleven years (1884–1895) as a student in the United States, first at Grinnell College, a center of Social

Gospel evangelism, then at Andover Theological Seminary and Yale Divinity School. During this first of a number of lengthy stays in the United States, Katayama was strongly influenced by the reformist social gospel doctrines of Richard T. Ely. In addition to Crump's brief account of this period, there is Katayama's autobiography.[38]

Abe Iso, another of the founding members of the Japanese Socialist Party, was already a Christian minister when he arrived in the United States in 1891 to study at the Hartford Theological Seminary. Abe was influenced by Edward Bellamy's *Looking Backward* as well as by Christian Socialist students at Hartford. That early Japanese socialist thought was strongly flavored by American Christian Social Gospel, Bellamy's utopian nationalism, Fabianism, and Henry George's theory of the single tax should not be surprising. Like the American SP, the SDP took a reformist position that shied away from the class struggle. This position however was not to last beyond the decade.

Soon after the SDP was organized, Kotoku Shusui, the only non-Christian among its founders, came to the U.S. Although his visit to the United States in 1905 was short, Kotoku made contact with a wide range of the American Left, and his experiences would have a major impact on the direction of the Japanese party. Kotoku had been invited by Albert Johnson, a veteran radical activist from the San Francisco Bay Area, who introduced Kotoku to anarchism, especially the writings of Peter Kropotkin. In 1906, Kotoku established relations between the SDP and the SP and for a short time joined the SP as a member. Kotoku broke with the SP over its reformism and its support for racial exclusion. In 1907, he and other leaders of the SDP wrote an open letter taking the SP to task for its racist policy, a criticism to which the SP did not reply. Albert Johnson also put Kotoku in touch with the SLP, which attempted to get Kotoku to move away from anarchism.

Kotoku had hoped to establish a revolutionary base in the United States where Japanese socialists could operate much as Russian exiles operated in Switzerland. In 1906, he brought together Japanese socialists in the Bay Area as the *Shakai Kakumeito*, or the Social Revolutionary Party. The first SRP meeting in Oakland was attended by about fifty men and women. Yuji Ichioka, in *Issei, The World of Japanese Immigrants to America* has provided the most detailed study of the context in which early Japanese immigrant socialists, including Abe, Kotoku, and others, operated.[39] The *Kakumeito* always remained tiny and was never successful in organizing Japanese workers.

The establishment of *Kakumeito* attracted the immediate attention of the SLP. Olive Johnson, an SLP party leader, immediately wrote to the *Kakumeito* inviting them to join the SLP and IWW, but the *Kakumeito* leaned heavily towards terrorism of the sort practiced by the Russian Social Revolutionaries. None of its members seem to have joined the SLP, which had strictly rejected anarchism, but it did cooperate with the IWW in getting the Japanese not to scab during the seaman's strike of 1906. Kokuto, meanwhile, had returned to Japan in 1906 and pushed the SDP towards a more anarchist position. In 1910, he was arrested and in the next year executed along with eleven other socialists in the so-called High Treason Affair, a trumped-up plot to assassinate the emperor.

The attraction of anarchism was easily as strong among Chinese radicals in the first two decades of the century as it had been among Kotoku and the early Japanese social democrats. A full-length study of the Chinese-American Left remains to be written, but indispensable survey articles and bibliographies have been published by Him Mark Lai.[40] Lai's studies provide a guide through a bewildering number of left-wing and Marxist organizations active in Chinese-American communities from the teens through to their demise in the 1950s.

The first well-known radical intellectual to immigrate to the United States was Jiang Kanghu who arrived in 1914. Jiang had established the Socialist Party of China in 1911. Like the Japanese SDP, the SP of China adopted an eclectic agenda and incorporated both anarchist and Marxist doctrines. In 1914, the Socialist Party of China was banned as subversive by the government of Yuan Shikai in Beijing, and Jiang fled to the United States.[41] Soon after his arrival, Jiang established the Chinese Socialist Club in San Francisco. Later that year, Jiang wrote and published *China and the Social Revolution*, which, according to H. M. Lai, was the first socialist work by a Chinese in America. Jiang was appointed to teach Chinese literature at Berkeley where he published a volume of translated poetry and worked as a cataloguer in the Chinese collection at the Library of Congress.

By the time of Jiang's return to China in 1920, socialist workers organizations had been established in Boston, New York, and San Francisco; and a short-lived monthly magazine *Laodong Chao* (Labor Tide) was being published in New York. During the red scare of 1919, the Chinese Workers Club in New York had been raided and IWW literature was confiscated. The largest of the clubs, in San Francisco, established the Unionist Guild, which remained in existence into the 1920s. The attraction of Indian, Japanese, and

Chinese intellectuals and workers to anarchism and syndicalism was not merely an intellectual infatuation. The establishment of the IWW was a momentous breakthrough as it marked the first opening for Asians into the American working-class movement. Although few if any Asians had joined the SLP, which had loudly advertised its opposition to the racial policies of the SP, hundreds of Japanese, Chinese, and Indian workers flocked to the call of the IWW.

In 1908, Takeuchi Tetsugoro and other former members of the Social Revolutionary Party established the Labor League of Fresno. The Fresno Labor League worked with the IWW to organize over two thousand of the four thousand Japanese grape pickers in the Central Valley area. In 1913, when the IWW established Local 283 in the Alaska Ketchikan cannery, its membership included over a hundred Japanese, Chinese, and Filipino workers. In the same year, when the IWW called a strike of 2,800 hop pickers in Wheatland, California, hundreds of Japanese were among the strikers. In 1925, an IWW leader reported to the Survey of Race Relations of the Pacific Coast that a third of the IWW's membership in Portland, Oregon was Chinese. The IWW's welcome to Asian workers was so well known, notorious to some, that its folklore maintained that the nickname Wobblies was originated by a Chinese laundryman who mispronounced the letter W.

Ichioka's coverage of early Japanese labor organizing is the most comprehensive account to date of the largely unwritten story of the Asian workers and the IWW.[42] It includes detailed accounts of the Fresno Labor League and detailed analysis of the decision of Wyoming locals of the United Mine Workers of America to accept Japanese miners as members in 1913, the first AFL affiliate to break the anti-Asian race barrier.

IV. The Bolshevik Revolution and the Turn Towards Communism

The triumph of the Bolsheviks in 1917, the establishment of the Communist Party in 1919 and the organization of the Comintern in 1920 completely changed the world in which Asian immigrant radicals worked. The subsequent career of Katayama Sen is emblematic of this new political era. After the execution of Kotoku and the others in the High Treason Affair, Katayama found himself unable to continue political work in Japan. He returned to the United States in 1914 and settled in New York where he published the newspaper *Heimin* (The Commoner) from 1916 to 1919. In that year, Katayama became one of the founding members of the American Communist Party. In the 1920s, Katayama helped organize the Japanese Workers Association, which had branches in New York, Seattle, San Francisco, and Los Angeles. In the 1930s, Katayama went to Moscow where he served as a representative of the Comintern. Katayama died in Moscow and was buried in the Kremlin.

Both the Bolshevik revolution and the May Fourth movement of 1919 in China radically transformed the political terrain of the Chinese Left in America. According to H. Mark Lai, in December of 1919, Oi-Won Jung, a Chinese-American who was a member of the *Kuomintang* Party, and had been active in the Chinese Socialist Club, established the *Xinshehui*, (New Society) in San Jose, California "to study capitalism and communism and the radical politics of the New Russia."[43] The organization of this Marxist study group paralleled the political ferment that was occurring among radical intellectuals all over China and would lead to the establishment of the Chinese Communist Party (CCP) in 1921.

The Chinese student group that founded the CCP in France is well known because it included Zhou Enlai and Deng Xiaoping, and it has been the subject of a number of studies.[44] Less well known is that among the students who came to the United States were a number who became prominent in the Chinese communist movement. Among the *Xiaonienzhongguo* (Young China) group of progressive students who arrived in 1922 was Chen Gongbo, one of the founding members of the CCP in Shanghai the preceding year. Another was Chiang Wentian who would return to China and join the party in 1925. While Chen soon split with the CCP to join the leftist *Kuomintang*, Chiang would become general secretary of the CCP as leader of the "Returned Student Faction," a position he maintained until 1932 when he was replaced by Mao Zedong.

Later arrivals included Chi Chaoting, an underground member of the CCP who became the first Chinese member of the American CP in 1926. Chi was a student at the University of Chicago where he edited the *Zhi-Cheng Quao Sheng* (Voice of the Chicago Chinese). He went on to become a prominent economist and journalist. Zhao Jiansheng, also known as Jao Shushi, arrived from Paris in 1938 to edit the *China Salvation News* in New York. Zhao returned to China to become a political commissioner of the Communist New Fourth Army, and eventually head of the CCP central organization department, but in 1955 he was ousted from the party for "anti-Party activities."

Although H. Mark Lai's essays have opened the door to research in this area, much less is known about Communist activists who were Chinese-Americans. These included Benjamin Fee, Xavier Dea, Lin Jianfu, and Chu Tong, all of whom joined the CP in the 1920s and became prominent organizers in Chinese-American communities. Still less is known about leftists outside the CP such as the novelist H. T. Tsiang, the progressive journalist Y.K. Chu, or Grace Lee Boggs who became active in the Trotskyist movement.[45] Lai reports that by 1930 about fifty Chinese had become CP members and the party had established a Chinese bureau with branches in San Francisco, New York, Philadelphia, Boston, Chicago, and Madison.

In the late 1920s, the Chinese branches of the CP worked to organize the Chinese-American community around support for the Communist movement in China. Xavier Dea and Ben Fee were instrumental in organizing the San Francisco Chinese Students Association which claimed a membership of three thousand, including high school students. After Chiang Kai-shek had turned on the CCP and the left wing of the *Kuomintang* (KMT), the association was active in supporting the left wing of the KMT and the CCP while the CCBA backed the ascendant right wing of the KMT. IN late 1927, the CP gained control over the national Chinese Student Alliance. CP members Mei Juao and Thomas Hu held posts as successive editors of the *Chinese Students Monthly*, which published articles by Borodin, M.N. Roy, Earl Browder, and others.

The CP cadre were also instrumental in organizing the *Kungyu* (Workers After Hours) Club, which in 1929 was active in the successful Chinese Laundry Workers Union strike. The *Kungyu's* support for the CP's calls for "work or bread," and unemployment insurance led to the organizing of the San Francisco Chinese Unemployed Alliance. The Alliance organized mass demonstrations against the CCBA demanding jobs and housing, and it sent a large Chinese contingent to participate in unemployed workers' demonstrations in San Francisco's business district. The Chinese Workers Center was organized to help find employment, food, and housing for unemployed Chinese workers. It operated for a year with about one hundred members, until closed by the police as a subversive Communist stronghold during the 1934 San Francisco General Strike.

In the early 1930s, a number of *Kungyu* activists organized a Chinese branch of the Trade Union Unity League's Needle Trades Industrial Workers Union and attempted without success to organize the growing number of garment workers in San Francisco's Chinatown. In 1934, the International Ladies' Garment Workers Union hired Ben Fee to organize Chinatown garment workers, but he was ousted by Jennie Matyas because of his CP membership after two not very successful years. Matyas would be no more successful until 1938 when women garment workers at the factory of the Chinese-owned National Dollar Store struck. After a 105-day strike, the ILGWU was successful for the first time in getting an employer to recognize a Chinatown union local. Unfortunately, within a year the National Dollar Store closed its factory.[46]

In 1937, *Kungyu* had established the Chinese Workers Mutual Aid Society which stressed worker education, unionism, class-consciousness, and links to militant unions. The CWMA had five hundred or more members and was able to survive into the early 1950s.[47] In New York, the CP was less successful in organizing the Chinese community. Nevertheless, two significant developments occurred independently. One was the establishment of the Chinese Hand Laundry Association (CHLA) and the other was the entry of thousands of Chinese seamen into the National Maritime Union. Peter Kwong's *Chinatown, New York, Labor and Politics 1930–1950*[48] is an excellent analysis of both of the events in the context of class and nationalist struggles. Renqiu Yu's *To Save China, To Save Ourselves; The Chinese Hand Laundry Alliance of New York*[49] is a more detailed historical account of the rise and fall of the CHLA.

In 1933 the New York City Council, at the behest of white laundry operators, passed an ordinance that required one-person laundries to pay a $25 annual fee and to post a $1000 bond. This ordinance was clearly aimed at the 3,500 Chinese laundry establishments in New York. When the laundrymen approached the CCBA to intervene, the CCBA demanded that each laundryman pay one dollar before it would look into the matter. The laundrymen then organized the Chinese Hand Laundry Alliance (CHL) to represent their own interests. They had the assistance of Y. K. Chu, editor of the progressive *Chinese Journal of Commerce*, and an outspoken critic of the CCBA. Chu was a member of the Left KMT and had earlier helped to oust the Right KMT organization in Philadelphia and replace it with a branch of the All China Workers and Peasant Revolutionary Party, a united front group opposed to Chiang Kai-shek. The CHLA and its lawyers pressed successfully for a reduction of the onerous Laundry Tax to ten dollars and a one hundred dollar bond.

The CHLA continued to represent the interests of the Chinese laundrymen despite the efforts of the CCBA to destroy it. Because the CHLA was considered to represent petty bourgeois interests, the CP was slow to recognize its significance. It was Chu Tong, a CP member, who became the Association's English-language secretary and wrote an analysis of the proletarian nature of the owner-operated hand laundries that gained CP support. The CHLA remained unremittingly and consistently critical of the CCBA, gave early support for other progressive movements in the Chinese community, and issued calls for a united front against Japanese aggression in China. In surviving these increasingly severe CCBA attacks, the CHLA represented a viable alternative to the long-standing dominance of the Chinatown merchant elite.

In New York in 1933, the Marine Workers Industrial Union (MWIU), predecessor of the National Maritime Union, was organized as an alternative to the conservative and corrupt Seamen's International Union, which had long been a foe of the thousands of Chinese seamen who worked for private shipping lines. The MWIU opposed any racial discrimination either in the union or in hiring and welcomed black and Asian sailors. In 1936, when the MWIU called a strike, three thousand Chinese sailors joined after the union agreed to take on the issues of particular concern to them: equal treatment, a uniform wage scale, and the right of Chinese alien sailors to shore leave.

The 1930s were a period of intense, often violent struggle for Asian-American workers in the fields as well as on the docks. Although the Wyoming locals of the UMW had accepted Japanese members as early as 1913, their acceptance remained the exception in the AFL well into the 1930s. Japanese farm laborers in California were joined in the 1920s by a growing force in Filipino and Mexican farm workers. The autobiography of Karl Yoneda,[50] a Japanese-American Communist and labor organizer, provides details of various strikes and organizing attempts in Southern California. According to Yoneda, in 1930 the Agricultural Workers Industrial Unity League, a section of the CP's Trade Unions Unity League, sent organizers into the Imperial Valley of California to organize the Mexican, Japanese, and Filipino farmer workers. A number of the AWIU organizers were arrested and convicted of criminal syndicalism. Among them were Horiuchi Tetsuji and twenty other Issei. Despite the efforts of the International Labor Defense, Horiuchi and the others were ordered deported. The ILD arranged to have them go to the Soviet Union rather than face certain imprisonment in Japan.

In 1933, the Filipino Labor Union (FLU) was formed by Filipino lettuce pickers in Salinas after the AFL turned down their request to organize a local. Within a year, the FLU had organized two thousand members and joined with the AFL Vegetable Packers Association in the 1934 Monterey County strike. The FLU demanded recognition from the growers and a raise in wages of Filipino workers from twenty cents to forty cents per hour. After two workers were killed by growers during the walkout, the federal government offered mediation. The vegetable packers accepted the offer of arbitration, but the FLU refused to lower its demands. As a result, the FLU was branded a Communist front group, and its strike leaders were arrested. The strike was defeated when local vigilantes burned down the Filipino strikers' camp. It was not until 1936 that Filipino and Mexican farm workers were able to persuade the AFL to grant a charter to the Field Workers Union Local 30326, an integrated Filipino-Mexican union.

The NMU's success in organizing Chinese seamen represented a major blow against racial exclusion as did the growing power of the CIO within the union movement. In 1934 the Alaska Packers Union, an AFL affiliated union, hired Karl Yoneda as its organizer in the San Francisco area. The Alaska Packers quickly became the most integrated union in the region. By 1937, the local had elected Karl Yoneda as first vice president, Ben Fee as second vice president, and C. Cabellero as third vice president. The International Longshoreman's and Warehouse Union, a stronghold of the Left, was also active in recruiting Asian members in the San Francisco area. The ILWU gave strong support to the CP's calls for the United States to aid China in its war against Japanese aggression. By 1937, the ILWU began to organize Hawaii's dockworkers. Later the ILWU would organize thousands of Asian-American agricultural workers, hotel and restaurant workers, and service workers in Hawaii.

IV. Conclusion: A Different Looking Glass

The history of radical movements in America is the history of possibilities. The history of Asian immigrant radicalism is the history of alternatives within those possibilities. The experience of Asian workers and the labor movement in Hawaii offers a looking glass through which we might see what those alternative worlds might have been like.[51]

Until the 1960s, the ruling elite in Hawaii was a white colonial oligarchy and the working class was overwhelming Asian. The planters successively imported different Asian nationalities, Chi-

nese, Japanese, Okinawan, Korean, and Filipino and organized
plantation work, wage structures, and social life in ways designed
to pit ethnic groups against one another. Since the racial divide in
Hawaii between white and various shades of brown coincide with
the planter oligarchy and plantation labor, the overwhelmingly
Asian immigrant working class in Hawaii, despite its serious ethnic
divisions, did not construct its class-consciousness around a theory
of racial supremacy.

At the turn of the century, the first labor organizations in
Hawaii were, to be sure, organized around ethnic solidarity. The
Japanese Higher Wage Association was founded in 1908 and the
Federation of Filipino Labor in 1911. In 1909, seven thousand
Japanese workers unsuccessfully struck the Oahu plantations for
four months, in what became the last great ethnic strike in Hawaii.
After their defeat the Japanese were evicted from their plantation
housing and Filipino and Korean workers were brought in. In
1920, the Higher Wages Association and the Federation of Filipino
Labor jointly called a strike that pulled over eight thousand workers out of the fields. Despite poor planning and lack of coordination, the strike lasted for six months. Even though over twelve
thousand people were evicted from their homes and the FFL
lacked an adequate strike fund, the owners sustained substantial
losses and made some concessions before the workers returned to
the fields.

By themselves, Hawaii's plantation workers could make few
gains against a planter oligarchy that controlled not only the land
but the territorial government. In addition, as Noel Kent has
shown, Hawaiian capital was itself dependent on mainland and
British capital and thus was at the mercy of trade and financial
decisions made in San Francisco, Washington, and New York. As
a result, it was virtually impossible for Hawaii plantation workers,
no matter how unified or militant, to succeed while isolated from
a larger working-class movement.

In 1930s, when the ILWU began its effort to organize labor in
Hawaii, it found a militant workforce that could be unified across
ethnic lines with relative ease. The ILWU would soon "march
inland" to successfully organize plantation workers. With the
strength of a national union that controlled the docks in the islands
and on the West Coast, Hawaii's plantation workers were able to
gain serious wage concessions for the first time and eventually the
best medical and retirement benefits in the industry. In turn, the
labor movement spawned a new generation of progressive activists
within the Democratic Party. These Democrats, many of whom

had grown up on the plantations, overturned a half century plus of conservative control of the territorial legislature in what has been called the Democratic revolution of 1958.

Hawaii, of course, did not become a workers' paradise—far from it. One of the prices that the progressive Democratic had to pay for statehood was the abandonment of any plan for radical land reform. As a result, the Hawaii plantation economy has given way to a service economy as agricultural land has been converted to golf courses and hotels. Although many of the sons and daughters of immigrant plantation workers now make up the middle class, Hawaii remains a highly stratified society, still dependent on mainland and Asian capital, with a new working class of recent immigrants from Korea, the Philippines, and Vietnam as well as an underclass of native Hawaiians and Samoans. The ILWU has been forced to organize service workers in the hotels and restaurants, and it remains to be seen if its successes can be repeated in the postindustrial society.

Had the labor movement in the United States welcomed Asian workers into its fold, it most likely would still not have triumphed over capitalism. On the other hand, it would undoubtedly have been a more democratic and successful movement, and as in Hawaii, a movement more able to appeal to universal values of brotherhood. The significance of Asian-American history for the history of the working class in the United States is that the history of a working-class America without the stories of Asian Americans can tell us no more than the photograph of Promontory Point without the Chinese.

Notes

1. Sucheng Chan, in a perceptive essay comparing Asian and European immigration to the United States, in *Immigration Reconsidered: History, Sociology and Politics,* ed. Virginia Yans-McLaughlin (New York, Oxford University Press, 1990) suggests fruitful points of comparison and contrast.

2. Ronald Takaki, *Iron Cages: Race and Culture in the 19th Century* (Seattle: University of Washington Press, 1979) 229.

3. Mary Coolidge, *Chinese Immigration* (New York: Henry Holt, 1909).

4. Paul Siu, "The Sojourner," *American Journal of Sociology.* 58

(1952):34–36. His 1953 dissertation has been recently published as *The Chinese Laundryman; A Study in Social Isolation*, ed. Jack Wei-kuo Tchen (New York: New York University Press, 1987).

5. Gunther Barth, *Bitter Strength; A History of the Chinese in the United States from 1850–1870* (Cambridge: Harvard University Press, 1964).

6. See my "Origins of Chinese Immigration to the United States" in *History, Life and Influence of the Chinese in the United States* (San Francisco: Chinese Historical Society of America, 1976) and Zo Kil Young, *Chinese Immigration to the United States* (New York: Arno Press, 1979).

7. Alexander Saxton, *The Indispensable Enemy: Labor and the Anti-Chinese Movement in California*, (Berkeley and Los Angeles: University of California Press, 1971).

8. Stuart Creighton Miller, *The Unwelcome Immigrant: The Image of the Chinese In America, 1785–1882* (Berkeley and Los Angeles: University of California Press, 1969).

9. Roger Daniels, *The Politics of Prejudice, The Anti-Japanese Movement in California and the Struggle for Anti-Japanese Exclusion* (Berkeley and Los Angeles: University of California Press, 1962).

10. Lucie Cheng and Edna Bonacich, *Labor Immigration Under Capitalism: Asian Workers in the United States Before World Ware II* (Berkeley and Los Angeles: University of California Press, 1984).

11. Ping Chiu, *Chinese Labor in California, 1850–1880: An Economic Study* (Madison: State Historical Society of Wisconsin, 1967).

12. Charles Crocker cited in Ping Chiu, 50.

13. Lucy M. Cohen, *The Chinese in the Post-Civil War South: A People Without A History* (Baton Rouge: Louisiana State University Press, 1984).

14. See Kirsten Farmelant, "The Coming of the Chinese to North Adams," unpublished paper, Brown University, 1992.

15. Renqui Yu, *To Save China, To Save Ourselves: The Chinese Hand Laundry Alliance* (Philadelphia: Temple University Press, 1992), 9.

16. Philip Foner, *American Socialism and the Black Worker, From the Age of Jackson to World War II.* (Hamden, Ct.: Greenwood Press, 1977), 378.

17. Foner, *American Socialism and the Black Worker*, 67.

18. Tomas Almaguer, and Karl Yoneda, "100 Years of Japanese Labor History in the USA" in *Roots: An Asian American Reader*, ed. Amy Tachiki et al. (Los Angeles: UCLA Asian American Studies Center, 1971) 150–158.

19. Elmer C. Sandemeyer, *The Anti-Chinese Movement*, Illinois Studies in the Social *Sciences*, vol. 24, 1939. See also Milton R. Konvitz, *The Alien and Asiatic in American Law* (Ithaca: Cornell University Press 1946) and Frank Chuman, *The Bamboo People: The Law and Japanese Americans* (Del Mar, California: Publishers Inc., 1976).

20. Sucheng Chan, ed., *Entry Denied; Exclusion and the Chinese American Community, 1882–1943* (Philadelphia: Temple University Press, 1991). Hyung Kim, *Asian Americans and the Supreme Court* (New York: Greenwood Press, 1992) contains a number of important essays on Asians and the Supreme Court as well as documents. Bill Ong Hing's recent *Making and Remaking Asian America Through Immigration Policy, 1850–1990* (Stanford: Stanford University Press, 1993) is a broad survey and demonstrates how changes in immigration law have enabled huge changes in the social demography of Asian America.

21. Chan, *Asian Americans, An Interpretive History* (Boston: Twayne Publishers, 1991), 90.

22. See, for example, Roger Daniels, ed., *Anti-Chinese Violence in North America* (New York: Arno Press, 1978); Howard A. Dewitt, *Anti-Filipino Movements in California: History, Bibliography and Study Guide* (San Francisco: R&E Research Associates, 1976); Yuji Ichioka, *Issei, The World of First Generation Japanese Immigrants 1884–1924* (New York: The Free Press, 1988); and Joan Jensen, *Passage from India; Indian Pioneers in America* (New Haven: Yale University Press, 1988).

23. Carlos Bulosan, *America is in the Heart, A Personal History* (New York: Harcourt Brace and Co., 1946).

24. Eve Armentrout Ma, *Revolutionaries, Monarchists, and Chinatowns: Chinese Politics in the Americas and the 1911 Revolution* (Honolulu: University of Hawaii Press, 1990).

25. See, for example, the sociological studies of nineteenth-century Chinese society in America by Lyman Stanford, *Asians in the West* (Reno: Desert Research Institute, 1969).

26. See Delbert McKee, "The Chinese Boycott Of 1905–1906 Reconsidered; The Role of Chinese Americans" *Pacific Historical Review* 55 (1986).

27. Chong-sik Lee, *The Politics of Korean Nationalism* (Berkeley and Los Angeles: University of California Press, 1963).

28. Kingsley Lyu, "Korean Nationalist Activities in Hawaii and the Continental United States, 1900–1945," Part I (1910–1919) and Part II (1920–1945), *Amerasia Journal* 4, no. 1 (1977):23–90 and no. 2 (1977):53–100. See also Linda Shin, "Koreans in America, 1903–1945" in Tachiki et. al. *Roots*, 200–206 and H. Brett Melendy, *Asians in America, Filipinos, Koreans and East Indians* (Boston: Twayne, 1977).

29. See Bruce Cummings, *The Origins of the Korean War: Liberation and the Emergence of Separate Regimes, 1945–1947* (Princeton: Princeton University Press, 1981); also see Robert A. Scalapino and Chong-sik Lee, *Communism in Korea*, 2 vols. (Berkeley and Los Angeles: University of California Press, 1972).

30. See Martin Bernal, *Chinese Socialism before 1907* (Ithaca: Cornell University Press, 1976). Also important is his essay "The Triumph of Anarchism over Marxism in China 1906–1907" in *China in Revolution: The First Phase 1900–1913*, ed. M.C. Wright (New Haven: Yale University Press, 1968), 97–142. See also Robert A. Scalapino and George T. Yu, *The Chinese Anarchist Movement* (Berkeley: Center for Chinese Studies, Institute for International Studies, 1961).

31. Jensen, *Passage, passim.*

32. See Sucheta Mazumdar, "Colonial Impact and Punjabi Emigration to the United States" in *Labor Immigration*, ed. Lucie Cheng and Edna Bonacich, 316–336.

33. *Ibid.*

34. Harish Puri, *Ghadar Movement, Ideology, Organization and Strategy* (Amritsar: Guru Nanak Dev University Press, 1983) is the most detailed study of the movement.

35. Jensen's *Passage* recounts the Bellingham riots and the *Komagata Maru* Incident in detail.

36. On Smedley's career as a radical activist and journalist, see Janice R. MacKinnon and Stephan R. MacKinnon, *Agnes*

Smedley, *The Life and Times of An American Radical* (Berkeley and Los Angeles, University of California Press, 1988).

37. John Crump, *The Origins of Socialist Thought in Japan* (New York: St. Martin's Press, 1983).

38. Sen Katayama, *Asian Revolutionary, The Life of Sen Katayama*, trans. Hyman Kublin (Princeton: Princeton University Press, 1960).

39. Ichioka, *Issei*, chapter 4.

40. Him Mark Lai, "A Historical Survey of Organization of the Left Among the Chinese in America" in *Bulletin of Concerned Asian Scholars* 4, no. 3, (Fall 1972):10–21 and "The Chinese Marxist Left in America to the 1960's" in *Chinese America: History and Perspectives*, 1992, 3–82.

41. See Martin Bernal, "Triumph of Anarchism," 97–142.

42. Ichioka, *Issei*, chapter 4.

43. Lai, "The Chinese Marxist Left in America to the 1960's," 7. 44. See, for example, John K.C. Leung, "The Chinese Work-Study Movement in France," (Ph.D. diss., Brown University, 1983).

45. H.T. Tsiang self-published three novels, *And China Has Hands, China Red*, and *Hanging on Union Square*, and a volume of poetry, *Songs of the Chinese Revolution*. His work was criticized in the *New Masses* as suffering from bourgeois individualism, and he was shunned by the CP. Y.K. Chu was a critic of the CCBA and an early supporter of the Chinese Hand Laundry Alliance. He wrote *Chinatown Inside Out* (New York: Barrows Mussey, 1936), a somewhat sensationalized expose under the pseudonym Leong Gor Yun.

46. The history of the ILGWU and Chinese garment workers is a sorry one. Patricia Fong's brief article "The 1938 National Dollar Store Strike" in *Asian American Review* 2, no. 1, is still the only account of the strike.

47. Most of information in the preceding five paragraphs is from Lai, "The Chinese Marxist Left in America to the 1960's."

48. Peter Kwong, *Chinatown, New York, Labor and Politics 1930–1950* (New York: Monthly Review Press, 1979).

49. Renqiu Yu, *To Save China, To Save Ourselves*.

50. Karl Yoneda, *Ganbatte! Sixty Year Struggle of a Kibei Worker*

(Los Angeles: Asian American Studies Center, University of California, 1983).

51. Hawaii is too often ignored in the study of the American working class. Noel Kent's *Islands Under the Influence* (New York: Monthly Review Press, 1983) is a study of the political economy of the islands from the perspective of the capitalist world system, which provides a critical context. Edward Beechart, *Working in Hawaii: A Labor History* (Honolulu: University of Hawaii Press, 1985) is a political history of the labor movement in Hawaii from its beginnings to the late 1950s. Ronald Takaki's study, *Pau Hana: Plantation Life and Labor in Hawaii* (Honolulu: University of Hawaii Press, 1983), ends with the 1930s and emphasizes the growing class-consciousness in the daily life and work of the multicultural plantation work force. Milton Murayama's bildungsroman, *All I Asking For is My Body* (San Francisco: Supa Press, 1975), is a brilliant account of growing up in a plantation culture.

TEN

Haitian Life in New York and the Haitian-American Left

Carole Charles

Any account of the development of progressive political practices and ideas within the many Haitian communities in the United States in general, and in New York in particular, must look at the formation and growth of the community. Two important elements have shaped political struggles and the development of leftist ideas within the community in New York: the organized opposition to the thirty-year dictatorship of the Duvalier regime and the struggles against the racist policy of the U.S. government toward the Haitian people as well as negative portrayals of them. Since the early 1960s, the significant Haitian flows of immigration to New York City coincided with the increasingly repressive policies of the Duvalier regime.

Haiti is distinctive in many ways. The richest colony in the New World during the eighteenth century, its wealth came from the production of sugar, coffee, and cotton. Nonetheless, two hundred years after the most successful slave revolution in human history, the first black republic and the second independent state in the Western Hemisphere is in shambles. Haiti is now the poorest country in the hemisphere. With an estimated population of around six million, the average annual per capita income was only

$270 in 1980. The World Bank estimated during that same period more than 80 percent of the population had an average income under $150. Other indicators of poverty were: malnutrition, high infant mortality, and low levels of education in the rural areas. Moreover, Haiti is extremely dependent on foreign assistance. From 1972–1981 foreign assistance financed approximately 70 percent of the total of Haitian development expenditures.[1]

A counterpart to the poverty is the extraordinary concentration of wealth and privilege. In 1981, 4 percent of the population received more than 46 percent of the national income. This concentration of wealth and power in the hands of a small elite residing in the capital led to a centralized structure of decision making in all spheres of life.[2] The Haitian bourgeoisie, which controls the most important economic sectors yet includes only 2 percent of the population, derives its wealth from the exploitation of the peasants and the urban working classes.

The most important characteristic of the ruling elite, composed of black and mulatto landowners, merchants, and military chiefs, has been a systematic policy of exclusion and denial of basic rights for the majority of the people. Since independence, the Haitian ruling elite has opted for a national program defined by dependence and collusion with foreign capital. Such parasitism had led to the U.S. occupation of the country from 1915 to 1934, an occupation that led to the establishment in 1957 of the Duvalier regime. Thereafter, with the succession of Jean-Claude Duvalier at the death of his father in 1971, Haiti became synonymous with Duvalier family eccentricities, and no distinction could be made between the Duvalier family and the state. The "contribution" of the Duvalier era was increased state kleptocracy and institutionalized state violence. The Duvaliers eliminated all political life in the country, establishing a regime of terror. It is within that context that the massive arrival of Haitians to the U.S. began.

Estimates of the number of Haitians living in New York City are problematic. Census data put the total number in the early 1980s at fifty thousand: 1,680 in the Bronx, 30,260 in Brooklyn, 3,620 in Manhattan and 14,340 in Queens. The remainder were in Staten Island and other counties of the New York metropolitan area. These data, primarily based on the 1980 census, did not take into account arrivals after 1980, the undocumented, or "entrants."

Haitians have been part of the New York area political landscape since the early 1920s. A relatively small number of Haitian immigrants were present in the period of the Harlem Renaissance movement and were very active in progressive trade union politics in the fur industry. By the early 1960s, many Haitian political exiles, all opponents of the Duvalier regime began to arrive. While in 1961, there were around seven thousand Haitians in New York, by 1967 the number had increased to more than forty thousand. Many were undocumented. During the last 1970s and early 1980s, the flow had increased with the arrival of refugees and the undocumented. By that time, around 350,000 Haitians were estimated to be living in the New York metropolitan area.

One important feature of the Haitian community in New York is that it lacks geographic concentration. Haitians are scattered throughout the city, with the largest communities in Brooklyn, followed by Queens and Manhattan. In Brooklyn, Haitians are located primarily in Crown Heights, Flatbush, and East New York. In Manhattan, there are clusters on the Upper West Side between 96th and 112th Streets, from Columbus Avenue to Broadway, and from 125th to about 168th Streets in Harlem. In Queens, Haitian immigrants are found in large numbers in Corona, East Elmhurst, Queens Village, Cambria Heights, and, more recently, in Rosedale and Elmont. Haitians live in the midst of crowds of lower- and middle-class African Americans, Jamaicans, Trinidadians, Colombians, Hasidic Jews, and Italians.

Although there is no Haitian district, there is a clear collective consciousness of being Haitian, which is reinforced by language, nationalism and a distinct meaning of blackness. This uniqueness finds expression in numerous Haitian organizations, including clubs, student organizations, churches, political groups, community organizations, and private businesses. These organizations are usually differentiated by class, color, and regional place of origin, which encourages a tendency toward division and heterogeneity in the community.

The early Haitian immigrants in New York City found jobs mostly in factories. Over time, with more knowledge of English and more experience of the labor market, some began to move into white-collar jobs, starting at the lowest positions. Financial and service institutions on Wall Street hired them. A few others went into business on their own, opening gas stations, or working as electricians, cleaning contractors, or grocers. The women went to work in hospitals and nursing homes as nurse's aides and increasingly as registered nurses. Many worked as maids. By the 1960s, many were employed as secretaries in private firms and a few in African missions to the U.N.

The bulk of Haitian workers have concentrated in manufacturing and services as semiskilled and unskilled labor. Since the

1980s, about 65 percent of Haitians work in hotels, restaurants, hospitals, and retail services industries. Many of these firms employ between six and one hundred workers. Only a small percentage of these workers earned less than the minimum wage of $3.35 in 1980. Many of the industries that hire both legal and undocumented Haitian migrants are unionized. Haitians participate at a substantial rate and are particularly active in trade unions like the National Union of Hospital and Health Care Employees, the International Ladies Garment Workers Union, and the Fur and Leather Workers Union.

Haitians, like other Caribbean immigrants in the United States, have created voluntary associations that help reinforce the experience of belonging to the same group. These associations have varying goals. Some are oriented toward maintaining cultural and social links with Haiti; others are economic and political organizations; some strive to meet the spiritual and religious needs of their members; others are geared toward an integration into U.S. society that does not imply complete assimilation.

The Development of Haitian Organizations

The history of Haitian political and social/community organizations can be divided broadly into six phases. Between 1957 and 1964, most of the organizations that emerged were political and religious. They were concerned primarily with issues related to Haiti. A second phase (1965–1972) saw the emergence of some community organizations. The flow of War on Poverty money that resulted from the civil rights movement induced Haitians to enter the arena of ethnic competition for federal money and program funds.[3] The third phase (1972–1982) coincides with the massive flow of undocumented immigrants and "entrants." During this period, new strategies were developed. Some organizations began to focus on issues of assimilation into mainstream American society, but the bulk of activities centered around struggles against the Duvalier regime and against racist U.S. immigration policies. This period of intense political activities was led by Left-oriented groups and associations. The fourth phase (1982–1986) was characterized by the massive mobilization against the portrayal of Haitians as a nation of AIDS carriers. By 1985, there were around 250 Haitian organizations in the New York metropolitan area. The downfall of the Duvalier dictatorship in 1986 began a new era in the history of Haitian political and social organizations. Many organizations began to develop projects for and within Haiti. A high percentage disappeared when their leaders returned to Haiti to participate in the transition process. The last phase began with the uprooting of the Duvaliers and the election in 1990 of Jean-Bertrand Aristide. A new political outlook began to take shape.

The Role of Politics in the Community

Political activities have always been the hallmark of the Haitian migrant population in New York. Most of the early Haitian migrants were political exiles. For them, New York was a place of transit, a place to organize opposition against the Duvalier regime.[4] This was expressed not only in the proliferation of political groups and the multiplicity of political activities, but also in the discourse that explained the causes of Haitian migration as solely political. Paquin's testimony on political mobilization in the community during its first years of formation is illustrative:

> Apartment 15-B in the Hotel Alexandria, located at 103rd and Broadway in Manhattan, was the headquarters of the opposition. It also became a screening and orientation center, a kind of Ellis Island for new Haitian refugees between Papa Doc country and the U.S. unknown.[5]

Political activities took different forms, from organizing raids to cultural events. The process began with the transfer from Haiti in 1957 of political confrontation among political leaders. All the main political actors who opposed Duvalier in the 1957 election settled in New York. Eugene Magloire, an army general who held power between 1949 and 1956, lived first on the East Side of Manhattan and later moved to Jamaica Estates, an affluent neighborhood in Queens. Louis Dejoie, the mulatto and bourgeois candidate, resided with his group on Manhattan's Upper West Side. Daniel Fignole, the populist candidate who had been an interim president in 1956–1957, was based in Brooklyn.

The first invasion attempted by Haitian exiles against the Duvalier regime, in 1958, was launched from the U.S. and was organized by mulattoes who were former members of the army linked to the Magloire regime. All the exiled political leaders and groups were part of it, however, as revealed in Paquin's account:

> At Roger's two room apartment on Broadway and 103rd Street, there was pandemonium. People all around were

talking at the same time. No Haitians went to work this morning of July 29th 1958. They were all relishing the idea of going to their last pay check, and showing their revulsion and hostility for "le blanc" who had squeezed their labor to the very last cent of the minimum wage or even far less, since most of them were illegal, thus helpless. They were all going back to Haiti by the first available plane.[6]

Although New York was defined as a transit place, it was also a place to organize political opposition to the Duvalier regime. Such political perceptions of the migration process permeated all dimensions of cultural life in the community. No activity escaped political scrutiny.

During the early 1960s, all political actions and discourse remained under the leadership of old and traditional Haitian politicians. Brooklyn was the center of these activities. Fignole, with his organization Movement of Peasants and Workers (MOP), published a journal, *Construction,* and organized monthly political meetings. Magloire controlled the "Haitian Coalition." The coalition owned a radio station that transmitted directly to Haiti, as well as a newspaper, *Le Combattant.* In addition, there were other organizations created by former army officers like the Haitian Revolutionary Armed Forces (FARH) an Revolutionary Movement of November 12th (MR12N). In 1965, one of the founders of FARH organized a second invasion when he created a parallel organization called *"Jeune Haiti,"* mainly comprised of young Haitian men from the mulatto and black elite of the southern region of Haiti.[7]

The displacement of traditional political groups by new leftist groups entailed no change in the conception of the migration process that permeated political discourse and action in the community. For example, *Sel,* the organ of a group of Catholic priests exiled from Haiti in 1969, explained that emigration existed because of the dictatorship, exploitation, and imperialism. If these problems were resolved, there would be no more poverty, repression, or emigration. Thus, the task was to work to change Haiti.[8]

Leftist politics began to emerge in the community around 1970. The movement began in Europe and Montreal under the leadership of students and intellectuals who had connections to or had participated in the struggles of the progressive democratic movement in Haiti between 1963 and 1969. Between 1966 and 1967, many young Haitians were recruited in New York for clandestine activities. In 1969, some returned to Haiti to organize an urban guerrilla movement. The failure of this project and the massive repression that followed produced a wave of migration.

In 1970, a new organization, *Resistance Haitienne*, was created in New York. It was based in a coalition of traditional politicians and leftist groups. In January 1971, this new organization held the first large anti-Duvalier demonstration in front of the United Nations in New York. This event marked the beginning of the hegemony of the anti-Duvalier Left in the community. The death of Francois Duvalier in 1971 accelerated the process.[9] By the late 1970s, there were some twenty political groups in the New York area. Some of these groups also had membership in other U.S. cities and in Montreal, Europe, and Latin America. Among them were the United Party of Haitian Communists (PUCH), the Party of Haitian Workers (PTA), *En Avant*, the Haitian Revolutionary Organization for Patriotic Action (ORHAP), *Voie Democratique*, the Haitian Liberation Movement (MLH), the Committee for the Defense of Haitian Peoples Rights (KODDPHA), the Assembly of Haitian Democratic Forces (RFDH), Unity, Practices, Unity (INIP), the "Jean-Jacques Acaau" Brigade, and the "Gerald Baker" Brigade. To these should be added the various women's groups whose membership often overlapped with some of the previous groups. The Organization of Patriotic Haitian Women (UFAP) is an illustration.[10]

UFAP was an organization created in the early 1970s to mobilize Haitian women, to organize them politically around antidictatorial and anti-imperialist issues. From the onset, UFAP rejected all forms of feminism that ignored class exploitation. For UFAP, the oppression of women could only be superseded by revolution. The women's movement had to work first for the liberation of Haiti in order to create conditions for women's emancipation. UFAP would have a short political life, disappearing from the scene by the late 1970s. Internal conflicts within the organization on strategic issues and the return of many members to Haiti destroyed it. When a democratic movement began to surface in Haiti around 1980, it included many Haitian women who had lived in the diaspora, had participated directly in women's struggles, and who had returned to Haiti.

The Haitian commercial media illustrates the impact of transnationalism in the community, and also reflects its political and ideological struggles. Three widely read French-language Haitian newspapers published in the United States have circulation in North America, France, and Haiti. They differ in perspective and ideological makeup. One of the papers, *Haiti Progress,* has a definite radical political orientation and opposes Haitian integration into U.S. society. The paper concentrates on analyses of historical experiences of third-world and progressive societies and on criticism of U.S. imperialist intervention. It promotes radical change in Haiti. The second paper, *Haiti en Marche,* follows a social democratic tendency with a strong nationalist discourse. It has a clear anticommunist flavor, but also argues for change in Haiti. Based in Miami, it informs its readers about racial conflicts in the U.S. The third paper, *Haiti Observateur,* is the oldest in the community. It has a fairly conservative orientation and claims to present objective journalism. Stories and information provided in the three newspapers focus primarily on issues and concerns in Haiti. At times, the journals also publish stories and take editorial positions on issues related to U.S. society and New York City politics.

The other media, radio and television programs, are also differentiated along the same lines. The oldest radio program, *L'Heure Haitienne,* a student program at Columbia University, is like *Haiti Progress,* Left-oriented. For most members of the community, whatever their politics, *L'Heure Haitienne* was *ti radio* (our little radio). Nobody would miss that program. Another program, *Moments Creoles,* broadcasts on an important radio station, which is owned by prominent African-Americans. *Moments Creoles* takes political positions similar to *Haiti Obervateur.* Since 1986, the most important radio and television programs have correspondents in Haiti.

The hegemony of the Left in the New York community of the 1970s was even more evident among cultural groups. Theater and musical groups with great followings like *Troupe Kouidor, Cercle Culturerl Mapou, Choeur Tambou Liberte, Association Culterelle Soley Leve, Theatre Choucoune, Haiti Club,* and *Association Toussaint Louverture* were part of the network. There were also journals, bulletins and reviews, like *Etincelles, Arc-en-Ciel, Luttes, Kako,* and *Sel.* In addition, the Left influenced many student organizations and clubs as well as professional organizations like the Association of Haitian Writers and the Association of Haitian Teachers.

Although the hegemony of progressive ideas was not translated into an increased membership in these groups, politics permeated all dimensions of life in the community. For example, in January 1973, the U.S. ambassador to Haiti, Clinton Knox, a black American, was kidnapped and exchanged for twelve political prisoners. The action was supposedly carried out by communists. There was a big demonstration of support for the kidnapping in

New York. Money was collected to help the twelve Haitians in six Catholic churches having a number of Haitian parishioners. Conferences and forums organized by KODDPA on human and democratic rights in Haiti at the time involved cultural and theater groups of different political persuasions.

The strong influence of a political and ideological discourse that urged against integration into U.S. social life, even affected groups like the Haitian Unity Council, which promoted integration and participation in U.S. politics. This organization was created in the early 1970s under the leadership of a Haitian priest by some Haitians with a social background in the mulatto bourgeoisie and the black middle class. It was considered the first Haitian-American organization (as opposed to a Haitian organization). This created a major controversy in the community and many members of the organization, including the priest, were ostracized. They were perceived as traitors to the national cause. The organization had a journal, *Unity*, which was published in French and English. The main objectives of the organization, as an editorial stated, were to reach "la majorite silencieuse" (the silent majority of Haitians, a term borrowed from the Nixon era), and to promote the Haitian cause. *Unity* was thus engaged "in an aggressive action of promoting what is Haitian." *Unity* wanted to be the "champion of these dynamic ideas that have governed our destiny as a small but free nation in its most noble and constructive undertakings."

The Struggle Against Racism and Exploitation in New York City

> The Haitian dreams of coming to New York. He comes to New York, but he'll never be an American. Why? He is an entity. He has a cultural background. He is somebody. He won't deny his past, because his past belongs to the greatest of Occidental nations. We were the first ones to vanquish Napoleon (a Haitian student, in the *New Yorker*, March 1975).

Although this statement might be taken as exceptional and sophisticated, it expresses a sentiment common to Haitians across race, gender, and class lines. Pride in the Haitian Revolution is part of the cultural and ideological social fabric of Haiti. There are few Haitian political and social statements that do not make reference to Haiti's independence. The Haitian Revolution of 1791–1804 is the basis on which Haitians define themselves as a racial and ethnic group, perceive and evaluate others, and create their identities. It also serves as a powerful cohesive ideology for political mobilization against U.S. racism or other forms of discrimination. Haitians often express their resentment against the exploitation and oppression inherent in U.S. society, as the following statement made by a female worker illustrates:

> The job I do is for an animal. It's the same day after day. No matter how fast I work, my boss always complains about my slowness. He speaks to me disrespectfully because I am black and foreign. He knows I don't have an alien card and won't argue with him. He might report me to immigration or fire me.[12]

Although the United States offers more economic opportunities, because of their historical experience, particularly of race and nationalism, most Haitian immigrants despise the racial stratification and racial inequality of the society. They even tend to distance themselves from the American racial categories that create hierarchies by skin color. This distance from race is reinforced by the politicization of most cultural and social activities in the community, all of which reinforce, in turn, their nationalist identity.

In a 1973 article on the cultural dimensions of Haitian emigration, Ernst Verdieu, a member of *Sel* stated, *"Pour que les Haitiens connaissent reellement un affrontement racial, il faudrait qu'ils recontrent alors les barrieres. Mais dans la mesure ou ils ne sont pas concernes, ils se contentent d'assister a cet affrontement sans y prendre part."*[13]

As the article shows, confronting U.S. racism was conditioned by the prevailing political agenda. From this perspective, the incorporation of Haitians into the U.S. labor market was not seen as a form of integration in U.S. life because integration would have meant a loss of identity. To confront issues of racism would have only been possible if Haitians had defined themselves as black members of U.S. society. But Haitians were mainly observers. In that vein, the absence of any reference to race in the actions of groups that aimed for the politicization and mobilization of Haitian immigrants during the 1970s and 1980s clearly indicated that class, nationalism, and a different meaning of Blackness had been the main parameters through which Haitian struggles evolved in the United States. Moreover, the nationalist discourse of the Left reinforced workers' racial and national pride in Haiti's history. Thus, the primary political concern was how to maintain and promote a Haitian identity that shunned integration in U.S. society and its capitalistic values. The answer was political action oriented to Haiti.

In 1986, a popular movement emerged in Haiti. This movement developed into *Operasyon Dechoukaj*, a popular uprising that led to the departure of the Duvaliers and would have significant impact on political life abroad. Many progressive organizations were caught by surprise. Nonetheless, with the uprooting, the dynamic of the struggles shifted to Haiti. Many organizations and political activists were forced to realign themselves. To some, the disconcerting aspect of the movement was the dominance of the grassroots segments of the Catholic Church, the *ti legliz*, in the popular movement.

Operasyon Dechoukaj marked the opening of political space. As a result, many would return to Haiti to participate. At the same time, the most important progressive organizations, as well as the political parties of the Right, began to expand their activities. Political groups and coalitions of the Left like CONACOM, KID, and FNCD created chapters in New York, Montreal, and Miami. Likewise, political parties of the Right and Center-Right like the MIDH of Marc Bazin, the PDCH of Sylvio Claude, and the RDNP of Leslie Manigat also established international branches.

Other more radical groups that have militated in the community were not able to transcend their divisions in order to create an alternative. Moreover, by the 1990s, they were unable to formulate a new agenda. Opposed fiercely to any electoral strategy, many did not even support the candidacy of Aristide. They could not see that the campaign/movement of the Aristide camp was part of the development of the mass movement in Haiti, even though the campaign was openly organized by many democrats and radicals who had lived in the diaspora.

The victory of Aristide marked a qualitative shift. The redefinition of the diaspora as the "10th Department" implied the inclusion of the immigrant communities in the political life of the country. Thereby, the struggle for change in Haiti could be directly connected to the struggles of the communities in the United States. Haitian immigrants play an important role in support of programs of solidarity for the social and economic reconstruction of Haiti.

The 1991 September coup against the Aristide government closed these avenues. Nonetheless, since Aristide's overthrow, many new organizations have emerged. Their new feature is a more international character. Many of these organizations announce solidarity with the Haitian struggle, like Haiti Reborn, Americans for Aristide, and Haiti Solidarity, and work in alliance with U.S. organizations in support of the return of democracy in Haiti.

Conclusion

The creation of a large Haitian community in New York began in the late 1950s with the arrival of political exiles, many of them members of the traditional elite and the middle class. Over time the flow increased and the community expanded. Haitians are now scattered throughout the five boroughs of New York and the metropolitan area. The community is divided along class, color, and gender lines. Although most Haitians are integrated into the secondary sector of the New York economy, there are a significant number of white-collar workers.

With the development of the diaspora community, many organizations have emerged. These organizations vary in their goals. Some are oriented toward maintaining cultural and social links with Haiti. Others are economic and political organizations. From its inception, the community has been caught in a tension vis-à-vis its form of integration into U.S. life. The first settlers and, subsequently, most leaders in the community gave priority to nationalist politics. This nationalism was dominated by leftist ideology, and, up to 1986, the experience of the migration process was perceived as a transitory phase. New York was an extended arena of Haitian politics. The uprooting of the Duvalier dictatorship brought some changes in these political practices, forcing many to redefine their political agendas. New York continued to be an extended space for political struggles originating in Haiti. With the victory of Aristide in the elections of 1990, a new perspective began to emerge. The political coup of September 1991 temporarily closed the blossoming of that hope for real social change. The restoration of Aristide in 1994 revived that hope.

Notes

1. J. DeWind and David Kinley, *Aiding Migration: The Impact of International Development Assistance on Haiti* (Boulder: Westview Press, 1988).

2. M. Hooper, "The Monkey's Tail Still Strong," *NACLA* (December-November, 1984):286.

3. N. Glick-Schiller, "The Formation of an Haitian Ethnic Group" (Ph.D. diss., Columbia University, 1975).

4. It was almost impossible for the Duvalier regime to organize

support groups in the various communities of the diaspora. The opposition controlled all political activities. Anyone with official ties to the Haitian government was systematically denounced and scorned.

5. Lyonel Paquin, *The Haitians: Class and Color Politics* (New York: Multitype, 1983), 162.

6. *Ibid.*, 163.

7. Julien Jumelle, "L'Opposition Politique dan l'Emigration Hatienne," *SEL* 10 (1973):38–51.

8. *SEL* 1971, 1973, 1975.

9. Jumelle, "L'Opposition," 38–51.

10. The list of Haitian political organizations is more exhaustive. The few attempts to classify them have been done by Julien Jumelle, and Joseph P. Antonio, "Soutiens et Resistance au Pouvoir Duvalieriste." In Collection CETIM *Haiti briser les chaines* (Suisse: Favre Editions, 1984).

11. *Unity* 30 (1976):3.

12. Susan Buchanan, "Language and Identity: Haitians in New York City." *International Migration Review* 13, 2 (1979):22.

13. Ernest Verdieu, "Aspects Culturels de l'Immigration" *SEL* 10 (1973):50.

ELEVEN

"El Salvador is Spanish for Vietnam": A New Immigrant Left and the Politics of Solidarity

Van Gosse

A new kind of social movement has arisen in the United States since the late 1950s. Tentatively naming itself the "Latin America solidarity movement" in the 1970s, as the U.S. war in Central America heated up after 1980, it became known as the "Central America solidarity movement."[1] There are two ways of explaining this movement. One may see anti-interventionist sentiment regarding Central America as the major legacy of mass opposition to the Vietnam War. Clearly, many North American solidarity activists had that experience as an essential element of their worldviews. At least through Ronald Reagan's reelection in 1984, this movement's most basic agitational line around Central America was "No More Vietnams!" But Vietnam is not by any means the main referent point. Since the last 1950s, a small but powerfully rooted Christian Left has germinated, with its own leitmotifs. Many "faith-based" activists went to various Latin American countries as missionaries in the 1950s, 60s, and 70s, where they directly experienced popular struggle and repression. For them, solidarity was its own distinct phenomenon, "A New Thing in the Americas," as the title of one mass-produced tabloid from the dissident Catholic Quixote Center framed it in 1981.

What truly distinguishes these efforts is the central role played by Latin Americans in the U.S., in tandem with the unprecedented "temporary emigration" of North Americans to Cuba, Chile, Nicaragua, El Salvador, and elsewhere. Here is the clearest contrast with the Indochina war. Activity within the United States by the Socialist Republic of Vietnam or the National Liberation Front would have merited espionage and treason trials, respectively, of the Vietnamese and any U.S. citizens who worked with them. No such legally fraught undertakings affected the Central America movement. The presence of thousands of U.S. citizens from all fifty states throughout Central America became ubiquitous in the latter half of the 1980s. This phenomenon built upon earlier emigrations to Cuba beginning at the onset of the sixties. Equally important were the tides of refugees who concentrated in various urban areas of the U.S., where their status as political exiles was widely recognized by city and state governments and by the Catholic and mainstream Protestant churches. Central American revolutionaries organized in the emigré milieus. They also maintained a high-profile "political-diplomatic" presence, becoming accepted presences in congressional offices, in university-sponsored debates, and even on network television.

The most important aspect of Central American activism within North America, however, has been the practice of organizing a movement of North Americans as an "external front" of the internal war of liberation. Rather than building fraternal networks in their own communities, action typical of the old immigrant Left, the Central Americans devoted their organizing efforts to those citizens who could affect U.S. policy, raise money, and provide "personal accompaniment" through tours and delegations to the region. Nor have they tried to initiate any political movement in the U.S., such as the old immigrant-based Communist Party, which drew in the native-born in a common project for social change.

The post-Vietnam syndrome shared by peace activists of all ages, and a resurgent Christian humanitarianism evoking both Social Gospel and Catholic social action traditions, provided a fertile ground for the solidarity movement of the 1980s. But without the intentionality of the exiles, the Central America movement that dominated U.S. Left politics in that decade would have existed in embryo at best, with the rapid ascent and more rapid eclipse characterizing a succession of protest outbursts since the cold war began.

This "new immigrant Left" (which might more accurately be called an exile or refugee Left) is new, therefore, because it defines itself through not one but two immigrations: that of Americans from both sides of the divide towards each other. This movement-building process reflects experiences stretching back to the 1950s. One can find in this history obscure campaigns in countries as diverse as British Guiana, Uruguay, Honduras, and Panama. But each major phase of the solidarity movement relied upon a strong exile presence in the U.S. Without either that presence *or* an ongoing, day-to-day connection outside the U.S.—as became possible during the 1980s in Nicaragua—solidarity efforts have been small-scale and haphazard.

The evolution of the solidarity movement involved three stages: Cubans in the late fifties and early sixties; primarily Chileans and Puerto Ricans in the struggles of the seventies; and Salvadorans, Nicaraguans, and Guatemalans in the eighties. Elsewhere I have described in detail the political history of that latter movement from 1979 through its apogee in 1987. This essay focuses on the events that led up to the founding of the Central America movement in 1979–1980, and emphasizes the deep roots of what transpired in the eighties, however newly minted the solidarity movement then seemed.

The Sixties: Cuba and the Rediscovery of Anti-Imperialism

There is a story handed down among veterans of the Socialist Workers Party (SWP) that during his organizing tour on the East Coast in late 1955, Fidel Castro approached the party's New York City printshop, asking them to run off a leaflet, only to be unceremoniously dismissed.[2] This anecdote has several layers of irony: in mid-1960, the Cubans here and their allies would permit the Trotskyists, who had belatedly discovered the virtues of *fidelismo*, to enter the Fair Play for Cuba Committee (FPCC) in order to ensure FPCC's organizational growth while maintaining it autonomy from any single force on the U.S. Left. Nine years later, the Cuban revolutionaries—now barred from any activity on the mainland—would again seal a high-level deal with U.S. Leftists, in this case the leadership of the rapidly imploding Students for a Democratic Society. The result was the Venceremos Brigade, which brought thousands of young radicals to Cuba to cut sugarcane and imbibe revolutionary ideas. Concealed in this fourteen-year trajectory is the Cubans' role in rearranging relations among U.S. radicals, turning the latter away from the traditional party model to something more amorphous, rather like Castro's *Movimiento Revolucionario 26 de Julio*, the rebel army *cum* youth movement, which smashed the well-organized Batista regime in a few years of hit-and-run guerrilla struggle.

An early observation one can make about the cold war's solidarity movements, then, is that they stand in an ascending relation to the decline of Marxist parties in the U.S. since 1945. This appears to be a contradiction, for it was class-conscious Marxist parties that championed "internationalism" and solidarity in the first place. In the era spanned by Presidents Theodore and Franklin Roosevelt, the Socialist and then Communist Parties had been the main generators of solidarity with Latin America, from the SP's campaign against U.S. intervention in Mexico in the teens to the close ties between U.S. Communists and their Latin counterparts from the 1920s on.

This tradition was unraveled by the Cuban Revolution. From the earliest days of U.S.-based *fidelismo*, the Communists and others were repeatedly displaced by nonparty individuals, ad hoc groups, and minor parties, which established their own direct relationships with the emigrés, and, through them, the revolution itself. In 1957–1958, when the struggle in the Sierra Maestra fascinated much of mainstream America, the harried, hunkered-down U.S. Left turned a blind eye. On the occasions when it did look at Cuba, this Left distrusted the young Castro's lack of a political program, and the apparent anticommunism of his 26th of July Movement. Carleton Beals, the venerable radical journalist who made his name interviewing Sandino in 1928, spoke for many in "Rebel Without A Cause?" a June 29, 1957 *Nation* article, where he suggested that the amoral adventurism of Cuba's rebel youth was little better than fascism. Many on the Left, from the neo-Marxists at the *Monthly Review* to the pacifists at *Liberation*, simply ignored Cuba in those years. The CPUSA, and others with a similar viewpoint on international affairs such as the *National Guardian*, faithfully reflected the ups and downs in the relationship between the Cuban Communists and the *fidelistas*. As if to mark themselves off from this vacillation, the SWP was especially hostile, referring to Castro in 1958 as an "unprincipled . . . opportunist."[3]

The Cubans in the large exile community drew lessons from

the disinterest of North American radicals. The multitude of 26 de
Julio Patriotic Clubs from New York's various boroughs, Union
City, New Jersey, and Bridgeport, Connecticut staged a massive
"thank you" rally in late June 1957 outside the New York Times'
offices instead of the National Guardian.[4] Although the Old Left
turned away, there was a massive display of North American
solidarity with the Cubans in those years. College students and
recent U.S. army veterans wandered into the exile offices on
Manhattan's Upper West Side, begging to be allowed to enlist.
Others tried to smuggle themselves into the Sierra. Young Cubans
and young North Americans showered the crowd with leaflets at
Yankee Stadium, ran up the Cuban flag at Rockefeller Center, and
practiced combat maneuvers in wooded areas of Bergen County.
Amateurish seagoing expeditions to reinforce Castro from Texas
and south Florida were repeatedly foiled. Gunrunning in particular
seemed to bond young men from both cultures. Meanwhile, high-
level support was demonstrated by anticommunist liberals, social
democrats, and others throughout the elite press, including Time,
Life, the Chicago Tribune and the major wire services, as Castro
recognized by awarding hand-minted gold medals to twelve U.S.
journalists at an April 1959 ceremony in Cuba's Washington D.C.
embassy. Working hand-in-glove with exile leaders, perhaps anticipating future votes in the Spanish-speaking areas of his Harlem
district, Representative Adam Clayton Powell, Jr. became the de
facto congressional spokesman of the Cuban-American community (much as Vito Marcantonio had earlier represented pro-independence Puerto Ricans both in el barrio and on the island). What
the Cubans learned from this experience was that solidarity need
not be ideologically based, and was best when it came without
preconditions. The trick was to go looking for it.

And look they did, from 1959 to 1961, before the Bay of Pigs
made pro-Castro activity of any sort nearly impossible. Even prior
to the formation of the FPCC in the first months of 1960, Cuba
aimed a tourist campaign at African-Americans, highlighting the
difference between segregated Miami and integrated Havana.
FPCC itself was founded outside the confines of the Left. If
functioned in 1960 and 1961 as an amalgam of Nation-style old
liberals, fiery youth, and incipient black nationalists (with paid
organizers supplied covertly by the Socialist Workers Party), all
under the direction of Robert Taber, the CBS journalist and friend
of Castro who founded the organization with the private encouragement of Cubans in New York. Key among the latter were Dr.
Carlos Santos Buch, from a prominent family of middle-class

Castro supporters, and Cuba's UN delegate Raul Roa Khouri, son of Foreign Minister Raul Roa. FPCC's rapid decline can be dated from Santos Buch's January 1961 testimony before the Senate Internal Security Subcommittee that "Raulito" Roa had supplied most of the cash to pay for the April 6, 1960 *New York Times* ad that launched Fair Play. Throughout its one year of notoriety, the FPCC represented itself publicly as an organization of U.S. citizens seeking objectivity in relations with the revolutionary government. However, at every point, this ad hoc coalition was backstopped by Cuban-Americans, who provided much of the original membership, spoke at rallies, gave Spanish classes, hosted "fiestas," and assured the Yankees that U.S. government insistence on Castro's domestic unpopularity was a Big Lie.

The most vivid example of what this Cuban-American presence meant was on display whenever Castro himself came to the U.S. Besides the forty thousand mainly Latino New Yorkers who flooded Central Park on April 24, 1959 to see him receive official keys to the city, an even more powerful reminder of solidarity's power surfaced when the now ostracized Castro stayed in Harlem in September 1960. Most accounts of this tumultuous event focus on the mass sympathy and excitement demonstrated by Harlemites, who ringed the Theresa Hotel in vast numbers to cheer the Cuban leader as he welcomed Khrushchev, Nasser, and Nehru into their midst. But urging on this African-American response were Cubans, Dominicans, Puerto Ricans, and others from the Spanish-speaking Caribbean who engaged in a running war of words, eggs, and fisticuffs with the anticommunists (often Eastern European emigrés), who showed up to circle the hotel in cars and pick fights.

The speed with which this exile support fell apart is startling. The largest single factor was the mounting exodus of anti-Castro Cubans, who were favored as political refugees by both public and private organizations. Mutual accusations of treason and violent animosity within the Cuban-American community were assured under these circumstances. For a time at least, pro-Castro sympathizers held their own, continuing to stage rallies that outnumbered those of their rivals well into 1960. But by 1961 the tide had turned.

One incident played a major role in bringing public disfavor down upon the once popular exile *fidelistas*: the case of Francisco "the Hook" Molina, a 26th of July militant. During Castro's September 1960 visit, a brawl broke out in a restaurant between pro- and anti-Castro militants, and in the melee a little girl was shot and killed. The one-armed Molina was arrested and tried in a near-hysterical atmosphere, though a vociferous defense campaign was waged by young New Leftists and members of the Workers World Party,with covert CPUSA backing.[5] This trial augured a more sweeping repression of the 26th of July movement's U.S. wing. Many *fidelistas* returned to Cuba, and vigilante violence escalated in communities like Hoboken and Tampa. During 1962, the 26th of July movement representatives (already forced to register as "foreign agents") were called before the House Committee on Un-American Activities, hundreds of Cubans were interrogated by the Immigration and Naturalization Service, and following the missile crisis, leaders of New York's *Casa Cuba* were arrested as "saboteurs," effectively crushing a once solid constituency.[6] For the next thirty years, a virulent anti-Castroism would be the litmus test for political, social, and cultural acceptability among Cubans in the U.S. Despite the best efforts of a few young Cuban-Americans in the Antonio Maceo Brigade, formed in the early 1970s, the prorevolutionary current within this immigrant community has remained a tiny, despised minority.

The FPCC was a significant building block of the early New Left, however much its example was later submerged. The nuances of Fair Play's relationship to the Cuban Revolution typified what would come later. Individuals and local groups in the U.S. would respond to a crisis through the mediation of exiles as well as personal experience abroad and become radicalized. Solidarity of this episodic character cropped up repeatedly during the 1960s. Three episodes are indicative of this milieu and of the separate strands of the secular and religious Left, which, when linked to an immigrant base, would eventually spawn successful movements. In a delayed reaction to the 1965 U.S. invasion of the Dominican Republic, the North America Congress on Latin America (NACLA) was formed in late 1966 by young activist-intellectuals with quiet church backing, as a research center to expose the political economy of informal empire in Latin America. A year later, a group of Maryknoll fathers and nuns were expelled from Guatemala just before setting up a Christian guerrilla front, indicating the effects of the post-Vatican II radicalization of the Latin American church upon thousands of North American missionaries who went south in the fifties and sixties to fight poverty and communism. A third initiative was the previously mentioned Venceremos Brigade.

Lacking the exile influence, none of these efforts led to an ongoing solidarity organization for the Dominican Republic, Guatemala, or Cuba. NACLA adopted a hemisphere-wide focus and decided early on that it would pursue counterhegemonic research rather than grassroots activism. Similarly, the Maryknolls kicked out of Guatemala had only an indirect immediate influence. Though several went on to long careers in solidarity organizing, the best known were Thomas and Marjorie Melville, who married each other immediately after their superiors put them on a plane to Mexico: their prominence in the U.S. came as members of the famous Catonsville Nine.[7] The role of the Venceremos Brigades should not be scanted, since they brought about the first nationwide organizing campaign opposing U.S. imperialism in Latin America since the long-forgotten FPCC, sending over thirteen hundred young Yankees to Cuba between November 1969 and August 1970 amid massive publicity. But unlike the FPCC, the ongoing brigade and its related milieu (including the Center for Cuban Studies and the Cuba Resource Center) never attempted to create a national solidarity organization, keeping its focus exclusively on bringing people to Cuba and feeding the returnees into other movements. It would require more dramatic and immediately accessible crises—the overthrow of Chile's socialist government and a resurgence of pro-independence feeling among Puerto Ricans—to give a "movement" character to the slowly accumulating solidarity movement.

The Seventies: Sectarianism and Solidarity

During the 1970s, radicalized exiles and immigrants from Chile, Puerto Rico, and numerous other countries, primarily in the Southern Cone and the Caribbean, learned how to call upon the unfocused energies of a U.S. New Left that was simultaneously maturing and disintegrating. Spurred by the Venceremos Brigade's example and the quieter efforts of returned churchpeople to influence their own institutions, a range of solidarity networks rapidly developed. Though they registered many successes, the efforts of that time were also marked by a climate of internecine feuding. This competitive behavior reflected a simple truth about any exile movement in a new country: to the extent that activists are united at home, they can present themselves abroad forcefully and even compel a united front among foreign allies. Conversely, to the extent that a movement is disunited and at odds with itself, it will play out its conflicts in an exaggerated, often petty fashion on foreign stages.

Thus the dynamic potential for an immigrant or exile Left, and therefore for a solidarity movement, largely relied on an external unity, even an imposed one. Without such unity, there was the continuous potential for "one, two, many" solidarity movements, to twist one of Che Guevara's then popular maxims, as North Americans chose between rival ideological perspectives. At the worst, this meant extolling one or another party as the truly "proletarian" force in a given country, though most tried to avoid this sort of play-acting with somebody else's revolution.

One veteran North American organizer for both the Venceremos Brigade and various Puerto Rican solidarity efforts remembers the maelstrom of competing interests during the seventies thusly: "it was so difficult to do anything then—you had all these parties, and each one of them had to be represented at every meeting, had to have its say, for the whole thing to work." In fact, exile parties and their North American friends often became so inextricably mixed that it is hard to tell where one began and the other ended.

To start with Chile: this movement hardly existed while Allende was in power in 1970–1973. A founding conference for the Non-Intervention in Chile (NICH) network was held in Madison, Wisconsin in 1971, but it remained very small. Instead, a crucial impetus for the sudden growth of Chile solidarity following the September 11, 1973 coup of General Augusto Pinochet came from North Americans returning precipitously, like the Reverend Joseph Eldridge, who helped found the Washington Office on Latin America in 1974, or the late Robert High, who became National Coordinator of NICH when it assumed its identity as the "anti-imperialist" wing of Chile Solidarity in 1975.[8]

In the last months of 1973 and into 1974, these returnees found themselves in a milieu of spontaneous grassroots organizing by a wide range of groups already familiar with a coalitional style of mobilization from years of antiwar protests.[9] Local coalitions and emergency committees formed under a variety of names and programs: the Los Angeles Coalition for the Restoration of Democracy in Chile, the Boston Chile Action Group, the Michigan Committee for a Free Chile, the Colorado May Chile Be Free Committee, the Chicago Citizen's Committee to Save Lives in Chile, the Oregon Fair Trial Committee for Chilean Political Prisoners, and many others.[10] A new element was added to this from-the-bottom-up dynamic when U.S. Communists stepped in. Their organizational resources and capacity, which still dwarfed that of any other national Left organization, allowed CP members to rapidly achieve leadership over the various strands of Chile solidarity.

The CPUSA was aided by being the only national organization that could legitimately claim to represent the *Unidad Popular* (UP). The latter was a classic Popular Front, led by the Chilean Socialist Party and Salvador Allende, in which Chilean Communists played a key role, along with four lesser parties. The U.S. Socialist Party had disintegrated in 1972, and in any case the Chilean socialists were not members of the Socialist International and had for some years declared themselves a revolutionary, Marxist-Leninist organization—albeit one committed to the parliamentary road. U.S. Communists were the only ones with the international contacts and a shared political perspective who could take up the UP's cause here. In early 1974, a first National Chile Solidarity Conference was held at the CPUSA's instigation, succeeded rapidly by a second and larger conference on February 8–9, 1975 in Chicago.[11] From these two conferences emerged the first national solidarity network since the FPCC, the National Coordinating Center in Solidarity with Chile.

The CPUSA and the politics of Popular Unity faced a serious challenge. Many of the North Americans who had lived in Chile and several U.S. citizens killed in the coup's first days supported the Movement of the Revolutionary Left (MIR). The MIR had remained outside Allende's government, criticizing it for reliance on bourgeois legality and inciting factory takeovers while preparing for armed struggle. The MIR's argument appeared to be rendered truthful by facts: Allende had been overthrown by the same military men in whom he placed his trust.

From its 1974 founding, the NCCSC, despite its strong CPUSA influence, contained an Anti-Imperialist Caucus (AIC) consisting of the Berkeley, San Francisco, and Seattle NICH groups plus several other key committees. This caucus quarreled repeatedly with the NCCSC over the correct definition of Pinochet's junta— Was it "fascist," as the UP in exile maintained, and the MIR denied, pointing to the lack of a working-class base as in classical fascist states? More practical were arguments over money and speaking tours of exiled Chilean leftists. In 1975, for instance, the AIC accused the NCCSC staff of sabotaging the tour of MIR leader Carmen Castillo. The most fundamental struggle was over the definition of solidarity itself. MIR supporters and other New Leftists in the AIC argued that the Chilean coup should be put into the context of the South American revolutionary struggle and the global confrontation with U.S. capitalism. Working people here should be educated to see their oppression as essentially the same as that faced by the workers of Chile, with the same enemy in the transnational corporations like ITT and Kennecott Copper that had undermined Allende. This approach required an ideological organizing style, a longer-term perspective, and a focus on less influential sectors of the U.S. body politic. As the Seattle NICH put it: "It is central to our work to educate the people in the U.S. to the issues of 1) How did the repression in Chile come about? and 2) How is the Chilean experience relevant to the people of the U.S.?"[12]

The majority in the National Coordinating Center network did not agree with this approach, stigmatized within the CPUSA as "ultra-left."[13] The Statement of Principles adopted at the NCCSC's Second National Conference's emphasized that "solidarity is sought from all those who favor the restoration of human rights and democracy in Chile and are opposed to fascism. No other condition is imposed"—meaning no allegiance to socialism, armed struggle, or Allende. This pragmatic, goal-oriented strategy won out because it drew upon the prestige associated with UP activists in exile. It was "drafted on the bases of the perspectives for the international movement in solidarity with Chile as outlined by Jose Miguel Insulza, representative of the Chilean anti-fascist resistance." And rather than an explicitly anti-imperialist national program situating the Chilean struggle in a wider American context, the winning position was for an immediate "human rights" campaign to "ACHIEVE VERY CONCRETE AND STRATEGIC GAINS [caps in original]," implicitly by getting as close to powerful liberals and mainstream institutions as possible, so as to stigmatize the junta in the eyes of Western liberal opinion by any means necessary.[14]

Late in 1975, the AIC pulled out of the National Coordinating Center network, and held a national conference to refound the NICH as a national membership organization. Thereafter, the differences within the solidarity movement were in the open. Though divisions could be temporarily submerged when a clearcut issue arose, such as the widespread protests against the participation of the Chilean navy's "torture ship" *Esmerelda* in the 1976 Operation Sail activities, they were exacerbated by the arrival of Chilean political refugees after early 1976, when Pinochet opened some of his prisons. Much of the movement, especially church groups, became involved in sponsoring exiles, including the first Marxists the U.S. had ever accepted as legitimate contenders for asylum.

The total number of Chileans politically active in the United States never constituted an "immigrant base" in the traditional sense. Although there may have been several thousand living in the U.S. for one reason or another, only a few hundred were involved in the Chile solidarity movement: fifty in Washington D.C., a hundred in New York, perhaps another hundred in Northern California, and smaller groupings elsewhere.[15] However much they imported sectarian rivalries, the presence of these exiles strengthened the movement, bringing a human factor into the equation. Members of the MIR joined NICH committees around the country, where translated MIR "cadre manuals" were widely used for internal education, while CPers developed close fraternal ties to Chilean socialists and communists.[16]

The top Chilean leftist who relocated to the U.S. was the former foreign minister, Orlando Letelier of the Socialist Party. He played a central and notably nonsectarian role in generating concern over Chile, maintaining good relations with all wings of the solidarity movement—the NCCSC, the NICH, the church groups led by WOLA—by positing himself as a diplomat above the fray. Ironically, his brutal assassination by Chilean agents in downtown Washington provided the solidarity movement's emotional climax, gave it a rallying cry, and revealed how fragile was its unity. After the September 21, 1976 carbombing, which also killed Ronni Karpen Moffitt, Letelier's associate at the Institute for Policy Studies, (IPS), a major funeral was planned. But intense disagreements over its format and style lasted up until the last moment. The leadership of the national NICH, based in New York, wanted a militant protest march, loud and forceful. UP representatives and their U.S. supporters, including people from IPS and the NCCSC, intended a solemn cortege, befitting Letelier's rank and the gravity of the situation, to be led by UP leaders flying in for the occasion. The NCCSC refused to compromise, insisting that the UP leaders' visas were at stake, and ten thousand people marched silently, the largest turnout ever for a Chile solidarity demonstration.

The reality of a divided movement persisted through the late 1970s. The NICH took the lead in street actions and exposing the relations of U.S. capital to the Pinochet regime, while the much larger NCCSC focused on lobbying Congress and high-prestige cultural events. The NCCSC founded the Chile Legislative Center in Washington in 1976, which was accepted into the human rights advocacy community led by the Coalition for a New Foreign and Military Policy. Tours in 1977 and 1978 of Chilean *nuevo cancion* stars Quilapayun and Inti Illimani featured U.S. celebrities like Jon Voight, Pete Seeger, Jane Fonda, Rip Torn, Leonard Bernstein, Holly Near, Tom Paxton and Peter, Paul, and Mary as performers and speakers such as Senators Edward Kennedy, James Abourezk, and George McGovern.[17]

As late as 1978, the Chile solidarity movement remained quite strong, as indicated by a major anti-Pinochet trade union conference, initiated by Senator Kennedy and the United Steelworkers of America. Within two years, however, it was largely defunct at the national level, though organizing continued at the local level.[18] Meanwhile, as another crisis brewed, the base of the Chile solidarity movement did not so much die out as gravitate into the upsurge around Nicaragua and El Salvador in 1979–1980.

The trajectory of the Puerto Rico solidarity movement of the 1970s resembled that of the movement around Chile. The distinct difference was that Puerto Ricans from the *Partido Socialista Puertorriqueno* (PSP) initiated and led the main solidarity organization, the Puerto Rican Solidarity Committee (PRSC). The latter grew out of the Committee for Puerto Rican Decolonization (CPRD) and other groups in the New York/New Jersey area. The CPRD started to publish the English-language magazine *Puerto Rico Libre!* after an August 18, 1972 demonstration of thousands at the United Nations headquarters in New York. This in turn led to the Puerto Rican Solidarity Day Committee, created to promote a massive Madison Square Garden Rally for Puerto Rican independence on October 27, 1974.[19] Twenty thousand people turned out to hear speeches and performances from an impressive array, including Ossie Davis, Phil Ochs, Holly Near, Piri Thomas, James Forman, Irwin Silber, Angela Davis, Jane Fonda, Dave Dellinger, Pete Seeger, Russell Means, and even a young Geraldo Rivera, then a local television reporter. Messages were read from several Nationalist Party members imprisoned since the 1951 armed assault on the U.S. Congress, more contemporary political prisoners, and Bernardine Dohrn, leader of the Weather Underground Organization. Shortly after this impressive event, the Solidarity Day Committee, which had established affiliates around the U.S., became the PRSC at a conference in Newark, New Jersey on March 1–2, 1975.[20]

From the first, the Puerto Rican Solidarity Committee was strongly influenced by the PSP. The Executive Director of the PRSDC and first Executive Secretary of the PRSC was Alfredo Lopez, a PSP member, and the PSP's charismatic general secretary, Juan Mari Bras, was the only island political leader who spoke at the Madison Square Garden rally. Given the realities of U.S. politics, both official and Left, this influence could hardly be stated officially, and at its founding conference the PRSC pledged to work "according to the needs of [the] Puerto Rican national liberation struggle," while adopting "a position of non-exclusion of any political tendencies."[21] In reality, however, the PRSC began as an alliance of the PSP with an array of post-New Left "anti-imperialist" tendencies (the PSP was also part of the NCCSC's Anti-Imperialist Caucus).

In the early 1970s, the PSP was a new and dynamic party. Yet it also had deep roots in the Puerto Rican Left, allowing it to effectively displace the old Communist Party of Puerto Rico as the commonwealth's main Marxist-Leninist organization. It had begun as the *Movimiento Pro-Independencia* (MPI) in 1959, a regrouping of people from the *Partido Independentista Puertoriqueno* (the PIP, always the largest pro-independence force on the island, affiliated with the Socialist International), and others once close to the Communist Party. Over the course of the sixties, the MPI grew into the leading force in radical student and antiwar politics. It also built a base within the labor movement. In 1971, it declared itself the PSP, a vanguard dedicated to achieving national independence through electoral means, but without renouncing the armed struggle. The early seventies were the party's heyday, as *independencismo* briefly flourished on the island in tandem with a wave of labor unrest and widespread repression.[22] Not surprisingly, it was also a propitious time to germinate a solidarity movement in the U.S., drawing together a base in the substantial Puerto Rican immigrant community, post-Vietnam anti-imperialism among whites, and the nationalist solidarity of African-Americans and other people of color.

From its founding, the PRSC declared that its future "depends on our ability to link up the struggle of the Puerto Rican people with the concrete present and long-term interests of many sectors of the American population.[23] It mirrored the New Left's definition of solidarity as a common fight stemming from a raised consciousness among people oppressed by class, color, or colonial status. The PRSC's first national board read like a Who's Who of the multiracial Left of that time, with the key civil rights leader Ella Baker, Clyde Bellecourt of the American Indian movement, Amiri Baraka, the Rev. Ben Chavis of the National Alliance Against Racist and Political Repression, Dave Dellinger, Arthur Kinoy, Irwin Silber of the *Guardian*, Jim Haughton of Harlem's Fightback, Corky Gonzalez of the Denver-based Crusade for Justice, former SNCC leader Phil Hutchings, and various others.[24]

By late 1976, the PRSC had functioning chapters in twenty U.S. cities, from New Haven to San Diego, and it played a strong role in 1976 countercelebrations with the PSP's call for a "Bicentennial Without Colonies." However, it was increasingly disrupted by a minority identified with the Prairie Fire Organizing Committee (PFOC), supporters of the Weather Underground Organization. This factional grouping charged that the PRSC was *not* "anti-imperialist" because it did not have the correct relationship to struggles for liberation within the U.S. To put it in the vernacular of the day, the leadership of several chapters, in particular the San Francisco PRSC plus some national staff members, asserted that the PRSC had severely deviated, refusing to recognize "the obstacles of white supremacy and national chauvinism among the ranks of white workers," since "sectors of the white working class do benefit from imperialism at this time."[25] The Prairie Fire supporters wanted the PRSC to recognize publicly that the only revolutionary sectors in the U.S., and thus the only possible sources of solidarity, were African-Americans and other nationally oppressed peoples.

The PFOC also believed that the PRSC's close relationship to the PSP was inappropriate. Strong believers in armed struggle as the only road to liberation, the PFOC and others, including Puerto Ricans from parties hostile to the PSP's dominance, implied in various ways that the PSP was committed to a "legalistic" solution because of its focus on UN decolonization proceedings, and Rep. Ron Dellums's "transfer of powers" congressional resolution. The PRSC minority wanted instead an explicit endorsement for those Puerto Ricans who had chosen the illegal route, not just the aging Nationalist political prisoners, but also the new *Fuerzas Armadas de Liberacion Nacional* (FALN), which carried out various notorious bombings within the U.S. in the 1970s.

The problem of the PRSC's "close political relationship" to the PSP was stated clearly by national staffer Dana Biberman, assessing her own work on the "Campaign to Free the Five Nationalist Political Prisoners":

> This campaign was probably the first time in the PRSC's history that we have worked so closely with more than one Puerto Rican organization [e.g. the Nationalist Party as well as the PSP]; and this process clearly revealed the weaknesses in our having had a close political relationship with only one Party/organization in the Puerto Rican national liberation movement—the Puerto Rican Socialist Party. That relationship has been invaluable to our work, but we have tended to see our solidarity work through their perspectives and strategies only, and have not fully understood what it means for us—in practice—to build

solidarity with the *whole* national liberation movement. There is not presently a national liberation front in the struggle for Puerto Rico's independence, and until there is one built, we must fully respect all of the many different parties and organizations that are part of and lead the independence movement.[26]

That it would be impossible to "build solidarity with" and "fully respect" many disparate organizations with radically opposed strategies, and of greatly varying political weight, was not yet fully understood. One final indication of the problems besetting the PRSC is that at its second national conference, February 18–20, 1977 in Chicago, the 34 candidates contesting for twenty national board seats included representatives from at least three Puerto Rican parties and every possible fraction of the U.S. Left: the PFOC, the CPUSA, the Workers World Party, the Socialist Workers Party, the Republic of New Africa, the Mass Party Organizing Committee, and others.[27] The conference plenary heard major political presentations from "Che" Velasquez of the PSP's Central Committee and Luis Angel Torres of the *Frente Revolucionario Anti-Imperialista*, a coalition of several small parties opposing the PSP's electoralist line. The bulk of the conference was devoted not to strategizing a national program of action, but parliamentary maneuvers over whether or not to permit debate on competing "draft political statements"[28]

Under these circumstances, no organization could have long prospered. The PRSC steadily declined after 1977 as *independentista* sentiments receded in Puerto Rico. Although it had brought together Puerto Rican activists with mainland radicals, and helped raise the island's profile on the U.S. Left, the PRSC developed no effective strategy for building a "mass organization" that could influence U.S. policy. To achieve this influence would have required a much more instrumental approach to U.S. politics, including a refusal to permit interventions by North American parties with their own agendas.[29] These were the lessons drawn by the exiles who initiated the Central America movement that lasted throughout the next decade.

The Eighties: "Guaranteeing the Needs"

Key to the Central America movement's success and long life was the circumstance that each of the Central American revolutionary movements (Nicaragua's *Frente Sandinista de Liberacion Nacional* [FSLN], El Salvador's *Frente Farabundo Marti para la Liberacion Nacional* [FMLN], Guatemala's *Unidad Revolucionario Nacional Guatemalteco* [URNG] achieved sufficient formal unity to speak in one voice in the U.S., presenting relatively few openings for disputatious North American leftists. It is hardly incidental that during this period the U.S. Left became oriented to "single-issue" movements untouched by the polemics of the past.

Only a minority of the most conservative congressmen in the Reagan/Bush era could not attest to the decade-long barrage of telegrams, letters, phone calls, constituent delegations, pickets, and sit-ins at their local offices regarding aid to the Nicaraguan Contras and the "death squad government" of El Salvador. At its peak in the mid-1980s, this activity involved some two thousand local groups, spearheaded by a host of national organizations and networks such as the Pledge of Resistance, Witness for Peace, the Committee in Solidarity with the People of El Salvador (CISPES), Neighbor to Neighbor, the Network in Solidarity with the People of Guatemala (NISGUA), the Nicaragua Network, the Coalition for a New Foreign and Military Policy, the Commission for U.S.-Central American Relations, the Quixote Center's Quest for Peace, the Sanctuary movement, the Religious and Inter-Religious Task Forces on Central America, the Sister City networks, MADRE, and the SHARE and New El Salvador Today Foundations; most of these organizations drew upon donor bases numbering tens of thousands. Although this movement was hardly "mass" on the scale of the Vietnam antiwar protests, it functioned as a recognized interest group at the left end of the liberal spectrum, pushing the Democratic Party into a prolonged struggle with the Reagan administration, which ultimately provoked the Iran-Contra affair.

Two alternative strategies and organizational patterns for the U.S.-based solidarity movement existed, each corresponding to a particular country, Nicaragua or El Salvador. The much smaller Guatemala wing of the Central American movement, also largely refugee-inspired, always operated within the shadow of these larger tendencies.[30]

Nicaraguan exiles played a crucial role in gearing up the late-breaking wave of U.S. solidarity with Nicaragua just before the revolutionary victory of July 19, 1979. They helped found the National Network in Solidarity with the Nicaraguan People, created at a February 1979 conference in Washington D.C. with sponsorship from the Catholic Church (the Maryknoll Order), labor (the United Auto Workers), and leading liberals (Senator

Edward Kennedy). Most of these refugees soon returned home to help rebuild their nation. In the absence of a pro-Sandinista exile community, the FSLN preferred a pluralist, loosely structured movement in the U.S., a pattern that prevailed for the rest of the decade. The FSLN's main contact with U.S. solidarity activists was in Nicaragua itself, the clearest example of that doubled process of immigration referred to at this essay's beginning.

The massive short-term emigration of U.S. citizens to Nicaragua during the 1980s is a unique phenomenon in the cold war's history. To give a sense of scale, Debra Reuben, executive director of the renamed Nicaragua Network, estimated in 1987 that ten thousand North Americans had gone south as political tourists, temporary harvest laborers, peacemaking "witnesses" in conflictive zones, or long-term technical volunteers like the engineer Benjamin Linder, killed by the Contras at the height of the U.S.-backed border war. This kind of contact was precisely what the ban on travel to Cuba was intended to prevent, and it continually refreshed the spirit and local base of solidarity. It also obviated the need for an exile presence. National coordinators and grassroots Nicaragua solidarity organizers in the U.S. routinely got their political analysis and practical needs assessment directly from the Sandinistas. At one time or another thousands of North Americans met with top FSLN leaders like President Daniel Ortega and Interior Minister Tomas Borge.

The pattern of Nicaragua solidarity organizing vividly highlighted the dynamism of a decentralized model. Sometimes it seemed as if not a thousand flowers, but a thousand different, idiosyncratic material aid projects had bloomed. While the wide-open space for local initiative ultimately generated an extraordinary amount of practical aid, in goods and services, it also proved difficult to focus the energies of this very diverse base. The pitfalls of this localism were rendered most vividly when the plethora of Nicaragua-oriented groups found themselves in an unholy alliance during Ronald Reagan's second term with the "moderate" mainstream of the Democratic Party, led by House of Representatives Speaker Jim Wright. The Democrats were determined to maintain control over foreign policy by opposing the Reagan administration's proxy war in Nicaragua, and treated the solidarity movement as very junior allies, demanding acceptance of whatever compromises in aid to the Contras that the party leadership engineered.

Nonetheless, the Contra war *was* hamstrung by these combined efforts, which proved enormously frustrating to the Reagan administration, setting out on a collision course with the Constitution via the efforts of Lieutenant Colonel Oliver North. Two Nicaragua-focused projects in particular creatively drew upon the autonomist tendencies and the upsurge of faith-based activism in the 1980s to directly influence U.S. policy.[31] One was the Pledge of Resistance, which sprang up in hundreds of congressional districts from late 1984 on, establishing a nationwide network of up to eighty thousand people formally pledged to commit civil disobedience in case of a U.S. invasion. Even more impressive, and longer-lasting, was Witness for Peace, perhaps the purest distillation of the new "emigrant" mode for North American activists. WfP was entirely focused on putting U.S. citizens into Nicaragua, but with a specific, concrete task: "witnessing" and peacekeeping by a public, nonviolent presence in the war zones of northern Nicaragua. Ultimately, the corroborated, detailed reports of thousands of these witnesses helped expose Contra human rights abuses in the mainstream U.S. press such as the *New York Times*, and reached many members of Congress. Witness for Peace was especially successful at recruiting its long- and short-term volunteers outside the usual areas of Left-liberal influence.

Salvadoran exiles, on the other hand, decided early on to organize a highly structured and tightly integrated movement in the U.S., one that could implement a program synchronized with the overall strategic priorities, and even the specific tactical needs, of both their guerrilla army and the unarmed *movimiento popular* in city and countryside. Most of the refugee organizers from the late 1970s on, even before five different political-military organizations formed the FMLN in October 1980, were supporters of one of the five, the *Fuerzas Populares de Liberacion* (FPL).[32] The FPL's practice in El Salvador combined the rigorous emphasis on personal commitment of both Marxist-Leninist and radical Christian base-building methodologies. Those habits of one-on-one recruitment, self-discipline, and developing complementary organizations to carry out different tasks with different sectors, were all carried over to the U.S. by a core of Salvadorans and a larger number of North Americans who translated this technique and ethos into their own pragmatic, entrepreneurial terms. Starting in 1980 with CISPES, and branching out to other organizations, campaigns, and projects, what one veteran Washington observer called "the interlocking corporate directorship of the El Salvador solidarity movement" scored impressive successes.[33]

The opposition to U.S. intervention in El Salvador, epitomized by the popular political slogan that forms this essay's title, was a genuinely spontaneous phenomenon. All over the U.S., El Salvador committees sprang into existence, some of them stemming from earlier work around Chile or Nicaragua, but many of them begun in smaller cities or on campuses with no history of Latin American solidarity. The achievement of the Salvadoran exiles and their core of North American associates was to channel this upsurge into CISPES, which in the early eighties already claimed many hundreds of chapters and affiliates.

A much greater achievement, in retrospect, was the cohesion and dynamism displayed by the El Salvador movement in the latter part of the eighties, after Ronald Reagan's reelection in 1984, when it began practicing what Salvadoran Communist Party head Schafick Handal called "new forms of militant solidarity":

> It is no longer solidarity through street protests nor internationalists who join us in our war fronts. It is that popular forms of action in El Salvador are coupled by numerous delegations of organizations and popular sectors of the United States . . .[34]

Public attention, and the bulk of the grassroots anti-interventionist ferment, had shifted to Nicaragua, with the unending battle over Contra aid. Instead of dispersing and declining, the various El Salvador-focused organizations developed new modes of work. They raised millions of dollars in material aid, as well as millions of dollars to fund their own organizing efforts, using the same professional methods employed in the mainstream: direct mail, phonebanking, major donor visits, sustainer programs, and all the rest. CISPES, and others like the NEST and SHARE Foundations, were able to maintain a strong staff presence around the country, which in turn supported a much higher level of volunteer activity by local groups. These groups and others also provided powerful "accompaniment" both in-person and long-distance for the unarmed Salvadoran opposition, then rebuilding after the early eighties bloodbath. Before 1985 only a handful of solidarity activists had ever visited El Salvador; by 1988 it had become a routine event in dozens of committees. These delegations, and thousands of telexes and phone calls every month to Salvadoran officials and the U.S. embassy, were of crucial importance in protecting the unarmed opposition. This human rights work was also a vehicle for rebuilding congressional concern. After the 1984 presidential victory of Christian Democrat Jose Napoleon Duarte, a much admired figure in Congress, the space for meaningful lobbying had shrunk to nil.

This revived solidarity network prepared for the anticipated urban insurrection that the FMLN cadre spoke of with increasing openness. In January 1989, an emergency national meeting of CISPES organizers in Washington was told they had just "ninety days" to wait, a phrase remembered with some embarrassment and much joking in later days. As it happens, the long-delayed offensive began on November 11, 1989, and ultimately brought an end to the war, convincing both Salvadoran and U.S. governments that there could be no military victory over the FMLN. In its drumbeat of protest before, during, and immediately after the offensive, and in the steady pressure maintained during the drawn-out negotiations from April 1990 to December 1991, the El Salvador-focused organizations at long last managed to cut off substantial portions of military aid in September 1990.

Epilogue

Whether the Central America movement was a final stage in the succeeding waves of cold war anti-interventionism, the stored-up residue of all that came earlier, or whether it truly augurs something "new"—a long-term model for citizen diplomacy and transnational action—remains to be seen. Despite the large, very radical Haitian community in the U.S., there has been no solidarity movement with Haiti equivalent to those that accompanied the struggles of the eighties. The only elements of the Central America movement that moved over to Haiti work were those associated with the religious Left, notably the Quixote Center, though some mainstream black political constituencies have offered support at the elite level, akin to the role they played in the eighties' other major solidarity movement with South Africa.

Nonetheless, the United States is certainly bound to a multicultural future, as the new immigration patterns show no sign of abating. With this prospect, it seems likely that the immigrant/emigrant dynamic so important to recent politics will only expand in scope and force, bringing with it renewed possibilities of radical change.

Notes

Besides documents and her own oral history, Linn Shapiro, a fellow historian, also greatly improved this essay by several acute readings. I also thank Geoff Thale for useful insights on several key issues.

1. In 1987, I wrote a from-the-inside-looking-out account, " 'The North American Front': Central American Solidarity in the Reagan Era" in *Reshaping the U.S. Left: Popular Struggles in the 1980's (Volume III of The Year Left)* ed. Mike Davis and Michael Sprinker (London: Verso, 1988). Since then, I have investigated the prototype of the Latin American solidarity movement in *Where the Boys Are: Cuba, Cold War America and the Making of a New Left* (London: Verso, 1993).

2. This tale was related to me by former SWP leader Peter Camejo in February 1993. He had heard it from someone else many years before.

3. Gosse, *Where the Boys Are*, 123–29, especially 125.

4. See the *New York Times*, July 1, 1957, reporting on a rally of four hundred people, where a signed album of congratulations was presented.

5. Besides the daily press, details on the Molina defense campaign were provided by one of its leaders, Marvin Gettleman, in a January 14, 1992 telephone interview.

6. See the *National Guardian*, November 22 and December 6, 1962 and January 17 and March 14, 1963 for more detail on various of these cases.

7. Among this group were Blase Bonpane, who founded the Office of the Americas, a southern California solidarity center in the 1970s and 1980s, and Gail Phares, who helped found the Network in Solidarity with the People of Guatemala in 1980 and Witness for Peace in 1983. The Melvilles produced a remarkable autobiography, *Whose Heaven? Whose Earth?* (New York: Knopf, 1971), required reading to understand the roots of the solidarity movement.

8. Interviews with Joseph Eldridge, May 30, 1989 and Robert High, December 10, 1988.

9. This is how Susan Borenstein, who became executive secretary of the National Coordinating Center in Solidarity with Chile, remembers the wave of spontaneous demonstrations the day after the coup in all major cities and on many campuses. In Philadelphia, for instance, where she was then living, she called the Women's International League for Peace and Freedom, the American Friends Service Committee, and Resist, all previously allied in the antiwar struggle, for a September 13 demonstration, which

turned out two hundred people at the federal building and led to the formation of the Philadelphia Chile Emergency Committee (interview, November 8, 1988).

10. These names are taken from the Credentials Report of the first National Chile Solidarity Conference, held in early 1974 in New York City, in Susan Borenstein Personal Papers [hereafter SBPP].

11. As an example of the CPUSA's prominence in the second conference, 22 of the 142 voting delegates were from national organizations, and nine of the 22 votes were held by the Communist Party and associated organizations, including the Emma Lazarus Federation of Women's Clubs, the National Alliance Against Racist and Political Repression, the Anti-Imperialist Committee in Solidarity with African Liberation, Trade Unionists for Action and Democracy (TUAD), and the Young Workers Liberation League. While quite a few other delegates (such as those representing the Fur and Leatherworkers Joint Board of New York, the World Federation of Trade Unionists and Illinois TUAD among the sixteen labor delegates) were also presumably close to the CP, clearly a majority of votes were held by independent local committees, and it appears to have been a highly democratic affair (from the Credentials Report, in SBPP).

12. A proposed amendment in "Response to the Proposed Definition of the Anti-Imperialist Caucus (AIC) of the National Coordinating Center in Solidarity with Chile (NCCSC)," by Seattle Non-Intervention in Chile (n.d., presumably 1975, in SBPP).

13. The disparate churchpeople constituted a de facto third wing of the movement, with no single "line." They were distinguished more by their personal style and theological roots, in contrast to the "partyness" of new and old leftists. Many religious activists based institutions worked outside of the NCCSC in any case, a point made by Susan Borenstein (interview, November 8, 1988). The major Protestant denominations, the National Council of Churches, Church World Service and the Justice and Peace Office of the U.S. Catholic Conference all made major contributions to solidarity, especially in lobbying for the restrictions placed on aid to Chile during the Carter years.

14. All quotations are from a February 19, 1975 mailing containing the credential report and all proposals and resolutions adopted at the Second National Conference, in SBPP. The confer-

ence's repeated emphasis on mobilizing "broad constituencies," moving to the center to take the moral high ground, was summarized succinctly in a self-critical Statement on Perspectives:

> . . . to a certain extent, we ourselves lacked an understanding of the political nature of the demand to restore human rights and to free all Chilean political prisoners. Because the issues contain a strongly moral and humanitarian character, there has been a general tendency to leave the initiatives around them to broad, humanitarian organizations not necessarily integrated with the Chile solidarity movement.
>
> As we have gained more experience over the last year and a half, the significance of the human rights campaign has been further clarified. We are striving to build a movement in support of Chile that—in the US—is a reflection of the anti-fascist struggle within Chile. Not only must this be made true by seeking to involve broad constituencies, as is the case in Chile, but also by accurately reflecting the political context of that struggle.

Despite the opaque, neutral character of this comment, it is clear that CPers were concerned that the solidarity movement could be marginalized by the unexpected success of the new liberal, human-rights organizations such as Amnesty International.

15. Interview with Linn Shapiro, member of DC-NICH in the later 1970s, October 9, 1993.

16. Resistance Publications in Oakland, California (closely connected to the NICH), published both the English-language *Resistance Courier: Bulletin of the Movement of the Revolutionary Left Outside Chile,* and also the *Miguel Enriquez Collection: Documents from Chile on Party-Building,* named for the MIR's secretary-general, who had died in combat on October 5, 1974. Linn Shapiro describes the membership of the NICH and its connection to the MIR as follows: "There were NAmerican leftists, unaffiliated with any political party. There were NA leftists affiliated with parties or pre-party formations. There were Chilean MIRistas or MIR-supporters. And then there were NAmericans who were very personally and politically close to the MIR" (Letter, Shapiro to Gosse, October 21, 1993). U.S. Communists meanwhile drew upon a formal relationship that then still had great historical resonance.

17. Borenstein interview, November 8, 1988. When the

NCCSC eventually constituted itself as an organization rather than a "coalition of coalitions," it became simply the National Chile Center, the word "solidarity" being seen as too Left by that time. The principal officers were Detroit City Councilwoman Mary Ann Mahaffey as president, Professor John Coatsworth of the University of Chicago as vice president, and Abe Feinglass of the Amalgamated Meatcutters as treasurer (interview with Susan Borenstein, November 19, 1988).

18. Both the NICH and the NCCSC were gone by 1980, though when the *Chile Alert* newsletter was founded in 1983, it went to over two hundred local contacts around the country (communication from Linn Shapiro). The return of many of the Chilean exiles circa 1980 had a paradoxical effect: while it may have contributed to the break-up of Chile solidarity as a nationally coordinated movement, it also gave local organizers a direct relation in Chile itself.

19. See first issue of *Puerto Rico Libre!* (1973); Letter, Reverend David Garcia to Philip Wheaton, May 13, 1974, in Ecumenical Program for Inter-American Communication and Action (EPICA) Papers, Washington D.C.; interview with Digna Sanchez, December 27, 1988.

20. See program for Madison Square Garden rally, also *Puerto Rico Libre!*, November 1974, both in EPICA Papers.

21. "Political Statement/Discussion Document for Founding National Congress of the Puerto Rican Solidarity Committee, March 1 and 2, 1975," in EPICA Papers.

22. This sketch is largely based on an interview with Jose Soler, former head of the PSP's U.S. section, November 14, 1988.

23. *Ibid.*

24. "Independence for Puerto Rico! Political Statement of the Puerto Rican Solidarity Committee," leaflet in EPICA Papers.

25. "Minutes of the PRSC Board Meeting, December 11–12, 1976, NYC," in EPICA Papers.

26. From "Evaluation of the Campaign to Free the Five Nationalist Political Prisoners," from Dana Biberman, PRSC Staff and National Coordinator [late 1976], in EPICA Papers.

27. "Puerto Rican Solidarity Committee National Conference/

Nominations for At-Large Board Members" [brief biographies], in EPICA Papers.

28. All of the above is taken from the "Synopsis of PRSC National Conference, February 18–20, 1977, Chicago, Ill.," in EPICA Papers. Following their defeat at this conference, the PFOC forces were forced out, and founded the New Movement in Solidarity with Puerto Rican and Mexican Liberation. It was hardly coincidental that the PSP itself was internally riven by these same debates in 1976–1977, losing its earlier momentum. I have not attempted to deal here with yet another sectarian battle that polarized the PRSC internally, involving the New York-based *El Comite*-MINP, which upheld a class orientation focused on Puerto Ricans living in the U.S., as opposed to the PSP's emphasis on a single struggle by all Puerto Ricans for independence.

29. Many a Byzantine tale could be told about how most of the existing U.S. Left parties found themselves out in the cold when it came to the Central American movement, but a few examples should suffice. One is that San Francisco CISPES, the "home chapter" for the largest of the solidarity organizations, had the effrontery to publicly maintain for many years an outright policy of exclusion: no member of a Leninist cadre organization was permitted to belong. Conversely, the disdain felt by party leftists for their Central American confreres (so reminiscent of the attitude towards the Cubans at another time), is indicated by the CPUSA leadership's willingness to hold a party convention on the same weekend in November 1983 as a fullscale national demonstration in Washington D.C.—even though the party-linked U.S. Peace Council had played a major role in the coalition sponsoring that march. And anyone wanting further evidence of how sectarianism could cripple a solidarity movement needed only to look at the U.S.-Grenada Friendship Society prior to the U.S. invasion, mired in infighting between the CP and the SWP. One exception was in the loose network of labor-based solidarity committees, which became a haven for partisans of all sorts, but still did much good work; another was MADRE, the major national women's network around Central America with twenty thousand supporters, which had a strong presence of activists associated with the CPUSA.

30. In 1984, the largest solidarity network, the Committee in Solidarity with the People of El Salvador (CISPES), briefly proposed to its sister (and much smaller) networks, the NNSNP and NISGUA, that all three merge together into a single, powerful

solidarity alliance for Central America or even the hemisphere (the author helped frame this grandiose proposal outlining an "Alliance for the Americas"). It was defeated at NISGUA's national conference in June of that year because of the solid opposition of the Guatemalan refugees that led the small number of Guatemala-specific committees within NISGUA, such as Chicago's Organization in Solidarity with Guatemala (OSGUA).

31. Given its focus on exiles and the dynamics of immigration/emigration, this essay has given only passing attention to the centrality of the Christian Left from the 1960s on in providing an individual and institutional base for solidarity organizing, and a discourse of justice and human rights that legitimated the movement. Because of various celebrated martyrdoms (Archbishop Oscar Romero; the four U.S. churchwomen killed in El Salvador on December 2, 1980), as well as the highly visible presence of revolutionary Christians in Central America's revolutionary movements, the 1980s brought faith activism—the Christian witness—to the fore, even as the traditional anticlerical U.S. Left parties quickly receded in importance.

32. The other four organizations in the FMLN were the *Ejercito Revolucionario del Pueblo* (ERP), the *Partido Comunista Salvadoreno* (PCS), the *Resistencia Nacional* (RN), and the *Partido Revolucionario del Trabajadores Centroamericanos* (PRTC). All had some level of representation and activity in this country within the Salvadoran community, but none invested the time and effort in building and maintaining a national structure over the long-term, as did the FPL.

33. Given space constraints, this is a necessarily reductionist picture of El Salvador solidarity organizing, scanting the work of important organizations with their own trajectory, such as Neighbor to Neighbor, a nationwide grassroots lobby important in both Nicaragua and El Salvador work, or *El Rescate*, the major human rights center in Los Angeles. Another FMLN party, the National Resistance (RN), played a main role in the labor solidarity networks. Most complicated is the religious sector, especially the Sanctuary movement, where no one group of exiles had a dominant influence. Having said all that, it remains true that over thirteen years, CISPES and its host of related organizations (including the Washington Center for Central American studies, the U.S.-El Salvador Institute for Democratic Development, the National

Agenda for Peace in El Salvador) were collectively the leading force at both the grassroots and national levels.

34. Schafick Jorge Handal, *Che Guevara and Latin America* (Liberation Communications Center, n.p, n.d.), 13–14. This was a speech given at a July 1, 1988 conference in Havana, Cuba.

Contributors

Paul Buhle directs the Oral History of the American Left, Tamiment Library, NYU, and is author or editor of twenty-one books, including *Marxism in the United States*, the *Encyclopedia of the American Left*, *The American Radical*, and *C.L.R. James: The Artist as Revolutionary*.

Dan Georgakas teaches in the Labor Education and Advancement Project of Queens College; he is author of *Greek America at Work*, special theme editor of the *Journal of Hellenic Diaspora*, and coeditor of the *Encyclopedia of the American Left* and *New Directions in Greek American Studies*.

Carolle Charles teaches sociology at Baruch College.

Mary E. Cygan is an assistant professor of history at the University of Connecticut, Bridgeport.

Van Gosse, director of the Center for Democracy in the Americas, is author of *Where the Boys Are: Cuba, Cold War America and the Making of a New Left*.

Robert G. Lee teaches Asian-American Studies and is an assistant professor of American civilization at Brown University.

Douglas Monroy is an associate professor of history at Colorado College and author of *Thrown Among Strangers: The Making of Mexican Culture in Frontier California*.

Stan Nadel is a visiting professor of history at SUNY-Plattsburgh.

Michael W. Suleiman is an assistant professor of political science at Kansas State University.

Michael Miller Topp is an assistant professor of history at the University of Texas–El Paso.

Maria Woroby is a former research assistant at the Immigrant History Research Center and currently librarian at Augsburg College, Minneapolis, Minnesota.

Name Index

Subject Index

McKees Rocks Strike, 130
Mensheviks, 91
Mesabi Range Strikes, 131
Mexican American War, 12
Mexican American Youth Organization (MAYO), 36
Mexican Revolution, 17, 21
Michigan Committee for a Free Chile, 310
Military Intelligence Bureau, 167
Milwaukee Bay View Massacre, 150
Milwaukee Central Trades Council, 63
Modern Greek Proverbs (by Takis George), 219
Modern Greek Studies Association, 225
Modern Quarterly, 92
Mobelarbeiter union, 57
Monterey County Strike, 281
Monthly Review, 305
Morgn Freiheit, 94
Moscow Trials, 99, 203
Movement of the Revolutionary Left (MIR), 311, 313
Movements Creoles, 296
Movimiento Estudiantil Chicano de Aztlan (MEChA), 35, 36, 37
Movimiento pro-Independencia (MPI), 315
Movimiento Revolucionario 26 de Julio, 305, 306
Mujer Moderna, 21
"My Palikar" (American Playhouse), 220

Nader's Raiders, 243, 244
Naier Geist, 85
Naprzod, 160
Narodna Volia, 190, 196, 205
Nash Shliakh, 199
Nation, The, 210, 305
National Association for the Advancement of Colored People (NAACP), 105
National Chile Solidarity Conference, 312

National Committee of Americans of Polish Descent, 173
National Coordinating Center in Solidarity with Chile, 311, 312, 313
National Dollar Store strike, 279
National Guardian, 222, 305, 306
National Labor Union, 5, 52, 53
National Maritime Union, 220
National Network in Solidarity with the Nicaraguan People, 318
Navajos, 11
Needles Trade Industrial Workers Union, 278
Neighbor to Neighbor, 318
Neoconservatism, 107, 108, 109
NEST Foundation, 321
Network in Solidarity with People of Guatemala, 318
Neue Kolnische Zeitung, 50
Neue Volkszeitung, 64
Neue Zeit, 54
New Deal, 96, 100
New Masses, 96
New Order, 202
New Republic magazine, 108
New York Intellectuals, 100
New York Teachers Strike, 107
New Yorker Volkszeitung, 58, 64, 65
Newspaper Guild, New York, 223
Newspaper Guild, San Francisco, 219
Nicaragua Network, 318, 319
Non-Intervention in Chile (NICH), 310, 311, 313
North American Committee on Latin America (NACLA), 308
Nowe Zycie, 161
Nuovo Mondo, 140
Nymphs of the Valley (by Kahlil Gibran), 240

Occupational Health and Safety Act, 244
Office of Strategic Services (OSS), 214